Joshua McConnell

Life-Cycle Flexibility

Joshua McConnell

Life-Cycle Flexibility

Designing, Evaluating and Managing "Complex" Real Options

VDM Verlag Dr. Müller

Impressum/Imprint (nur für Deutschland/ only for Germany)
Bibliografische Information der Deutschen Nationalbibliothek: Die Deutsche Nationalbibliothek
verzeichnet diese Publikation in der Deutschen Nationalbibliografie; detaillierte bibliografische
Daten sind im Internet über http://dnb.d-nb.de abrufbar.

Coverbild: www.purestockx.com

Verlag: VDM Verlag Dr. Müller Aktiengesellschaft & Co. KG
Dudweiler Landstr. 99, 66123 Saarbrücken, Deutschland
Telefon +49 681 9100-698, Telefax +49 681 9100-988, Email: info@vdm-verlag.de
Zugl.: Cambridge, MIT, Diss., 2007

Herstellung in Deutschland:
Schaltungsdienst Lange o.H.G., Berlin
Books on Demand GmbH, Norderstedt
Reha GmbH, Saarbrücken
Amazon Distribution GmbH, Leipzig
ISBN: 978-3-639-10258-1

Imprint (only for USA, GB)
Bibliographic information published by the Deutsche Nationalbibliothek: The Deutsche
Nationalbibliothek lists this publication in the Deutsche Nationalbibliografie; detailed
bibliographic data are available in the Internet at http://dnb.d-nb.de.

Cover image: www.purestockx.com

Publisher:
VDM Verlag Dr. Müller Aktiengesellschaft & Co. KG
Dudweiler Landstr. 99, 66123 Saarbrücken, Germany
Phone +49 681 9100-698, Fax +49 681 9100-988, Email: info@vdm-publishing.com
Copyright © 2008 VDM Verlag Dr. Müller Aktiengesellschaft & Co. KG and licensors
All rights reserved. Saarbrücken 2008

Printed in the U.S.A.
Printed in the U.K. by (see last page)
ISBN: 978-3-639-10258-1

TABLE OF CONTENTS

TABLE OF TABLES

4

TABLE OF FIGURES

5

8

1 INTRODUCTION

Complex systems exist in an uncertain environment and have behaviors that can be difficult to predict. These uncertainties can result in outcomes that have serious consequences for the users of the system. Making "good" decisions about the system under this uncertainty is non-trivial. This leads to the need to find some way of coping with this uncertainty. For this research, flexibility is the means with which uncertainty is addressed.

Designing flexibility in a physical system is one method for managing uncertainty. However, designing flexibility in a physical system is but one of several tasks that must be accomplished in a complex system if the designed flexibility is to be deployable and of value. While designing physical flexible systems may not be straight-forward, other potential challenges exist throughout a flexible system's life-cycle.

How to create "cradle to grave", or life-cycle flexibility as a way to cope with uncertainty in complex systems is the research topic addressed in this dissertation. The research presents a Life-Cycle Flexibility (LCF) Framework, which is a comprehensive and systematic tool for addressing uncertainty with flexibility in complex systems. The LCF Framework provides for integrated design, evaluation and management activities that span physical and social system dimensions. Additionally, the LCF Framework, as the name implies, spans the entire life-cycle for flexibility. The LCF Framework starts with creating the needed support mechanisms in an enterprise so that it is capable of developing and managing flexible systems.

A second major concept that is presented in this research is the notion of leveraging multiple value streams from certain technologies and technical architectures. This research forwards the notion that some technologies and technical architectures, called Dual Value Design (DVD) technologies and technical architectures, will possess multiple value streams; some coming from inherent value and others coming from the ability of the technology or technical architecture to create a more flexible system that is better able to deal with an uncertain future.

Two case studies were chosen to test the ideas presented in the LCF Framework and the DVD concept. The case studies of interest for this research are both technologically complex physical system embedded within a complex social system, with linkages within and between the physical and social portions of the system.

The two case studies considered in this research are;

1. A large commercial aircraft making use of blended wing body technologies and the private aircraft manufacturer enterprise it would be embedded in,
2. Intelligent Transportation System (ITS) capabilities applied to managed lanes in an urban metropolitan setting and the various stakeholders involved in such a regional transportation system.

It is anticipated that for the two case studies chosen for this research, designing, evaluating and managing flexibility is not a trivial task.

This chapter begins by discussing the relationship between system complexity, uncertainty and the need for flexibility, before moving into additional discussion on the unique challenges posed by providing flexibility in complex systems. The research questions are then presented, followed by a brief introduction of the two main concepts introduced in this research; the concept of Life-Cycle Flexibility and the concept of Dual Value Design. The chapter ends with a summary of the research contributions and an overview of the organization of the remainder of the thesis.

1.1 COMPLEX SYSTEMS, UNCERTAINTY AND FLEXIBILITY

Several different definitions of what makes a system complex and different types of complexity have been proposed, summarized by Sussman (Sussman 2000). Two key characteristics relevant to this research are the uncertainty in the environment that the system is embedded in and the difficulty in predicting system behavior. These uncertainties drive the need for flexibility in the system.

Systems that exhibit these complex, large-scale, interconnected, open attributes are called CLIOS (Complex, Large-Scale, Interconnected, Open Socio-technical) Systems, as defined in Sussman et al., (Sussman et al. 2007). A CLIOS System, or simply a complex system, can be conceptualized as being composed of a physical system embedded within a social system, as graphically represented in Figure 1-1.

14

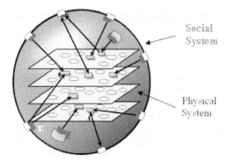

Social
System

Physical
System

Figure 1-1 CLIOS Representation of Nested Complexity: Physical system "nested", or embedded, within a social system. Figure modified from (Sussman et al. 2007)

Complex systems have evolved and appear in many parts of modern society. Just a few examples of complex systems could include: regional, national or international power grids, space-based constellations of communication satellites, national health care systems, military and security forces, and passenger and freight transportation systems (Magee and de Weck 2002). These types of systems have grown in size, complexity and importance for several reasons. Five potential drivers in system complexity are (Moavenzadeh 2007):

- Population growth
- Economic growth
- Increased urbanization
- Increased dependence on infrastructure
- Increased role of technology in society

These five drivers have evolved and interacted so that society as a whole has become more dependant on technological-based systems to support larger populations and a higher standard of living. As expectations from a growing population increase, the systems designed to support society have themselves grown and become more complex. As a result, complex systems have become increasingly important as society has become ever more reliant on them. As a result, disruptions in these systems have become more critical over time. Further, these systems have become more inter-connected as society has globalized, meaning disruptions may no longer be local events.

Disruptions that arise in complex systems are often difficult to effectively fix for a number of reasons. First, complex systems are composed of many different physical and social subsystems which interact in a difficult to understand manner, which makes prediction difficult. Second, the decisions made to change the system impact several areas (measured in money, time, political capital, environmental effects, social impacts, and others), making trade-offs between areas necessary but difficult. Third, changes

15

made to the system are often not only directed at current issues but also anticipated or desired future issues; this is inherently difficult due to uncertainty, where uncertainty can reside in the system itself and in the surrounding environment. Fourth, due to evaluative complexity, agreement between different stakeholders on the value of coping with disruptions is difficult to achieve (Sussman 2002).

Dealing with uncertainty when designing, implementing and sustaining solutions to problems in complex systems is the major focus of this research.

For this research, a Life-Cycle Flexibility (LCF) Framework is developed and is then applied to two complex system case studies. The case studies were chosen to act as a test bed to exercise the LCF Framework and DVD concept and to better understand flexibility in these respective case study domains. A brief description of the case studies follows.

1.1.1 AIRCRAFT ENTERPRISES

Large aircraft comprised of 100+ seats and comparable cargo capacity are some of the most technologically advanced systems in existence. The enterprises that support the design, manufacture and distribution of these large aircraft are themselves complex global systems, with supply chains spanning multiple nations. The large commercial aviation industry has been seen as an area of "strategic trade" (Krugman 1986), making it a "critical part of the US industrial base in terms of skilled production jobs, applied research, foreign exports, and inter-industry multiplier effects" (US International Trade Commission 2001), and the source of continuing international trade conflicts. Fierce competition in the large aircraft duopoly between Boeing and Airbus has led to the introduction of new technologies and launch processes for aircraft, such as the new Boeing 787 Dreamliner which Boeing hopes will "change the rules" on how aircraft are launched (Pritchard and MacPherson 2004), and the restructuring of the Boeing enterprise around the concept of becoming a "systems integrator", with the aim of reducing costs and risks and speeding up the system development process (MacPherson and Pritchard 2003). The ability to "change the rules" on aircraft is even more apparent on the Boeing conceptual Blended Wing Body (BWB) aircraft. With a more seamless integration of fuselage and wing structure, the BWB creates a new aircraft technical architecture with improvements in multiple areas over the extant tube and wing technical architecture. Together with the financial risks undertaken by the aircraft manufacturers often "betting the firm" when a new aircraft is launched, the technological, enterprise and political challenges create a complex system.

1.1.2 GROUND TRANSPORTATION SYSTEMS

Ground transportation systems form the backbone of modern societies, providing the means to move people and goods around cities and across and between countries. With issues such as increasing traveler demand, congestion, safety, environment impact and suburbanization, among others, the technical challenges involved in designing an effective, efficient and sustainable transportation system have never been more difficult. The challenges involved with a transportation system go beyond the technical. Financing the large capital investment needed for infrastructure like railroads, airports, and roadways poses a challenge even for the richest of nations. Political issues surrounding the placement of large, intrusive infrastructure in one neighborhood versus another or choosing one mode over another creates challenges in building coalitions of political support for any transportation solution. Social and cultural challenges associated with changing demographics, land use changes and economic prosperity create changing norms and expectations for transportation system usage and equity issues between rich and poor. Taken together, these technical, economic, political, institutional, social, and cultural challenges create a complex system.

The following section expands on the existence of uncertainty in complex systems and the potential for flexibility as a means of coping with this uncertainty.

1.1.3 UNCERTAINTY AND FLEXIBILITY IN COMPLEX SYSTEMS

The management of uncertainty is of particular importance in a complex system. This is because a complex system, more so than traditional engineering on a smaller scale, impacts more aspects of society and is longer lasting. This means that there are more sources from which uncertainty can arise and that the uncertainty can grow larger, due to long time scales and multiple subsystems (de Neufville 2004).

Uncertainty appears in many forms, such as technical uncertainty, economic uncertainty, scheduling uncertainty and political uncertainty. These areas have been recognized and tools have been developed in the past to deal with each. For example, factors of safety are included in the technical design to accommodate technical uncertainty; management reserves are created to address financial uncertainty; and work in major government programs is spread over many congressional districts to reduce political uncertainty.

Unfortunately, while these actions can be effective in reducing the uncertainty that is targeted, the system-wide uncertainty may not be significantly reduced. For example, including factors of safety may significantly increase economic costs which may increase the uncertainty of political support in government programs. Or spreading the design and manufacture over several political districts may decrease political uncertainty but can make the management of the system more complex and may increase scheduling uncertainty. These "siloed" fixes for uncertainty can act to push the uncertainty from one part of the system to another, rather than lower system-wide uncertainty. Solutions are needed that reduce uncertainties across multiple dimensions.

For this research, an emphasis is placed on examining flexible solutions to deal directly with uncertainties stemming from future market demand and fuel prices in the BWB case study and travel demand and relative mode share in the ITS case study. The effect of these flexible solutions on other aspects of the system, such as political viability, or the effect of system characteristics such as stakeholder fragmentation, are examined as well in a more qualitative manner.

17

From the MIT Engineering Systems Division Terms and Definitions Version 12, flexibility is defined as (Allen et al. 2001):

> *Flexibility: property of a system that is capable of undergoing changes with relative ease*

This research primarily studies flexibility as a means of transforming the physical system configuration or operation to deal with uncertainty. The emphasis of the research is on designing real options "in" the physical system, as opposed to real options "on" a system, which deal less with the actual technology and more with the use of the technology, such as scheduling flexibility in program management. This approach of designing options "in" a system as opposed to "on" a system comes from previous work done by de Neufville (de Neufville 2004) and others.

The concept of real options is based on financial options. Real options give decision makers specific alternative courses of actions that can be pursued in the future, depending on changing needs. Financial options give the option holder the right, but not the obligation, to take some action now or in the future at a predetermined cost. Real options are similar in concept to financial options, but in reality, additional complexities may exist, such as the ability to actually exercise the option or uncertainty surrounding exercise costs.

Real options provide a decision maker the freedom to act in response to a changing environment, by creating flexibility in the system. The concept of real options can be used to help create flexibility in a system and tools such as real options analysis for valuation can be used to quantitatively evaluate the benefits associated with options.

In the real options literature, the "standard" real options have been presented as relatively straightforward additions or changes to a system to create flexibility. The "standard" real option is then embedded in a "standard" system, where "standard" system here means lack of need to consider system characteristics such as enterprise architecture, politics or management processes. This "standard" real option is then evaluated with a "standard" real option evaluation process that makes use of relatively straightforward quantitative-based techniques.

For the research considered here, "complex" real options in complex systems are of interest. A "complex" real option is envisioned as being composed of more than a single or simple change or addition to a system to create flexibility. Rather, the "complex" real option is likely composed of interconnecting technological, organizational and process components. A "complex" real option may then be embedded in a complex system, which has technical and social system components and the behaviors that go along with this.

For "complex" real options in complex systems, "standard" real option evaluation processes may not be adequate to address the complexity in the option and the system. Instead a new process may be needed. This research will go on to present a new evaluation process designed to analyze "complex" real options in complex systems, called the Life-Cycle Flexibility (LCF) Framework. .

The following section introduces and discusses the research questions that were addressed in this research.

1.2   RESEARCH QUESTIONS

The following two questions define the emphasis of this research.

1. How do "complex" real options and "standard" real options differ across the life-cycle of an option, including design, evaluation and management activities?

Previous work on real options has focused on "standard" real options, or options that create flexibility through relatively simple additions or modifications to a system. In comparison, very little work has been done in the past on "complex" real options, or options that have multiple, interconnected technical, organizational and process components.

The design of a "complex" real option is defined here as being composed of more than a single or simple change or addition to a system to create flexibility. Rather, the "complex" real option is likely composed of interconnecting technological, organizational and process components. The utility of the "complex" real option then depends on successfully integrating action along the multiple dimensions of technology, organizations and processes. For example, changes in managerial processes, properly structured and written contracts, and the availability of appropriate technologies may all be necessary to ensure that the "complex" real option will have some utility and that the flexible system can be deployed and the options exercised. Consideration of only one of these dimensions may result in the "complex" real option being unusable in practice. Additional discussion on the definition of "complex" real options can be found in Section 2.6.

Because a "complex" real option involves more components that must all be present for the option to be deployed and exercised, it is anticipated that significant differences will exist throughout the life-cycle between "standard" and "complex" real options. For the purposes of this research three main phases of interest for the life-cycle of an option are considered: the design phase, the evaluation phase and the management phase. Each is briefly discussed below. A more detailed discussion can be found in Section 3.1.2.
- **Design Phase** – The design phase of the option life-cycle contains activities needed for conceiving and designing the option. This can included activities across multiple domains. For example, technical design activities may be needed if the option depends on technologies or technical architectures. Additionally, if the option will require new way of management for the

19

enterprise, the enterprise itself may need to be partially re-designed to accommodate the requirements of a flexible system.

- **Evaluation Phase** – The evaluation phase of the option life-cycle contains activities needed to evaluate the option for the purpose of determining whether the proposed flexibility is worthwhile. Since the "complex" real option may contain components from the technical, organizational and process domains, the evaluation will likely be composed of multiple quantitative and qualitative evaluation techniques.

- **Management Phase** – The management phase of the option life-cycle contains activities needed to allow for option purchasing, managing and exercise. The purchase of the option may involve more than "writing a check" and can include actual construction and deployment of flexible physical systems. Managing the option involves the ability to actively monitor the system and the environment, making modifications to the option over time, if needed. The exercise of the option involves making the decision on whether or not to exercise the option and then implementing any changes to the system or its operation if the option is actually exercised. After the option is exercised, the system again may need to be managed and monitored, especially if there are multiple options in the system. System management and monitoring activities are also needed to address unknown unknown uncertainties.

The research seeks to understand how "standard" and "complex" real options differ over the life-cycle of the option in design, evaluation and management activities.

2. *How should real option processes be modified to systematically and comprehensively design, evaluate and manage "complex" real options?*

Previous work on real options has mainly centered around processes for evaluating options, with some work also on processes for designing real options. Creating a flexible system must encompass more than just designing and evaluating flexibility. Additional activities may be necessary, such as; creating an enterprise and institutional environment conducive to including flexibility in designs, knowing when to exercise flexibility, understanding how to implement flexibility, and possessing the ability to evaluate the environment to respond to emerging trends that were not previously anticipated. Creating a framework that can help guide designers and decision makers through all the facets of flexible systems is necessary, leading to the creation in this research of the Life-Cycle Flexibility Framework.

The following section provides an initial overview of the Life-Cycle Flexibility Framework. Additional discussion of the LCF Framework is presented in Chapter 3.

1.3 LIFE-CYCLE FLEXIBILITY FRAMEWORK

This research argues that the current methods of designing and evaluating flexibility in systems are not adequate for designing "complex" real options in complex systems. We suggest a new framework, the Life-Cycle Flexibility Framework, that may be more capable of dealing with the challenges posed by "complex" real options in complex systems. The Life-Cycle Flexibility (LCF) Flexibility is presented in Figure 1-2.

Current tools and practices for designing flexibility in a system are inadequate for a number of reasons, as follows:

  i. Quantitative analysis tools do not take into account difficult to quantify parameters such as distribution of costs and benefits among stakeholders or political realities that may make it difficult to implement solutions,
 ii. Qualitative tools are not sufficient by themselves to fully develop technical systems or determine the effects that technical, social, economic and political systems have on one another,
iii. In practice, professionals charged with either system design or implementation are not trained in or aware of methods to create and implement flexible systems, and
 iv. The ability of enterprises to create support for or implement flexible systems in practice is often questionable.

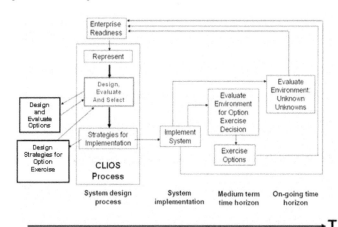

Figure 1-2 LCF Framework.

From this discussion, the following definition of life-cycle flexibility is proposed:

Life-cycle flexibility addresses multiple aspects of uncertainty over all phases of a system's life-cycle in an integrated fashion, with the goal of creating a flexible

21

*system capable of coping with uncertainty. The Life-Cycle Flexibility Framework
is a comprehensive framework for helping the user address life-cycle flexibility
considerations in a systematic manner during design, evaluation and management
of the system.*

The following section presents a second concept introduced in this research, that of dual value design in certain technologies and technical architectures.

1.4   DUAL VALUE DESIGN

A second concept introduced in this research is the idea of designing technologies and technical architectures that have dual benefit streams. These benefit streams are; an inherent value that stems from the choice of technologies or technical architectures, and a flexibility value stream, stemming from flexibility created by a specific technology or technical architecture. We call this Dual Value Design (DVD).

The sum total of these two value streams is the total value of using DVD technologies.

$$\text{DVD value} = \text{inherent value from technology} + \text{value from flexibility}$$

The DVD concept can be interpreted in two ways.

First, the choice of a technology or a technical architecture used in a system will have some inherent value, which could be reason for its selection. Additionally, there is the potential that the technology or the technical architecture may also possess attributes that could be used to create flexibility in a system. This flexibility would have some additional value and should be accounted for in a benefit-cost analysis.

Second, the inclusion of flexibility in a system may have some cost associated with it. This means that something has been added or modified in the system, either through a new or modified technology or technical architecture. This technology or technical architecture creates flexibility, but has a cost associated with it. If this cost of including a real option is too high compared to the benefits gained from flexibility, the flexibility may not be deemed worthwhile. This is especially true when stakeholders consider that the real option may never be used and are therefore reluctant to spend money to purchase the option, even if it is shown to have value. However, if the technology or technical architecture itself has some inherent value in addition to providing flexibility, the benefits associated with the technology or technical architecture are increased, as there are benefits from both flexibility and inherent value. By considering the inherent value of the technology or technical architecture, the benefit-cost analysis may be changed in a direction more favorable to the inclusion of the technology or technical architecture in the system.

Additional discussion of DVD technologies and technical architectures is presented in Chapter 3.

Note, that the DVD concept is not itself a separate contribution to this research apart from the LCF Framework. Rather, the DVD concept is another way to describe flexible systems.

The following section discusses the research contributions.

1.5 CONTRIBUTIONS OF RESEARCH
This research offers unique and new contributions in several areas.
- First, the LCF Framework is presented as a new methodology for designing, evaluating and managing "complex" real options in complex systems. As "standard" real option evaluation processes are not adequate for evaluation of "complex" real options, a new methodology is needed that can explicitly address the complexity.
- Second, as a part of the LCF Framework, a new quantitative analysis process is presented. This quantitative analysis process makes use of sophisticated modeling techniques. Additionally, the quantitative modeling explicitly takes into account both physical and social system characteristics of importance. These sophisticated modeling techniques are needed to support the LCF Framework and properly evaluate "complex" real options in complex systems.
- Third, the concept of dual value design is forwarded. This concept is useful in helping to account for all value streams of a particular technology or technical architecture choice in a system.
- Finally, new application areas for real options were studied in the two case studies; the use of a blended wing body technical architecture and ITS capabilities on managed lanes as real options are areas with little previous research attention.

The following section describes the organization of the dissertation.

1.6 ORGANIZATION OF THESIS
An overview of this thesis is presented below. A summary of the research, graphically showing how the research fits together, is presented in Figure 1-3.

23

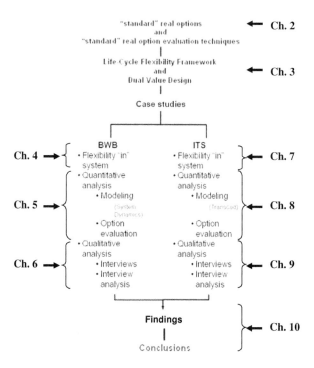

"standard" real options
and
"standard" real option evaluation techniques   ← **Ch. 2**

Life-Cycle Flexibility Framework
and
Dual Value Design   ← **Ch. 3**

Case studies

	BWB	ITS	
Ch. 4 →	• Flexibility "in" system	• Flexibility "in" system	← **Ch. 7**
Ch. 5 →	• Quantitative analysis • Modeling (System Dynamics) • Option evaluation	• Quantitative analysis • Modeling (Transcad) • Option evaluation	← **Ch. 8**
Ch. 6 →	• Qualitative analysis • Interviews • Interview analysis	• Qualitative analysis • Interviews • Interview analysis	← **Ch. 9**

Findings   ← **Ch. 10**

Conclusions

Figure 1-3 Diagram of research design.

Chapter 2 starts with a review of the literature for uncertainty and flexibility. In the review of the uncertainty literature, a framework is presented for categorizing and organizing uncertainty. The literature review on flexibility covers an overview of flexibility in a variety of systems, then concentrates on real options. An overview of the concept, mathematics and processes involved with real options are discussed. The chapter concludes with a comparison of "standard" real options and "complex" real options.

Chapter 3 furthers the discussion of processes associated with real options as reviewed in the literature from the prior chapter and presents a new framework for looking at flexibility in systems, called the Life-Cycle Flexibility (LCF) Framework. This framework integrates and adds to existing frameworks for complex systems, namely the Complex Large Interconnected Open Socio-technical (CLIOS) Process, and real options. The LCF Framework is presented step-by-step to walk the reader through each portion and discuss in detail the need for the individual steps and the overall LCF Framework.

Also in Chapter 3, the concept of DVD technologies and technical architectures is presented. DVD concept is that some technologies and technical architectures not only have an inherent value, but also have added value by embedding flexibility in their design.

Chapters 4 through 9 cover the two case studies used in this research; a Blended Wing Body type commercial aircraft (BWB) and the Intelligent Transportation System (ITS) managed lanes in Houston, Texas case studies. These two case studies were chosen to test out the LCF Framework and DVD concept. The two case studies represent a range of technical architectures (BWB) and technologies (ITS) of interest, types of technical systems (BWB is a product and ITS is a networked system), and social systems (commercial aircraft manufacturing is a private enterprise and the Houston transportation systems is managed by a variety of government agencies with private stakeholders influencing the system). The organization of these chapters is in a parallel structure, with each case study consisting of three chapters. The BWB case study appears in Chapters 4 – 6 and the ITS case study follows in Chapters 7 – 9.

Chapter 4 and Chapter 7 introduce the two case studies used in this research. Chapter 4 presents the Blended Wing Body case study, while the Houston Intelligent Transportation System (ITS) managed lane case study is introduced in Chapter 7. Each chapter provides an overview of the technologies and technical architectures of interest as well as the current situation surrounding each case study. Both chapters end with a description of the options of interest for the two case studies.

Chapter 5 and Chapter 8 provide the quantitative analysis of the options of interest for the two case studies. In the BWB case study a system dynamics model was built to better understand the interactions between passenger demand, airline operations, aircraft manufacturer's corporate strategy and aircraft architectures. The results of this model were used to quantitatively better understand the options presented by the BWB technical architecture. In the Houston ITS case study a traffic demand model was built using Transcad to better understand the effect of managed lanes on the behavior of the Houston transportation network. The results of this model were used to better understand the options for the Houston ITS case study.

Chapter 6 and Chapter 9 provide the qualitative analysis of the options of interest for the two case studies. For each case study, examples of flexibility currently being pursued and behaviors that were being engaged in relevant to flexible systems was investigated for the purpose of better understanding the feasibility of designing options into these respective systems. The data that was collected for both of the case studies was obtained from public source material and interviews with people either directly involved in the system or with expert knowledge of the system.

Chapter 10 presents a synthesis of the case studies, integrating the results over both the quantitative and qualitative analysis performed for each case. Chapter 10 then re-visits the Life-Cycle Flexibility Framework and examines the lessons learned and the applicability of the framework. Finally, conclusions and suggestions for future work are made at the end of Chapter 10.

The following chapter provides a review of the literature on complex systems, uncertainty and flexibility.

1.7 REFERENCES

Allen, T. et. al. (2001) ESD Terms and Definitions, Version 12. ESD Working Paper Series, ESD-WP-2002-01, esd.mit.edu.

Brach, M. (2003) Real Options in Practice, Wiley Finance, New Jersey.

Copeland, T. and v. Antikarov. (2003) Real Options: A Practitioner's Guide, Thomson, New York.

de Neufville, R. (2004) Uncertainty Management for Engineering Systems Planning and Design, Monograph draft for Engineering Systems Division.

Dixit, A. and R. Pindyck. (1994) Investment Under Uncertainty, Princeton University Press, New Jersey.

Dodder, R., J. McConnell, A. Mostashari and J. Sussman. (2005) The Concept of the CLIOS Process: Integrating the Study of Physical and Institutional Systems Using Mexico City as an Example, ESD working paper, esd.mit.edu.

Huchzermeier, A. and C. Loch. (2001) Project Management Under Risk: Using the Real Options Approach to Evaluate Flexibility in R&D, Management Science, v. 47, n. 1.

Hull, J. (2002) Introduction to Futures and Options Markets, 5th Ed. Prentice Hall, New York.

Kulatilaka, N. (1993) The Value of Flexibility: The Case of a Duel-Fuel Industrial Steam Boiler, Financial Management, v. 22, n. 3.

Krugman, P. (1986) Strategic Trade Policy and the New International Economics, MIT Press.

Lax, D. and J. Sebenius. (2004) Anchoring Expectations, Negotiation, v. 7, n. 9.

Mun, J. (2002) Real Options Analysis: Tools and Techniques for Valuing Strategic Investments and Decisions, John Wiley and Sons, Inc., New York.

MacPherson, A. and D. Pritchard. (2003) The Global Decentralization of U.S. Commercial Aircraft Production: Implications for Employment and Trade, Futures v. 35.

Magee, C. and O. de Weck. (2002) An Attempt at Complex System Classification, MIT Engineering Systems Division Working Paper Series, ESD-WP-2003-01.02, esd.mit.edu

Moavenzadeh, F. (2007) Conversation concerning complex systems.

Myers, S. (1977) Determinants of Capital Borrowing, Journal of Financial Economics, v..5.

Pritchard, D. and A. MacPherson. (2004) Industrial Subsidies and the Politics of World Trade: The Case of the Boeing 7e7, The Industrial Geographer, v. 1 n. 2.

Reuer, J. and T. Tong. (2007) Real Options Theory in the Advances in Strategic Management Series, Volume 27, Elsevier, forthcoming.

Royer, I.(2001) Stopping-Champions of Failing Projects, Academy of Management Conference, Washington D.C.

Schwartz, E. and L. Trigeorgis. (2001) Real Options and Investment Under Uncertainty: Classical Readings and Recent Contributions, MIT Press.

Sussman, J., R. Dodder, J. McConnell, A. Mostashari, S. Sgouridis. (2007) The CLIOS Process: A User's Guide, Working Paper.

Sussman, J. (2002) Collected Views on Complexity in Systems. MIT Engineering Systems Division Working Paper Series, ESD-WP-2003-01.06, esd.mit.edu

Sussman, J. (2000) Ideas on Complexity in Systems: Twenty Views. Engineering Systems Division Working Paper, ESD-WP-2000-02, esd.mit.edu.

Trigeorgis, L. (2002) Real Options: Managerial Flexibility and Strategy in Resource Allocation, MIT Press, Massachusetts.

United States International Trade Commission. (2001) Competitive Assessment of the U.S. Large Civil Aircraft Aerostructures Industry, Washington DC.

Wilson, James Q. (1989) Bureaucracy, Basic Books, New York.

Zhao, T. and Tseng, C. (2003) Valuing Flexibility in Infrastructure Expansion, J. of Infrastructure Systems, v. 9 n. 3.

2 UNCERTAINTY AND FLEXIBILITY

Chapter 2 provides a review of the literature on uncertainty and flexibility, as embedded in complex, or engineering, systems. Various types of uncertainties are presented and analyzed along the dimensions of knowledge about events and probabilities. Several strategies are then presented for coping with uncertainty, with an initial proposal for how these strategies can be mapped to the multiple types of uncertainty previously presented. One of these strategies, flexibility, is then discussed in greater detail, looking at flexibility in various literatures and applications. Real options, a concept that helps operationalize flexibility, is then reviewed, emphasizing the concept of "standard" real options and "standard" real options quantitative analysis techniques for valuing flexibility. Finally, an overview of real option processes that appear in the literature are reviewed, with the intent to determine if these processes are adequate for designing, evaluating and managing "complex" real options in complex systems.

Figure 2-1 shows how the literature fits into the overall research process.

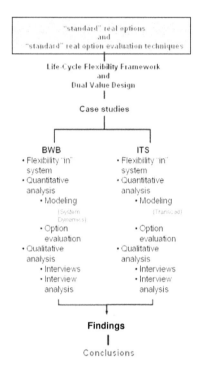

Figure 2-1 Research process with current stage highlighted.

This chapter seeks to better understand the second research question: **How should real option processes be modified to systematically and comprehensively design, evaluate and manage "complex" real options?** Specifically, this chapter aims to review the literature on "standard" real options and present a definition of "complex" real options. By providing an initial comparison between "standard" and "complex" real options the underlying need for a framework to design, evaluate and manage "complex" real options is presented.

2.1 COMPLEX SYSTEMS

We begin this chapter with a discussion of systems that are complex. The following definitions of engineering systems, complex systems and CLIOS Systems are presented to show different perspectives of complexity in systems.

> *Engineering System*: "a system designed by humans having some purpose; large-scale and complex engineering systems, which are of most

interest to the Engineering Systems Division (at M.I.T.), will have a management or social dimension as well as a technical one". (Allen et al. 2001)

Complex System: "a system with components and interconnections, interactions, or interdependencies that are difficult to describe, understand, predict, manage, design, or change". (Allen et al. 2001)

CLIOS System: A Complex Large-scale, Interconnected, Open Socio-technical System is a class of socio-technical system where the interaction between social, political, economic, institutional structure with physical systems is of critical interest and a driver of complexity. A CLIOS System can be conceptualized as being composed of a physical system and institutional or policy "sphere" (composed of organizations both formal and informal) as graphically represented in Figure 2-2. (Sussman et al. 2007)

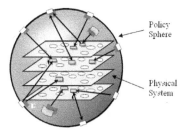

Figure 2-2 CLIOS Representation of Nested Complexity: Physical system "nested" within a policy system (policy sphere). Figure from (Sussman et al. 2005)

While there are many examples of complex systems (or engineering systems or CLIOS System), such as transportation systems, aerospace systems, energy systems, manufacturing systems and telecommunication systems (Magee and de Weck 2002), all of the above systems share similar characteristics, including complexity in the social and technical aspects of the system. For the purposes of this research, complex, engineering and CLIOS Systems are considered inter-changeable.

Several different definitions of what makes these types of systems complex have been proposed, summarized by Sussman (Sussman 2000). These include system characteristics such as:
- Large systems
- Many subsystems
- Unknown relationships / emergent behavior
- Multiple time scales
- Non-linear effects
- Multiple actors, viewpoints, priorities and capabilities

- Difficult to predict future behavior

A key characteristic relevant to this research is the difficulty in predicting system behavior, which is a cause of uncertainty.

Difficulty in predicting system behavior can stem either from the complexity within the system itself or from the environment the system is embedded in.

In the first case, the system is complex enough that it is difficult to predict how it will react to a particular input. In the second case, the inputs to the system from the environment are uncertain. The second case, uncertain inputs from the environment, are usually the primary concern when studying flexibility. However, for this research, as the system is defined as being comprised of both a physical and a social system, the interaction between these systems can also lead to difficult in predicting the system behavior. Specifically of interest for this research is better understanding how the behavior of the system may differ from what is expected, given the inputs of interest.

The management of uncertainty is of particular importance in complex systems. This is because a complex system, more so than traditional engineering on a smaller scale, impacts more aspects of society and is longer lasting. This means that there are more sources from which uncertainty can arise and that the uncertainty can grow larger than in traditional engineering (due to long time scales and multiple subsystems) (de Neufville 2004).

The following section examines uncertainty in more detail, focusing on different ways of defining and classifying uncertainty.

2.2 UNCERTAINTY

Uncertainty is of interest because its presence can affect the output of a system. Achieving a desired system output drives decision making regarding design and operation of systems. Uncertainty in the inputs to the system creates uncertainty in how designs and management strategies should be tailored to best achieve desired system outputs. Ignoring uncertainty when making design and management decisions can result in decisions that lead to undesirable system outputs. However, reducing or otherwise coping with uncertainty can also be costly in terms of resources and time.

Uncertainty in complex systems appears in many forms, such as technical uncertainty, economic uncertainty, scheduling uncertainty and political uncertainty, to name a few. These areas have been recognized and tools have been developed to deal with each. For example, factors of safety are included in a technical design to accommodate technical uncertainty, management reserves are created to address cost uncertainty and work in major government programs is spread over many congressional districts to reduce political uncertainty. As systems become more complex, the amount and complexity of the uncertainty itself in these systems increases, making it challenging to adequately design strategies for coping with the uncertainty. We proceed to review the uncertainty literature.

Uncertainty first became of interest to scholars in the study of games of chance, such as roulette or craps (Bernstein 1998, Hacking 1984). This type of uncertainty, called aleatory (pertaining to luck) uncertainty comes from the randomness of events occurring. Uncertainty began to be extensively studied in the literature starting in the early 1900's in the field of economics. Knight was the first to separate out risk and uncertainty, calling risk a situation where probabilities can be assigned to events, while uncertainty in a situation can not be expressed in terms of a specific probability (Knight 1921).

Note, that risk is often defined as the product of the probability of an event and the consequence of the event. In this context, the probability of an event occurring is often described as being the uncertainty surrounding the event. Note, this definition of uncertainty is different from Knight's, where uncertainty in that context is on events whose occurrence can not be reduced, or are at least difficult to reduce, to a probability.

Keynes later made this same differentiation by describing probable and uncertain events, where a particular number coming up in a game of roulette is probable while future prices, interest rates or the prospect of war is uncertain (Keynes 1937). For example, a specific roulette number has a definitive probability associated with it, while a future price could take almost any value.

More recently, Knightian uncertainty has been revisited with the argument that the definitions of risk and uncertainty forwarded by Knight are the same. It is argued that the difference is not that decision makers can not assign probabilities to some events, but that they choose not to assign probabilities to some events. This subtle shift changes the nature of the problem from one that deals with a lack of the probability's existence to one that is a lack of information about these probabilities. This has led to a reclassification of uncertainty as ether fundamental uncertainty or ambiguity (Dequech 2001). Fundamental uncertainty has been defined as events that can not be imagined but may occur in the future. Ambiguity is defined as the uncertainty about the probability of an event that could theoretically be known if there was more information present.

Other fields outside of economics have taken different views on uncertainty. Risk analysis and technical fields have been concerned with uncertainty related to quantity types and model forms (Morgan 1990). Quantity types include uncertainty concerning the general knowledge of a process, such as values of decision variable, randomness, linguistic imprecision and subjective judgment. Modeling uncertainty comes from a model's approximation of the real world system of interest and the uncertainty involved in how well the model then approximates the system of interest.

Other fields and subfields often look at uncertainty defined over a set of functional divisions. For example, the field of management lists uncertainties in the areas of performance, schedule, development, technology, market and business (Browning 1998). Uncertainties in space system design have been classified into development, operational and modeling uncertainties, where subsets of these uncertainties can include political, requirement, development cost, schedule and technology uncertainties (Walton 2002).

As is apparent in the literature, there are a variety of topologies for classifying uncertainty, each with its own merits and areas of applicability.

Because of the wide variety in classification techniques that the utilities of these classifications to different fields, we are not confident that a single framework can adequately address all dimensions of uncertainty, while still maintaining some value without becoming too cumbersome.

As was mentioned earlier in this section, different uncertainties require different coping strategies. For a generalizable process of coping with uncertainty, as is proposed in the next chapter on the Life-Cycle Flexibility Framework, a generalizable classification of uncertainties would be helpful. A generalizable classification on uncertainties would allow different coping strategies to be mapped to different uncertainties, independent of domain. For example, it is difficult to directly compare technology, political, and modeling uncertainties, as the domains and functions are very different. It is therefore difficult to determine if there are general coping strategies that would be applicable to these different types of uncertainty. For example, flexibility as a strategy for coping with uncertainty is the focus of this research. However, without a framework for classifying uncertainties, it is unclear if flexibility is appropriate for any or all of the technology, political or modeling uncertainty just mentioned.

Figure 2-3 is an attempt at a framework that is generic enough to classify a wide range of uncertainties, while still helping achieve the goal of being useful in helping select strategies for coping with uncertainty.

One potential way of characterizing uncertainty is over three dimensions. These three dimensions are: uncertainty over the type of event that may occur, uncertainty of the probability of an even occurring and the reducibility of the uncertainty.

Other dimensions could be added as needed, such as uncertainty over the consequences if an event should occur or where the knowledge or skill to deal with uncertainties resides. However, this is left for other researchers. Figure 2-3 presents different types of uncertainty along these three dimensions.

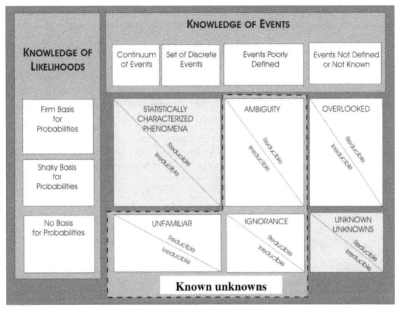

Figure 2-3 Types of uncertainty, organized around knowledge of events, event occurrence probabilities and reducibility (based on Stirling 1998 and Hastings and McManus 2004).

From Figure 2-3, six types of uncertainty are identified. Note that three of these types are grouped together into the known unknown category. A brief definition for each of these types of uncertainty is suggested below.

Statistically characterized phenomenon – The uncertainty surrounding possible events, as well as their accompanying probabilities, are well known. This describes a decision tree, where events and probabilities can all be mapped out. Reducibility refers to the ability to collapse the probabilities closer to certainty. For example, a theoretical coin has a 50-50 chance of coming up heads or tails. The events (heads or tails) are known, as is the probability, thought the actual outcome is not known until the coin is flipped. While the probabilities for heads or tails for a theoretical coin are irreducible, experimentation can be run on an actual coin, the person flipping the coin and environmental conditions, to try and reduce the probability of the theoretical coin to one that more closely approximates a real coin. For example, a real coin could be weighted, slightly increasing the probability that heads will come up.

Known unknowns – The set of uncertainty, including unfamiliar, ambiguous and ignorance classes, where there are unknown events or probabilities but we are cognizant of these. Ideally, either with the passage of time or with concentrated effort (learning, research, etc.) these will be resolved into statistically characterized phenomenon.

> **Ambiguity** – Uncertainty surrounding the probability of an event occurring. This would be like a decision tree where the probabilities are not known for certain but the event branches are known. For example, when flipping a real coin that is known to be weighted, the events of heads and tails are still known, but the probability with heads or tails coming up is uncertain.

> **Unfamiliar** – Uncertainty surrounding the different events that can occur or events not well defined. This would be like a decision tree where all the branches of the tree are not known. For example, this is like rolling a multi-sided dice when the number of sides are known but the character of the sides is not known (i.e. the number on the side of the dice), meaning the probability of an event is known but the event outcome itself may not be known.

> **Ignorance** – Uncertainty surrounding both probabilities and events, as little is known about the probabilities and events. For example, a child may not know what flipping a coin is all about – the outcomes and probabilities are uncertain.

Overlooked – Event would have been well defined if it had been thought about. This is different than ignorance, as it is in our realm of knowledge, but we forgot to consider it a priori or it was not known to be important.

Unknown unknowns – Events and probabilities not defined or could not be defined at all a priori. Once the even occurs, it is no longer an unknown unknown, an may reveal an entire new class of considerations to be taken into account into the future. What constitutes a true unknown unknown is open to interpretation. In its purest form, an unknown unknown is completely unknowable, before the event occurs. In a different sense, the unknown unknown may only be unknown to a certain stakeholder but not to others; if greater information sharing occurred across stakeholders the uncertainty could be resolved or reduced.

This research primarily addresses one type of uncertainty, that of statistically characterized phenomenon, though the Life-Cycle Flexibility Framework, presented in the following chapter, provides some guidance on addressing other types of uncertainty as well. For brevity, for the remainder of this paper, unless stated otherwise, uncertainty will be primarily referring to the statistically characterized variety.

The following chapter discusses different coping strategies for coping with uncertainty.

2.3   COPING WITH UNCERTAINTY

In coping with uncertainty, there are multiple strategies that can be deployed in complex systems. Relevant strategies are needed for coping with both negative (worse than expected) as well as positive (better than expected) outcomes associated with uncertainty

(Dean 1951). Three basic strategies have been identified by de Neufville, including: reducing the uncertainty in the system, increasing system robustness and increasing system flexibility (de Neufville 2004).

1. **Reducing uncertainty in the system** – While all aspects of uncertainty can not be eliminated or even reduced, it is possible to reduce some uncertainty. For example, through demand management techniques, uncertainty related to market or social pressures can be reduced.
2. **Increasing system robustness** – Increasing system robustness over a range of possible futures is the traditional means of addressing uncertainty in technical systems. For example, design factors of safeties are included in civil structures to account for uncertainty in loading and operating conditions.
3. **Including flexibility in the system** – Creating a system that can actively transform or better facilitate a future transformation, so as to better anticipate or respond to changing environmental and operating demands is a third way of addressing uncertainty. In this definition flexibility is different from robustness in that flexible systems actively transform to meet changing needs, while robust systems can passively perform under a variety of changing conditions.

Hastings and McManus have defined six outcomes for systems that can cope with uncertainty; reliability, robustness, versatility, flexibility, evolvability and interoperability (Hastings and McManus 2004). Hastings and McManus have described outcomes as a desired attribute of the system that is the result of a mitigating or exploiting strategy. It would seem that some of these six, such as robustness, versatility, flexibility, and evolvability could also be considered system strategies that are useful in creating specific system outcomes. Robustness and flexibility are defined similarly to the definitions found in de Neufville. For the other two strategies:

1. **Versatility** – Ability of the system to do jobs not originally included in the requirements document or to do a variety of jobs well.
2. **Evolvability** – Ability of the system to serve as the basis for new or upgraded systems with new capabilities.

Several "illities" appear in the MIT Engineering Systems Division Terms and Definitions document that deal with uncertainty; flexibility, agility, robustness, adaptability, modularity (Allen et al. 2001). Again, definitions of strategies such as flexibility are similar to ones previously presented (though subtly different as will be discussed in the following section, especially for flexibility) and the definitions for other strategies are presented below:

1. **Adaptability** – Similar to the above definition of flexibility, but while flexibility requires an outside agent as an effector for change, an adaptable system can change from an internal effector. [1]

---

[1] Where the system boundaries are defined makes the difference between a flexible and adaptable system questionable. If a transportation system is defined as including the transportation institutions that plan, design construct, operate, manage and maintain the system, then it is unclear how this could be anything

2. **Modularity** – Degree to which system components can be developed and changed independently of one another.

Other authors have forwarded additional strategies for dealing with uncertainty, such as minimizing the impact of uncertainty (Piepenbrock 2006) or resiliency (Sheffi 2005).

1. **"Ignoring" or minimizing impact of uncertainty** – Instead of actively designing coping mechanisms for uncertainty, the system can be redesigned to minimize the impact of uncertainty on it, allowing the system to "ignore" the uncertainty. For example, an enterprise could be designed to produce a product at a steady rate. As shown in Figure 2-4, this rate could be constant and below the uncertainties introduced by changing market demand. In this case, the supplier gives up the potential to increase production during peak demand, but gains the ability to reduce the impact that uncertain demand has on production.

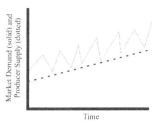

Figure 2-4 Minimizing impact of demand uncertainty on supply. (based on Piepenbrock 2006).

2. **Resiliency** – The ability to contain then quickly recover from uncertain events.

From the above descriptions, it seems apparent that there is substantial overlap between strategies. For example, the difference between flexibility and adaptability seems only to reside in where the agent that effects the change resides – external or internal to the system. Also, the difference between flexibility and agility only seems to be a function of time – systems that have agility can respond to changes at a faster rate. Perhaps because of the subtle differences, or similarities, between many of these "illities", Ross has rolled several of these into a general "illity" of "changeability" (Ross 2006).

No research has been found to date that systematically compares these types of strategies to one another, for the purpose of determining relative strengths and when it is appropriate to apply certain strategies. This task is needed, but is made more challenging by the apparent overlap between the strategies discussed, as these strategies

---

but an adaptable system, as almost all stakeholders that can change the system are considered part of the system. However, if the terms flexible and adaptable are applied only to the physical system, then these terms can have the added significance of implicitly looking at the need for policy intervention. IE, flexible systems will need outside intervention (policy intervention) to make changes, while adaptable systems will be able to change on their own without needing additional intervention from policy makers.

do not appear to be mutually exclusive. Whether these strategies form an exhaustive set of strategies is also unknown.

Also making the distinction between strategies more of a challenge is an apparent dependence of strategies at a lower level to create strategies at a higher level in the system. For example, the B-52 bomber has been described as a flexible system[2] because of its ability to be modified so that it can accomplish many combat missions, such as close ground support and release of precision munitions, which were not originally envisioned during its design as a strategic bomber (Saleh et al. 2001). Modifications have included new munitions systems (hardware) and flight profiles (operational). These modifications have taxed the B-52's airframe in ways not intended in the original requirements, for example, with increased weight loads from newer precision munitions. With the exception of a general strengthening of the secondary airframe starting in the early 1960's (Globalsecurity.org 2006), the robustness in the original airframe structural sub-system of the B-52 has enabled the overall B-52 weapon system to become flexible. In this case, a robust structural sub-system seems to enable a flexible, or evolvable, system.

Many of the above strategies for coping with uncertainty can be applied to both physical and social systems.

For example, Ho and Lui describe the rationale and benefit behind increasing the foundation strength of a parking garage so that floors can be added in the event of increased market demand for parking spaces, creating flexibility in the parking garage by making its size expandable (Ho and Liu 2003). In a social systems application Forman describes how a group of armed services, environmental groups, researchers, and businesses were formed into a coalition to support the V-22 tilt-rotor Osprey successfully during four years of programmatic and budget hostility, creating robustness in the political domain against program cancellation (Forman 2000).

While many strategies exist as a means of coping with uncertainty, this research will primarily focus on the strategy of flexibility. The following section discusses flexibility in more detail.

2.4 FLEXIBILITY

This section discusses flexibility in more detail. The section begins the discussion with a general survey of flexibility in different domains. Then, the concept of real options is introduced, followed by an overview of real option quantitative analysis techniques. The next part of the section then discusses the primary inputs used in real option analysis techniques and the challenges present when applied to "complex" real options in complex systems. Finally, the section closes by discussing the concept of real options "in" systems.

---

[2] While Saleh describe the B-52 as a flexible system, it would seem to fit more in line with the definition provided for evolvability.

2.4.1 SURVEY OF FLEXIBILITY

As in the discussion of uncertainty, there are many different dimensions and definitions for flexibility, between disciplines and even within disciplines. As a small sample:

- In the systems design literature, Saleh defines flexibility as either the ability to modify the mode of operation (i.e. changing a mission) or the attribute (i.e. the value of a parameter) of a system (Saleh 2002). Saleh had also earlier defined flexibility in terms of the ability to handle changes in requirements from those defined during the design process (Saleh 2001).
- In the flexible manufacturing literature, a large number of flexibility definitions and dimensions are identified, as covered in de Toni and Tonchia (de Toni and Tonchia 1998). A select few of these include the ability to change manufacturing line volumes, product mixes, change delivery rates or add new product lines (Suarez et al. 1991), the ability to change the speed or scope of manufacturing activities (Parthasarthy and Sethi 1992), or the flexibility at the machine, cell, plant or corporate levels (Gupta 1993).
- Within networks, Moses defines flexibility as the ability to add new nodes to the network or to make new connections between the nodes (Moses 2003).
- Within the business community, flexibility has been defined as the ability to shift factors of production or transfer resources within the corporate network (Linda and Christos 1996)
- In an institutional setting flexibility has been described as the ease in making new decisions on the basis of fixed constitutional rules (Hosli 1998).

Even within the discipline of complex systems, a variety of definitions for flexibility persist, such as :
- Property that allows systems to change with relative ease with only a small increase in system complexity [Allen 2002]
- Ability of design to satisfy changing requirements after system has been fielded [Saleh 2001]
- System capable of actively adjusting to shocks [de Neufville 2004]

While all of the above definitions and dimensions of flexibility have differences, the underlying theme of them all seems to be the ability to allow a system to undergo change with greater ease or lower costs than if no considerations of flexibility were present.

The reasons for these changes (shocks, changes in requirements, etc.), the level of the system that is impacted (machine, plant, organization, etc.) or the exact type of flexibility to be designed into the system (operational, attributes, decisions, etc.) will vary from system to system and from application to application.

Since the emphasis of this research is complex systems, with both physical and social systems present, it seems that the best course of action for the system would be to take aspects from all of the above types of flexibility and apply them where needed, as opposed to being constrained to any one definition. Therefore, the definition of flexibility that will be used for this research is as follows:

The ability for a system to actively transform, or facilitate a future transformation, to better anticipate or respond to changing internal or external conditions.

2.4.2 OPTIONS

Flexibility as a concept has been operationalized with the use of options. An option represents at its most fundamental level a freedom of choice amongst alternatives, once new information has been revealed. Options have a formal definition and mathematics, both of which will be described in the following section, but the fundamental thinking behind options have predated both by thousands of years.

Brach gives an overview of the history of options. Some of the earliest option contracts dating back to 1800-1500 BC have been found written on stone tablets in what is today Syria and Iraq, representing a derivative on real assets such as grain and metal. One of the most famous early option examples was in the Dutch tulip market in the 1600's. Here, options on future tulip bulbs were traded. As the demand for tulips far exceeded the supply, tulip prices soared. The tulip options allowed future tulip prices to be locked in. If the tulip price further increased the option could be exercised and the tulip purchased at the lower price. If tulip prices decreased, the option expired unexercised and the tulip was purchased at market prices. The first formal exchange of options (and futures) occurred with the opening of the Chicago Board of Trade in 1848, with trading in options beginning in the 1870s. Trading of the first options based on stocks in 1973 coincided with the future Nobel prize winning publication of Black and Scholes paper that showed how call options on stocks could be properly priced. The Black-Scholes formula coming from this paper, and other variations, became the basis for option valuation in financial markets and helped lead to the expanse of option trading in the market (Brach 2003).

The options described above are called financial options, because they are options on financial assets or commodities traded in financial markets. In contrast, options on real assets or projects are called real options, a term first used by Myers (Myers 1977). The need for real options came about as a way to address shortcomings in corporate project evaluation tools, such as discounted cash flow and net present value analyses. Relatively recently, projects have been evaluated using discounted cash flows (DCF) and net present values (NPV), which estimate the future cash flows and discounts them to a present value so projects of different time horizons and cash flows can be compared. However, dissatisfaction arose with these techniques because of the perceived undervaluing of projects that contained flexibility and strategic interactions. These flexibility and strategic interactions were perceived to have value that was not being represented in the quantitative values generated by DCF and NPV (Schwartz et al. 2001).

Myers identifies four main problems with DCF; estimating the discount rate, estimating future cash flows, estimating project impact on other projects and estimating project impact on future investment opportunities. Myers further classifies projects that are good at cost reductions or cash cows that offer stable returns and are not part of generating future strategic value as being ideal candidates for valuation with DCF, while opportunities with high growth or intangible opportunities should be valued with real options (Myers 1987).

While the basic shortcomings of the DCF method, introduced in 1907 by Fisher (Fisher 1907), have long been known, adequate means of addressing them had not been developed. For example, in Dean's 1951 book, he identifies the lack of flexibility taken into account with DCF processes and proposes four alternatives for coping with shortcoming, ranging from applying professional judgment informally to applying different handicaps to the mathematical analysis (Dean 1951). Work in decision trees (Hertz 1964) and simulation (Magee 1964) was forwarded as quantitative methods of valuing flexibility and strategic investments.

The lack of quantification of the flexibility and strategic interactions in projects was seen as biasing project selection towards projects that had a higher short-term return on investment, harming longer-term corporate and national interests, due to underinvestment because of undervaluation (Hayes and Abernathy 1980). While the long-term benefits of activities such as R&D or investing in new technology development were seen, how to quantify them still remained a mystery: "beyond all else, capital investment represents an act of faith, a belief that the future will be as promising as the present" (Hayes and Gavin 1982).

Not until the mid-1980's did real options begin to be used and studied in corporate decision making. Myers was one of the first to suggest that option theory had the best theoretical promise for valuing investments that have significant operational or strategic options (Myers 1987). First used primarily in the natural resource industries (Borison 2005), where swings in prices of 25-40% were common (Brennand and Schwartz 1985), real options were included in the financial calculations of firms. One of the first examples in the literature is that of options on a copper mine, where the option of when to begin and end operations could be contingent on the future price of copper prices in the world copper market (Brennand and Schwartz 1985).

Formally, an option is defined as:

> *The right, but not the obligation, to take some action at a future date at a predetermined price.*

The essential pieces of this definition are that the option grants the options holder the ability to take some action at a cost that will be determined before the actual event occurs. For example, with a stock option, the option holder can choose to buy a share of stock at a predetermined price sometime in the future. If the price of the stock on the open market is cheaper than the price point the holder can buy at, the option is not used. If the market price is more expensive, the holder can exercise the option, buy the stock at the agreed upon price and realize the difference between the purchase price and the market price (and the price of the option) as profit. Thus, the option holder has paid a price (the option price) for the flexibility to buy or not buy the stock at a predefined price. While this flexibility has long been identified as valuable, the actual value that it has was not quantifiable by rigorous means until the advent of the Nobel prize winning Black-Scholes (Black and Scholes 1973, Merton 1973) method, and later follow-on methods.

An overview of "standard" option pricing methodology is presented below, where "standard" pricing methods are defined as the relatively straightforward analysis techniques commonly found in the real options literature. This work is presented as an overview of existing quantitative evaluation methods. For this work, however, the focus will be on evaluation of "complex" real options in complex system.

2.4.3 BACKGROUND TO MATHEMATICS BEHIND REAL OPTIONS

The mathematics driving Real Options Analysis (ROA) is based on the same mathematics used to calculate prices for financial options. Figure 2-5 below shows the stock price of AOL Time Warner, a typical asset, over the course of a year. The purpose of the mathematics is to calculate the value of an option for an asset that exhibits a stochastic nature, such as the AOL stock price.

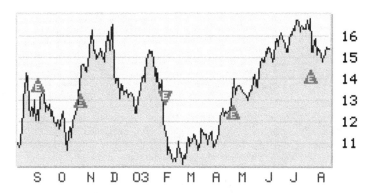

Figure 2-5 Annual price of AOL Time Warner stock.

As can be seen from Figure 2-5, the instantaneous price of the asset can be very unpredictable. This stochasticity makes it difficult to set a number that represents the value for an option on the asset.

The value of an option comes from two parts: the intrinsic and extrinsic value (Hull 1995, Summa and Lubow 2002). The intrinsic value is the value that could be obtained from exercising the option now. If the option is "in the money" it has some intrinsic value, while if the option is out of the money the option's intrinsic value is zero. The extrinsic value is essentially the time value of waiting to exercise the option. If the option is deep in or out of the money, unless the underlying asset is subject to extreme volatility, it is unlikely the price will move substantially and the extrinsic value is low, meaning there is

43

little value in waiting. However, if the option is close to the money, either in or out, there is value in waiting as the option may move into the money or deeper into the money. In this case the extrinsic value is high. The intrinsic and extrinsic value is shown below for a call option in Figure 2-6. The solid line is the intrinsic value, the dotted line is the total value and distance between them is the extrinsic value.

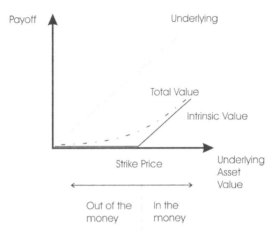

Figure 2-6 Payoff diagram for call option.

There are multiple "standard" methods for determining the value of an option. The easiest to use are closed form solutions to the underlying differential equation. The most famous example of this is the Black-Scholes equation which is the closed form solution of a European call option. Other closed form solutions have also been found for a variety of different options, such as put options or options with dividends. Mun provides a variety of these closed form solutions in his work (Mun 2002). While these are by far the easiest way to compute the value of an option, the appropriateness of using closed form solutions for finding real options values is questionable. The closed form solutions are solutions for the underlying partial differential equation (PDE), solved with different boundary conditions. While this may adequately represent basic financial options, such as a European call option, for more "complex" real options, it is unlikely that an existing closed form solution is available, or can even be found.

Where this is true, a second method then is to solve by some means the underlying PDE. Typically some form of numerical methods is necessary to solve the PDE for the desired option.

A third, and popular, approach is to use a discrete time approximation of the underlying asset value and option price. The most common, called a recombining binomial lattice, was developed by Cox et al. (Cox et al. 1977). This process is relatively simple to use and the results can be easier to explain and justify. This is opposed to needing to understand complex mathematics or numerical techniques, or to "just trust" the output value, as is necessary in using the solution source for the first two methods.

The final method for solving for option value is through the use of simulations. Different authors have used different approaches to simulation, though the underlying idea is to use the simulation to understand how the uncertainty and option unfolds over time. With the addition of Monte Carlo analysis, a distribution of the results can be obtained and the mean value of the option found. A benefit of simulations is the ability to value "complex" real options or options in "complex" systems that may be too difficult or impossible to characterize with the more "standard" analysis techniques above. These are summarized below in Table 2-1.

Table 2-1 Overview of mathematical methods used to solve for option pricing.

Mathematical Classification	Option Pricing Method	Description	Strengths	Weaknesses
Analytical	Analytical Solution of PDE	Analytical solution directly solves the PDE, producing one closed form solution. The most elegant and easy to use solution, of which Black-Scholes equation is the most famous example.	Simple to use once the solution is found. Very elegant and requires almost no computation time or resources.	Finding the analytical solution is very difficult or impossible in many cases. Each solution is only good for the boundary conditions that were applied to the PDE when solving. Because it is so easy to use and because the boundary conditions may not be apparent, the equation can easily be misused. Also, because it is so easy to use, there is a tendency to distrust the number that "pops" out – as it is difficult to explain how the option value was obtained.
Numerical Methods	Finite Difference / numerical integration of PDE	A numerical method for solving the PDE when analytical solutions can not be obtained or would require too much effort.	Can be used to solve for option prices under a much larger set of boundary conditions. Many well known methods exist for solving PDEs with this method.	Difficult to use unless conversant in mathematics, meaning that most practitioners and decision makers would not use this method. As it is very mathematically intensive, it is hard to explain how the option price was obtained to decision makers. Difficulty in implementing rapidly increases when multiple underlying are present.
Lattice	Multi-nomial lattices for representing stochastic DE	A discrete method to represent the stochastic differential equations. Can be combined with Monte Carlo or other simulation methods to increase accuracy.	Easy to use and easy to explain where the option prices "come from". Can be used in a low computationally intensive form to get a rough approximation of the option price. This is currently the most popular method for calculating option prices.	Not the most accurate of methods, especially at lower levels of resolution. Difficult to calculate multiple underlying and non-constant parameters (can be done to a certain extent).

Mathematical Classification	Option Pricing Method	Description	Strengths	Weaknesses
Simulation	Monte Carlo or other simulation of stochastic PDE	A simulation of the underlying price. Monte Carlo is the most popular method, combining thousands of simulations to represent the stochastic nature of the price.	Relatively easy to use and requiring low mounts of mathematical skill and knowledge. Many software packages are available to conduct Monte Carlo analysis. Can be used to simulate option prices when multiple underlying or non-constant parameters are present.	Can be computationally intensive. May not be theoretically precise.

2.4.4   Generating Real Option Parameter Values

When using standard valuation techniques for real options, one of the largest difficulties is with the determination of values for the parameters used in solving for the option price. The five parameters, listed Table 2-2, all present various degrees of difficulty in quantification. The problems stem from the change in application, i.e. moving from financial options to real options. Many of the assumptions and data sources that are used in obtaining these values when finding the price of financial options either do not exist or need to be modified for real options. This section deals with the various methods available for generating values for the five parameters above. First a brief overview of each of the five parameters is given, followed by an overview of the different methods available for finding values for these parameters.

2.4.4.1   Overview of the Five ROA Parameters

Table 2-2 lists the five parameters used in real options valuations are: current price, volatility, time to expiration, strike price, and interest rate.

Table 2-2 Five parameters used in real option valuation techniques.

S	=	value of the underlying asset
σ	=	volatility or standard deviation of the underlying variable
R	=	continuously compounding risk-free rate of return
D	=	continuous dividend payouts
T	=	time until payout

Value of underlying asset - The value of the underlying asset refers to the underlying asset that the real option provides an option on. In financial option theory the underlying asset, or just underlying, is a stock and the current value (or price) of the underlying is therefore the current price of the stock. In real options valuation, this is perhaps the hardest of all parameters to determine. The reason for this is that to determine a current value of an underlying, an appropriate underlying must first be determined.

For some real options this appears deceptively easy. For example, if we want an option to purchase land that can be used for petroleum production, it would seem that the proper underlying would be the price of petroleum on the open market. Therefore, if petroleum prices increase, the potential value of the field increases (i.e. the potential to sell more oil at a higher price), the option would be exercised and oil wells would be drilled. However, even oil prices on the open market may not be an appropriate underlying, as the type of oil may differ from the composite oil prices that are listed.

Unfortunately, most real options problems are not even this straight-forward. The proper choice of an underlying for most options is very difficult. For example, suppose we wanted an option on whether to build a subway system in a city. What would be a good underlying that would indicate if the new subway additions should be built or not? Number of subway travelers? Number of public transportation travelers? Total number of travelers? Property value prices? Cost of building a subway system? Cost of providing other modes of transportation? All of these ways of measure, and more, would go into any decision made for building a subway system. Is one of these more important than the others and should therefore become the underlying? Unlike financial options, there is no clear choice on what the underlying is so that a current value can be obtained.

A common, though not uncontroversial method, of obtaining an underlying asset is through the Mutual Asset Disclaimer (MAD) method, where the object itself with no flexibility included is used as the underlying asset. The rationale here is that the NPV of the project without flexibility is the best approximation of what the project would fetch on the open market if it were put up for sale (Brealey and Myers 2003, Copeland and Antikarov 2003).

Most real options theory discusses the choice of one underlying. In the above subway example, it is clear that multiple factors would affect any decision on whether to build the subway or not. This seems to point to the need for an analysis that takes into account multiple criteria when used to value the option and when creating decision rules on when to purchase and when to exercise the option. Also, since the factors that are important for making the decision to build a subway vary from city to city, from country to country and from time to time, there could be a necessity for the choice of an appropriate set of criteria to be dependant on the specific application.

Volatility - Volatility is another difficult to quantify parameter that is open to interpretation. Ideally, the volatility provides a measure or bound of uncertainty involved with the underlying asset. The difficulty comes with how to measure this volatility. Should it be a historical measure taken since the beginning of the creation of the underlying? Or should it be only the more recent volatility – like the volatility experienced over the last several years, which may be a better indicator of future events. In complex systems, especially those that deal with the political domain, sudden jumps can also occur, such as from a change in regulation, that makes modeling the volatility more challenging. Luerman suggests three approaches to modeling volatility; historical data, simulation and educated estimates (Luerman 1998). Copeland and Antikarov and

Mun both suggest an increased role for Monte Carlo analysis to estimate and aggregate volatility, where appropriate (Copeland and Antikarov 2001, Mun 2002).

Time to Expiration - The time to expiration is one of the easier parameters to determine. While in financial options the expiration time is explicitly set when purchased, there is no such comparable rule with real options. However, while there is in effect no deadline to many decisions, an expiration time can be set that is useful for the decision or tied to some outside factor. Returning to the subway example, the deadline for making a decision on building the subway may be imposed by the political administration to show they are getting something done, it may be tied to the availability of federal matching funds, or dependent on when the next round of elections occur. In any case, while all have some measure of arbitrariness, it is set as a measure of what is useful.

A key difference between financial options and real options is the length of time that the option is open. Financial options are typically measured in lengths of weeks or months. Real options may run into the years or decades. Aside from the challenge of projecting out realistic parameters, such as volatility, that far into the future, additional considerations should be noted. Specifically, the value of a financial option goes to zero once the time expires. In real options, the same assumption is made, though in reality the option may not actually lose all its value at the time of expiration. For example, expanding on the subway example, if the option in question was the purchasing of land and the future decision to build a subway, the option exercise decision in the future is to either build the subway on the purchased land or not. The cost of the option was the current price of the land. In option theory, if we decide to let the option expire after some time by not building the subway the option value would go to zero. This is obviously not true as the land still has some value. It may no longer have value as land that can be used to build a subway on, but it still has some value.

Strike Price – While the strike price, i.e. the price at which the option is exercised, is predefined and set by contract in financial options, the actual strike price may vary over time for real options. Any number of factors could change the strike price, such as unexpected costs, partners renegotiating contracts or shifts in technology. These become especially important when the expiration time is long and the strike price depends on transactions between multiple actors.

Interest Rate - The interest rate is supposed to represent the risk free interest rate. While this can easily be taken as the return from a very low risk asset, like Treasury Bills, whether this is really appropriate is open to debate. The risk free rate is supposed to be free of *private* risk – that is risk that is applicable to a particular venture, as opposed to *market* risk. The elimination of private risk still allows many different "risk free" interest rates to be set. In our oil field example, possible choices could be the return offered from T-bills, from the stock market or from petroleum commodities. All of these are free from private risk of investing in a particular oil field, but carry much different market risks and rates of return. Additional factors, such as options depending on decisions of government actors, may complicate proper interest rate selection further. Even if the project itself does not have options built into it, if the uncertainty of the interest rates are high enough, there is value to waiting to see what future interest rates will be before embarking on a project, giving the project an option like feature (Ingersoll and Ross 1992).

The overview of real options analysis techniques presented above suggest that while option valuation techniques are improving, the practice still has a significant amount of art in the process.

Further, it is not clear that the "standard" real option analysis techniques will ever be able to adequately evaluate "complex" real options in complex systems. This is because "complex" real options in complex systems involve more than a single or simple change or addition to a system to create flexibility. Rather, "complex" real options in complex systems involve interconnected system attributes across a variety of technical, organizational and process dimensions.

Creating an analysis methodology capable of taking into account the multiple dimensions of "complex" real options in complex systems is the subject of the next chapter on Life-Cycle Flexibility.

Before moving into the following chapter on the Life-Cycle Flexibility Framework, new directions for options and existing processes for evaluating real options are discussed in the following two sections.

2.4.5 THE CONCEPT OF REAL OPTIONS "IN" SYSTEMS

The concept of real options applies the concept of financial options to real assets. *Prior work on real options has mostly originated from the economic and management domain, with the consequence that the technical system has been treated like a black box.* The vast bulk of the real options literature has designed options around the physical system, concentrating on areas such as program management, corporate strategy and market entrance. Typical examples of real options that appear in the literature include:

- Valuing pharmaceutical R&D at Merck as a series of successive options that can be exercised to progress to the next stage or not exercised to terminate a project (Nichols 1994).
- Kester explicitly links capital budgeting decisions and long range planning to provide for improved competitive position with new growth opportunities (Kester 1984).
- Kester also characterized the sequential introduction of inter-related products into the market to learn from prior product placements and to understand erosion in market share (Kester 1993).

The number of applications in different industries also varies substantially. Merton and Copeland and Keenan identify many industries and how they use real options in practice, such as in pharmaceutical R&D, power plant phased construction, the making of movie sequels, and modularity in production systems (Merton 1998). Additional examples are shown below in Figure 2-7.

49

Situations generating real options, by sector

Aerospace and defense
Valuing options in customer contracts (eg, the cancellation of features)

Assembly and machinery
Timing of investment in new factories

Automotive
Valuing decisions to modify new car designs well into product development cycles

Banking and securities
Valuing real estate leases

Chemicals
Timing of investment in new factories

Consumer/packaged goods
Learning options for new product R&D and test marketing

Electronics
Entry or exit options in the PC assembly business

Energy
Learning options in timing the development of oil and gas fields

Insurance
Valuing such contingency features as loans against value of policies

Media and entertainment
Planning new product launches

Metals
Learning options in timing the development of new mines

Pharmaceuticals and medical products
Establishing priorities among prospective R&D projects

Pulp and paper
Timing of forest harvesting

Retail
Timing of expansion into foreign markets

Telecommunications
M&A programs for geographic expansion

Transportation
The option to extend or contract routing structures (eg, railroad spurs)

Figure 2-7 Real options in practice: a variety of industry and real option examples. Figure taken from (Copeland and Keenan 1998).

A notable early exception to treating the technical system as a black box was the design of an industrial steam boiler to have the flexibility to operate using either oil or gas, depending on the current market prices for each (Kulatilaka 1993).

In this theme of incorporating specific features into the design of the system, de Neufville has called this process designing real options "in" a system, as differentiated from designing real options "on" a system, which requires no special technical knowledge of the system (de Neufville 2004). Research efforts along these lines include the following examples of real options "in" system:

- Adding flexibility in the amount of water capacity a dam can store or release, depending on electricity prices (Wang and de Neufville 2006).
- Design of a building that allows it to be reconfigured either as an office or laboratory, depending on the real estate market for office space, lab space and the future needs of the occupants (Greden 2005).
- Sizing the foundation of a parking garage so additional floors can be added at a later date if demand materializes (Zhao and Tseng 2003).
- Design and deployment of a constellation of low earth orbit satellites that can be augmented with additional satellites if demand increases (de Weck et al. 2003).

The following section discussed existing real option processes.

2.5 REAL OPTION PROCESSES

Existing processes for using real options have focused on the quantitative evaluation of the real option.

While there are a number of variant frameworks proposed for valuing real options, a sample of which is presented below, all have the common theme of seeking to extend more traditional discounted cash flow techniques that are widely used in project evaluation to real option analysis. Three frameworks for valuing real options taken from Copeland, Mun and Amram are presented below.

The framework that Copeland (Copeland and Antikarov 2003) proposes is divided into four steps. Step one requires the determination of a value for a "base case" project that has no flexibility built into it using standard DCF techniques. Step two calls for explicitly identifying and modeling the critical uncertainties involved with the project and understanding how these develop over time. This is to be accomplished with either the use of historical data or management estimates. Step three creates a decision tree that can be analyzed to identify the places where management possesses managerial flexibility. At these points, flexibility can be built into the project. Step four then uses real option valuation techniques, such as Black-Scholes, a lattice or simulation, to determine the value of the option. The value is compared to the cost of the option to determine desirability of purchasing the option.

The framework proposed by Mun (Mun 2002) has many similarities to the one described in Copeland, but has the significant difference of looking at combinations of projects to determine how options interact across a portfolio of projects. Mun's framework is presented in eight steps. Step one involves qualitative management screening of projects that are suitable for inclusion of options. Step two estimates a NPV for the inflexible base case, similar to that proposed in Copeland. Step three advocates the use of Monte Carlo analysis to help identity the critical parameters affecting uncertainty and their sensitivity, with the most critical and sensitive being the best candidates for applying options. Step four asks for appropriate real options to be created, followed by their quantitative evaluation in step five. Step six goes beyond evaluation of options in a single project to understand how a portfolio of projects, each with options, behaves. The intent is to better understand the value of the options working together and to help optimize resource allocation between projects and options. Step seven and eight include reporting the results and updating the analysis over time, if necessary.

Amram's four step framework (Amram and Kulatilaka 1999) is similar to the two frameworks previously presented, but goes into more detail in the process of how to design real options. Step one frames the application, relying heavily on user experience and judgment to determine what applications are appropriate for using options and what options are appropriate to use. Amram goes into some detail in this step, discussing identification of the following; the decisions (in terms of what are the relevant decisions and who is making them), the critical uncertainty, the decision rules for when to exercise an option, and the search for an appropriate framework for pricing, such as the availability of market data or not. Step two quantitatively evaluates the options. Step three analyzes the results along the dimensions of critical values for decision making, appropriateness for the strategy space and the investment risk profile. Finally, step four recommends and iteration to determine if the option can be better designed or expanded to increase value.

The framework proposed by Copeland and Mun explicitly call for using real option valuation techniques to supplement the DCF analysis of an inflexible base case project, with the real option value calculated adding to the basic value. Mun takes this a step further at the back end by placing the options into a larger context of a portfolio of projects and explicitly calling for option interaction effects to be considered once option value has been calculated. Amram expands on the point of explicitly calling for decision rules and decision makers to be identified a priori during the option development.

The shortcomings of existing real option processes will be discussed in the following chapter on Life-Cycle Flexibility. However, in general, these frameworks do not consider the set of interacting technology, organizational and processes concerns that appear in "complex" real options in complex systems.

2.6 "COMPLEX" REAL OPTIONS IN COMPLEX SYSTEMS

As discussed in Wang and de Neufville (Wang and de Neufville 2006), real options are often not as easy to design and evaluate as financial options. As noted in Brach, the reasoning for this is that financial options essentially only have two dimensions of interest: time to maturity and the difference between the observable price and the exercise price. However, for real options, multiple dimensions of interest exist (Brach 2006). These dimensions can include, but are not limited to:

- Time to maturity is uncertain for real options
- Real options can be partially reversible, such as the salvage price of a project after an option to abandon has been exercised
- The cost of capital may increase when waiting to exercise a real option, making a delayed expansion more costly
- The future uncertainty faced with real options may not be a continuation of past trends
- Real options may be path dependant, unlike financial options.

While financial options can exhibit mathematical complexity when their value is calculated, within real options a spectrum of complexity across multiple dimensions exists. At one end of the spectrum are "standard" real options and at the other are "complex" real options.

The design of "standard" real options has been presented in the literature as relatively straightforward additions or changes to a system to create flexibility. The "standard" real option is then evaluated with a "standard" real option evaluation process that makes use of relatively straightforward quantitatively-based techniques. These evaluation techniques can include such tools as the Black-Scholes equation or binomial lattices. "Standard" real options also assume that the option holder has the managerial flexibility to react to changing conditions by choosing whether or not to exercise the option at a future date.

In comparison, the design of a "complex" real option is envisioned as being composed of more than a single or simple change or addition to a system to create flexibility. Rather, the "complex" real option is likely composed of interconnecting technological, organizational and process components. The utility of the "complex" real option then depends on successfully integrating action along the multiple dimensions of technology, organizations and processes. For example, changes in managerial processes, properly structured and written contracts, and the availability of appropriate technologies may all be necessary to ensure that the "complex" real option will have some utility. Consideration of only one of these dimensions may mean for the "complex" real option that the flexible system cannot be successfully deployed or the option exercised.

The following definition for "complex" real options is proposed:

> "A complex option is composed of multiple components across a variety of dimensions, such as technical, financial, political, organizational and legal. All components are necessary for the option to be deployed and exercised; no single component is sufficient.

A continuum illustrating the levels of complexity for real options, along with examples, is shown in Figure 2-8.

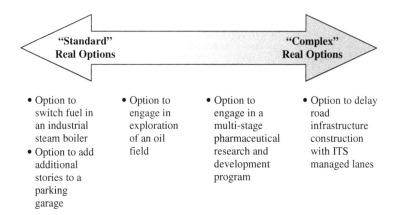

"Standard" Real Options			"Complex" Real Options
• Option to switch fuel in an industrial steam boiler • Option to add additional stories to a parking garage	• Option to engage in exploration of an oil field	• Option to engage in a multi-stage pharmaceutical research and development program	• Option to delay road infrastructure construction with ITS managed lanes

Figure 2-8 Continuum of examples of real options, from "standard" to "complex".

The examples of real options presented in Figure 2-8 are discussed in more detail below.

- **Option to switch fuel in an industrial steam boiler** – The option to switch operation of a steam boiler between two different types of fuels, such as oil and gas, as described in Kulatilaka, allows the option holder the flexibility to take advantage of whichever fuel is selling at a lower price (Kulatilaka 1993). This option is a "standard" real option because the design of the option is a relatively straightforward technical modification of a typical steam boiler. The evaluation of the option can also be accomplished adequately using "standard" real option evaluation techniques, such as a binomial lattice. The management of the option is also straightforward, requiring the option holder to simply "pull a switch" to activate the option and change the fuel type used in the boiler.
- **Option to add additional stories to a parking garage** – The option to increase the size of support columns during construction of a parking garage to create the option to add additional stories at a later date allows the option holder to postpone a build decision on the additional stories until market demand can be determined (Zhao and Tseng 2003). This option is a "standard" real option because the design of the option is a straightforward increase in the size of the support columns. The evaluation of the option can also be accomplished using "standard" real option evaluation techniques such as binomial lattices. The management of the option is also straightforward with the option holder observing the demand for the parking spaces and exercising the option to build additional parking spaces when the demand reaches a high enough level.

- **Option to engage in exploration of an oil field** – The option to engage in the exploration of an oil field is a multi-phased option that allows the option holder to engage in a series of exploration, drilling and production activities, if the oil field is found to contain adequate amounts of oil and the market price of oil justifies further drilling and production investments (Brennan and Schwartz 1985). This option is more complex that a "standard" real option primarily because of the additional challenges involved in evaluation. Instead of a one-stage project that can be evaluated with "standard" real option evaluation techniques, this option can be considered a compound rainbow option. The compound rainbow option has multiple later stage options embedded within earlier options and are affected by multiple sources of uncertainty. Evaluation of this option would require a greater sophistication than provided by "standard" real option techniques.
- **Option to engage in a multi-state pharmaceutical research and development program** – The option to engage in a multi-state pharmaceutical research and development program allows the option holder the ability to continue, abandon or sell a R&D program at any stage depending on the success of previous stages, anticipated success of future stages and the current market value of the drug under development (Copeland and Antikarov 2003). This option is more complex than "standard" real options because of the challenges involved with the evaluation and management of the option. Like the oil field exploration example above, this option is also a compound rainbow option. However, while the oil field option could be considered proprietary, meaning a single company has rights to develop a field, the pharmaceutical R&D program could be taking place in a competitive environment. In a competitive environment, the option holder may not be able to appropriate the entire value of the option, resulting in the timing and value of the option being influenced by other competitors (Smit and Trigeorgis 2004). This makes the option evaluation and management more complex than a "standard" real option.
- **Option to delay road infrastructure construction with ITS managed lanes** – The ability to deploy ITS technologies on a managed lane to create the option to delay conventional infrastructure construction to a future date is an example of a "complex" option examined in this research. For this option, additional complexity beyond a "standard" real option is observed along the dimensions of design, evaluation and management. The design of the ITS capabilities requires a simultaneous design of a technical component and an organizational component. The ITS capabilities are only effective if they are actively managed, which is much different than traditional infrastructure which can be deployed without active management. Since active management of the road network is not a standard activity for transportation organizations, design of the organizational capabilities to match the technical capabilities is non-trivial. The evaluation of the option is also more complex than "standard" real options. First, the metric of interest is variable depending on the type of enterprise operating the system; public enterprises may be interested in societal benefits while private enterprises may be interested only in revenue generated through tolls. Second, deployment of ITS capabilities on a single facility can affect the entire road network. Without the proper design, benefits on a single facility can be offset by consequences on

other links in the network. Sophisticated modeling techniques, such as the use of regional traffic demand models are necessary to determine the benefits derived from the ITS option. The management of the ITS option is also more complex than "standard" options. Multiple stakeholders are associated with the option and can directly or indirectly affect the option value and ability to exercise. Political considerations, public concerns and internal division within the option holder's own enterprise can all make the management of the option more challenging than the assumption of managerial flexibility common for "standard" real options.

Table 2-3 and Table 2-4 help illustrate the differences between financial options, "standard" real options and "complex" real options.

Table 2-3 "Standard" and "Complex" financial and real options.

Option Type	Option Type	
	"Standard"	"Complex"
Financial	Discussed in literature on financial options. Examples include call options, put options, etc.	Existence of "complex" financial options in question. Potential examples could include options in large scale and sophisticated portfolios, with the portfolio manager operating in financial, political and business environments to affect the option values.
Real	Discussed in literature on real options. Examples include dual-fuel industrial steam-boiler and variable level parking garage.	Discussed in this research. Examples include the use of ITS in managed lanes and the use of BWB type aircraft to gain commonality across airplane families, involving such considerations as; technologies, enterprise architectures, corporate strategies, metrics, legal/liability concerns and politics.

Table 2-3 shows the difference between "standard" and "complex" financial and real options. "Standard" financial and "standard" real options are the classifications used here to describe the majority of the financial and real options literature. The options are relatively straight-forward and are evaluated with "standard" option evaluation methods, such as those described in Section 2.4.3. "Complex" real options are the type discussed in this research. The existence of "complex" financial options is uncertain. There are certainty very complicated financial options, but it is not clear if there are "complex" financial options.

Table 2-4 shows the difference between combinations of different types of real options "in" systems. To date, the concept of real options "in" systems is relatively new. Several examples of past analysis looking at real options "in" system were given in Section 2.4.5. Most of these could be considered "standard" real options in "standard" systems. For this research, "complex" real options in "complex" systems are of interest.

Table 2-4 "Standard" and "complex" real options and "standard" and "complex" systems.

System Type	Option Type	
	"Standard" Real Option	"Complex" Real Option
"Standard" System	Discussed in literature. Examples include dual-fuel industrial steam-boiler and variable level parking garage.	NA
"Complex" System	Discussed in literature. Examples include option to expand water supply systems or the variable level parking garage in a more realistic setting.	Discussed in this research as options with multiple components embedded in systems with characteristics such as containing multiple stakeholders or being large. Examples include the use of ITS in managed lanes and the use of BWB type aircraft to gain commonality across airplane families.

The difference between "standard" and "complex" real options was the topic of discussion earlier in this section. The distinction between "standard" and "complex" systems refers back to the discussion on complex systems presented in Section 2.1. In summary, the complex system will have additional complexity, such as being large or having multiple stakeholders with multiple viewpoints, which either do not exist or are not critical to consider with "standard" systems.

"Complex" real options in complex systems therefore refers to options with multiple interconnected components across several domains that are embedded within systems

that have characteristics such being large, having uncertainty and influenced by multiple stakeholders with fragmented goals and priorities.

While the "standard" real options analysis discussed earlier in this chapter seem to consider complex systems, the actual analysis conducted in many of these cases did not explicitly address many of the characteristics that make the systems complex, though there are a few cases where the system complexity was explicitly considered, such as the analysis conducted by Ramirez (Ramirez 2002).

In actuality, since all real options exist in the "real world", which is a very large complex system, all real options are in a "complex" system. When the system can be considered "standard" and when it should be considered "complex" depends on the specific instance and a matter of judgment. To illustrate, the variable level garage example is re-visited.

As presented in the literature, the garage example is a "standard" real option in a "standard" system[3]. When explicitly considering the system, the characterization of a "standard" real option in a standard system would hold if the garage was owned and operated by a sole proprietor in the middle of a small town. However, the garage example could be considered a "standard" real option in a "complex" system if the garage was part of a multi-national conglomerate involved with transportation systems operating the garage in the middle of a large metropolis. Challenges that exist from operating a large enterprise, dealing with stakeholders hostile to the expansion of the garage or trying to influence zoning regulations on the height of buildings are all factors that could make the system more complex. These challenges may not exist or may be of more moderate scale for the sole proprietor in the small town and hence do not need to be taken into account.

The combination of the "complex" real options and the "complex" system creates the class of options of interest for this research; "complex" real options in complex systems.

It should be noted that while Table 2-4 displays "standard" and "complex" real options and systems, in actuality two considerations need to be addressed. "Standard" and "complex" are simply two points on a continuum, as shown in Figure 2-8. Real options and systems can be more or less complex. This creates a two-dimensional space of that would describe real options of some complexity in a system of some complexity, as shown in Figure 2-9.

---

[3] The garage example in the literature does not explicitly consider the system that the garage is embedded within, such as stakeholder resistance to the addition of stories, legal or zoning concerns, or enterprise architecture issues. Since these are not explicitly considered, they are assumed not to be important for the design, evaluation and management of the option, so therefore the system is considered as a "standard" system.

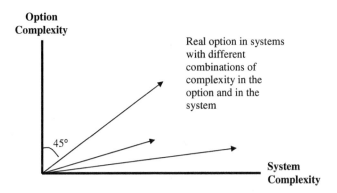

Figure 2-9 Space of possible real options in a system, as measured by degree of complexity in both the real option and the system. Note, that it is assumed that system complexity will always be as great or greater than the option complexity, by definition.

Another consideration is the difference between the level of complexity in the real option and the system and the level of complexity in the analysis of that option. A real option and the system may be very complex, but simplified to allow analysis. This would have the effect of making a "complex" real option in a complex system appear for analysis purposes as a "standard" real option in a standard system. The validity of this simplification will depend on the specifics of the system and the option.

The result of the complexity existing in the real option and in the system creates a need for a process that can handle this set of interconnecting technical, organizational and process considerations. From the literature review on complex systems, uncertainty, flexibility, real options and valuation processes, this type of process does not seem to be available. Therefore, there seems to be the need to create such a process. To our knowledge, the Life-Cycle Flexibility Framework is the first such attempt at creating a process for designing, evaluating and managing "complex" real options in a complex system.

2.7 CHAPTER SUMMARY

A summary of the concepts from the literature on complex systems, uncertainty, strategies for coping with uncertainty, flexibility and real options is presented in Table 2-5.

Table 2-5 Summary of major points from literature review.

Complex Systems
Complex system characteristics make predicting future behavior difficult, leading to uncertainty. The difficulty in predicting behavior comes from two reasons: • Complexity from the system itself • Uncertain environmental inputs
Uncertainty
Many types of uncertainty exist, over multiple dimensions
No single, generic framework for classifying, and therefore identifying common characteristics across uncertainties, has been found in the literature
There is a need for a framework that allows comparison of uncertainties so that strategies for coping with different kinds of uncertainty can be identified. A framework is presented to allow comparison across uncertainties to facilitate choosing strategies for coping with the uncertainty, in Figure 2-3.
Strategies for Coping with Uncertainty
Multiple strategies exist for coping with uncertainty
Relative strengths and weaknesses across strategies, as well as when it is appropriate to apply individual strategies, is an open topic
Many of the strategies can be applied to both technical and social systems
Flexibility
Many different definitions and types of flexibility are apparent, varying over domains and applications
The underlying theme of flexibility seems to be a system trait that facilitates change at a lower cost than if flexibility was not present
Real Options
Real Options are a way to operationalize the concept of flexibility
Quantitative evaluation techniques, based on financial options evaluation techniques, encounter challenges when applied to real options
Previous literature on real options have been applied to "standard" real options
"Standard" evaluation techniques do not seem appropriate when applied to "complex" real options in complex systems
A new evaluation technique is needed for "complex" real options in complex systems, as "standard" evaluation techniques are not adequate. The LCF Framework in Chapter 3 will address this need.

A presentation of the Life-Cycle Flexibility Framework is presented in Chapter 3.

2.8 REFERENCES

Allen, T. et. al. (2001) ESD Terms and Definitions, Version 12. ESD Working Paper Series, ESD-WP-2002-01, esd.mit.edu.

Amram, M. and N. Kulatilaka. (1999) Real Options: Managing Strategic Investment in an Uncertain World, Harvard Business School Press, Massachusetts.

Bernstein, P. (1998) Against the Gods: The Remarkable Story of Risk. Wiley, New York.

Black. F. and M. Scholes. (1973) The Pricing of Options and Corporate Liabilities, Journal of Political Economy, v. 81.

Borison, A. (2005) Real Options Analysis: Where are the Emperor's Clothes?, Journal of Applied Corporate Finance, v. 17 n. 2.

Bolye, P. (1998) A Lattice Framework for Option Pricing with Two State Variables, The Journal of Financial and Quantitative Analysis, v. 23, n. 1.

Brach, M. (2003) Real Options in Practice, Wiley Finance, New Jersey.

Brealey, R. and S. Myers. (2003) Principles of Corporate Finance, 7th ed, McGraw-Hill, New York.

Brennan, M. and E. Schwartz. (1985) Evaluating Natural Resource Investments, Journal of Business, v. 58 n. 2.

Browning, T. (1998) Modeling and Analyzing Cost, Schedule and Performance in Complex System Product Development, MIT PhD Thesis, Massachusetts.

Copeland, T. and v. Antikarov. (2001) Real Options: A Practitioner's Guide, Texere, New York.

Copeland, T. and P. Keenan. (1998) Making Real Options Real, The McKinsey Quarterly, n. 3.

Cox, J., S. Ross and M. Rubenstein. (1979) Option Pricing: A Simplified Approach, Journal of Financial Economics, v. 7.

Dean, J. (1951) Capital Budgeting: Top-Management Policy on Plant, Equipment, and Product Development, Columbia University Press, New York.

de Neufville, R. (2004) Uncertainty Management for Engineering Systems Planning and Design, Monograph draft for Engineering Systems Division, esd.mit.edu.

de Weck, O., R. de Neufville, M. Chaize. (2004) Staged Deployment of Communication Satellites in Low Earth Orbit, Journal of Aerospace Computing, Information and Communications, v. 1 n. 3.

Dequech, D. (2001) Fundamental Uncertainty and Ambiguity, Journal of Economic Issues.

De Toni, A. and S. Tonchia. (1996) Lean Organization, Management by Process and Performance Measurement, International Journal of Operations and Production Management, v. 16 n. 2.

Dodder, R., J. McConnell, A. Mostashri, S. Sgouridis, J. Sussman. (2006) The CLIOS Process: A User's Guide to CLIOS. Material for FAMES Course, MIT.

Faulkner, T. (1996) Applying 'option thinking' to R&D Valuation, Research Technology Management, May/June96, v. 39 n. 3.

Fisher I. (1907) The Rate of Interest : Its Nature, Determination and Relation to Economic Phenomena, Macmillan, New York..

Forman, B. (2000) The Political Process and Systems Architecting, in M. Maier and E. Rechtin, The Art of Systems Architecting, 2nd ed., CRC Press, New York.

Globalsecurity.org (2006) B-52 Stratofortress History, http://www.globalsecurity.org/wmd/systems/b-52-history.htm.

Greden, L. (2005) Flexibility in Building Design: A Real Options Approach and Valuation Methodology to Address Risk, MIT PhD Thesis, Massachusetts.

Gupta, D. (1993) On Measurement and Validation of Manufacturing Flexibility, International Journal of Production Research, v. 31 n. 12.

Hacking, I. (1984) The Emergence of Probability: A Philosophical Study of Early Ideas about Probability, Induction and Statistical Inference, Cambridge University Press, Cambridge, England.

Hastings, D. and H. McManus. (2004) A Framework for Understanding Uncertainty and its Mitigation and Exploitation in Complex Systems, Engineering Systems Symposium, MIT, esd.mit.edu.

Hayes, R. and W. Abernathy. (1980) Managing Our Way to Economic Decline, Harvard Business Review, July-August.

Hayes, R. and D. Garvin. (1982) Managing as if Tomorrow Mattered, Harvard Business Review, May-June.

Hertz, D. (1964) Risk Analysis in Capital Investment, Harvard Business Review, January-Feb.

Ho, S. and L. Liu. (2003) How to Evaluate and Invest in Emerging A/E/C Technologies under Uncertainty, Journal of Construction Engineering and Management, v. 129 n. 1.

Hosli, M. (1998) The Flexibility of Constitutional Design: Decision Making and Efficiency in the European Union, Institute for Advanced Studies Paper #97, Austria.

Howell, S., A. Stark, D. Newton, D. Paxson, M. Cavus, J. Pereira, K. Patel. (2001) Real Options: Evaluating Corporate Investment Opportunities in a Dynamic World, Prentice Hall, New York.

Hull, J. (2002) Introduction to Futures and Options Markets, 5th Ed. Prentice Hall, New York.

Ingersoll, J. and S. Ross. (1992) Waiting to Invest: Investment and Uncertainty, Journal of Business, v. 65 n. 1.

Kasanen, E. (1993) "Creating Value by Spawning Investment Opportunities," Financial Management, Autumn..

Kester, C. (1993) Turning Growth Options into Real Assets, Capital Budgeting under Uncertainty, ed. R. Aggarwal. Prentice-Hall, New York.

Kester, C. (1984) Today's Options for Tomorrow's Growth, Harvard Business Review, v. 62 n. 2.

Keynes, J. (1937) The General Theory of Employment, Quarterly Journal of Economics, v. 51.

Knight, F. (1921) Risk, Uncertainty and Profit, Harper Torchbooks, New York.

Kulatilaka, N. (1993) The Value of Flexibility: The Case of a Duel-Fuel Industrial Steam Boiler, Financial Management, v. 22, n. 3.

Linda, A. and P. Christos. (1996) Valuation of the Operating Flexibility of Multinational Operations, Journal of International Business Studies, v. 27 n. 4.

Luehrman, T.A. (1998a) Investment Opportunities as Real Options: Getting Started on the Numbers, Harvard Business Review, Jul-Aug.

Magee, C. and O. de Weck. (2002) An Attempt at Complex System Classification, ESD Working Paper 2003-01.02, esd.mit.edu.

Magee, S. (1964) How to use Decision Trees in Capital Investment, Harvard Business Review, v. 42 Sept.-Oct.

Mason, S. and R. Merton. (1985) The Role of Contingent Claims Analysis in Corporate Finance, Recent Advances in Corporate Finance, pp. 7 –54, Edited by Altman, E. and M. Subrahmanyam, Illinois.

McManus, H. and D. Hastings. (2005) A Framework for Understanding Uncertainty and its Mitigation and Exploitation in Complex Systems, 15th Annual INCOSE Symposium, New York.

Merton, R. (1973) Theory of Rationale Option Pricing, Bell Journal of Economics and Management Science, v. 4 n.1.

Merton, R. (1998) Applications of Option Pricing Theory: Twenty Five Years Later, American Economic Review, n. 3.

Morgan, M. and M. Henrion. (1990) Uncertainty: A Guide to Dealing with Uncertainty in Quantitative Risk and Policy Analysis, Cambridge University Press, Cambridge, England.

Moses, J. (2003) The Anatomy of Large-scale Systems, ESD Internal Symposium, WP-2003-01.25, esd.mit.edu

Mun, J. (2002) Real Options Analysis: Tools and Techniques for Valuing Strategic Investments and Decisions, John Wiley and Sons, Inc., New York.

Myers, S. (1977) Determinants of Corporate Borrowing, Journal of Financial Economics, v. 5.

Myers, S. (1987) Finance Theory and Finance Strategy, Midland Corporate Finance Journal, v. 5 n. 1.

Nichols, N. (1994) The New Pharmaceutical Paradigm, Harvard Business Review, v. 72 n. 1.

Parthasarthy, R. and S. Sethi. (1992) The Impact of Flexible Automation on Business Strategy and Organizational Structure, Academy of Management Review, v. 17 n. 86.

Piepenbrock, T. (2006) Presentation to Lean Aerospace Initiative, January 25, 2006.

Ramirez, N. (2002) Valuing Flexibility in Infrastructure Developments: The Bogotá Water Supply Expansion Plan, MIT Masters Thesis, Massachusetts.

Ross, A. (2006) Managing Unarticulated Value: Changeability in Multi-Attribute Tradespace Exploration, MIT PhD Thesis, Massachusetts.

Rubenstein, M. (2000) On the Relation Between Binomial and Trinomial Option Pricing Models, Working Paper RPF-292 Haas School of Business, University of California, Berkeley, haas.berkeley.edu/finance/WP/rpflist.html.

Saleh, J., D. Hastings, D. Newman. (2001) Extracting the Essence of Flexibility in System Design, ESD Working Paper WP-2001-04, esd.mit.edu.

Saleh, J., E. Lamassoure and D. Hastings. (2002) Space Systems Flexibility Provided by On-Orbit Servicing: Part I, Journal of Spacecraft and Rockets, v. 39 n 4.

Schwartz, E. and L. Trigeorgis. (2001) Real Options and Investment Under Uncertainty: Classical Readings and Recent Contributions, MIT Press, Massachusetts.

Sheffi, Y. (2005) Resilient Enterprise: Overcoming Vulnerability for Competitive Advantage, MIT Press, Massachusetts.

Shi, H., M. Aktan. (2002) Effect of Implementation Time on Real Options Valuation, Proceedings of the 2002 Winter Simulation Conference.

Smit, H. and L. Trigeorgis. (2004) Strategic Investment: Real Options and Games, Princeton University Press, New Jersey.

Spetzler, C. (1968) The Development of a Corporate Risk Policy for Capital Investment Decision, IEEE Transactions on Systems Science and Cybernetics, SSC-4.

Stirling, A. (1998) Risk at a Turning Point? Journal of Risk Research, v. 1 n. 2.

Suarez, F., M. Cusumano and C. Fine. (1991) Flexibility and Performance: A Literature Critique and Strategic Framework, Sloan working paper 50-91, MIT, Massachusetts.

Summa, J. and J. Lubow. (2002) Options on Futures: New Trading Strategies, Wiley and Sons, New York.

Sussman, J., R. Dodder, J. McConnell, A. Mostashari, S. Sgouridis. (2007) The CLIOS Process: A User's Guide, Working Paper.

Sussman, J. (2000) Ideas on Complexity in Systems: Twenty Views. Engineering Systems Division Working Paper, ESD-WP-2000-02, esd.mit.edu.

Trigeorgis, L. (1993) The Nature of Option Interaction and the Valuation of Investments with Multiple Real Options, Journal of Financial and Quantitative Analysis, v. 28 n. 3.

Walton, M. (2002) Managing Uncertainty in Space Systems Conceptual Design Using Portfolio Theory, MIT PhD Thesis, Massachusetts.

Wang, T. and R. de Neufville. (2006) Identification of Real Options "in" Projects, Annual INCOSE Symposium, Florida.

Zhao, T. and Tseng, C. (2003) Valuing Flexibility in Infrastructure Expansion, J. of Infrastructure Systems, v. 9 n. 3.

3 LIFE-CYCLE FLEXIBILITY (LCF) FRAMEWORK

Chapter 3 presents a new framework for comprehensively considering flexibility in complex systems. Following from the previous chapter's discussion, the Life-Cycle Flexibility (LCF) Framework is an attempt to address short-comings in existing frameworks intended for design and evaluation of "standard" real options. There is a perceived need to explicitly consider the additional challenges that are present when dealing with flexibility in complex systems. Therefore, there is a need for an evaluation process more sophisticated than "standard" real option evaluation processes. To address the needs associated with "complex" real options in complex systems, the LCF Framework incorporates concepts from existing processes for designing and evaluating complex systems and real options. Explicit consideration of both technical and social system characteristics are embedded into the framework.

This chapter begins by establishing the need for the LCF Framework. The chapter then discusses the LCF Framework, step by step, starting with the existing CLIOS (Complex Large Interconnected Socio-technical) System Process, which itself is designed to address complex systems. During the discussion of the LCF Framework, the concept of Dual Value Design (DVD) is introduced. DVD technologies and technical architectures provide dual value streams from inherent benefits and flexibility benefits associated with a complex system.

Figure 3-1 shows how the LCF Framework and DVD concept fit into the overall research process.

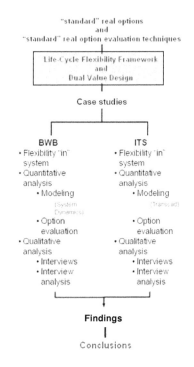

"standard" real options
and
"standard" real option evaluation techniques

Life-Cycle Flexibility Framework
and
Dual Value Design

Case studies

BWB
• Flexibility "in"
  system
• Quantitative
  analysis
    • Modeling
      (System
      Dynamics)
    • Option
      evaluation
• Qualitative
  analysis
    • Interviews
    • Interview
      analysis

ITS
• Flexibility "in"
  system
• Quantitative
  analysis
    • Modeling
      (Transcad)
    • Option
      evaluation
• Qualitative
  analysis
    • Interviews
    • Interview
      analysis

Findings

Conclusions

Figure 3-1 Research process with current stage highlighted.

This chapter seeks to better understand the second research question: **How should real option processes be modified to systematically and comprehensively design, evaluate and manage "complex" real options?** Specifically, this chapter presents the LCF Framework as a potential answer to this research question. The case study results in Chapter 4-9 are presented as a means of exercising this framework and better understanding the difference between "standard" and "complex" real options. This understanding of the differences between "standard" and "complex" real options was then used to refine the LCF Framework. The discussion on the LCF Framework presented in this chapter is the refined LCF Framework that was developed in an iterative process over the course of conducting the case studies.

3.1 OVERVIEW OF NEED FOR LIFE-CYCLE FLEXIBILITY

Current methods of designing, evaluating and managing "complex" real options in complex systems are not wholly adequate.

From this assertion comes the motivation for developing the LCF Framework.

This is because both the real options themselves are complex, often being composed of inter-related technical, organizational and process characteristics, and the system these options are embedded in are also complex.

Individually, we assert that current tools and practices for designing flexibility in a system are inadequate for a number of reasons, such as:

    i.   Quantitative analysis tools do not take into account difficult to quantify parameters such as distribution of costs and benefits among stakeholders or political realities that may make it difficult to exercise ("trigger") options,

    ii.   Qualitative tools are not sufficient by themselves to fully develop technical systems or determine the effects that technical, social, economic and political systems have on one another,

    iii.   In practice, professionals charged with either system design or implementation are not trained in or aware of methods to design, evaluate and manage flexible systems, and

    iv.   The ability of institutions to create support for or implement flexible systems in practice is questionable.

The Life-Cycle Flexibility Framework is envisioned as being complementary to existing considerations for design, evaluation and management, as opposed to a replacement process, shown in Figure 3-2.

Figure 3-2 Life-Cycle Flexibility Framework complementing existing design considerations.

This means that activities in the life-cycle framework are not meant to replace existing activities associated with system design, evaluation and management. Rather, the LCF Framework should be considered more as an additional set of activities that should be completed when designing or analyzing a flexible system.

Expanding on this thinking, "traditional" design considerations include the fundamental activities and analyses needed to design a system. For example, if the project is manufacturing a car, traditional design considerations would need to include design and evaluation activities associated with determining an appropriate engine size, braking distance, vehicle weight, and emission levels, to name just a few. As engineers and managers have begun to master these basic "traditional" design considerations, additional considerations have been included in the design and evaluation of the car. More sophisticated considerations, such as manufacturability, maintainability, and reliability are all examples of "traditional life-cycle considerations" that may be included in the design and evaluation of the auto. These "traditional" life-cycle considerations are in addition to the "traditional" design considerations; the life-cycle considerations do not replace or negate the need to address the basic set of design considerations.

Continuing this reasoning, new strategies have relatively recently been proposed by the MIT Engineering Systems Division, among others. These have been called the "-illities" of design, of which flexibility is one (Allen et al. 2001). Adding an "-illity" such as flexibility to a design and evaluation process for the system again builds on existing considerations, as opposed to replacing them. In this case, if a flexible auto design is desired, design and evaluation of the flexibility does not mean that the "traditional" design and life-cycle considerations can be forgotten. Rather, all need to be considered.

For the Life-Cycle Flexibility Framework, life-cycle considerations linked to the desire to design and evaluate flexibility in a system are addressed. The life-cycle considerations of the flexibility in the system are the primary focus of the LCF Framework, as opposed to providing a comprehensive framework that explicitly includes all other considerations as well. Even though the LCF Framework does not try to explicitly address these other types of considerations, that does not mean they do not need to be addressed.

A condensed version of the LCF Framework is presented in Figure 3-3.

Additional detailed discussion of the framework will occupy much of the rest of this chapter.

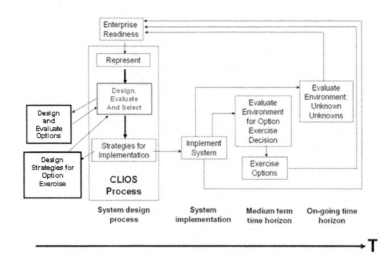

Figure 3-3 Condensed version of the LCF Framework.

From this discussion, the following definition of life-cycle flexibility is proposed:

Life-cycle flexibility (LCF) is a framework to comprehensively address multiple aspects of uncertainty across both physical and social systems, with the goal of creating a flexible system capable of coping with uncertainty. The Life-Cycle Flexibility Framework explicitly addresses flexibility along all the phases of the life-cycle.

The above definition of the LCF Framework can be decomposed into two major parts. The first is the recognition that "complex" real options in complex systems will have multiple dimensions that need to be addressed, in both the physical and social systems. The second is the recognition that flexible systems may be fundamentally different than non-flexible systems. This difference is due to the need to actively manage and, potentially, introduce changes to the system over time (i.e. exercise the option). As the flexible system needs active management and may change over time, this increases the need to understand life-cycle considerations, as the system needs to be designed from the outset to support future change.

The following two sections discuss these two perspectives of LCF. The first section is a discussion of the various drivers that have been identified as important to the LCF

71

Framework. The second perspective in the following section is a discussion of the six identified phases in an option's life-cycle.

3.1.1 FIVE DRIVERS IN LCF

Uncertainty surrounding future conditions is the reason that flexibility may be needed in a system. In "standard" real options, relatively simple changes are made to the system to create the flexibility. And in "standard" real option analysis processes, relatively straightforward techniques are used to evaluate the option value. However, for "complex" real options in complex systems, additional considerations may need to be taken into account if the option is to provide the intended value. These considerations acted as drivers, or critical considerations that were taken into account when the LCF Framework was constructed. The drivers that were explicitly identified are as follows:

1. The presence of uncertainty surrounding future system needs and performance.
2. The need for enterprise and institutional architectures that enable the ability to design and/or exercise an option that has been designed into the system to address technical uncertainty
3. The need to take into account transaction costs that increase the total costs associated with the option. Transaction costs may encompass more than economic costs, such as the expenditure of political capital in the exercise of options
4. The need for the ability to monitor the system so that the current state of the system is known well enough to make a decision regarding when or if an option should be exercised
5. The recognition and ability to cope with sources of uncertainty that are unknown at time = 0, called unknown unknowns

These five drivers are discussed in more detail below.

Technical uncertainty – The first driver, technical uncertainty, is of the type traditionally looked at in the real options literature. The initial process involved in designing and evaluating options that deal with technical uncertainty are no different between "standard" real option processes and the LCF Framework. However, as the options of interest may not be "standard" real options, but are instead "complex" real options in complex systems, additional design and evaluation machinery is built into the LCF Framework, compared to "standard" real options processes.

Enterprise and institutional architectures – An enterprise with the desire to create a flexible system needs to have the ability to conceive, design, analyze, implement and then potentially exercise a flexible system. The enterprise must have an architecture that not only facilities the ability to conceive and design the flexible system, but also the ability to actively manage the flexibility that has been designed in the system.

For public enterprises interested in flexibility, both enterprise and institutional architecture considerations need to be addressed. At the institutional, or "rule making", level, the appropriate enterprise needs to have been vested with the legal authority for designing, evaluating and managing a flexible system. The need for an appropriate institutional architecture is applicable more to public, rather than private, enterprises. This is because public enterprises have to cope with the additional constraint of operating as a government agency.

Transaction costs – In the real options literature, the cost typically associated with the use of flexibility has been the direct cost of adding flexibility to the system, or in option parlance, the option cost. The exercise cost, or additional cost needed to change the state of the system by exercising the option, is also considered in the realm of real options literature. Not considered are additional transaction costs associated with purchasing or exercising the option. For financial options, these transaction costs can include monetary costs such as broker fees, but can also include other costs such as the time and information costs associated with finding a broker and ensuring that they are reputable. For "complex" real options in complex systems, given the potential large scope of the technical system and the number of stakeholders involved in some manner with the option during its life-cycle, it seems evident that the transaction costs may not be negligible. Rather, these transaction costs may have a cost that are significant, or on the same order of magnitude as the option purchase and exercise costs, and therefore should be explicitly considered.

Monitoring the system – Unlike financial options, where the information on movement of an underlying asset is continuously collected, reported and easily obtainable, the same may not be true for real options. Information is needed to make the determination of when or if to exercise an option. Being able to identify the appropriate information that needs to be collected, and then collect, analyze, disseminate and act on the information in a timely manner is non-trivial.

Unknown unknowns – The real options literature dealing with flexibility has concentrated on uncertainties that can be identified a priori, specifically statistically characterized phenomena. As shown previously in Figure 2-3, these types of uncertainties are but one type that can be encountered. It is assumed here that the known unknown variety of uncertainty can, with effort or assumptions, be analyzed in a similar manner to the statistically characterized phenomena type of uncertainty.

However, unknown unknowns are assumed to require a completely different coping strategy. As unknown unknowns are by definition not known, and therefore not considered, during the design process, it is unclear if it is possible to systematically and purposefully (rather than by luck) design flexibility in a physical system to address unknown unknowns.

Rather, it would seem that unknown unknown uncertainties create the need to design flexibility in the enterprise or institutional architectures, rather than the physical system. A flexible enterprise or institutional architecture could allow for a faster change in standard operating procedures to allow the enterprise or institution to adapt to the unexpected circumstances affecting the system.

73

For "complex" real options in complex systems, the five drivers presented above have the potential to dominate the considerations affecting an organization's ability to design, evaluate and manage a flexible system. Therefore, addressing these concerns during the design and deployment of the real option is assumed to be beneficial. This is assumed beneficial because it is assumed that not taking these drivers into account will result in the option delivering a lower value than originally expected.

The next section discussed the second part of the LCF Framework definition, namely life-cycle considerations that may affect the option.

3.1.2 LIFE-CYCLE OF A REAL OPTIONS

The design of real options in a system explicitly creates the ability of the system to change over time. The characteristic of flexible systems to be designed to change over time is different than for non-flexible systems. For non-flexible systems, once the system is deployed, it is typically static and does not change over time, or the cost of change is higher than that for a flexible system. For flexible systems, once the system is deployed, it must be actively managed; the environment and system performance must be repeatedly scanned to determine if and when a real option should be exercised. Once exercised, the system may then experience substantial change. For some real options, multiple exercise decisions must be made.

Presented in Figure 3-4 is a detailed overview of the life-cycle of an option. The mapping between these detailed steps in the option life-cycle and the three main phases of the option as presented in the first research question are also shown.

The remainder of this section presents a discussion for each of the phases of the life-cycle depicted in Figure 3-4.

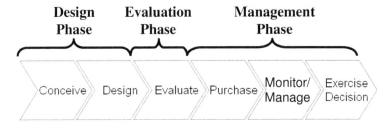

Figure 3-4 Life-cycle of option.

3.1.2.1 Conceiving an Option

The ability to conceive of an option, shown in Figure 3-5, is a fundamental requirement for designing real options in systems. Here, "conceive" is broadly defined. It includes the ability of the key personnel, such as engineers or program manager, to consider including flexibility in the system. The ability to "conceive" of using flexibility is also applied at the enterprise and institutional level. In this context, the ability of an enterprise to consider using flexibility means that the rules and incentives in the enterprise are aligned with regularly using flexibility as a coping strategy to deal with uncertainty.

These two dimensions of "conceive" are not independent of one another; rather they form a feedback loop between one another. The ability of individuals to conceive of flexibility is a prerequisite for the enterprise as a whole to conceive of flexibility. However, if the enterprise does not have an environment that will be hospitable to flexibility, it is unlikely flexibility will be conceived by personnel as a viable strategy to cope with uncertainty. Once the enterprise considers flexibility a desirable strategy for coping with uncertainty, future engineers and managers can then be instructed in considering flexibility during regular system design activities. Each of these two aspects of "conceiving" of flexibility is discussed.

Figure 3-5 Ability to conceive option.

3.1.2.1.1 *Ability to Conceive Real Option: Personnel Experience with Real Option*

One of the main challenges to adopting or designing flexibility in systems is lack of prior experience and organizational norms as regards flexibility in systems. While uncertainty has been and continues to be a concern in the design of systems, the mechanisms for coping with uncertainty have tended towards risk management, or the reduction of the probability that negative consequences will occur. Combined with the practice of making design decisions based on fixed specifications, the methods for coping with uncertainty have tended to be static, such as the use of factors of safety (de Neufville 2004).

Comparing this lack of experience and tradition in designing real options into physical systems to the experience and traditions in the financial world, several differences appear. First, the very idea, or paradigm, that designing flexibility in a physical system is a possibility may be overlooked or not considered. Second, even when flexibility is considered, because there is a lack of prior experience there is no real design process in place for considering flexible solutions. This lack of prior experience as a whole means there are not as many basic options to choose from, compared to financial options where basic call and put options can be built on to create more advanced options. For example, in financial options, much time and effort is devoted to creating exotic options as investment vehicles for specific needs. These exotic options, such as butterfly or collar options (Hull 2002), are created from basic call and put options. These exotic options serve additional investment purposes and can be created without having to recreate the basic set of options, providing a fundamental set of well understood option "building blocks", with which to work. These building blocks may not be present for "complex" real options in complex system.

3.1.2.1.2 *Ability to Conceive Real Option at the Enterprise and Institutional Level*

Options are instruments that can not exist in a vacuum. Rather, they require a substantial amount of supporting infrastructure, from the existence of basic institutions to the existence of proper incentives.

In the case of financial options, multiple institutions are present. At a basic level, the existence of a market system is needed on which to trade the option itself and the option's underlying asset, such as stocks on a stock market. Other related infrastructure is present as well, such as stock brokerages, which facilitate easy transactions between option sellers and option buyers. Additionally, the existence of supporting institutions and organizations, such as legal courts and the Securities Exchange Commission help enforce option contracts and ensure that the market and the options are not being manipulated unfairly.

For real options the supporting institutions may be different than for financial options. At a minimum, supporting institutions are needed to allow the design, purchase and exercise of options. If the supporting institutions do not support these activities, then it is unlikely that flexibility in systems is feasible. The complete set of supporting institutions needed for flexibility in systems is not known. But at a minimum, supporting institutions that do not forbid flexibility and incentivize people to make use of flexibility are needed.

Public institutions are a good example of an institutional architecture that may forbid flexibility in systems. To exercise an option, program managers would need the ability to make a system change, such as expanding, contracting, starting, or terminating a program. However, funding, by law, can only be used in the manner that it was appropriated. Without prior approval, it may be illegal for the system to be changed as called for when exercising options.

Many common incentive structures in place in private enterprises are also not aligned with using some types of flexibility. For example, the flexibility to contract or terminate a program could have value for the enterprise. However, the incentives for a manager may not be aligned with options to terminate or reduce a program, as early program termination could be interpreted as a failure and negatively affect the manager's career.

3.1.2.2 Design and Evaluation of Options

The design and evaluation of "standard" real options is more challenging than financial options. And the design and evaluation of "complex" real options in complex systems, shown in Figure 3-6, is more challenging than for "standard" real options. For "complex" real options in complex systems, the difficulty posed by the physical system, the social system or the interaction between the two can create barriers to the design and analysis of the system. The challenges may be daunting enough so that even if a "complex" real option in a complex system is designed, no tools are available to adequately analyze it. This could result in either the option being purchased without more than a qualitative sense of its value, or it could result in the option not being purchased because no quantitative analysis could be conducted to justify the investment.

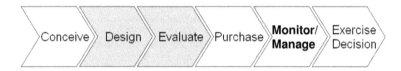

Figure 3-6 Design and evaluation of options.

3.1.2.3 Purchasing and Managing an Option

The difference between "complex" real options in complex systems and financial options are evident in the purchasing and management phases. The ability to purchase and managed a financial option is typically a straight-forward activity. A pre-existing option is identified, or an option is created, then priced and sold. The terms of the option are well known and agreed upon, such as the sale price, the identities of the option seller and owner, the terms of the sale and the rights granted to the new option holder. Typically, once the option is sold, the former option owner has no further control over the option or the new option holder. Further, the stakeholder who purchases the option is the same stakeholder who manages the option, or at least there is alignment between the interests of the option purchaser, the option owner and the option manager – i.e. the stakeholder who determines if and when the option should be exercised.

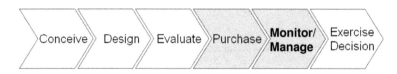

Figure 3-7 Purchase and management of option.

In "complex" real options in complex systems some of these assumptions may not hold. For example, in the sale of an option from one party to the next, the sale may not be "complete", meaning that *all* of the rights, benefits and costs of the option are not transferred from one stakeholder to another. Instead, the rights, benefits and costs may be shared in some manner between parties. This creates problems when interests are not aligned between the various stakeholders that all have a stake in the option.

Another challenge with "complex" real options in complex systems is that the option purchaser, owner and manager may all be different stakeholders. This can be common with government-funded systems, where one government entity may design a system, another may fund the system and still another entity may operate the system. This fragmentation of option ownership may enable or inhibit decision making that would not occur if there was sole ownership and management of the option. Since different stakeholders bear different levels of costs and benefits, the decision on when to purchase an option or when to exercise an option may be different if the stakeholder making the decision only sees the benefits from the decision and a reduced cost.

The ability to identify and observe information in a timely fashion is also a critical when considering options. In financial options, the needed information, such as a stock price, is pre-identified and easily observable, often in real or near real time. For a "complex" real option in complex systems, the ability to identify, observe or gather information in a timely manner may not be present. In some cases, the needed information may not be observable, either in real time or from historical records. Timeliness can also be a problem if option decisions are being made on information that is only collected infrequently, such as census data.

Related to the availability and observability of needed information is the believability of this information. For financial options, stock price information is believable, as there are standard institutions for providing the information to the public. Since there may be no standard or highly reliable method for gathering the information needed in real options, a greater reliance on estimates or beliefs made by the option holder may be needed. Especially if the life of the option is long lasting, the option holder may have to repeatedly scan for information or make estimates, updating their belief on current values. As has been shown in the past, people tend to "anchor" their perceptions of uncertain situations by fixating on initial estimates, even if the initial estimate is wrong or changes over time (Lax and Sebenius 2004). For options with a lack of available or observable information that rely partially on the option holder's estimates, this can distort the valuation and exercise decision for the option.

3.1.2.4 Ability to Exercise Options

The ability to exercise an option at will, shown in Figure 3-8, is a critical part of realizing the value of an option. Exercising at will requires that the option holder can actually exercise the option, can exercise the option at the appropriate time and does not lose out on the option value through high transaction costs. For financial options, the ability to exercise the option is built into the option itself, for most cases. In cases where the option holder can not exercise the option at will, such as options with a vesting time, there are clear rules that state when an option holder can exercise the option.

The timing of financial option exercise is also not usually an issue. The valuation of an option assumes that the option will be exercised at the optimal time, to maximize the payoff. For financial options, this is typically relatively easy to do, either directly by the option holder observing the market or with a standing order to a financial broker, who will exercise, buy or sell the option at a predefined price point. Typically, the transaction costs for exercise (and for other aspects of the option, such as purchase and information observation) are relatively small, compared to the value of the option, with costs decreasing over time due to competition, such as the emergence of online trading houses.

Figure 3-8 Option exercise.

For "complex" real options in complex system, the ability to exercise an option can not always be taken for granted. In some cases, such as the classic example of the dual-fuel boiler whose operation can be switched between gas or oil depending on current prices (Kulatilaka 1993), the option holder (i.e. the owner of the boiler) may quickly make the decision to exercise the option and switch the fuel source for the generator. In other cases, such as a large corporation or a government agency, the option holder may not be the final decision maker, or there may be multiple decision makers or veto points. The ability to exercise an option in these cases may be opposed by other stakeholders or not institutionally supported. For example, in a military acquisition program, options designed into a system that could provide the flexibility to terminate part of the project or switch funding to a different priority could be opposed on political grounds by congressional members or explicitly forbidden by the rules of government appropriations (Wilson 1989). In this case, the option holder (the program manager), may not be able to exercise the option[4].

In some cases, the will to exercise the option is not stymied from an external source, but from the option holder. In cases where the benefits from exercising the option and the personal incentives for the option holder to exercise the option are not aligned, the option

---

[4] Thinking through this problem, it is likely that the program manager would be able to anticipate these types of problems and avoid purchasing the option in the first place. While this would not change the valuation of the option, it would lead to reduced use of flexibility in the system as the challenges involved could be seen as negating the value. At the least, it acts as a constraint on the types of flexibility that are deemed feasible to include in the system.

may not be exercised. For example, in a program with an option to abandon, the willingness of the program manager to exercise the option and terminate the project may not align well with the program manager's personal incentives, as aborting a project could be interpreted as a project failure and have a negative impact on the manager's career; indeed, an "anti-champion" often has to step in to stop the project (Royer 2001).

Also presenting a challenge is the exercise of the option at the optimal time. Option valuation techniques calculate the value of the option with the assumption that the option will be exercised at the optimal time. If this timing is off, either with exercise later or earlier than optimal, the option value will change. For financial options, the time between when an order to buy, sell, or exercise is given and when the order is executed is typically small. For real options, this may not be the case. This can be partially due to the nature of the option itself, such as the option to expand production in a plant that may require additional plant capacity to be physically constructed. However, this can also be due to lack of complete control the option holder has on the option. Take for example the option to build additional stories on a parking garage if demand materializes (Zhao and Tseng 2003). If the parking garage expansion is opposed by neighbors or environmental groups, the resulting protests or lawsuits could slow down or prevent the exercise of the option.

Determining the effect on option design, evaluation and management from the above six life-cycle considerations is non-trivial. For some of the above challenges, such as delay of option exercise, a direct estimate can be calculated using real option mathematics, with a sensitivity analysis being performed a priori to determine the effect of delays on option exercise, if this is a concern. For other challenges, such as legal liabilities, a quantitative estimate of legal liabilities can be made using appropriate methods or judgments and added back into the option valuation process to determine the effect on option value. Finally, challenges, such as political resistance or misalignment of incentives, may be more difficult to estimate the direct effect on the option valuation. In these cases, a qualitative analysis that determines sources and solutions for overcoming such challenges may be the best analysis possible.

Due to the wide variety of challenges facing "complex" real options in complex systems over the life-cycle of the option, the need for the LCF Framework seems reasonable.

With the case made for the need for the LCF Framework, the actual framework will be presented below. The framework will be presented incrementally, with each new piece presented building on the preceding discussion.

3.2   INTEGRATION OF LCF INTO THE CLIOS PROCESS

It is proposed that the LCF Framework would function well as an expansion to the existing CLIOS (Complex Large-scale Interconnected Open Socio-Technical Systems) Process. The CLIOS Process is used as "an organizing mechanism for understanding a system's underlying structure and behavior, identifying strategic alternatives for improving the system's performance, and deploying and monitoring those strategic alternatives" (Sussman et. al 2007).

As the purpose of the LCF Framework is to help in the design, evaluation and management of "complex" real options in complex systems, the use of the CLIOS Process, itself used in design and evaluation of complex systems, was judged to be an appropriate process on which to build.

How the LCF Framework builds on the CLIOS Process is explained below in the remainder of this section. The CLIOS Process is presented as a baseline and then each step in the LCF Framework is presented. The order of presentation roughly matches the chronological order in which an analyst or manager would use the LCF Framework. It is noted that while the LCF Framework is presented in a linear, sequential order, feedback between all steps is very likely to occur.

3.2.1 CLIOS PROCESS

An overview of the CLIOS Process is presented here. A full discussion of the CLIOS Process can be found in Sussman et al. (Sussman et. al 2007). The CLIOS Process consists of three main phases: representation; design, evaluation and selection; and implementation. The goal of the representation phase is to fully understand the system as it currently exists, as well as articulating the relevant problems and desired future goals for the system. The design, evaluation and selection phase has the deliverable of a fully designed system that has been evaluated and determined to be of use in dealing with the critical problems identified in the representation phase. The last phase, implementation, explicitly addresses challenges to implementation of the chosen system design and guides the CLIOS Process user to consider strategies related to the physical and social systems that can be used to overcome barriers to implementation.

While the CLIOS Process itself does not provide answers or provide specific tools to use to complete analysis tasks, it does provide a comprehensive process that can organize and structure the design and analysis. This structure is important because of the challenging and multidisciplinary nature of the analysis and decision making needed to solve problems associated with complex systems.

The twelve-step CLIOS Process, divided into three phases, is presented in Figure 3-9. Additional steps added to the CLIOS Process to create the LCF Framework will be discussed in the following sections, starting with the decision process that determines if there is a need for the LCF Framework to be used.

81

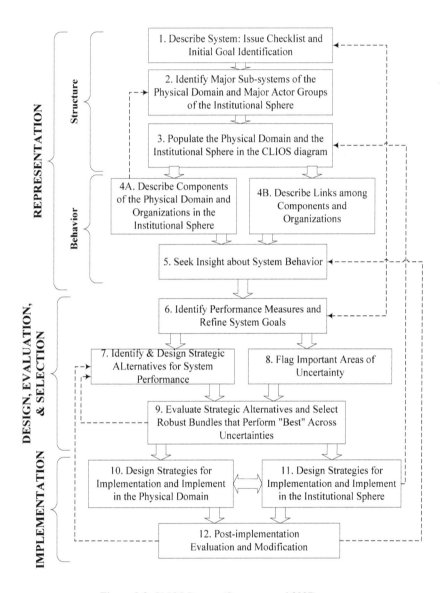

Figure 3-9 CLIOS Process (Sussman et. al 2007).

3.2.2 Decision to Use LCF Framework or Standard CLIOS Process

During the activities of understanding the system behavior (CLIOS Process Step 5) and system uncertainty (CLIOS Process Step 8), the CLIOS user must make a determination on whether it is even appropriate to use the LCF Framework. For example, if there is low uncertainty associated with the system, then adding flexibility is of low additional value and hence there is likely little need to use the LCF Framework. However, if the system has considerable uncertainty associated with it and there is the desire to explicitly address the uncertainty using flexibility as a strategy, then the LCF Framework may be relevant. An overview of the decision making process to decide on whether to use the LCF Framework is presented in Figure 3-10.

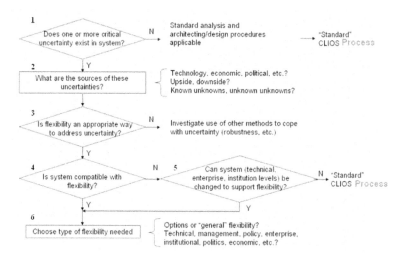

Figure 3-10 Flow chart to make decision on whether or not to employ the LCF Framework.

Each step in the decision process presented in Figure 3-10 is discussed. Note, the following paragraph refers to steps in the decision process presented in Figure 3-9, as opposed to steps in the CLIOS Process.

The first decision point, represented by the upper left diamond requires the CLIOS Process user to determine if some critical uncertainty exists in the system. If uncertainty is not important to the system, then the LCF Framework is not needed. However, if critical uncertainties exist in the system, then the source of those uncertainties should be understood before proceeding, as called out in the second step. This step is necessary as the needed tools and capabilities may vary as a function of the type of uncertainty present in the system. Once the sources of uncertainty have been identified and understood, a decision on whether flexibility is the appropriate strategy for addressing the uncertainty should be made, shown in the third step. Other strategies for addressing uncertainty exist, such as robustness or uncertainty management (de Neufville 2004), and may be more appropriate for the specific system of concern. Step four examines if the system as currently envisioned is capable of supporting flexibility. If not, step five addresses whether the system could be modified to support flexibility. For example, in the government arena, program managers or bureaucracies may not have the authority or the legal standing to make decisions regarding a change to the system without explicit authorization from higher up in the bureaucracy or Congress (Wilson 1989). If the system is currently compatible with flexibility, or if it is felt that the system can be designed to support flexibility, then the type of flexibility that would be of most use should be chosen, as shown in step six. The appropriate choice of flexibility would depend on the type of uncertainty found in the system and the preferred strategy for addressing the uncertainty. It is likely that step six can not be completed until later in the design process.

Figure 3-11 shows how the decision process for using the LCF Framework fits into the CLIOS Process.

The next section examines the steps in the LCF Framework that address uncertainty.

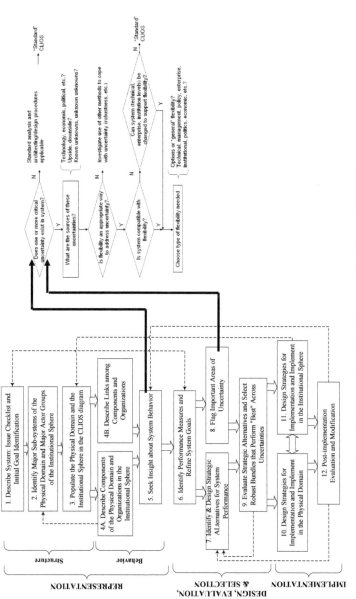

Figure 3-11 Integration of decision to use flexibility and CLIOS Process.

Decision process entered after considering Steps 5 and 8 in the CLIOS Process

3.2.3 ADDRESSING TECHNICAL UNCERTAINTY

To address technical uncertainty, "standard" real options design and analysis methods exist that may either be appropriate as is or with some modifications. A number of sources have put forward a general methodology for the design and analysis of flexibility, as discussed in the literature review of flexibility in Section 2.5.

The LCF process for designing and analyzing technical flexibility is shown below in Figure 3-12.

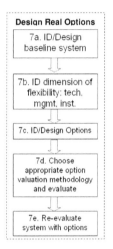

Figure 3-12 LCF Framework steps for designing and evaluating real options.

Each of the steps in Figure 3-12 is described below. These steps are labeled as steps 7a through 7e, as these steps are sub-steps from the CLIOS Process Step 7, as shown in Figure 3-13.

Step 7a has the objective of identifying or designing a baseline system. The baseline system is a system designed to solve the critical problems identified in the representation phase of the CLIOS Process, but does not include any flexibility. It is assumed that in large, complex systems, in many cases it may not be possible to immediately design a flexible system. This is because of bounded rationality, or the cognitive or knowledge limits, of the designers (Simon 1957). Rather, a system that meets many or most of the needs of the system would be the baseline system and through a series of iterative changes, the baseline design can be changed to include flexibility in the system. Where bounded rationality is not an issue, the step of first designing a baseline system could be dispensed with and a flexible system could be designed immediately.

Once the baseline system has been designed, the type of flexibility that is desired and appropriate for the system is identified, as shown in Step 7b. Note, that this is the same as the final step in the decision process presented in the previous section. As noted in the previous section, it is anticipated that the act of deciding on the type of flexibility will be an integral part of the system design process; hence the step is included as Step 7b.

As a first step, deciding on an option type includes making decisions on whether the flexibility to be designed will be related to technical, program management, strategic planning, enterprise or institutional system aspects. In much of the real options literature, real option case studies at the program management and strategic planning levels have been primarily discussed. Several examples of this can be found in Schwartz and Trigeorgis (Schwartz and Trigeorgis 2001). The concept of applying flexibility within physical systems or with technology can be found in de Neufville (de Neufville 2004). Outside of the option literature, flexibility applied to enterprises (Sheffi 2005) and institutions (Zuckerman 2001) have also been studied.

At a more detailed level, a specific type of flexibility that is appropriate can be determined, such as strategic, tactical, or operational flexibility (de Neufville 2004). At an even more detailed level, the specific characteristics of the desired flexible system can be decided upon, such as degree of access to the system, system's responsiveness to change and time horizon for change (Nilchiani 2005).

In Step 7c, after the appropriate type of flexibility has been decided upon and the necessary parameters determined, the act of designing flexibility in the system can proceed. Some of the most common option archetypes are listed below in Table 3-1. The actual act of designing flexibility in the system will likely follow commonly established design principles and methodologies as set out in the specific enterprise conducting the system design. However, it is believed that consideration of the option archetypes may be useful when designing the option.

Table 3-1 Basic option archetypes (Copeland and Antikarov 2001).

Option Archetype	Description
Option to wait or defer	Gives the right to put off making a decision or making a commitment, which reduces uncertainty by giving the option holder more time to gather information or see how events unfold
Option to abandon	Gives the right to halt activities in the event that a downside future is revealed
Option to change scale – expand or contract	Gives the right to change the scale of system to better match current conditions, i.e. expand if the future is better than expected or contract if the future is worse than expected
Option to grow	Gives right to invest in project that has potential to grow, such as investment in technology that could grow into an entirely new line of business
Option to switch	Gives the right to shift the current direction of a project
Compound options	Upon exercise, presents the option owner with additional future options

Evaluation of flexibility, shown in Step 7d, is of importance before a commitment to including flexibility in the system design has been made. The evaluation is important as including flexibility in the system may have a cost associated with it, such as a purchase price or an exercise price. An evaluation would help determine if the benefits achieved from flexibility are worth any additional costs incurred.

While the costs associated with adding flexibility in the system may be relatively straightforward to calculate, the benefits associated with flexibility are not as easy to determine. Valuation techniques such as real options analysis is a way in which the benefits of flexibility can be quantified. Multiple types of "standard" real options analysis methods were presented in the literature, in Section 2.5. As was discussed in the literature review, because of the limitations of "standard" real options analysis methods, these may not be suitable for "complex" real options in complex systems. For this research, the use of more sophisticated modeling techniques, such as system dynamics and travel demand models, were used to help evaluate the "complex" real options. Comparison of the benefit distributions generated for flexible and non-flexible systems allowed a value of flexibility to be determined. Additional detail on the quantitative analysis techniques used in this research are presented in each of the case study quantitative analysis chapters, Section 5.1 and Section 8.1. Additional detail on the qualitative evaluation techniques used are in Section 6.1 and Section 9.2.

Finally, the system as a whole should be re-evaluated once flexibility has been included, to ensure that it continues to meet its performance objectives and cost constraints, as shown in Step 7e. This means that for complex systems, the inclusion of flexibility may have affected the system in ways not anticipated and the entire system should be re-evaluated to determine system level costs and benefits.

Figure 3-13 illustrates how the option loop is integrated into the CLIOS Process.

During the five steps just presented, the additional consideration of Dual Value Design (DVD) can be addressed. DVD does not appear as a separate step, as it is more of a design philosophy, rather than an explicit action to be taken. In brief, DVD emphasizes obtaining the maximum value possible for a system. In the context of flexibility, this means that design choices should be undertaken to create value streams both from inherent benefits and from flexibility benefits. Designing and evaluating this flexibility would likely occur throughout the five steps presented above.

A more detailed discussion on the DVD concept is presented.

3.2.4   DUAL VALUE DESIGN (DVD) TECHNOLOGIES AND TECHNICAL ARCHITECTURES

Defined for this research, DVD technologies and technical architectures seek to more fully account for value by including both inherent benefits and flexibility benefits.

The value derived from DVD stems from two sources, one type is from inherent value and the other value from flexibility. The sum total of these two value streams is the total value of using DVD.

$$\text{DVD value} = \text{inherent value from technology} + \text{value from flexibility}$$

The DVD concept can be interpreted in two ways.

First, the choice of a technology or a technical architecture used in a system will have some inherent value. Additionally, there is the potential that the technology or the technical architecture may also possess attributes that could be used to create flexibility in a system. This flexibility would have some additional value and should be accounted for in a benefit-cost analysis.

Second, the inclusion of flexibility in a system may have some cost associated with it. If the cost of including a real option is too high, it may not be deemed worthwhile. This is especially true when stakeholders consider that the real option may never be used and are therefore reluctant to spend money to purchase the option, even if it is shown to have value. However, if the technology or technical architecture itself has some inherent value in addition to providing flexibility, that addition of the inherent value could change the benefit-cost analysis in a favorable manner.

The presence of these dual benefit streams depends on the design of the option. The two interpretations of DVD are both illustrated below with an example.

To illustrate the first interpretation, consider the use of Intelligent Transportation Systems (ITS). As will be discussed in Chapter 7, ITS systems provide multiple inherent benefits, such as improved traffic management, increased information collection, easier toll collection, improved safety, etc. (Sussman 2000). When using ITS capabilities on a managed lane, the inherent capabilities could include improved toll collection, increased information collection, and use of congestion pricing schemes to manage traffic demand. All these inherent benefits are either enabled or improved because of ITS. Also, all of these inherent benefits are commonly recognized and discussed in the ITS literature. Thinking about ITS in terms of DVD, it becomes apparent that ITS capabilities can also be used to create flexibility. For example, considering ITS on a managed lane, the ITS enables the flexibility to switch the operational strategy of the lane over time. For example, the lane could be restricted to autos during certain times of day and to trucks during other times of day. This flexibility creates additional value that is not commonly recognized in the ITS literature or in practice. This likely means that when evaluating ITS capabilities the benefit steam coming from flexibility is being overlooked, resulting in ITS being undervalued.

A second example illustrates the second interpretation of the DVD concept. In the real options literature, an addition or a change to a system is proposed to create flexibility. This addition would not have been needed if it weren't for the desire to include flexibility in the system. As such, the cost of such an addition is weighed against the flexibility benefits to determine if it is worthwhile. The second way of thinking about the DVD concept is that the addition to the system that generates flexibility benefits may also have inherent benefits on its own.

For example, consider the desire to build an office building in a city. The desire would be to build the office building only if leasing prices are high, making the project worthwhile, though there is uncertainty in future leasing prices. Instead of committing to build in year zero, an option could instead be purchased. In this example, a piece of land could be purchased, reserving the space for a future office building. If the leasing prices increase in the future, the office building would be built and if leasing prices decreased, the building would not be built. In this case, owning the land creates flexibility and the cost of the flexibility is the purchase price of the land.

While the land just sits there waiting to either be built on or not, it has a flexibility value stream, but no inherent benefit value stream. However, with a very low additional cost, the land could be used as a parking lot, generating a revenue stream from parking fees. In the future, if leasing prices increase the building could still be built easily. In the meantime, the land now would have dual benefit streams, providing flexibility benefits and providing inherent benefits from the parking fees collected.

The concept of DVD is considered important for two reasons. First, the ability to properly access the complete value of a system is important in helping make trade-offs between choices. Understanding the value streams from a particular choice, in terms of inherent value and value from flexibility, is needed to make better decisions. Second, the ability to design flexibility in a system may be difficult due to resource constraints. Often, to include flexibility in the system requires that some additional resource commitment, such as funding, be made initial. While the inclusion of the option may result in improved system performance over the life-cycle of the system, the flexible system may still cost more initial than a non-flexible system. Obtaining the funds for this additional initial option cost in an environment where funding is constrained means that resources used to create flexibility are resources that can not be used for other projects, making the inclusion of flexibility difficult to sell to decision makers. The idea behind DVD, where the option has inherent value in addition to the value from providing flexibility, is that the resources dedicated to the option can contribute immediately to the system's overall benefits, in effect creating more "bang for the buck".

For this research, DVDs that are suitable for the two case studies have been identified. For the ITS in managed lanes case study, Intelligent Transportation System (ITS) technologies have been studied as a DVD. For the blended wing body type aircraft case study, the actual technical architecture of a blended wing body plane is studied as a DVD.

Note, that the DVD concept is not itself a separate contribution to this research apart from the LCF Framework. Rather, the DVD concept is another way to describe flexible systems.

Integration of the previously discussed steps for designing and evaluating options is integrated into the LCF Framework in Figure 3-13.

The next section discusses strategies for designing the option to overcome barriers to option exercise.

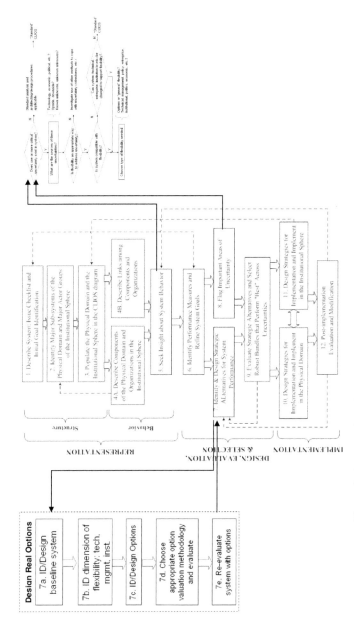

Figure 3-13 Integration of flexibility design and evaluation process with CLIOS Process.

92

3.2.5 DESIGN STRATEGY FOR OPTION EXERCISE

To fully understand the challenges associated with incorporating flexibility in a system, all the costs must be identified and addressed. Flexibility costs can be categorized into three major groups; option cost, exercise cost and transaction cost, as shown in Equation 3-1. In financial options, the option cost (or premium or price), is the amount of money that the option buyer gives to the option seller in exchange for the option contract. The exercise cost (or price) in financial options is the amount of money that the option holder can pay to exercise the option contract.

An economic transaction cost is, as defined by Dixit "anything that impedes the specification, monitoring, or enforcement of an economic transaction" (Dixit 1996). The concept of transaction costs, however, need not be confined to transactions between economic actors, but can include transactions within markets, within organizations and between political actors (Epstein and O'Halloran 1999). For financial options, transaction costs can include the monetary cost of paying for a broker to exercise the option as well as the costs in personal time, expense or energy in researching which option to purchase, finding a broker and ensuring that the broker is reputable. In general, the transaction costs are considered small or unavoidable, and are hence ignored.

Equation 3-1

Total costs of flexibility = option cost + exercise cost + transaction costs

Each of the three costs associated with including flexibility in a system needs to be analyzed and understood. The option cost is typically the most straightforward, as it is the direct cost in adding flexibility to the system. Without flexibility the system would have one cost point; adding flexibility changes that cost point. The difference in costs is the option cost. The exercise cost is a little more challenging to determine. Unlike the option cost, which is paid initial, the exercise cost is not paid until the option is exercised, some time in the future. During the design of the flexibility, this cost is estimated, but the true cost at the time of exercise may change from the initial estimates.

Transaction costs may be the most difficult of the three to estimate and account for, because of the large scope of costs that are involved and the inherent non-economic aspect of many of these transaction costs. It is anticipated that consideration of transaction costs are important for "complex" real options in complex systems. This is because for complex systems and "complex" real options, the presence of multiple stakeholders and transactions over a range of domains are likely. This is even more pronounced with flexible systems, as the potential for system change creates a greater number of transactions than in non-flexible systems. The flexibility makes the need for decision making, coordination and system change even greater, making the consideration of transaction costs important.

While transaction costs are anything that impedes or increases the cost of exchange, several transaction costs have become known by name (Definition of Transaction Costs, Wikipedia 2005), including:

- *Search and information costs* – cost incurred in determining availability of goods, lowest price, etc.
- *Bargaining costs* – costs stemming from process of actors reaching a mutually acceptable agreement
- *Policing and enforcement costs* – costs driven by monitoring and enforcing previously agreed upon contract

In general transaction costs come from two sources; those external to an organization and those internal to an organization. The external costs can again be divided into two categories: internalized costs and externalities. Internalized costs are costs borne by the actors directly linked to the transaction, while externalities are costs that are imposed by the transaction to other actors not involved in the transaction directly. External costs can come from transactions between economic actors, political actors or a combination of economic and political actors, as shown in Figure 3-14.

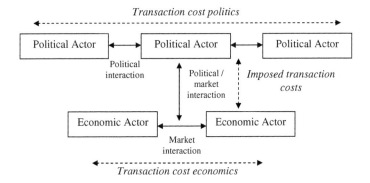

Figure 3-14 Schematic of external transaction costs between actors. Figure based on Epstein and O'Halloran (Epstein and O'Halloran 1999).

Internal transaction costs come from transactions within an organization, such as information costs or lack of an internal pricing structure. The organization of interest will vary depending on what is the relevant level of interest. This could range from interactions between teams, to transactions within an individual enterprise, to an extended enterprise comprised of multiple organizations, such as a supply chain. The notion of how to structure an organization to minimize transaction costs dates back to Coase's seminal work on the nature of the firm (Coase 1937). That work forwards the notion that the creation of a firm is appropriate when market-based transactions costs are high and internal transaction costs are lower.

Depending on the system, actors and flexibility in question different transaction costs may need to be explicitly considered during the design process. For example, if it is anticipated that external political transaction costs between actors will play a large role during option exercise, addressing the politics involved may be appropriate. Or, if the internal transactions of a large supply chain could pose difficulty in exercising an option due to interactions between supply chain members, the design of the supply chain may need to be examined and potentially changed.

Both flexible and non-flexible systems experience transaction costs. However, non-flexible system will experience these costs during the initial system implementation phase. Flexible systems will experience these costs not only during the initial implementation phase, but also at each option exercise point. Transactions costs associated with standard operations of the system are not considered in this research.

Figure 3-15 illustrates the basic process involved in identifying and considering transaction costs that may impact the system.

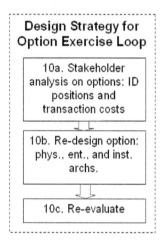

Figure 3-15 Strategy for option exercise loop, procedure for identifying transaction costs, and re-designing and evaluating system.

Each of the steps depicted in Figure 3-15 is described in more detail below. The three steps shown are numbered 10a through 10c. This corresponds with the CLIOS Process Step 10, which is concerned with developing strategies for system implementation. While these three steps are numbered 10a-10c, in actually they apply to both steps 10 and 11 in the CLIOS Process. Namely, strategies for implementation in both the physical system and social system should be considered where appropriate.

It should be noted that a fundamental difference exists between steps 10a-10c and Steps 10 and 11 in the CLIOS Process. Steps 10 and 11 in the CLIOS Process are meant to aid in system implementation immediately. This means implementation that moves the system from a paper design during the design phase into a fully actualized system that exists in the "real world". For a non-flexible system, implementation is of concern only once in the system's life-cycle. Once the system is deployed, it is unlikely to be removed. The CLIOS Process Step 12 has similarities, as it seeks to modify the system post-implementation. However, this post-implementation evaluation and modification may or may not be taken into account pre-implementation. The Steps 10a-c discussed here explicitly call for consideration of these post-implementation activities during the design process, pre-implementation.

However, for a flexible system, the implementation may occur multiple times. The initial implementation is comparable to that for a non-flexible system; namely, the system is deployed for the first time. However, every time a real option needs to be exercised this can be considered a new phase in system implementation. This means that challenges associated with the initial implementation, such as political resistance, will likely also appear during option exercise. As such, designing "implementation" strategies for multiple time periods over the option life is necessary; once for initial deployment and again each time the option is to be exercised.

Each step is discussed below.

The first step in this process, Step 10a, focuses on trying to identify and understand the positions of relevant stakeholders and the transaction costs that are likely to occur if the option holder were to try and exercise the option. Stakeholder analysis and transaction costs are two useful frameworks for identifying and understanding these issues, both between actors and within organizations. The exact analytical tools will be system and actor-specific, but will likely require a range of techniques. Stakeholder analysis and transaction costs are two useful frameworks for organizing these techniques.

Once the relevant stakeholder positions and transactions costs have been identified, in Step 10b, effective responses need to be created. This is important if the identified relevant stakeholders are powerful and may resist option exercise or if the transaction costs are high. An appropriate response will be dependant on the specifics of the stakeholders and costs. In general, a response could include changes to the physical system architecture, technology choice, enterprise architecture or relationship between stakeholders. If changes are required, the costs associated with the flexible system should be re-evaluated to ensure that the benefits obtained from the flexible system are worth the costs, as shown in Step 10c. Evaluating these costs may not be confined to an economic analysis.

Note, that in this case, enterprise architecture refers to only a few of the dimensions that can define a enterprise architecture, such as processes, organizational structure, policy/corporate strategy, information technology, products, etc. (Nightingale 2005). Instead, enterprise architecture refers primarily to the organizational structure, policy/corporate strategy of the enterprise, and the specific technological product (for this research, either a BWB aircraft or ITS capabilities).

Figure 3-16 illustrates how the strategy for option exercise loop is integrated into CLIOS.

The discussion on the LCF Framework that has occurred up to this point relate to activities that would occur during the design of the system and prior to the system being deployed. As the LCF Framework is useful for design, evaluation and management of the system, the steps just discussed cover the design and evaluation phase of the life-cycle. The management phase, to be discussed next, concerns activities that occur once the system has been deployed.

For the purpose of organizing the LCF Framework, the time point of $t = 0$ has been chosen to represent the time when the system is implemented. For simplicity, it has been assumed that implementation time is instantaneous. Time before implementation, $t < 0$, is dedicated to design and analysis of the system, which is where the CLIOS Process and all of the LCF Framework discussion up to this point are located temporally. After implementation, $t > 0$, the system is assumed to be operational and any modifications to the system, such as exercising flexibility, will impact the operation of the system. .

This time scale will be shown on LCF Framework figures starting with Figure 3-18.

The following section concerns the management of the system after it has been implemented. System management includes monitoring the system and exercising the option, if deemed appropriate.

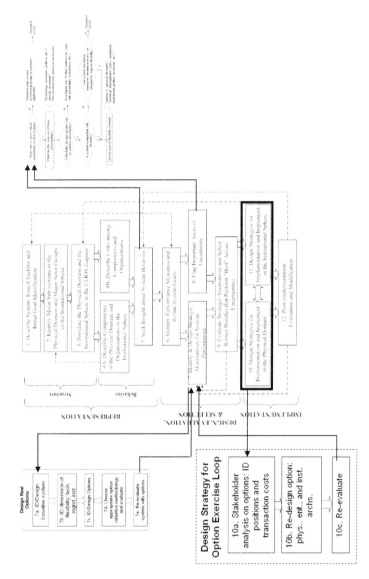

Figure 3-16 Integration of strategy for option exercise loop into CLIOS Process.

98

3.2.6 MANAGING THE SYSTEM

Managing the system once it has been deployed consists of two parts. The first part is monitoring the system. The second part is making the decision on whether or not the option should be exercised. Both are discussed below.

3.2.6.1 Monitoring the System

The ability to assess the environment to determine when to implement the option requires the gathering and assimilating of data on the status of the system. For financial options, the metric and data needed to determine if and when the option should be exercised, a stock price, is readily available on an instantaneous basis. For real options, the necessary data may not be present without proactive action to determine what data is needed and to then make plans to collect the data. The ability to collect, analyze and act on this information may require additions to the system.

Two activities are needed to enable system monitoring. First is the process of determining what information is desired for decision making. Second, once deployed the system needs to be monitored with some frequency to determine when conditions are appropriate to exercise the flexibility. If changes are needed in the system to facilitate information collection and dissemination, these changes should be made to the system during Step 7 of the CLIOS Process.

3.2.6.2 Exercise Decisions

The ability to evaluate the collected information and decide when to exercise the option is the other activity involved in managing the system, post-implementation. For financial options the decision rule, availability of information and rights granted to the option holder make option exercise decisions straightforward. However, for "complex" real options in complex systems, option exercise is not as straightforward. Enterprises not used to actively managing a system may find the active management required for flexible systems different than their standard operating procedures. For example, in many state Department of Transportation (DOT) agencies, the DOT is primarily a building organization. The DOT builds a facility and moves to the next project. The facilities are available for use but are not typically actively managed and the DOT does not have much experience in the management of facilities. However, this has been changing in recent years, as state DOT's move more into operations.

An additional issue is the potential for the same type of challenges faced by a system when it is initially deployed to be faced by the option holder again when an exercise decision has to be made. Changes to the system resulting from option exercise will likely encounter resistance, similar to when the system was initially implemented. The ability to overcome these challenges may be necessary to ever be able to exercise the option.

Figure 3-17 shows the process for managing the system. The process shown in Figure 3-17 is based on the same steps as the CLIOS Process. Originally, the CLIOS Process was intended to be used as a systematic process to guide design activities. Here, the purpose is to use it as an operational process. This means that the steps shown in Figure 3-17 would be used as a guide for organizations to follow in real time to help manage monitoring and option exercise activities.

The steps shown in Figure 3-17 could be considered a more detailed representation of the CLIOS Process Step 12, Post-Implementation Evaluation and Modification. However, the steps in Figure 3-17 are aimed primarily at deciding on whether or not to exercise the options.

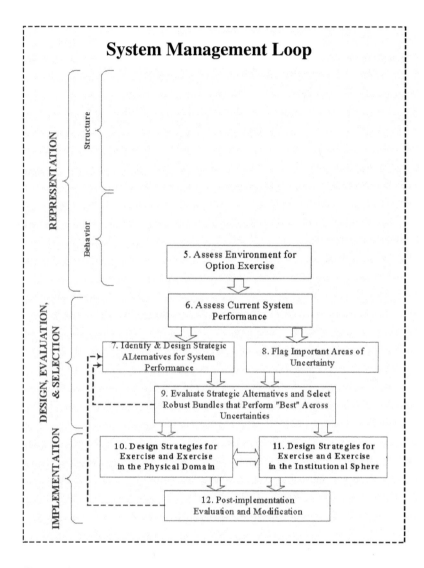

Figure 3-17 System management loop for evaluating environment and system for option exercise decision.

101

The structure of the monitoring loop is based on that of the CLIOS Process, with some steps modified (Steps 5 and 6) and some steps deleted (Steps 1 – 4). The spirit of the phases remains the same, but they are applied primarily to the option, rather than to the system as a whole. A discussion of each step is presented. To allow easier comparison of the original CLIOS Process steps, the original CLIOS Process step numbering is maintained.

Steps 5 and 6 call for an assessment of the environment and system performance. This is a new assessment from that done originally in the CLIOS Process during the design phase. These steps are needed because the time that could elapse between when the initial assessment was conducted and when the option may be exercised could be on the order of years or even decades. Over that time, the environment and system may have changed from that originally considered in the CLIOS Process.

Steps 7 and 8 also re-assess the system design and the relevant uncertainty. For example, given the time delay between option purchase and option exercise, the design of the option may need to be updated or modified. This could occur with telecommunication and software based real options, where the initial systems and software may need to be brought up to date before the option can be exercised.

Step 9 reconsiders the available option that has been purchased in the context of new alternatives that may have become available since the system was implemented. New alternatives may be more worthwhile to pursue than the existing option and should be considered.

Steps 10 and 11 access the potential for exercising the option. If option exercise is anticipated to encounter resistance, suitable strategies may need to be designed to facilitate option exercise.

Finally, Step 12 exercises the option and conducts post-exercise analysis and updates to the option, if needed.

Figure 3-18 illustrates how these steps are integrated into the CLIOS Process.

In Figure 3-18 note that time a scale has been added to denote an approximate chronological ordering of the various activities. Again, t<0 refers to design activities, t=0 refers to system deployment, and t>0 refers to system operation.

The following section addresses how the system could cope with unknown unknown uncertainties.

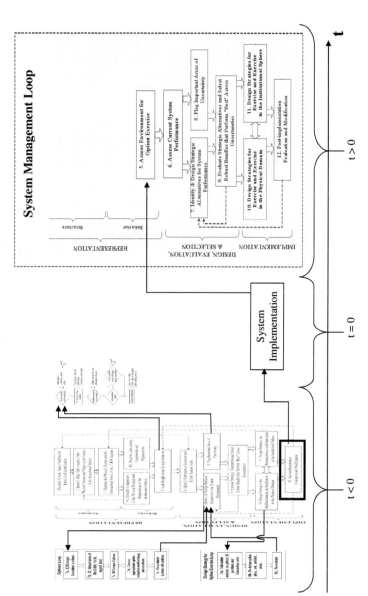

Figure 3-18 Integration of monitoring loop, used for deciding when and if an option should be exercised, into CLIOS Process.

3.2.7 COPING WITH UNKNOWN UNKNOWNS

The previous discussion regarding technical uncertainty focused on responding to changes in the environment that had been anticipated during the design process. Strategies and methods such as real options are designed to cope with and evaluate responses to these types of uncertainties. Not dealt with are unknown unknown types of uncertainty. Addressing this type of uncertainty in the system requires a substantially different approach than that discussed thus far.

It is anticipated that coping mechanisms for unknown unknowns will likely require enterprise and institutional strategies, rather than physical system strategies.

While unknown unknowns are not the focus of this research, some preliminary thinking on how to cope with these is presented. This is just a starting point, as considerable effort would need to be undertaken to adequately address this type of uncertainty.

Unknown unknowns in complex systems have many similarities to how companies deal with innovation. In firms, an inability to change technologies, operations and organizational structures in tandem with unanticipated changes to the environment or dominant technologies is a major source of firm failure (Foster 1986; Utterback 1996). This is in essence the problem of coping with unknown unknowns.

For firms, the ability to anticipate and adapt to changing conditions is difficult because not only does the technology or market conditions change, but the attributes that define good performance can also change, relative to the attributes previously established in the firm's enterprise (Christensen 2000). For firms to effectively cope with the unknown unknowns of future innovations, they often have to use tools that are outside of the toolset developed for managing their current product or service portfolios.

For example, von Hippel has shown that while listening to customers in the course of day to day business is a "good" habit, it may be a "bad" habit for firms trying to cope with disruptive technologies. Rather than listening to the existing customer base, the firm should seek out new types of information that is relevant to help them innovate, such as interacting with and learning from lead users who use technologies in new and novel ways (von Hippel et. al 1999).

Similarly to the way that firms adapt to previously unknown market conditions with innovations (or don't adapt in most cases), enterprises need a set of processes for adapting to unknown unknowns. The design of such an organization that can manage not only day to day activities but can also be constantly vigilant for the appearance of unknown unknowns is a challenge that has not been solved to date.

Figure 3-19 illustrates a process for monitoring the system so that previously unanticipated changes can be identified, evaluated and the system can adapt in a timely manner.

104

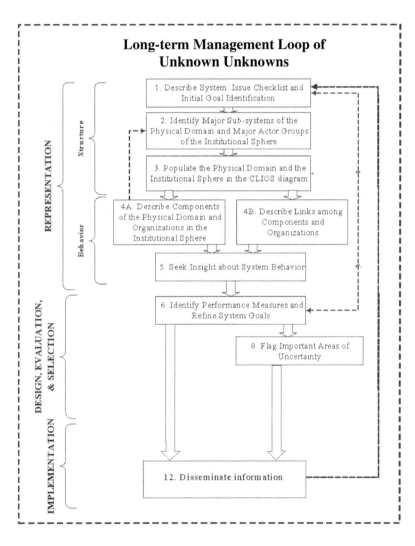

Figure 3-19 Long-term management loop for identifying and responding to unknown unknowns.

The activities in the long-term management loop are based on the CLIOS Process. Like the system management steps presented in Figure 3-17, these steps occur after the system has been implemented. A discussion of each of the steps is presented below.

Steps 1 – 5 are aimed at creating a better understanding of the system and the environment. The focus of these steps is to better cope with unknown unknowns by trying to understand broad changes in the environment, and how they would affect the current system.

Steps 6 and 8 are aimed at updating the system performance measures and uncertainties, based on observations made in Steps 1 – 5.

Finally Step 12 has as its goal the dissemination of information to parts of the organization that can act on the information. If some major change is found to be occurring, it may require that the system be changed in a major way. This could entail re-entering the design phase, essentially "re-booting" the entire process. This is envisioned as a need for the organization to recognize how the "world has changed" and then to re-prioritize or re-organize to appropriately address the change.

These activities are integrated into the LCF Framework in Figure 3-20.

Enterprise readiness to address the activities described in the LCF Framework is presented in the next section.

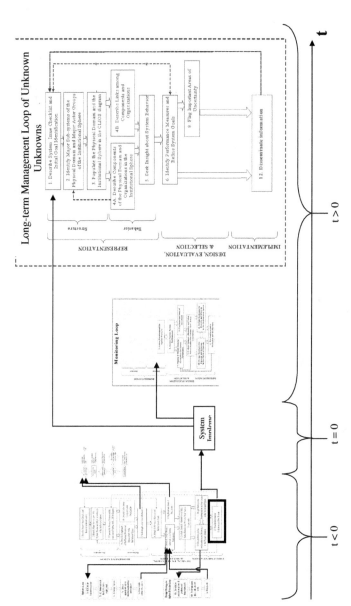

Figure 3-20 Integration of long-term management loop, used for evaluating system and increasing probability of detecting previously unanticipated changes in a timely manner.

3.2.8 ENTERPRISE READINESS

As all of the above activities discussed in the course of presenting the LCF Framework likely depart from most enterprise's standard operating procedure, requiring a change in the way the enterprise operates or even a change in the enterprises structure. Ideally, an enterprise would engage in many of the activities presented in the preceding discussion on the LCF Framework before creating flexible systems. However, it is unrealistic to believe that drastic changes can be made throughout the enterprise before any type of flexibility is designed in a system. Rather, it is anticipated that activities related to making the enterprise ready to design, evaluate and manage flexible systems would occur over time. For example, as new ideas concerning how to design flexibility in systems are brought forward, the enterprise would need to change if these ideas are to progress beyond individuals and become embedded into the organization's standard procedures and thinking.

Activities to facilitate enterprise readiness are likely to occur at three levels; personnel, enterprise and institutional. Personnel changes involve changes to individual's skill sets. Enterprise changes involve changes to enterprise's structure and behavior. Institutional changes involve changes to institutional rules enabling or restricting the use of flexibility.

Example of each are presented in Figure 3-21.

Personnel Readiness
• **Architecture** – Do personnel possess skills for architecting a flexible system?
• **Implementation** – Do personnel known how to interpret information to make decision on flexibility exercise?

Enterprise Readiness
• **Architecture** – Is structure and behavior of enterprise appropriate for dealing with applicable flexible system?
• **Implementation** – Are incentives aligned across stakeholders to overcome resistance to flexibility exercise?

Institutional Readiness (applicable for systems involving gov't)
• **Architecture** - Is it legal for enterprises dealing with government to credibly use flexibility?
• **Implementation** – Do structural incentives exist for exercising flexibility (market based, regulatory, etc.)?

Figure 3-21 Examples of change at personnel, enterprise and institutional levels.

Enterprise Readiness is included as Step 0 in the CLIOS Process, as shown in Figure 3-22, which is also the completed LCF Framework. Notice that the LCF Framework forms a feedback loop where changes to the system and environment eventually result in changes to the enterprise.

As the complete LCF Framework presented in Figure 3-22 is rather unwieldy, a condensed version of the LCF Framework is presented in Figure 3-23.

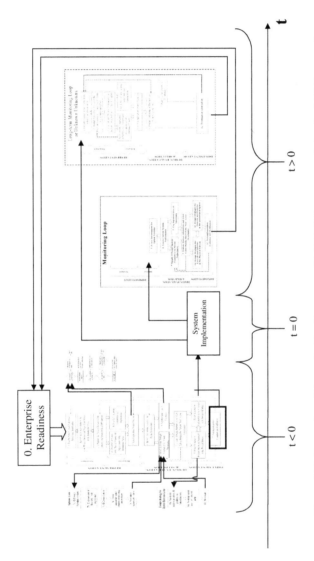

Figure 3-22 Integration of Enterprise Readiness step with CLIOS Process, completing the LCF Framework.

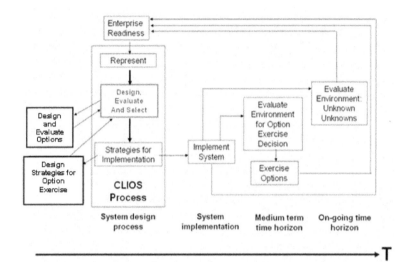

Figure 3-23 Condensed LCF Framework.

3.3 CHAPTER SUMMARY

This chapter presented a new framework to comprehensively consider flexibility and the effects its inclusion are anticipated to have on a complex system. It is thought that the LCF Framework, or a framework similar to it, would be needed to design, evaluate and manage "complex" real options in complex systems. The need for the LCF Framework was influenced by five drivers and the identified six phases in the life-cycle of the option. Considering these different drivers and life-cycle phases helped define the structure of the LCF Framework.

The LCF Framework was based on prior processes and evaluation techniques. The CLIOS Process in particular served as an essential baseline. Building on the CLIOS Process and using different aspects of the CLIOS Process in new ways served as the basis for the LCF Framework. Additionally, existing real option analysis processes were incorporated into the LCF Framework. In the end, the LCF Framework is a synthesis of multiple ideas and existing processes.

The concept of Dual Value Design was also introduced. The DVD concept is forwarded as a way of better understanding the total value associated with technologies and technical architectures. A DVD technology or technical architecture has two value streams associated with it; one from the inherent value associated with the technology or technical architecture and one from flexibility. Identification of DVD technologies and technical architectures are presented in the two case studies and the relative benefits from the inherent value and flexibility value are then studied.

Also included in the LCF Framework is the need to consider addressing unknown unknowns as a potentially separate type of process than that associated with real options. This will likely require changes to the enterprise or institutional architecture, as opposed to the physical system.

A summary of the major considerations discussed in this chapter are presented in Table 3-2.

Table 3-2 Summary of LCF Framework chapter.

Need for LCF Framework
Existing framework are not adequate to design, evaluate and manage "complex" real options in complex systems
The LCF Framework complements, as opposed to replaces, existing activities related to system design, evaluation and management
The LCF Framework addresses two major needs • Addressing physical and social system considerations • Addressing flexibility along all phases of the life-cycle
The need for the LCF Framework is generated by five drivers over six life-cycle phases

Five LCF Drivers
   • Evaluating flexibility in "complex" real options in complex systems
   • Consideration of the enterprise and institutional architectures
   • Consideration of transaction costs
   • Ability to monitor the system
   • Ability to cope with unknown unknown uncertainty

Six life-cycle phases
   • Option conception
   • Option design
   • Option evaluation
   • Option purchase
   • Option management
   • Option exercise decision

Dual Value Design
The DVD concept extends the value of a technology or technical architecture by considering: • Inherent benefits • Flexibility benefits
Unknown Unknown Uncertainties
Unkown unknown uncertainties will likely need coping strategies creating flexibility at the enterprise and institutional levels, rather than within the physical system

3.4 REFERENCES

Allen, T. et. al. (2001) ESD Terms and Definitions, Version 12. ESD Working Paper Series, ESD-WP-2002-01, esd.mit.edu.

Christensen, C.. (2000) The Innovator's Dilemma: The Revolutionary Book that will Change the Way you do Business, Harper Business Essentials, New York.

Christensen, C., S. Anthony and E. Roth. (2004) Seeing What's Next: Using the Theories of Innovation to Predict Industry Change, HBS Press, Massachusetts.

Coase, R. (1937) The Nature of the Firm, Economica, v. 4, No. 16, Nov. 1937.

Copeland, T. and v. Antikarov. (2001) Real Options: A Practitioner's Guide, Texere, New York.

de Neufville, R. (2004) Uncertainty Management for Engineering Systems Planning and Design, Engineering Systems Monograph submitted for the ESD Symposium, esd.mit.edu.

Dixit, A. (1996) The Making of Economic Policy: A Transaction Cost Politics Perspective, MIT Press, Massachusetts.

Dodder, R., J. McConnell, A. Mostashari and J. Sussman. (2005) The Concept of the "CLIOS Process": Integrating the Study of Physical and Institutional Systems Using Mexico City as an Example, MIT working paper, esd.mit.edu.

Epstein, D. and S. O'Halloran. (1999) Delegating Powers: A Transaction Cost Politics Approach to Policy Making Under Separate Powers, Cambridge University Press, Cambridge, England.

Foster, R. (1986) Innovation: The Attacker's Advantage, Summit Books, New York.

von Hipple, E., S. Thomke and M. Sonnack. (1999) Creating Breakthroughs at 3M, Harvard Business Review, Jan-Feb.

Nightingale, D. (2005) Class notes for Integrating the Enterprise Architecture course, taught at MIT.

Nilchiani, R. (2005) Measuring the Value of Space Systems Flexibility: A Comprehensive Six-element Framework, MIT Doctoral Dissertation, Massachusetts.

Schwartz, E. and L. Trigeorgis. (2001) Real Options and Investment Under Uncertainty : Classical Readings and Recent Contributions, MIT Press, Massachusetts.

Sheffi, Y. (2005) The Resilient Enterprise: Overcoming Vulnerability for Competitive Advantage, MIT Press, Massachusetts.

Simon, H. (1957) Models of Man, Wiley.

Sussman, J., R. Dodder, J. McConnell, A. Mostashari, S. Sgouridis. (2007) The CLIOS Process: A User's Guide, Working Paper.

Sussman, J. (2000) Introduction to Transportation Systems, Artech House, Massachusetts.

Utterback, J. (1996) Mastering the Dynamics of Innovation, HBS Press, Massachusetts.

Wang, N. (2003) Measuring Transaction Costs: An Incomplete Survey, Ronald Coase Institute Working Paper Series, Working Paper No. 2.

Wilson, J. Q. (1989) Bureaucracy, Basic Books, New York.

Zuckerman, B. (2001) Long-term Trends, Adaptation, and Evaluation in US Regulatory Policy, MIT Doctoral Dissertation, Massachusetts.

4 FLEXIBILITY IN BLENDED WING BODY (BWB) AIRCRAFT

Chapter 4 presents the first of three chapters on the Blended Wing Body (BWB) aircraft case study. The BWB case study was chosen to act as a test bed to exercise the Life-Cycle Flexibility (LCF) Framework and Dual Value Design (DVD) concept and to better understand flexibility in BWB aircraft. Chapter 4 provides an introduction to the aviation industry and the specific real options associated with the BWB case study. Figure 4-1 displays the current phase of the BWB case study research. Chapter 5 will present the quantitative analysis performed for the BWB case study, with the aim to better understand the value associated with BWB aircraft. Chapter 6 will conclude the BWB case study with a qualitative analysis, to better understand the practical challenges of "complex" real options in complex systems. Chapter 10 then will provide a synthesis of results across the two case studies investigated in this research; BWB aircraft and ITS in managed lanes.

This chapter begins with a history of the aviation industry, defined here as including both aircraft manufacturing and airline industries and their inter-relationships. This history focuses on the social system aspects of the aviation industry. Next, a history of key aircraft technical architectures are then presented, to show the evolution of passenger planes from a technological perspective. Following this history is a technical overview of the Blended Wing Body aircraft. The BWB aircraft is a concept plane that, if adopted, would create a new technical architecture for large commercial aircraft, with superior performance along several dimensions. Two sets of real options are then presented. These real options in systems are created from the technical architecture of the BWB aircraft. Finally, the benefits from the BWB technical architecture are framed in terms of the DVD concept, with both inherent and flexibility benefits identified and described.

While the BWB is a Boeing Aircraft Company concept plane, this research should not be interpreted as supporting any conclusions for or against the support of the use of the BWB. Rather, the case study serves as an example that is used primarily to illustrate the concept of LCF Framework and the DVD concept.

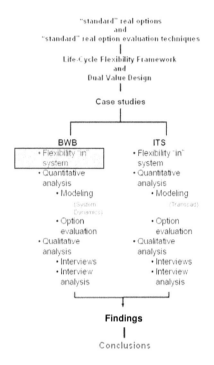

"standard" real options
and
"standard" real option evaluation techniques

|

Life-Cycle Flexibility Framework
and
Dual Value Design

|

Case studies

BWB
• Flexibility "in"
system
• Quantitative
analysis
• Modeling
(System
Dynamics)
• Option
evaluation
• Qualitative
analysis
• Interviews
• Interview
analysis

ITS
• Flexibility "in"
system
• Quantitative
analysis
• Modeling
(Transcad)
• Option
evaluation
• Qualitative
analysis
• Interviews
• Interview
analysis

Findings

|

Conclusions

Figure 4-1 Case study analysis with highlighted box showing current stage of analysis.

The following section provides and overview of the aviation industry, focusing on the aircraft manufacturing and airline industry segments.

4.1 HISTORY OF THE AVIATION INDUSTRY: MANUFACTURING AND AVIATION

The following section presents a brief overview of the birth and growth of the aviation industry, with an emphasis placed on aircraft manufacturers and airline operators. The purpose of this section is to better understand how the aviation industry has evolved over time to its present state and to understand the drivers behind this evolution.

4.1.1 THE EARLY YEARS

After the first powered flight by the Wright brothers at Kitty Hawk, North Carolina in 1903, the aircraft "industry" experienced rapid growth. Many small new firms sprouted up around the industrial world as entry barriers were low. Only a bit of daring, some engineering expertise and modest resources were needed. The new companies and inventors formed a craft industry located in a variety of barns, stables or any other available free space. Although it was the American Wright brothers that accomplished the first powered flight, the American air industry quickly fell behind the technology and manufacturing expertise being developed in Europe. By the start of World War I, in 1914, the 16 American aircraft manufacturers produced a sum total of 49 airplanes. However, with the import of European technology and superior aircraft designs developed during the war, American aircraft production reached 14,000 planes produced per year by 1918. With the end of World War I, the first of what would become many boom and bust cycles in the air industry occurred, as over $100M in military aircraft manufacturing contracts were canceled with the signing of the Versailles treaty. This bust was exacerbated by the fact that there was no longer a large export market that desired American planes and the commercial market did not yet exist as we know it today. By 1922 total production from American manufacturers was down to 263 airframes. (Bluestone et al. 1981)

4.1.2 THE INTER-WAR PERIOD

During the inter-war period American aircraft manufacturing began to geographically concentrate in two locations. Airframe manufacturers began to locate in southern California, where the good weather allowed them to test fly planes year round and there was an adequate supply of skilled and semi-skilled labor. Engine manufacturers began to locate in New England, where there was more of an industrial heritage and larger source of skilled craftsmen capable of working with metals. (Bluestone et al. 1981)

The American civilian aviation industry got its first real start with the passage of the 1925 Air Mail Act, which authorized the US Postmaster General to put out contracts for airmail service. The airmail contracts gave airlines their first reliable source of income, through airmail contract subsidies. Airmail service would be the dominate domestic aviation revenue stream for years until it was finally surpassed by passenger service. The lucrative airmail contracts allowed the airlines to grow in their early years, but in an unorganized fashion which later inhibited progress towards a more rational system. (Donohue and Ghemawat 1997).

While civilian airmail contracts were initially awarded on standard competitive bidding methods, military contracts were awarded through the winning of prototype airplane races, later called fly-offs. This competition based on technical performance has continued to be imbedded in US manufacturers to this day, even though price competition seems to have become more important to airlines than performance competition, a fact that has caused difficulty for Boeing in its current-day struggle with Airbus. At that time, rivalry between American and foreign firms was intense. This resulted in most profits being reinvested in research and development activities, leading to many important breakthroughs over the years. With Charles Lindbergh's solo trans-Atlantic flight in 1927, aviation became a glamour stock and investment money for manufacturers substantially increased and stock prices soared (Bluestone et al. 1981).

To help facilitate increased investment in infrastructure across the system, the Postmaster General proposed regulating the airline industry to award airmail contracts at the discretion of the Postmaster General. The resulting process ended up with the Postmaster General allowing the airlines to negotiate amongst themselves to divide up operations across the US geographically, with United Airlines in the north, American Airlines in the south and TWA in the middle of the country. These three airlines would continue to dominating the industry for years. The Postmaster General's authority was later curtailed by the Airmail Act of 1934 which re-established competitive bidding, but forbad the dominate three from bidding on new routes. As new airlines entered into the bidding process and bid low to establish market share, no carriers made money in the immediate following years.

This instability in the airline industry resulted in a congressional inquiry that concluded that the airlines would fail without some form of protection from competition, resulting in the passage of the Civil Aeronautics Act of 1938. The Civil Aeronautics Act regulated the airline industry until de-regulation occurred in the 1970s. The newly formed Civil Aeronautics Board (CAB) had the authority to regulate passenger fares and airmail rates, route entry and exit, merger and acquisitions, and inter-firm agreements. In general, the CAB gave out highly lucrative, long-haul and high density routes to help offset unprofitable, lightly traveled routes. Throughout the period of regulation, CAB prevented price competition between the airlines and prevented any new carriers from entering into the industry, except local carriers with limited market penetration ability.

With the sky rocketing value of aircraft manufacturers on Wall Street, the first round of mergers and acquisitions began to occur, resulting in three conglomerates; Boeing, Aviation Corporation and General Motors. Until the middle of the 1930's, these three conglomerates accounted for almost all market supply of airframes and engines. With charges of unfair practices and price gouging, congressional investigations into the air industry resulted in forcing the conglomerates to divest themselves of their air transport (air mail) services. The conglomerates were split up into manufacturers and air operators, resulting in the birth of the independent airlines[1], such as American Airlines, United Airlines, TWA, and Eastern Airlines. The aircraft manufacturers consolidated their manufacturing holdings, with some choosing to exit the airplane industry and pursue alternative technologies, such as Sikorsky's exit from constructing its flying boat to instead concentrate on trying to build a workable helicopter. (Bluestone et al. 1981)

---

[1] Prior to this point, these airlines were operational, but part of the airframe manufacturing conglomerates. (Heppenheimer 2003)

Figure 4-2 Sikorsky S-42 Flying Boat amphibious plane. Figure taken from
www.sikorskyarchives.com/s42.html

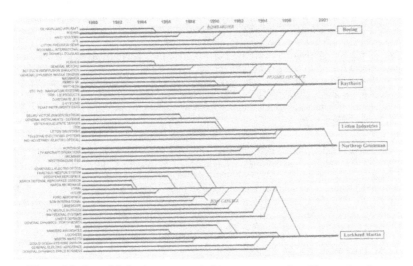

Figure 4-3 Consolidation in aerospace industry, to present day. Figure taken from
(Ferreri 2003).

On the civil airline operation side, airmail service had been the mainstay of operators'
business. By the early 1930's Boeing came out with the B-247, a plane capable of
carrying 10 passengers. Douglas followed up with the DC-2 and DC-3, which carried 14
and 21 passengers respectively. The DC-3 was the plane that "freed the airlines from

119

complete dependence on [air]mail pay. It was the first airplane that could make money just by hauling passengers." (Heppenheimer 2003) The DC-3 revolutionized air service by attracting passengers with low fares by spreading the operating costs over the number of seats flown, a similar economic model still used by most of today's airline operators (Heppenheimer 2003).

4.1.3 WORLD WAR II

With the approach of World War II, American airframe manufacturers began to receive larger and larger orders from around the world. Export was difficult because of the Neutrality Act, until its repeal in 1938. With Germany's aerial attack on Britain (Battle of Britain), President Roosevelt ordered 50,000 planes to be produced for the next year. This was in comparison to the 2,195 military aircraft that had been produced in the preceding year, marking the start of American industrial expansion in aircraft manufacturing that would last through the Cold War. (Bluestone et al. 1981)

With the shortage of skilled labor throughout the aviation industry and the need to efficiently produce planes, subcontracting and licensing agreements for technology sharing between companies became widespread, while before the war they were almost non-existent. Government contracting policy also changed during the start of the war. Due to the large inflationary pressures of the time, the traditional fixed cost contracts government had traditionally used with the aircraft manufacturers became unrealistic and cost plus fixed fee contracts became widespread and are still commonly used to this day in military contracts (Bluestone et al. 1981). These cost-plus contracts are widely seen as being lower risk and higher return than aircraft manufacturing in the commercial market (Newhouse 2007).

Over the course of the war, more than 300,000 airplanes were produced and the capitalization value of the entire aviation industry went from 44th to 1st in the U.S. By 1944, the United States was producing more airplanes annually than Germany, Japan and the United Kingdom combined. During the war many technological advances were made and by the end the planes began to take on the aerodynamic styling and performance characteristics that would dominate to the start of the jet age. (Bluestone et al. 1981)

4.1.4 POST WAR PERIOD

With the end of the war, aircraft manufacturing capability dramatically shrunk. During the war, new manufacturing capacity was introduced in the interior of the country, away from the coasts, to prevent attacks. With the end of the war, much of this inland capacity was chosen for closure by the air industry, as it was preferred to concentrate in the historic coastal locations occupied before the war. This sparked considerable regional political battles in congress, presaging the regional battles that would occur to present day with major military contracts. (Bluestone et al. 1981)

The 1950's saw aircraft shift from propeller driven planes to jet planes, starting with the military. By 1952 the world's first jet airline began carrying passengers in the British De Havilland Comet jet propelled aircraft. It was an immediate success due to its unrivaled speed of 480 mph, high cruising altitude that could fly over bad weather and smooth running engines that eliminated the vibrations associated with then conventional motors. However, three mysterious crashes of the Comet in 1953 and 1954, later found to be caused by fatigue cracks, did irreparable harm to the De Havilland aircraft company and allowed the American Boeing and Douglas companies to take the lead in civilian aircraft manufacturing for decades. (Heppenheimer 1995)

Figure 4-4 British Comet, world's first jet passenger aircraft. Figure taken from
http://www.geocities.com/CapeCanaveral/Lab/8803/pc08_mk1_galyp2.jpg

It was not until the end of the 1950's that the American commercial airliners began to embrace jet transports, with the Boeing 707 and Douglas DC-8, though jet aircraft were not universally used until the 1960's. The Boeing 707 became the most popular early jet aircraft, similar to the popularity previously enjoyed by the DC-3. The DC-8 entered service a year after the 707, but due to the lead developed by Boeing, Douglas lost its premier position in the civilian aircraft market. (Bluestone et al. 1981)

As the CAB prevented new airlines from entering the market and competition between airlines on ticket prices, airlines instead competed on service, aircraft speed and aircraft capacity. Competition on performance, instead of on price, by the airlines, was also transmitted to the airframer industry, where performance was valued more than price, as with the CAB's approval, prices could be passed on to the customer in terms of airfare increases (Newhouse 2007). Speed and comfort were big draws, leading to replacement of propeller fleets with new jet engine planes. The larger jets also allowed an increase in capacity to service the main trunk routes. However, the large-scale buying of new jet planes weakened the balance sheet of many airlines. This would later be exacerbated with the twin problems of increasing fuel prices and stagflation, which increased labor costs and reduced demand.

Figure 4-5 Boeing 707. Figure taken from
http://www.chicagocentennialofflight.org/images/images_aircraft/Boeing707_Boeing.jpg

Figure 4-6 Douglas DC-8. Figure taken from
http://www.boeing.com/companyoffices/gallery/images/commercial/dc8-03.html

The 707 also laid the ground for what would become a Boeing corporate strategy for decades in funding aircraft, and would play a part in today's World Trade Organization (WTO) battles between the US and Europe. In the early 1950's Boeing was unsure of the consumer demand for a commercial jet airliner and was hesitant to enter into the market. However, it devised the strategy of designing a jet aircraft that could be used, with some modifications, as both a military plane as an air refueling tanker and a civilian aircraft. The strategy was to design the military version first, convince the USAF to purchase the tanker and then with the order placed Boeing could recover much of its internal investment. Boeing planned to then convince the government to allow it to use the tanker manufacturing tooling for also producing the commercial version, and after the fees paid

122

to the government for doing so, would then still be able to recoup a large profit. (Lawrence and Thornton 2005)

Between Boeing's corporate dual use strategy for designing planes, the ill-fated crashes of the De Havilland Comet and Boeing's more timely responses to redesigning the 707 in response to customer needs[2], Boeing netted more civilian aircraft sales in the 1950's than de Havilland, Douglas and Convair, its next three closest competitors, combined, leading to eventual Boeing dominance in the civilian aircraft market. (Lawrence and Thornton 2005)

In the late 1950's and early 1960's the aircraft manufacturers entered into the new area of missile design, development and manufacture[3]. Initially, missile production constituted a small portion of their overall business, 5.7% in 1956, but by 1961 it was 44% of total sales. (Bluestone et al. 1981)

4.1.5   THE 1960'S AND 70'S

During the Vietnam War era, demand for both military and civilian aircraft jumped. At the end of the 1960's in only three years total industry employment increased by over a third, creating an extremely tight labor market and resulting in soaring labor costs. With limited labor options, aerospace labor unions worked together to force companies to meet the pay packages provided in the auto industry, and eventually exceeded that goal.[4] Also posing a challenge during this time frame was the rapidly growing airline industry, which created a large demand for civilian planes. This helped create a shortage in the necessary raw materials, causing a severe order backlog to develop. Overall, aircraft manufacturers' profits grew faster than all other industries and again became America's lead exporter during the mid- to late 1960's. (Bluestone et al. 1981)

During this time period, Boeing and other aircraft manufacturers began to respond to airlines' desire for more aircraft alternatives with a smaller seating capacity and shorter range. The result for Boeing was first the 727 and then the even smaller "baby Boeing", the, eventually, hugely popular 737. After losing its DC-9 market share to the Boeing 737, Douglas was forced to merge with the defense contractor McDonnell, forming McDonnell Douglas in 1967. (Lawrence and Thornton 2005)

---

[2] For example, Boeing quickly met a market challenge by Convair to produce commercial jets smaller than the 707 by proposing a smaller variant of the 707, the 720, to Convair's United Airlines customer, killing the order. (Lawrence and Thornton 2005)

[3] Interestingly, with the advent of missile technologies, it was not airframe manufacturers that were seen as being the best choice by the government to fulfill missile development and manufacturing contracts. Rather the systems knowledge of electronics manufacturers was seen as superior for this complex new technology and aircraft manufacturers only received 24% of total market share. It was not until later that aircraft manufacturer's prior experience with large-scale manufacturing and dealing with government contracts proved superior and aircraft manufacturers became the familiar aerospace manufacturers known today. (Bluestone et al. 1981)

[4] However, with the close of the Vietnam War and subsequent drop in demand, pay fell below that in the auto industry.

With large annual increases of more than 10% in civilian passenger traffic occurring by the mid-1960's, Pan American airlines believed that a large step-change in passenger carrying capacity was needed and believed that an aircraft with more than 350 seats would be required to meet expected demand. In response, Boeing designed and manufactured the large 747. At the time this was viewed as a huge risk, as the industry did not share Pan America's future forecasts on demand and further believed that supersonic transports were soon to arrive, making subsonic passenger planes obsolete. (Lawrence and Thornton 2005) While this did not play out, it is surprisingly similar to the situation repeated in the early 2000's when Airbus chose to pursue the A380 jumbo jet and Boeing was pursuing the Sonic Cruiser sub-sonic air transport. History seemed to repeat itself, as the fast passenger transport concept again did not materialize.

With the aircraft family of 707s, 727s, 737s and 747s that Boeing constructed, by the end of 1969 it dominated civilian aircraft manufacturing, leading to its eventual acquisition of McDonnell Douglas in the 1990s and the exit of firms such as Lockheed from the civilian aircraft manufacturing industry, leaving Boeing as the only 100+ seat aircraft manufacturer in the United States. By the end of the 1960's the U.S. had 90% of the world commercial aircraft orders and had built and sold 82% of the civilian jets in use at the time worldwide. (Lawrence and Thornton 2005)

By the end of the 1960's European aircraft manufacturers began to try and challenge the dominant American position in the aircraft manufacturing industry. A joint British and French governmental program lead to the development of the supersonic Concorde. Even after it was apparent that the project would not be profitable, at least in the short-term, the Europeans continued, making it clear a priority was the resuscitation of their domestic aircraft manufacturing industry. To enter the market with competitive products, a combination of risk sharing and capital financing between private industry and government was embarked on. Over time, the original consortium French and British interests expanded to include West Germany, Spain and the Netherlands, creating Airbus Industrie. (Bluestone et al. 1981) The first commercial plane to be produced by Airbus was the A300, a two engine short to medium range jet transport. Since then Airbus has followed the Boeing strategy of offering a range of planes to airlines, culminating in the recent development of the A380 super-jumbo jet that will compete with the smaller Boeing 747 and will give Airbus a complete family of planes from the 100+ to 550+ seat sizes.

Figure 4-7 European supersonic civilian jet, Concorde. Figure taken from
http://www.concordesst.com/

Figure 4-8 Airbus A300 short to medium range plane. First aircraft for Airbus
Industries. Figure taken from http://en.wikipedia.org/wiki/Airbus_A-300

The entry of the A300 was initially met with skepticism on the worldwide stage. As late
as 1968 during the design phase of the A300, there were no firm orders for the aircraft.
Nonetheless, when the plane first flew in the early 1970's it met its technical
specifications and was delivered on time and to budget. Additionally, the A300 was
designed to be more fuel-efficient than its older Boeing competitors and when the first
OPEC led oil crisis started in the 1970's the A300 was offered to airlines as a lower
operating cost alternative. Additionally, disastrous competition between Boeing, Douglas
and Lockheed for the same wide-body jet market segment left the smaller jet market
completely open to the new A300. With an additional energy crisis in the late 1970's and
the good performance of the new Airbus planes, by the end of the 1970's, after only nine

years in business, Airbus was outselling Boeing this market. (Lawrence and Thornton 2005)

In the middle of the 1970's the A300 had not provided the financial returns necessary to start a family of product lines. However, the Europeans were committed to developing a domestic aircraft manufacturing industry despite the early investment losses and work began on the A310. Starting with the A310, and for all its aircraft since then, Airbus has been a leader in technology innovation and manufacturing efficiency. (Lawrence and Thornton 2005) Airbus's success in today's environment can be at least partially attributed to its heritage of mastering process innovation, as opposed to Boeing's emphasis on product innovation, which was born from Airbus' entry into the aircraft manufacturing industry when it was already mostly mature (Piepenbrock 2004). It is only now that Boeing has started to compete on a similar process innovation platform, by introducing lean manufacturing techniques into assembly lines (the 737 has a shorter final assembly time than comparable Airbus planes and the 787 is anticipated to have an even shorter final assembly time) and technologies that aid in assembly (unitized composite fuselages) and improved operating performance (20% fuel-efficiency).

By the late 1970's there were increasing calls for airline deregulation, as when the poor balance sheets of legacy airlines were compared with the highly profitable and lightly regulated regional airlines, it appeared that airlines and the CAB were ineptly running the industry. In 1978 the Airline Deregulation Act was passed, allowing competition between airlines on prices for the first time since the 1930's. After deregulation, the airline industry experienced several changes, including:

- lowered costs and lower fares through competition
- increased fleet planning, as legacy airlines began to retire older planes and match planes with short and long range route segments
- due to prior poor operating results, legacy airlines had less ability to raise funds and began to turn to increasingly to aircraft leasing arrangements for new planes
- legacy airlines consolidated routes into the hub and spoke model, cutting direct connections between unprofitable city pairs
- increase investment in size and efficiency of hub airports and terminals to handle increased traffic
- increased cost competition pressures resulted in changed cabin configurations with decreasing leg room and increasing seat density
- new fare innovations allowing advanced ticket purchases and lower fares aimed at leisure travelers, eventually resulting in today's sophisticated computer reservation and yield management systems

4.1.6 THE 1980'S TO PRESENT

By the mid-1980's a series of mergers and airline bankruptcies resulted in consolidation of the industry, with 45 carriers leaving the industry and over 25% of the revenue passenger miles switching companies. By the mid 1990's, eight carriers had 89.4% of the domestic market share (Dana and Schmitt 2004).

While airlines compete on a variety of dimensions, such as destinations offered, flight frequency, customer service, and frequent flyer programs (Dana and Schmitt 2004), the low profit margins for airlines today make cost a primary concern. For example, in 2000, worldwide scheduled airlines had revenues of $329.1B, but net profits of only $3.9B.

This competition on cost has also affected the latest plane offering from Boeing and Airbus, the Boeing 787 Dreamliner and the Airbus A380. The Boeing 787 "Dreamliner", Figure 4-9, will be an ultra efficient mid-sized aircraft that will be capable of long-range flight. The 787 has several new technological innovations driving this efficiency, including a large use of composites that comprise 50% of the plane by weight, fly by wire technologies, an open avionics architecture and efficient engines. Additionally, the 787 will drastically change Boeing's prior outsourcing practices with a growing reliance on suppliers to ship Boeing completed assemblies for final integration, which is similar to past Airbus final assembly operations (Kotha et al. 2005).

Figure 4-9 Boeing 787 "Dreamliner". Figure taken from Boeing.com

The Airbus A380, Figure 4-10 and Figure 4-11, will be the largest commercial plane ever built, surpassing the previous record holder Boeing 747, capable of holding between 550 and 1000 passengers, depending on the configuration. The Airbus A380 continues to push technologies and outsourcing practices for Airbus, but the innovations on the Airbus A380 appear more incremental compared to the large jumps in innovation apparent on the Boeing 787. Cost efficiencies for airlines from the A380 come through scales of economies, due to the large number of passengers the A380 can carry, or room for alternative revenue generating sources onboard.

Figure 4-10 Airbus A380 jumbo jet. Figure taken from Airbus.com

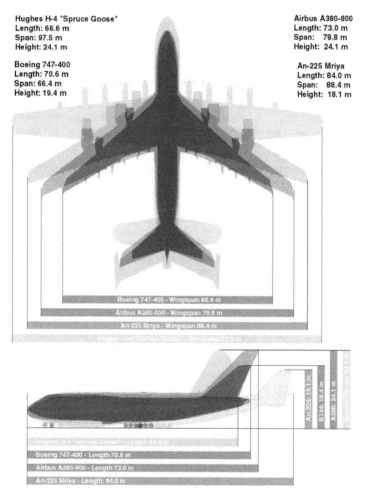

Figure 4-11 Comparison of several large aircraft, including A380 and B747. Note, the plane with the largest wingspan in this figure is the Spruce Goose, which holds the record for the largest wingspan on any plane ever built. Figure taken from http://en.wikipedia.org/wiki/Boeing_747

With the end of the Cold War in the early 1990's the aerospace sector went through its worst economic crisis since the end of WWII, as the general economic recession combined with a sharp reduction in military spending decreased revenues. The belief that bigger was better, combined with the encouragement of mergers from the defense department and the availability of financing from the banking system helped create a major consolidation in the industry. Currently, only four major aerospace firms exist in the U.S. market and only one, Boeing, competes in the 100+ seat commercial aircraft manufacturing sector. A similar consolidation has simultaneously occurred in the European aircraft manufacturing sector, with only Airbus left on the large plane commercial manufacturing side.

The aircraft manufacturing industry can be decomposed into four sectors: airframes, engines, avionics and systems (non-electrical system, such as landing gear, fuel systems, etc.). Currently, only Boeing and Airbus compete in the large airframe sector[5]. This is because of the large-scale complexity involved in designing and integrating both the technologies involved in aircraft as well as the large enterprises created for running global supply chains. The two integrators, Boeing and Airbus, have ultimate responsibility for not only the technical aspects of the aircraft but all the enterprise aspects related to production as well, including supply chain management, marketing, and after-sale support of customers. In the engine sector, there are also few competitors, mainly due to the technological complexity involved in aircraft engine design and manufacture. In the avionics and systems sector, these firms are typically highly specialized and substantially smaller than the firms found in other parts of the aviation industry. (Ferreri 2003)

Competition between manufacturers now occurs on a global scale. This is due to the high-costs involved with developing, manufacturing, selling and supporting an airplane and the subsequent need to spread the costs out over as large a production run as possible, resulting in international sales. As planes have become more complex technologically and as the international nature of sales and support have also grown in complexity, the major manufacturers have recently begun to change the nature of interactions with subcontractors. In the past, some areas of technology were closely held within the company and there was a refusal to outsource manufacturing tasks that dealt in these areas, such as wing design. Now, there is a growing acceptance on the part of the primes to embrace suppliers as partners where technological, financial and commercial risks are shared. (Ferreri 2003) For example, the wing design on the Boeing 787 is being outsourced to a foreign supplier for the first time in Boeing history.

---

[5] It has been hypothesized that some of the smaller jet manufacturers, such as Bombardier or Embraer, may increase their capabilities and gradually move into this market segment. Also, entry by other countries, notably Russia, Japan, India and China into this market segment have been predicted by some.

Assembly	727	737	747	757	767	777
Wings	D	D	D	D	D	D
Inboard flaps	D	F	F	F	F	D
Outboard flaps	D	F	F	F	F	F
Engine Nacelles	D	D	D	D	D	D
Engine Strut	D	D	F	D	D	D
Nose	D	D	D	D	D	D
Front fuselage	D	D	D	D	F	F
Center fuselage	D	D	D	D	F	F
Center Wing Box	D	D	F	D	D	F
Keel beam	D	D	D	D	D	F
Aft fuselage	D	D	D	D	F	F
Section 48	D	D/F	D	D	F	F
Stabilizer	D	D/F	D	D	F	D
Dorsal Fin	D	D	D	F	F	F
Vertical Fin	D	D/F	D	D	F	D
Elevators	D	F	D	F	F	F
Rudder	D	F	D	F	F	F
Passenger Doors	D	D	D	D	F	F
Cargo Doors	D	D	F	F	F	F

Figure 4-12 Foreign and domestic sources of past Boeing aircraft assembly production. Wing production has historically always been a Boeing manufacturing assembly, due to the technologies involved. D = domestically produced, F = foreign production. Figure taken from (Pritchard 2001).

This acceptance of the prime integrators towards viewing their preferred suppliers as partners rather than just suppliers is changing the manner in which the global supply chain is being organized and managed by the primes, as shown below in Figure 4-13. It is anticipated that this will lead to the evolution of some of the suppliers away from a subcontractor role to an increased capability role that is more along the line of a conditional partnership. This partnership will have greater collaboration between the prime integrator and the preferred partner such that the preferred partner works with the prime in the areas of planning, quality management and delivery logistics, as well as supplying the finished assemblies that will be incorporated directly into the final assembly. In this manner, these preferred partners will take on the role of a smaller integrator. (Ferreri 2003)

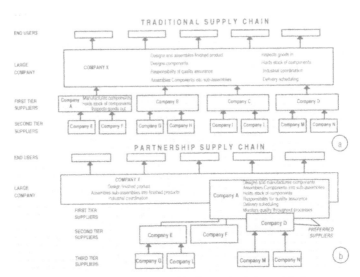

Figure 4-13 Traditional (a) and partnership (b) supply chain models for aerospace industry. For example, in the partnership supply chain model applied to the Boeing 787, Boeing would be "Company X" while Mitsubishi Heavy Industries, the Japanese company designing and building the wing assembly, would be "Company A". Figure taken from (Ferreri 2003).

This section completed a history of the aviation industry, focusing on the aircraft manufacturers and airlines. The following sections presents a history of aircraft technological architectures and technologies. While this section focused on a history of the social system, the next section focuses on a history of the physical system.

4.2   AIRCRAFT ARCHITECTURES, STRUCTURAL DESIGNS AND WINGS

This section presents a history of the evolution of aircraft technical architectures and technologies. The following section presents a technical overview of the BWB aircraft, which is a new technical architecture for airplanes.

While man has long been interested in the concept of flight, as evidenced by drawings such as those of Leonardo da Vinci in the 1400's, the modern era of flight can be thought to begin with the Wright flyer, piloted by Orville Wright in 1903.

Figure 4-14 Drawings from Leonardo da Vinci concerning manned flight, showing from left to right, a parachute, aerial screw and wings. Figure taken from http://www.museoscienza.org/english/leonardo/invenzioni.html

Figure 4-15 Wright flyer. Figure taken from http://www.libraries.wright.edu/icons/special/flyer.gif

With great interest in flight, technology progressed rapidly. However, by 1914 there was still no dominant aircraft architecture that had emerged, as evidenced by the multitude of fuselage types, wing designs, materials and landing platforms shown in Figure 4-16. (Anderson 2002)

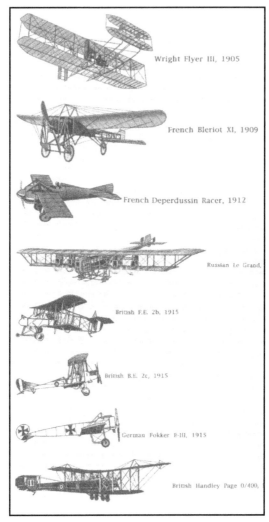

Figure 4-16 Early aircraft. Figure taken from (Anderson 2002).

One of the most visible areas of difference between the planes was in their fuselage. Fuselage construction varied considerably from the open fuselage of the Wright flyer (i.e. no fuselage, the Wrights sat or laid on the bottom wing and controlled the plane by shifting their body weight) to the completely enclosed fuselages of later planes. Not as visibly obvious was the difference in structural and manufacturing technologies that went into creating the fuselages. By 1908 three primary types of fuselage structures were employed. These were girder, monocoque and semi-monocoque.

- **Girder** – Girder structures were the most common structures early on. The construction was much like that in civil engineering applications, such as bridges. Girder construction had a box like structure composed of longerons, which ran the entire length of the fuselage, supported by struts and wires to form a lattice structure that could support vertical and side loads, as well as torsion about the longitudinal axis. Typically, most girder structures were constructed of wood and wire, though some of the aircraft manufactured by the German Fokker company had metal construction.

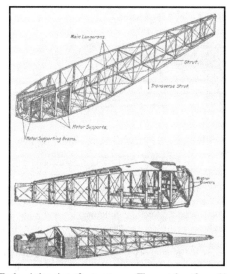

Figure 4-17 Early girder aircraft structures. Figure taken from (Anderson 2002).

- **Monocoque** – Monocoque (the French word for shell) structures were made by layering thin strips of a material, often wood, over a mold contoured to the desired fuselage shape. A typical technique was using three layers of wood, glued together with their grain pattern at right angles to each other as the only load bearing structure, with a layer of cloth glued to the inside and outside of the structure. The fuselage was often molded in two half shells that were then glued together to form the completed fuselage. One of the benefits of the monocoque structure over that of girders was that it was thin and light and aerodynamically

135

superior. However, because of the difficulty in manufacturing by this method, few planes of World War I vintage were made with this method.

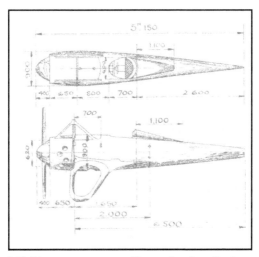

Figure 4-18 Monocoque structure. Figure taken from (Anderson 2002).

- **Semi-monocoque** – Semi-monocoque (or monocoque-girder or veneer type) structures are a combination of girder and monocoque structures, becoming popular during World War I. The semi-monocoque structure has an internal girder like structure, but with fewer members than a pure girder structure. The external skin is composed of panels, early on mostly of wood but later of metal, which are attached to the frame either by gluing, nailing, screwing or riveting. For the semi-monocoque structures *both* the skin and girder structure carry loads, to different degrees as materials and manufacturing technology progressed. By the 1930's semi-monocoque structures had become the dominant structural architecture. As the amount of loading carried by the skin increased, the term "stressed-skin" construction replaced semi-monocoque. Stressed-skin construction is still the dominant design used by commercial airplanes today. However, the move by Boeing to a unitized composite fuselage construction on the 787 is a change from this type of construction and it would be expected that the BWB fuselage would be composed in a similar manner.

136

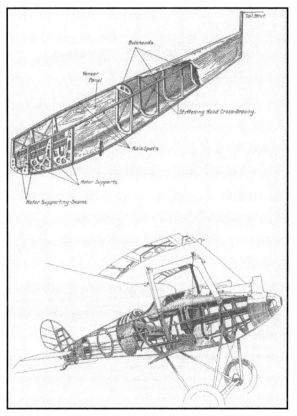

Figure 4-19 Semi-monocoque construction. Figure taken from (Anderson 2002).

One of the critical areas, if not the most critical, was in development of the wings. As evidenced in Figure 6, there was considerable work with both mono-wing, bi-wing and in some cases tri-wing (not shown in figure) architectures. While much work progressed on the cross-sectional shape of the wings, or the airfoil, which determines the aerodynamic properties of flight, considerable difficulties in the construction of the wings was encountered.   It was recognized that mono-wing architectures offered the greatest aerodynamic performance, as well as provided the pilot a superior view, which was important for aerial dog fighting and flying in general, due to lack of instrumentation. (Anderson 2002) However, due to a combination of the loads carried by the wings (the wings carry by far the largest aerodynamic loads on the airplane), then modern airfoil design and the state of materials technology, mono-wing designs were technically challenging to actually build and function adequately. Contemporary airfoil designs were thin, which left little room for internal wing structures. This made it difficult to design the thicker and stronger spars (main structural wing elements that run between the fuselage and the length of the wings acting as the main support) needed for a monoplane.

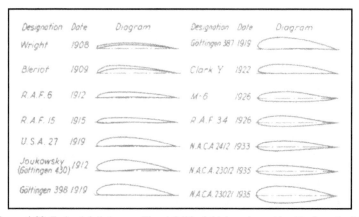

Figure 4-20 Early airfoil shapes. The airfoil had thickened considerably from the thin shapes used by the Wrights in 1908 (shown top left) to the N.A.C.A designs of the 1930's (shown bottom right). Figure taken from (Anderson 2002).

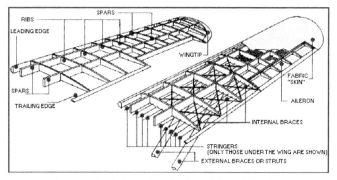

Figure 4-21 Modern wing structure. Figure taken from http://www.allstar.fiu.edu/aero/flight12.htm

With a bi-wing (or tri-wing) construction the aerodynamic loads could be spread out over two (or three) wings, meaning each wing structure only had to bear a fraction of the total loads. Additionally, with the wings wired together the resulting box like structure was sturdier than contemporary monoplanes. This was especially important for the stresses and strains involved with the violent movements associated with World War I style dog fighting. (Anderson 2002) Many contemporary monoplanes also experimented with using wires to brace the wings, as shown in Figure 4-22, however, higher than normal wing failure rates for monoplanes such as the Bleriot IX and Fokker E-I through E-III helped keep bi-planes the dominant wing architecture for the time. (Anderson 2002). It would not be until materials technology could improve that monoplanes would again become competitive and challenge the bi-plane architecture. (Heppenheimer 2003)

Figure 4-22 Bleriot XI, monoplane circa 1909, with wires supporting wing spars.
Figure taken from http://memorial.flight.free.fr/gallery/bleriot/66.jpg

Structural elements of the aircraft during the jet age have stayed essentially the same with stressed skin construction with ribs, stringers and spaces for added stiffness. While the structural elements have stayed the same, the design and manufacture of these elements has changed, due to improved design tools and computational abilities, such as finite element analysis, computational fluid dynamics, computer aided design/manufacture, etc.

The following section provides a technical overview of the Blended Wing Body type aircraft.

4.3   BLENDED WING BODY OVERVIEW

The Blended Wing Body (BWB) aircraft is a conceptual aircraft by Boeing that integrates the wing, fuselage, engines and tail of the aircraft to achieve substantial performance improvements over conventionally architected, "tube and wing" aircraft. As shown in Figure 4-23, the architecture of the BWB falls between that of conventional tube and wing and flying wing architectures.

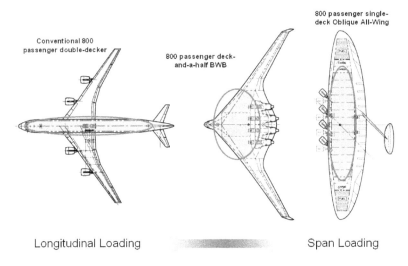

Conventional 800
passenger double-decker

800 passenger deck-
and-a-half BWB

Longitudinal Loading   Span Loading

Figure 4-23 Three aircraft architectures: conventional tube and wing, BWB and flying
wing. Figure taken from (Liebeck 2005).

The physical architecture of the BWB provides for several advantages over conventional
aircraft architectures. The integration of the wing and the fuselage allows for increased
span loading, or increased ratio of weight to wingspan, allowing increased weight for a
constant wingspan. This is due to the lift generating capability of the fuselage, meaning
the fuselage can help provide lift on a BWB, whereas a conventional tube fuselage
provides almost no lift, as shown in Figure 4-24.

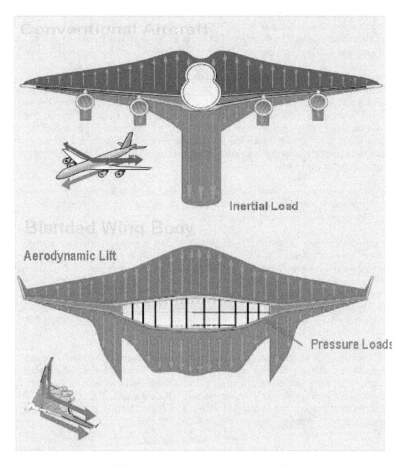

Figure 4-24 Loads and lifts generated by conventional and BWB architectures. Figure taken from (Liebeck 2005).

The geometry of the BWB also allows for increased aerodynamic performance, as the wetted area, or area exposed to airflow and hence friction forces, is reduced on a BWB when compared to a conventional aircraft architecture, holding passenger seating requirements constant (Liebeck 2005).

Because of the aircraft architecture, significant improvements in both weight and fuel burn can be achieved, comparing the BWB to a conventional architecture. Comparing across comparable technology levels, 800 passengers, 7000 n mile range for both BWB and conventional aircraft designs, the BWB has a 15% reduction in takeoff weight and a 27% reduction in fuel burn per seat mile (Liebeck 2004).

Overall, the BWB offers several advantages over a conventional aircraft architecture. Because of the large wingspan and resulting high L/D (lift to drag) ratio, the BWB has a reduced fuel burn compared to conventional aircraft. The placement of the engines on the BWB above or in the rear fuselage reduces noise. This is because engines hanging under the wing causes engine noise to be reflected off the ground. Because of the near elimination of noise outside airport boundaries, increased flight times in and out of airports may be possible, increasing the time of operations that the plane could be operated around the clock.

Together, these attributes form the "inherent benefits" of the BWB technical architecture. For this research, the lower fuel consumption is the primary inherent benefit that will be taken into account in the following chapter.

A key characteristic of the BWB of interest to this research is the "remarkable and unique" capability that the BWB has to be stretched and re-configured (Liebeck 2003). Two types of commonality have been identified as strengths of the BWB architecture: size commonality across families and commonality across applications. Increased commonalty across applications, such as commercial, military, reconnaissance, tanker and freight applications are outside the bounds of this research. Concentration on commonalty between aircraft sizes representative of different existing aircraft families will be focused on.

For conventional aircraft, derivative aircraft in the same family can be created by stretching the aircraft's fuselage along the length of the aircraft, among other means. In general, stretching the fuselage allows for increased aircraft size and for passenger aircraft, increased passenger carrying ability. For example, the re-designed 747-8 stretches the fuselage of the older 747-400 in two places, increasing passenger carrying capabilities by 51 seats, as shown in Figure 4-25.

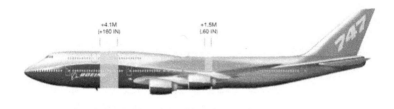

Figure 4-25 747-8, showing both locations were stretch is to occur. Figure taken from www.boeing.com.

For the BWB, due to the geometry, stretching occurs laterally. Whereas a conventional aircraft architecture can only be stretched so far, do to the extra weight and aerodynamic considerations, the BWB can be stretched considerably more, because of the lift benefit provided from the fuselage and the plane's geometry which add span and lift at the same time. This increased ability to stretch the plane allows plane designs that are technically and economically feasible to be made across several existing families, from sizes of the range 250-450 passengers. Mapped against current Boeing plane families these sizes encompass the 787, 777 and 747.

The cross section of the BWB can be divided into fuselage bays, with the number of bays varying as a function of BWB size and hence number of passengers. For example, the 250 seat BWB has four bays, while the 450 seat BWB has six bays. The total number and configuration of the bays have high commonality across the BWB family. A comparison of the 250, 350 and 450 seat BWB variants is shown in Figure 4-26 and a cross section of the bays for the 250 and 450 seat variants is shown in Figure 4-27

Figure 4-26 Fuselage bay modules for the 250, 350 and 450 BWB variants. Figures modified from (Liebeck 2005).

143

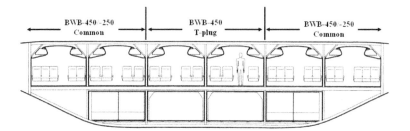

Figure 4-27 Cross section of BWB fuselage, showing bays for 250 and 450 variants. Figures modified from (Liebeck 2005).

When examining the level of commonality between planes in the BWB family, three levels of commonality can be observed: common (completely identical), cousins (similar parts, with differences such as change in skin gauge or hole locations, but identical geometry) and unique parts. The commonality for the BWB family of planes can be broken up into the following major subsystems: wings, cockpit, and fuselage. For all BWB family, the wings and cockpit are common across planes. The architecture of the blended wing, allows ample fuel volume for fuel needs for planes across the entire family. Parts of the fuselage are common across multiple planes, such as the outer fuselage bays shown in Figure 4-27, which are common for the 250 and 450 planes. In general, BWB fuselages are comprised of combinations of two or more distinct bays (Liebeck 2004). Nose gear and landing gear are common across all planes, as are interior cross section commonalities, such as galleys, lavatories, bag racks and seats. The transition between the nose and body and body and engines is unique to all planes, due to aerodynamic constraints.

Overall, by weight, 39% of the aircraft can be considered common, 33% cousin and 28% unique. Compared to point designed planes, this offers savings of 23% and 12% for non-recurring and recurring costs, respectively, if just the 250 and 450 planes were produced. Savings would further increase if additional planes, such as the 350, were also manufactured (Liebeck 2003).

To increase commonality across the BWB family, design at the family level, rather than point design, must be enforced. Designing for this commonality imposes additional constraints, that reduce performance for all planes in the family. For example, if the planes in the BWB were point designed, in many places skin thickness on the smaller planes could be reduced, due to lower loads, which would decrease the aircraft weight and improve performance (Liebeck 2003). However, this would decrease the number of common parts across BWB sizes, decreasing commonality. The performance penalties for commonality when optimizing over a BWB family consisting of a 272 and 475 person planes, compared to optimizing over each aircraft individually has been calculated as a takeoff weight penalty of 2% and 0.05% for the small and large aircraft, respectively (Willcox and Wakayama 2003).

Additional benefits of the BWB architecture that create synergies with the commonality are the reduced need to design for complex joints found on traditional tube and wing planes, such as the wing / fuselage and fuselage / empennage joints. These joints join highly loaded subsystems together at angles approaching 90 degrees. Also, current thinking for trailing edge control surfaces envision simple hinged surfaces, compared to current trailing edges that contain hinges, tracks and spoilers. These types of design simplifications made possible through the technical architecture result in about a 30% reduction of the number of parts when compared with conventional aircraft configurations.

In general, the technical architecture of the BWB is the enabler behind providing

> *the opportunity for an unusual level of commonality while the aerodynamic efficiency is maintained via the natural variation of wing area and span with weight. This implies significant reductions in part count and learning curve penalties in manufacturing. Enhanced responsiveness to fleet mix requirements is also implied. (Liebeck 2004)*

The increased ability to create commonality across a wide range of passenger loads is the second type of value of interest for the BWB case study, the value from flexibility. By designing the first plane in the series as a common plane, this creates the option for the second plane to either share the commonality and benefit from reduced costs and decreased development time or to instead be optimized around at a narrow market point and increase performance at the expense of the reduced development costs and times.

4.4 BWB TECHNICAL ARCHITECTURE AS A SET OF REAL OPTIONS

The application of BWB technical architecture as a real option has been identified as potentially having value in the commercial airplane industry. A description of the options and the manner that uncertainty in the market and environment is coped with is presented below.

1. **Option to launch derivative aircraft** – All modern commercial aircraft are part of a family of aircraft. Each aircraft in the family help to define a range of performance for the family as a whole. Typically, these dimensions include passenger / freight carrying capacity, flight distance, and functionality variants (passenger, freight, military, and tanker). Derivative aircraft in a family share many commonalities with one another, allowing economies of scale and increased learning curve benefits to be achieved by spreading costs and experience over all the aircraft in a family. New derivate aircraft cost significantly less to design and manufacture, in terms of both time and capital resources, due to commonalities with other family members.

    Previous research has looked at the value of considering the option value of developing and selling derivative aircraft (Miller and Clarke 2004, Miller 2005). The concept is that designing the first aircraft as the first in a family, as opposed to an optimized single aircraft, creates the option to develop additional aircraft in the same family in the future at a reduced cost and time than it would otherwise have taken.

This option is hypothesized to be the same for BWB and for tube and wing technical architectures. However, because of the geometry of the BWB and reduced part count, the BWB may improve on this option compared to the tube and wing architecture. For the purposes of this research, the BWB and tube and wing option below are considered the same. The following description describes derivatives that appear "within" a family of aircraft, such as the 737-600, 737-700, 737-800 and 838-900ER derivatives are all in the 737 family, but have been developed over time and share commonality with the original 737-100 produced in the 1960's (though over time this commonality ahs been reduced through successive design changes and technology upgrades). This option is important because several of the benefits from derivatives within families are also present in derivatives that go "across" families as well, which are described next.

    a. **Reduced exercise cost** – Because of the increased commonality between a baseline design and a future derivative, the future derivative can be developed at a fraction of the cost as the original family member. Price estimates for new planes start at about $10B, while for derivatives run between $1-3B in development costs (Ferreri 2003). This allows an airframer to enter the market with an updated plane for a fraction of the price of a completely new plane. This allows the manufacturer to respond at a later date to changes in customer needs, environmental changes (such as increases in fuel prices, or different regulations) or new competitor products.

    b. **Increased speed to market** – The derivative can also be brought to market faster than a totally new plane, given the leveraging of both prior designs and also increased experience with the original plane in the family. By coming to market faster, this allows the entire revenue stream to be moved forward in time, increasing net present value.

2. **Derivative capability expanded over larger family range** – While traditional tube and wing aircraft families are relatively homogenous in terms of technical specifications like passenger capacity and range, a BWB offers the ability to create families of aircraft that have a much larger difference in performance. For example, Willcox and Wakayama examine BWB families with passenger capabilities ranging from 272 to 475 passengers, with relatively small weight and performance penalties (Willcox and Wakayama 2003). The benefit of the large family made possible with the BWB architecture is that costs can be spread out over a wider range of aircraft, further increasing economies of scale and learning curve benefits. This ability allows for the creation of derivatives "across" families, with similar advantages as those described for derivatives within families, above.

4.4.1 BWB OPTION DECISION PATHS

For the options presented above, the expected decision paths are as follows. Under a competitive environment, it is expected that new derivatives and new aircraft will be developed and manufactured when: previous aircraft have reached their technological life expectancy, when existing aircraft are being significantly outsold by a competitor's aircraft offering or in response to a competitor's new offering. The decision to exercise the option and build either a new derivative or start a new baseline aircraft for a new size range is based on expected future return for the investment. The decision to exercise is also constrained by total resource availability at the enterprise level. This means that even if the time to exercise is optimum due to market conditions and/or competitor actions, constraints on funding availability will also determine if an option is exercised, i.e. if the exercise price can be paid.

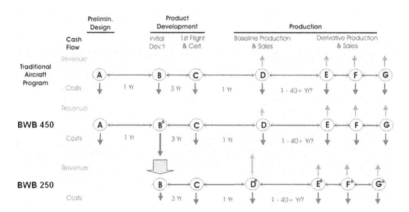

Figure 4-28 Typical option paths for BWB derivatives "across" families.

- A – preliminary design, similar between conventional and BWB programs
- B – initial development in conventional program
- B* – initial development in BWB, cost higher due to increased commonality, commonality can be used between BWB programs, shown here as initial development of BWB 250 followed by development of BWB 450
- C – first flight and certification, similar between conventional and BWB programs
- D – baseline production and sales, similar between conventional and BWB programs
- E, F, G – range of future derivatives for conventional aircraft
- D*, E*, F*, G* – range of future derivatives for BWB aircraft, derivates are time shifted forward in time, due to reduced design, development and tooling needs, costs are lower, present value of revenues are higher due to faster time on market

147

and increased market share (note faster time to market can be for first-mover or second-mover), and additional derivatives are possible due to reduced costs and development/manufacturing time

4.4.2 BWB AS A DVD TECHNICAL ARCHITECTURE

The BWB options presented above can be expressed in terms of the dual value design concept. As a reminder, dual value designs provide two benefits streams, one from the inherent value of the technology or technical architecture used and the second from the flexibility in the system. For the BWB options, the BWB technical architecture is the enabler for the DVD concept. That is, the BWB technical architecture provides both inherent value and flexibility value.

Note, that the DVD concept is not itself a separate contribution to this research apart from the LCF Framework. Rather, the DVD concept is another way to describe flexible systems.

The inherent value of using a BWB type aircraft comes from several sources. These include:

- Because of the aircraft architecture, significant improvements in both weight and fuel burn can be achieved, comparing the BWB to a conventional architecture. Comparing across comparable technology levels, 800 passengers, 7000 n mile range for both BWB and conventional aircraft designs, the BWB has a 15% reduction in takeoff weight and a 27% reduction in fuel burn per seat mile.
- The integration of the wing and the fuselage allows for increased span loading, or increased ratio of weight to wingspan, allowing increased weight for a constant wingspan. This is due to the lift generating capability of the fuselage, meaning the fuselage can help provide lift on a BWB, whereas a conventional tube fuselage provides almost no lift.
- The geometry of the BWB also allows for increased aerodynamic performance, as the wetted area, or area exposed to airflow and hence friction forces, is reduced on a BWB when compared to a conventional aircraft architecture, holding passenger seating requirements constant.
- The placement of the engines on the BWB above or in the rear fuselage reduces noise. This is because engines hanging under the wing causes engine noise to be reflected off the ground. Because of the near elimination of noise outside airport boundaries, increased flight times in and out of airports may be possible, increasing the time of operations that the plane could be operated around the clock.

The BWB options also appear to possess value from flexibility. The flexibility values that the BWB possesses are described below.

- The BWB has the potential to have increased commonality across aircraft families, allowing "cross-family" derivatives to be built. The commonality enabled by the technical architecture allows for: reduced parts count leading to

148

lower costs, higher scales of economy and improved learning curves. This has the following effects:

- o Flexibility through the option to build natural family of planes with large amounts of commonality
- o Ability to move faster in developing and building a new plane, compared to an optimized plane
- o Ability to reduce costs in developing and building a new plane, compared to an optimized plane
- The BWB also possesses the same flexibility value as conventional tube and wing planes: the ability to create "same-family" derivatives of the plane. It is not thought that the BWB technical architecture adds to this type of flexibility
- These options improve on the flexibility available for all aircraft, including tube and wing. These are:
  - o The flexibility to decide whether to build a plane or not
  - o The flexibility to decide on the timing of when to build a plane
  - o The flexibility to decide on what type of plane to build, or the technical performance of the plane

These flexibilities and the ones above interact. For example, when exercising the option of deciding what plane to build a BWB technical architecture enables the additional possibility of leveraging off of pervious BWB planes. Due to the increased commonality of the BWB technical architecture, with a cross-family derivative or a new optimized plane could be chosen as the type of plane to build

The above discussion lists multiple ways in which the BWB technical architecture possess both inherent and flexibility benefits. In this case study, these above flexibilities are in existence for tube and wing planes as well as a BWB architecture. However, it is thought that the BWB technical architecture improves on these benefits.

4.5 CHAPTER SUMMARY

Both the aviation industry and aircraft technology have changed significantly over the last half a century. The technology for aircraft has created a dominate technical architecture in the "tube and wing" plane that now allows commercial operations anywhere on the globe at a common service standard. The BWB technical architecture can be considered a disruptive technical architecture that allows for substantially improved performance, relative to conventional tube and wing architectures. As an example of DVD, the inherent values of the BWB are discussed, along with the types of flexibility that are embedded in the BWB technical architecture.

The following chapter continues the BWB case study by providing a quantitative analysis of the two sets of options presented above.

4.6 REFERENCES

Anderson, J. (2002) The Airplane: A History of its Technology. AIAA, Virginia.

Bluestone, B., P. Jordan and M. Sullivan. (1981) Aviation industry Dynamics: An Analysis of Competition, Capital and Labor, Massachusetts College, Massachusetts.

Clark, B. and J. Clarke. (2005) Investments Under Uncertainty in Air Transportation: a Real Options Perspective, Journal of the Transportation Research Forum, v. 44 n. 1.

Dana, J., Jr. and D. Schmitt. (2004) The U.S. Airline Industry in 1995, Kellogg School of Management, KEL042.

Donohue, N. and P. Ghemawat. (1997) The U.S. Airline Industry, 1978-1988 (A), Harvard Business School Case Study, 9-390-025.

Ferreri, D. (2003) Marketing and Management in the High-Technology Sector: Strategies and Tactics in the Commercial Airplane Industry, Praeger, Conneticut.

Heppenheimer, T. (1995) Turbulent Skies: The History of Commercial Aviation, Wiley, New York.

Heppenheimer, T. (2003) First Flight: The Wright Brothers and the Invention of the Airplane, Wiley, New York.

Kotha, S., D. Olesen, R. Nolan, and P. Condit. (2005) Boeing 787: The Dreamliner, Harvard Business School Case 9-305-101..

Lawrence, P. and D. Thornton. (2005) Deep Stall: The Turbulent Story of Boeing Commercial Airplanes, Ashgate, New York.

Liebeck, R. (2005) Design of Subsonic Transports, Presentation to MIT ESD.34 System Architecture, Massachusetts.

Liebeck, R. (2004) Design of the Blended Wing Body Subsonic Transport, Journal of Aircraft, v. 41 n. 1.

Liebeck, R. (2003) Blended Wing Body Design Challenges, AIAA/ICAS International Air and Space Symposium and Exposition, Ohio.

Liebeck, R.. M. Page, B. Rawdon (1998) Blended Wing Body Subsonic Commercial Transport, 36th Aerospace Science Meeting and Exhibit, Nevada.

Miller, B. (2005) A Generalized Real Options Methodology for Evaluating Investments Under Uncertainty with Application to Air Transportation, MIT Doctoral Dissertation, Massachusetts.

Miller, B. and J. Clarke. (2004) Application of Real Options to Evaluate the Development Process of New Aircraft Models, 4th AIAA ATIO Forum, Illinois.

Newhouse, J. (2007) Boeing vs. Airbus: The Inside Story of the Greatest International Competition in Business, Random House, New York.

Piepenbrock, T. (2004) Enterprise Design for Dynamic Complexity: Architecting & Engineering Organizations using System & Structural Dynamics, MIT Masters Thesis, Massachusetts.

Prichard, D. (2001) The Globalization of Commercial Aircraft Production: Implications for US Based Manufacturing Activity, International Journal of Aerospace Management, Vol 1, No. 3.

Willcox, K. and S. Wakayama. (2003) Simultaneous Optimization of a Multiple-Aircraft Family, Journal of Aircraft v. 40 n. 4.

5 VALUE OF FLEXIBILITY IN BLENDED WING BODY

Previously in Chapter 4, two sets of BWB real options were introduced. In Chapter 5, these real options are evaluated in a quantitative manner, to better understand the costs and benefits associated with each set of BWB options. Instead of trying to calculate a definitive value for flexibility added with using a BWB type technical architecture over a conventional architecture, this chapter presents results that look at the various aspects of flexibility and the factors that can affect it. The resulting analysis presented here demonstrates that the quantitative analysis of flexibility in a BWB plane is not a simple process, as it depends on a variety of factors including technical, organizational and strategic, as well as the underlying uncertainty in question.

Because the BWB options are "complex" real options in complex systems, a more sophisticated quantitative analysis technique was used in the evaluation process, compared with "standard" evaluation techniques for real options discussed in the literature. As a reminder, these "standard" real option evaluation techniques are described in Section 2.5. Figure 5-1 displays the analysis procedure for the current phase of the BWB case study research. The following chapter, Chapter 6, expands on the quantitative evaluation conducted here with a qualitative analysis of the BWB case study, to better understand the practical challenges associated with "complex" real options in complex systems.

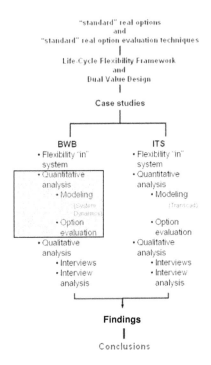

"standard" real options
and
"standard" real option evaluation techniques

|

Life-Cycle Flexibility Framework
and
Dual Value Design

|

Case studies

|

BWB	ITS
• Flexibility "in" system	• Flexibility "in" system
• Quantitative analysis	• Quantitative analysis
• Modeling (System Dynamics)	• Modeling (Transcad)
• Option evaluation	• Option evaluation
• Qualitative analysis	• Qualitative analysis
• Interviews	• Interviews
• Interview analysis	• Interview analysis

Findings

|

Conclusions

Figure 5-1 Case study analysis with highlighted box showing current stage of analysis.

The purpose of the quantitative analysis was to help better understand the flexibility associated with "complex" real options in complex systems, using the BWB case study as an example. For this purpose, a better understanding of where flexibility occurs and what its value is for a BWB type aircraft was sought. Also, the process that was used to obtain the results is central to this thesis, where the process refers to both the LCF Framework and the quantitative evaluation process used to value flexibility. In essence, this portion of the case study addresses the first research question, applied to the BWB case study: **How do "complex" real options and "standard" real options differ across the life-cycle of an option, including design, evaluation and management activities?** Specifically, this chapter seeks to better understand the design and evaluation portion of this research question.

To accomplish this purpose a quantitative analysis centered on the building and use of a system dynamics model of the aviation industry was conducted.

154

This chapter is composed of three main parts. The first part describes the quantitative evaluation process that was used for the quantitative evaluation. The second part describes the system dynamics model that was used in the quantitative evaluation. As will be described, this model is the main engine used in the evaluation process to generate quantitative results for the BWB "complex" real options in complex systems. The third part of this chapter presents the results and what we learned from them.

It is noted here that while the blended wing body aircraft is a concept being investigated at the Boeing Phantom Works Division, this research is looking at the BWB concept in a company-neutral manner. The ideas expressed here are not for a Boeing BWB concept per se, but rather apply to the BWB concept as a platform for providing flexibility in the large commercial aviation industry in general. Similarly, while examples are drawn from Airbus and Boeing, the modeling effort described in this chapter is geared towards a hypothetical pair of companies competing in a commercial aircraft duopoly. The characteristics of the companies used in the following examples can at best be referred to as characterizations drawn from prior Airbus and Boeing corporate strategies and product lines at different points in their respective corporate histories, as opposed to direct representations of Airbus and Boeing. In this way, the quantitative analysis can serve as a "proof of concept" for studying "complex" real options in complex systems.

5.1 CASE STUDY ANALYSIS PROCESS

The analysis process used for the case studies is based on a portion of the Life-Cycle Flexibility (LCF) Framework, specifically the part involved in quantitatively evaluating real options, as shown in Figure 5-2. As a reminder, a discussion of the entire LCF Framework is presented in Chapter 3.

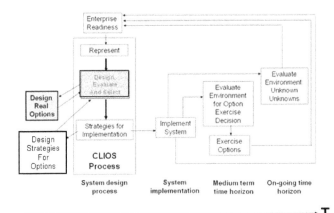

Figure 5-2 High level overview of LCF Framework, with components used in the research highlighted.

Note, that as a convenience to the reader, the case studies were written to stand alone. The case study analysis procedure described here is parallel to that described for the ITS case study in Section 8.1.

The quantitative analysis used for this research builds on prior real options analysis work. An emphasis in this research that has not received much attention in the real options literature is in the evaluation of "complex" real options in complex system. As previously discussed in Chapter 3, "complex" real options in complex systems have technical, organizational and process characteristics that are interconnected with one another. This differs from "standard" real options, which are characterized as a single relatively simple change or addition to a system that creates flexibility. Also, "standard" real options in "standard" system do not take into account organizational and process issues associated with the flexibility. "Standard" real options analysis techniques, as discussed in Chapter 2, are therefore not adequate for taking into account the complexities associated with the option and the system.

To better analyze "complex" real options in complex systems, a new analysis procedure was used to quantitatively evaluate flexibility, and applied to the BWB and ITS case studies. In general, the analysis procedure developed for this research utilizes at its core more sophisticated modeling techniques to better simulate the options and system of interest. For the BWB case study, an aviation industry system dynamics model was built to better understand the interaction between passenger demand, the airline industry and the aircraft manufacturing industry. The more sophisticated modeling techniques used in this research were deemed necessary to adequately capture the full richness of the issues surrounding the analysis of "complex" real options in complex systems.

As shown in Figure 5-3 and Figure 5-4 the quantitative evaluation process that was used for the BWB case study consisted of three main parts; generation of inputs, the system dynamics model, and the quantification of option value. An overview of the activities and purpose of these three main parts are described below.

Note, that as part of the LCF Framework, the quantitative evaluation of the flexibility is not the only evaluation that needs to be conducted. Rather, a qualitative evaluation of the "complex" real options in complex systems is conducted to better understand the practical challenges that exist. This qualitative analysis for the ITS case study is described in the next chapter.

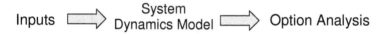

Inputs ⟹ System Dynamics Model ⟹ Option Analysis

Figure 5-3 Overview of three steps in BWB case study quantitative analysis.

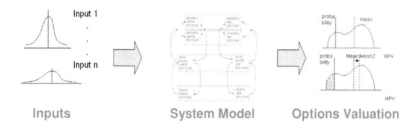

Inputs   System Model   Options Valuation

Figure 5-4 Quantitative analysis process for BWB case study, using system dynamics model of the aviation industry.

- **Inputs** – The inputs for the BWB case study that are important to the modeling need to be determined. These inputs can describe underlying passenger demand growth rates, fuel prices, competitor product offerings and business strategy. Since uncertainty surrounds some of these inputs, such as future fuel prices, this uncertainty could effect future system value and decision making. A probability distribution is then assigned to represent the uncertainty associated with these inputs. As shown in Figure 5-4, multiple inputs, each with a separate probability distribution can be used.
- **System Dynamics Model** – A system dynamics model was built to allow a better understanding of the interaction between passenger travel demand, the airline

industry and the aircraft manufacturing industry. The system dynamics model allows a better understanding of how different BWB options being considered affect aircraft order rates and aircraft manufacturer profitability. The model can be run multiple times using the probability distributions generated from the above discussion on inputs to understand how the system reacts under the input uncertainty. The outputs of interest from the model are aircraft order rates, which help determine aircraft manufacturer profitability associated with different BWB options under different input conditions.

- **Real Options Analysis** – Results from the system dynamics model with the input uncertainty are used to create probability distributions of the benefits associated with the specific BWB options. Benefits of interest for this research are profitability of the plane at the program and enterprise levels.

Comparing the probability distribution function averages for systems with flexibility and without flexibility yields the value of flexibility. For example, the NPV distributions for the profitability of a non-flexible and flexible plane are generated. A non-flexible solution could be building a plane in year zero, while a flexible solution could be delaying the plane design until a later year when future uncertainty is resolved. Comparing the average of the two NPV distributions would provide the value of flexibility. A more detailed discussion of this calculation is presented in the option analysis in 5.2.4.

Note that the valuation of flexibility through the comparison of the NPV distribution averages follows previous work (Tufano and Moel 1997, Clemons and Gu 2003, Greden et al. 2005, and Miller 2006). However, it is noted that other means of valuing the options could be considered, or that additional constraints in the valuation process could be added to make the evaluation more sophisticated. However, for this research, the comparison of averages is used. As this research serves as a proof of concept for the analysis of "complex" real options in complex systems, this means of valuing flexibility was deemed sufficient.

More detailed discussion of the system dynamics model used for this case study is presented in the next section.

5.2 SYSTEM DYNAMICS MODEL FOR AVIATION INDUSTRY

The purpose of the system dynamics model is to provide insight into different aspects of the commercial aviation industry and its behavior over time. The relationship between passengers, airlines and aircraft manufacturers was modeled, with the emphasis of the model on aircraft manufacturers. Specifically, the model seeks to show how changes in aircraft technical characteristics and aircraft manufacturing business strategies affect the relationship between airlines and aircraft manufacturers, such as aircraft orders and financial impacts.

For clarity of discussion, a high level overview of the model is presented, followed by more detailed discussion of each of the major objects in the model.

5.2.1 MODEL BASIS AND BACKGROUND

The commercial aviation industry system dynamics model presented here expands on an existing model of the airline industry as developed by Weil (Weil 1996). In his paper, Weil presents a generic industry model that can be adapted to multiple industries, including the aviation industry. Weil then customizes the model to the airline industry as an example, with a high level overview of the model shown in Figure 5-5.

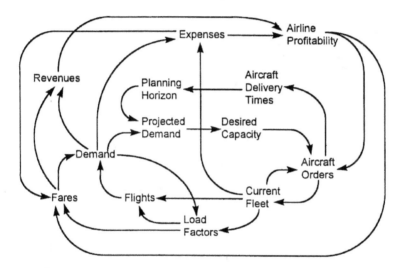

Figure 5-5 High level system dynamics model of the airline industry, as presented in (Weil 1996).

In the Weil model, interactions between passenger demand, airlines and airframers is modeled. However, the emphasis is on the airline industry and the relationship between the airline industry and passenger demand. Airframers and the relationship between airframers and airlines is highly simplified and the airframers are essentially represented by exogenous objects[1]. By not including the airframers as endogenous objects, there is

---

[1] An object is a "thing", or particular instance of a class. This terminology comes from object-oriented programming, which has as a fundamental goal the creation of modularity in the software code. As an example, "dog" would represent a class and "Lassie" would be an object, which is a particular instance of a dog. The class "dog" contains information about its characteristics and behaviors. The object "Lassie" describes the particular characteristics and behaviors of one dog, Lassie. (Wikipedia entry on object based programming 2007).

no feedback between the airlines and the airframers. The Weil model concentrates on the airline industry, with the bulk of the objects related to airlines, with the exception of the passenger demand and airframer objects highlighted in Figure 5-6.

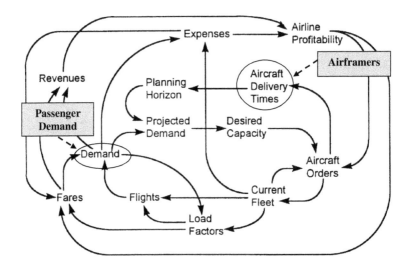

Figure 5-6 Weil model showing, pointing out passenger demand and airframer interactions with airline industry. Non-circled elements are all part of the airline industry model.

While the Weil model is excellent for demonstrating how small variations in the input of parameters can effect changes upstream, the model has several short-comings with respect to the needs of this research on "complex" real options in complex systems. These short-comings are discussed below.

- As the current research seeks to understand flexibility in the BWB, more emphasis on the airframer industry is needed. As a result, the airframer industry was explicitly modeled, similar to that shown in the Weil model for the airline industry, and fully integrated into the original Weil model. This change creates feedback between the airline and airframer industry, making the airframer industry endogenous to the model.
- The original Weil model seeks to understand broad industry trends. As such, it models the overall airline industry, as opposed to competitors within the airline industry. As such, the airframer industry is also modeled as a single aggregate industry that provides an aggregate product, a single plane. When modifying the

model, a better understanding of competing planes being offered by competing airframers was desired, so the model is disaggregated in two ways: first, two competing airframers are modeled. Second, each airframer offers two products to the airline industry; a narrow-body plane and a wide-body plane. A two competing airframer industry was deemed realistic, as the current airframer industry is essentially a duopoly between Airbus Industries and Boeing Commercial Aircraft Company. While each of these companies offers more than two products, the representation of these product lines were made both to simplify the model and also because it roughly approximates the types of planes that are sold to airlines to match needs. Smaller, narrow-body planes are in general used on shorter flights and larger, wide-body planes are used to connect city pairs further apart. The narrow-body planes represent products similar to the Airbus A320 family and the Boeing 737 family. The wide-body planes represent an average of the Airbus A330, A340 and A380 and Boeing 787, 777 and 747 lines. While these planes have seating capacities that vary between 200 – 550 seats, it was assumed the wide-body planes used in the model had about 300 seats.

- Since understanding how competing aircraft using different technical architectures (BWB vs. tube and wing) was of interest, increased specification of the performance of the planes being sold to the airlines was modeled. In the Weil model, only an aggregate cost determined the price of the airplanes. This was de-aggregated into three main cost components; operating expenses, capacity costs and fuel costs. Here operating expenses cover costs such as personnel and other variable costs, such as food and baggage handling. Capacity costs represent the costs associated with buying and owning a particular plane, such as the selling price for the plane and maintenance. The fuel costs represent the technological level of the plane, described in the model by the plane's fuel-efficiency. Together, these costs allow an exploration of trade-offs along several dimensions. The operating costs are mostly controlled by airline decisions, but can be greatly affected by technologies in the plane. For example, the adoption of the two-person forward-facing cockpit over a three-person cockpit over the last several decades, has greatly reduced operating costs. Trade-offs between capacity costs and fuel-efficiency can also be made, with airline deciding if they want a less expensive, but less technically advanced plane that may be more expensive to operate, especially if fuel prices increase in the future, or if they prefer a more expensive plane that is more fuel-efficient that could be cheaper to operate if fuel prices increase.

The changes described above are major changes to the Weil model in that the airframer industry is explicitly modeled, multiple aircraft are modeled, and competition between planes offered by airframers is explicitly modeled. Numerous other minor modifications were also made to the model to support these changes. Additional description of the aviation industry system dynamics model that was built and used for this research are presented in the section below.

5.2.2 AVIATION INDUSTRY SYSTEM DYNAMICS MODEL

This model focuses on the 100+ seat aircraft market; thus it excludes regional and smaller planes. The passenger demand is considered to have a single price elasticity curves that aggregates the behavior of business and leisure travelers on a single aircraft type, but differs over aircraft types (which represent different types of traveling patterns – i.e. short vs. long or domestic vs. international). Similarly, discrete firm behavior within the airline industry is beyond the scope of this model; i.e. the competition among airlines is not modeled and competing business models within the airline industry are not distinguished (e.g. legacy vs. discount airlines, ticket vs. amenity sales, etc.). A fundamental assumption of this model is that the airframe manufacturing industry market structure is a static duopoly, with only two competitors competing on both sales prices and the impact of technology on operating conditions (i.e. fuel-efficiency and operating costs). This precludes structural changes within the airframe manufacturing industry and as a result the rise of new competing airframe manufacturers or manufacturing business models (i.e. very light jets) was not included in this model. Finally, the behavior and impact of other stakeholders on the aviation industry, like governments, leasing companies, labor and capital markets, is not directly represented.

The end result is a system dynamics model composed of three main subsystems: passenger demand, an airline industry and an airframer industry. The airframer industry is further disaggregated into two competing companies. The structure of the system dynamics model is shown in Figure 5-7.

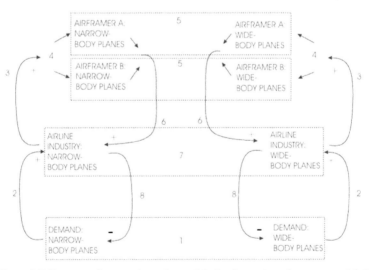

Figure 5-7 Structure of system dynamics model, showing major subsystems modeled and interactions.

162

An overview of each of these subsystems and the interactions between the subsystems is presented below. The remainder of the description in Sections 5.2.2 and all of 5.2.3 is taken almost entirely from a working paper written by the author and two other doctoral students who co-developed this system dynamics model (Lin et al. 2007).

5.2.2.1 Customer Demand

The customer demand object models customer demand for air travel and is based on *exogenous* economic conditions, such as GDP growth rates, and *endogenous* feedback from the airline industry objects in the form of fare prices and service quality. While demand for freight is also driving demand for airlines and consequently for aircraft, it is not modeled explicitly but considered only as a fraction of total demand.

5.2.2.2 Airline Industry

The airline industry object represents the airline industry in an aggregate form (i.e. all airlines are included as a single entity). The input into this object is customer demand and the output that connects this object to the airframe manufacturer object is new aircraft orders. Airlines use current unit profitability and price sensitivity as the only deciding factor in aircraft purchases (therefore the effect of fleet commonality is not included in this model formulation). The airline industry is divided into two segments; customers served by narrow- and wide-body planes. These two segments roughly match the breakdown of city pairs into short- and long-distance travel, or domestic/regional and international/intercontinental travel.

5.2.2.3 Airframers

The airframe manufacturing industry supplies planes to the airline industry and is structured in a competitive duopoly. Each aircraft manufacturer offers two products: a narrow and a wide-body aircraft. The two companies' offering in these market segments directly compete with each other. The aircraft products are differentiable in terms of their characteristics (capital and operating costs) *between* the companies and *over time within the same company* thus representing successive generations of aircraft.

5.2.3   OVERVIEW OF MAJOR OBJECTS AND INTERACTIONS

Each of the major objects and interactions labeled in Figure 5-7 are described below. The objects and interactions are presented in the functional order which they appear in the model. For example, underlying passenger demand affects the passenger demand/airline interaction (by lower ticket says, for example), which then affects airline profitability. These objects and interactions are both presented below.

1. **Customer demand object** - Total customer market demand is divided between demand for narrow and wide-body aircraft and equals total commercial passenger demand in the 100+ seat plane market. Customer demand is driven by general

163

economic conditions, fare prices and service quality (as measured by airline load factors).

2. **Customer demand / airline industry interaction** - Airline industry is positively affected by increasing customer demand.

3. **Airline industry / aircraft manufacturing industry interaction, part 1** - The demand for new aircraft is positively affected by increasing airline profits (profit effect on orders) and future desired capacity, where future desired capacity is targeted to meet forecasted changes in customer demand.

4. **Airline industry / aircraft manufacturing industry interaction, part 2** - The airline industry chooses which airframe manufacturer to order from in both the narrow-body and wide-body market segments based on the relative profitability of each manufacturer's existing plane offering. The profitability is the difference between revenue and costs, where the manufacturer can affect cost through the sale price (capital cost) and the fuel-efficiency (operating cost) of the airplane design. In general, higher cost planes are less profitable and result in lower order rates for an airframe manufacturer's plane.

5. **Airframe manufacturing object** - Corporate headquarters for each airframe manufacturer make trade-offs between the narrow-body and wide-body programs. Each program has the authority to make decisions on airplane sales price and design decisions affecting fuel-efficiency. Corporate headquarters makes the decision on when to launch a new plane, when to expand or reduce capacity and how to mediate between conflicts between the needs of both programs. E.g., ensuring that both programs do not try and launch a new plane simultaneously, as resources are constrained.

6. **Aircraft manufacturing / airline industry interaction** - As airframe manufacturers deliveries increase, airline capacity increases.

7. **Airline industry object** - Airline industry segments served by narrow and wide-body aircraft. This roughly corresponds to different city pairs, with long distance city pairs served by wide-body aircraft and closer city pairs served by smaller narrow-body aircraft.

8. **Airline industry / customer demand interaction** - As airliners' fleet capacity increases because of the addition of new planes, the number of flights offered increase, load factors decrease and fares decrease, causing an increase in customer demand.

The major elements and connections between elements within each of these subsystems is described below.

5.2.3.1 Customer Demand Object

The customer demand object models the underlying demand for air transportation and aircraft by focusing on passenger air transportation in the 100+ seat market. This focus ignores travel on regional, very light jets, corporate jets and general aviation and was done to simplify the model. This simplification was seen as reasonable, as 72.2% of the airline industry revenues were derived from passenger travel in 2000 (Mak and Enright 2002). An important assumption of the model is that while these additional segments are important and may make inroads into the 100+ seat passenger market, this market will continue to remain the dominant way in which customers utilize air transportation in the immediate decades.

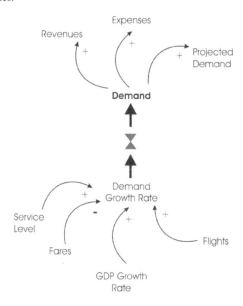

Figure 5-8 Customer travel demand.

The customer demand object is based on a stock and flow of the customer demand growth rate creating customer demand over time. The demand growth rate is influenced by four main inputs: GDP growth rate, ticket prices, fare and flight availability and airline service levels. GDP growth rates represent the underlying world economic conditions, which have been shown to be a highly correlated to passenger air traffic growth rates (Jiang and Hansman 2004). It is assumed that passengers are price sensitive, with lower prices leading to increased demand and higher prices acting to suppress passenger travel demand. The passenger price elasticity curve used is assumed to aggregate business and leisure customers preferences. An increased number of flight offerings increases passenger demand, as the frequency of flights and number of destinations increases, while simultaneously, load factors decrease, which represents an increase in airline passenger service quality.

The total demand affects both the airline's finances and future planning. Increased numbers of passengers increases revenues, but also increases total expenses (though may decrease expenses on a unit passenger basis). Current and previous demand also drive

165

the airline planning process, as future demand is forecasted based on the demand time series. In general, increasing current demand translates into increased future demand forecasts, which leads to needs for increased capacity to meet the forecasted growth in future demand.

5.2.3.2 Airline Industry Objects
The second class of objects are for the airline industry. It includes the following main sub-objects which will be described in detailed in following section.
- Airline finances and profitability object
- Airline profitability, planning and aircraft order rates object
- Airline fleet size

5.2.3.2.1 *Airline Finances and Profitability Object*
Passenger airlines garner the majority of their revenues through the sales of tickets to passengers, a trend that this model assumes will continue in the future[2]. The airline finance and profitability object models the relationship between fares and the effect on airline profitability, identifying the drivers affecting fare prices that airlines can reasonably charge.

---

[2] A recent exception to this pricing model is the experimentation that RyanAir, a European discount carrier is running with offering free airfares and charging passengers for incidentals, such as food services, to create a revenue stream (Capell and Foust 2006). Still, even if non-conventional revenue sources become commonplace the model assumptions still stand since (1) this revenue streams need to be adequate to cover expenses and (2) passengers are not given free-rides; they are still paying for the cost of their travels via other means.

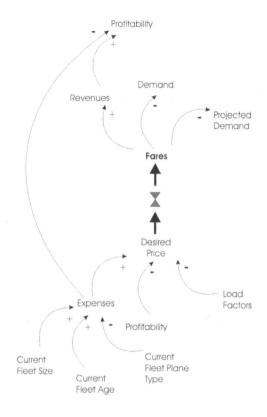

Figure 5-9 Airline finances and profitability.

A stock and flow of desired pricing and actual pricing charged by airlines for passenger tickets forms the basis of the airline finance and profitability object. The desired price for airlines is based on unit costs, passenger load factors, and profitability. Airlines are sensitive to passenger demand for seats, as represented by the load factors. As passenger demand drops, airlines attempt to compensate by lowering ticket price. Ticket price fluctuations are modified by expenses and profitability. Higher expenses caused by larger fleets, older fleets or inefficient fleets (i.e. non-fuel-efficient aircraft), drive ticket prices higher. Profitability has the opposite effect with declining profitability resulting in increasing ticket prices, in an attempt to increase profitability.

Actual passenger fares affect airline finances and planning, and feeds back into customer demand. For airline finances, increased fares increase revenue, which then increases profits. Increased fares tend to decrease passenger demand which also affects projected future demand as well.

5.2.3.2.2 *Airline Profitability, Planning and Aircraft Order Rates Object*

Airline profitability influences planning and aircraft order rates.   In general, as profitability increases, the desire for additional planes increases, to meet growth in forecasted passenger demand[3]. The unit profitability for the aircraft operated within each market segment of narrow and wide bodied planes from each airframe manufacturer is calculated by the airlines and this influences the relative orders of new planes. The more profitable a certain type and brand of plane is, the larger the relative percentage of orders that plane type and brand receive, compared to other types and brands. The order rate is driven both by unit profitability as well as desired capacity and in turn affects the planning cycle.

The planning cycle consists of actual demand driving the forecasts for projected demand, influenced by the airlines planning horizon. The projected demand creates a need for either new capacity, if projected demand is increasing, or a need to accelerate older aircraft retirements and slow order rates of new planes if desired capacity is decreasing. The airline planning process is influenced by the aircraft delivery rates, with longer delivery times requiring airlines to increase their planning horizons, to take into account the delay in receiving new aircraft. In general, as aircraft order rates are increased, the time it takes to deliver the aircraft increases, as production backlogs increase, as discussed in the following sections.

---

[3] The higher the number of decision makers in the industry the greater the potential of misestimation of the forecast due to "strategic exuberance." Weil 1996.

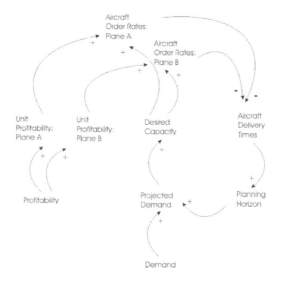

Figure 5-10 Airline profitability, planning and aircraft order rates.

5.2.3.2.3 *Airline Fleet Size*

The airline fleet size is dependant on the difference in rates at which new aircraft are delivered and old aircraft are retired. In general, larger fleets increase expenses (though larger new fleets may be less expensive than smaller older fleets, due to larger operating costs), increase the number of flights that are possible and decrease the load factor of passengers per plane, for a given number of passengers. The change in flight offerings and load factors further affect fares and demand. Increasing load factors (increased customer demand) driving ticket prices higher, which then serves to dampen demand, which can result in a decreased load factor. An increase in flights offered increases customer demand, as new destinations and increased frequency improve customer perceived value, which can lead to further increases in load factors.

169

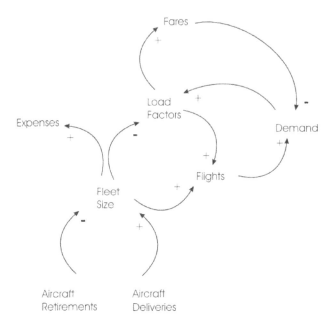

Figure 5-11 Airline fleet size.

5.2.3.3 Aircraft Manufacturing Production and Finances Object

Airframe manufacturers have passenger airlines as their direct customers, taking in aircraft orders and delivering completed planes, typically years after the order is placed. The airframe manufacturing industry has been modeled as two companies competing in a permanent duopoly, where competition is divided over two market segments that compete head to head; narrow and wide-body planes. Each manufacturer competes on providing a plane that tries to maximize the profitability function of the airline industry, of which the aircraft is only part.

Both airframe manufacturers employ an enterprise architecture based on highly independent aircraft programs. Decisions for aircraft design and some decisions for new product development and production capacity are made at the program level. An airframe manufacturer corporate "headquarters" object has also been modeled to help make trade-offs between programs concerning the distribution of scare resources, specifically the resources to start a new aircraft program and increase or decrease production capacity.

Product design is based on a trade-off between performance and cost. In general, it is assumed that there is a trade-off between performance and cost, with more technically advanced planes costing more to develop, resulting in a higher potential selling price. For this model, technological development is divided into two categories. First are short-term technology developments, represented by fuel-efficiency. In the model, high technology products are represented by planes that have higher than average fuel-efficiency, when compared with contemporary average product offerings. In the longer term, it is assumed that technology and process improvements can reduce operating costs by, for example, reducing the flight crew needed.

Each airframe manufacturer has a specific business strategy, combining product architecture and pricing. It is possible to alter the business strategy of an individual airframe manufacturer to emulate real world trends. For example, Airframer A may pursue a business strategy of offering planes of average performance at a low price, while Airframer B may focus on developing higher performing planes and charge a premium for the performance. The trade-off involved is the aircraft purchase price vs. the aircraft operating costs, including fuel consumption. Because there is uncertainty over time with regard to which would be the winning strategy, the competitive advantage may shift between manufacturers and airlines using each type of plane performance over time. This may happen if, for example, a highly fuel-efficient, and expensive, plane is produced and fuel prices sky rocket; airlines using this plane will benefit, as the savings in fuel consumption would outweigh the cost of purchasing the aircraft. The reverse can also be true, where the highly fuel-efficiency plane is a poor investment if fuel prices are lower than expected.

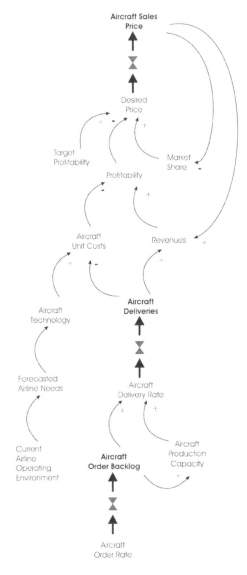

Figure 5-12 Airframer program production and finances.

The airframe manufacturer production and finances object is based on three stocks and flows. The first stock and flow is the aircraft order backlog, which describes the increase in plane orders depending on the airline aircraft order rate. For a given production capacity, the order backlog increases for increasing order rates. The second stock and flow is the number of aircraft deliveries, which is determined by the airframe manufacturer. The final stock and flow is the aircraft sales price, which is driven by the desired pricing strategy by the airframe manufacturers.

The aircraft delivery rate, and total deliveries, directly influences both revenues and unit costs. As the number of planes delivered increases, so do revenues. As the total number of planes delivered increases, unit costs fall, as it is assumed that each product has a learning curve that it moves down as an increased number of planes are delivered, decreasing unit costs over the entire production run.

Also affecting unit costs is the aircraft technology, with high technology planes increasing costs. The choice of aircraft technologies is based on airframers' forecast of future airline operating needs, based on historical data.

The difference of total revenues and expenses is the profitability of each program. Combined with the desired profitability and the current market share for each plane, the desired selling price for each plane is set. Increases in desired profitability drive prices higher, while declines in market share depress prices in an attempt to increase market share. The actual aircraft sales price the effects revenues and market share, with higher plane prices increasing revenues but also dampening market share.

5.2.4 INPUT UNCERTAINTY AND OUTPUTS OF INTEREST

Numerous inputs are used for the model. Most of the inputs are either assumed to be static or vary over time in a continuation of historic trends. A few of the inputs that were seen as being critical in affecting aircraft sales and had uncertainty surrounding their future values were used as inputs to better understand what about a BWB technical architecture would create flexibility, where these flexibilities would exist and what the value of these flexibility would be. A probability distribution around these inputs was created and used in the modeling. The inputs of interest that were investigated over different conditions were:

- **Uncertainty over future passenger demand growth rates.** This growth rate affects the future number of passengers seeking air travel. This in turns affects the airline new plane ordering rate. Finally, this impacts the sales and profitability of planes and the decision on whether or not to invest in offering a new plane or derivative. Lower than expected growth rates can decrease demand for new planes and make investment in a new product line unprofitable. In the model, passenger demand is a function of GDP growth rate, airline fares, airline service levels and the frequency of flights. The underlying driver of demand growth is the GDP growth rate, with the other factors changing the demand incrementally around the underlying trend established by the GDP growth rate.

173

As such, uncertainty in the GDP growth rate, and hence uncertainty in the basic trend for new aircraft orders was examined. Historic worldwide GDP growth rates, shown in Figure 5-13, were obtained for the last several decades and the underlying uncertainty extended into the future (World Bank 2006).

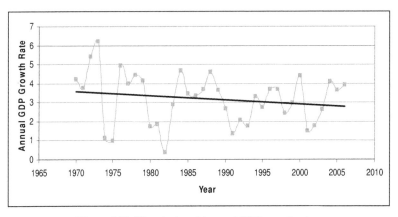

Figure 5-13 Historical world annual GDP growth rates.

- **Uncertainty over future fuel prices.** This uncertainty affects the cost structure for the airlines. Higher fuel costs lead to higher ticket prices which in turn suppress demand. Lower passenger demand lowers the demand for new aircraft. In order to help hold down fuel costs and to improve sales, airframers can introduce more fuel-efficiency aircraft, relative to older models and relative to their competitor. If the higher fuel-efficiency of a plane lowers costs, airlines are more likely to buy the fuel-efficient plane if they expect fuel prices to increase, all else being equal. However, typically planes with higher fuel-efficiency have a higher technology standard and may cost more relative to a lower fuel-efficient plane. As such, the airlines must make a trade-off between increased purchase costs and fuel-efficiency. This trade-off will change as fuel prices in the future change. The underling driver of fuel price changes was estimated with changes in the prices of oil. Historic uncertainty in crude oil (Inflation Data 2006), shown in Figure 5-14, was extrapolated to estimate future fuel price uncertainty.

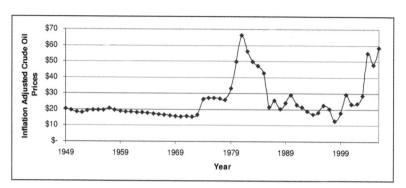

Figure 5-14 Historical inflation adjusted crude oil prices.

- **Competitor Product Offering.** Uncertainty regarding the type of product offered by the competing airframer affects plane valuation. A competing product better suited to the market, for example offering higher fuel-efficiency when fuel prices increase, can lower the value of one's own plane. As customers only have two competing airframer products to choose from, the industry is a zero-sum game, with gains in orders by one airframer resulting in a loss of orders at the other airframer. Instead of trying to capture the uncertainty involved in guessing competitor product offerings, scenarios were examined to look at flexibility in the BWB against multiple types of competing planes.
- **Competitor Business Strategy.** Competitors can compete on more than just airplane technical design. The business strategy of competitors also creates uncertainty. A competitor can compete on a first- or second-mover strategy and can compete by offering optimized planes with high performance or planes that share commonality across families, which lowers performance but also lowers prices. Instead of trying to quantify a competitor's business strategy, multiple scenarios were examined under different competitor business strategies.

The primary output of interest was the profitability of airframer decisions regarding aircraft design and production decisions. To determine the profitability of their decisions, the model outputs of interest were the total number of planes sold over a 20 year period and the timing of when the planes were sold. The total number of planes sold determines the total revenue stream captured with a particular plane and the timing of the sales affects the discounted cash flow, as planes sold in the future are worth less in present value terms than planes sold closer to the present day. To complete the determination of the net present value of the plane, the discounted expenses were also considered, primarily consisting of initial development costs at time zero for a new plane and additional development costs in the future for any derivative planes developed. Variable manufacturing costs during the production of each plane are also considered to capture the profit from each plane.

175

To generate this output, it was assumed that all airlines and airframers were rational agents that made decisions based on maximizing their net present value. Based on this assumption, it was assumed that if planes were technically exactly the same, airlines would buy them in equal numbers, but if the planes are different airlines would increase in likelihood of buying a plane that was expected to increase profitability. In the model, airlines can not know a priori what plane will maximize profits, as future uncertainty has not been resolved yet and the future conditions may change from when the plane was ordered.

For example, if current fuel prices are low, airlines may forecast continued low fuel prices and buy planes that are lower in cost but less fuel-efficient. If the future changes, the airlines may be stuck with a fleet that has a high operating cost due to the low fuel-efficiency of the fleet. This example is shown in Figure 5-15 with a changing order rate for two planes. Plane A is a low-cost, low efficiency plane and Plane B is a high-cost, high efficiency plane. At the start of the simulation, fuel prices are low and Plane A outsells Plane B. However, a sudden fuel price increase after a number of years causes the ordering patterns of airlines to reverse, with Plane B outselling Plane A until the end of the simulation.

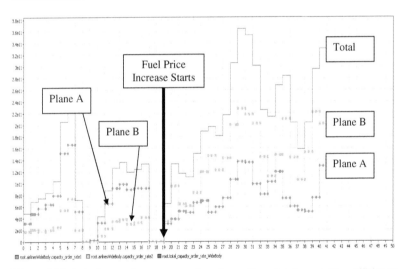

Figure 5-15 Ordering rate for two competing planes: Plane A is low-cost/low efficiency and Plane B is high-cost/high efficiency. Fuel prices start low and increase after about 20 years.

5.2.5 MODEL VALIDATION

The system dynamics model was validated in four ways. First, the structure of the model was seen as valid, given the similarities from expanding on the previously published and extensively used Weil model (Weil 1996). Second, the model was used to try and recreate historical outputs for such driving factors as passenger demand and capacity. A comparison of the historical passenger demand and aircraft capacity produced by the model with historical data is shown in the two figures, Figure 5-16 and Figure 5-17.

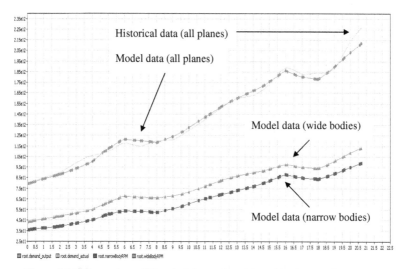

Figure 5-16 Comparison of historical data and model produced results for historical demand. Historical demand from 1984 – 2005 is shown in the figure.

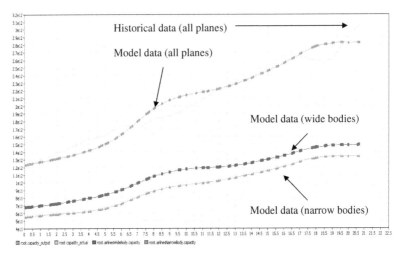

Figure 5-17 Comparison of historical data and model produced results for historical capacity. Historical capacity from 1984 – 2005 is shown in the figure.

Comparing the model produced data with the historical data shows that the model produced data is within 10% of the historical data for the 21 year period for which data was available. The ability to reproduce historical data creates comfort with using the model to extrapolate future behaviors. The third validation technique was in using the model to extrapolate the future demand and capacity needs to determine if similar results to forecasts made by Boeing and Airbus are obtained (Airbus 2006, Boeing 2006). As Boeing and Airbus each has forecasts that differ somewhat from one another, these forecasts were averaged together to compare with the model, with results shown in Figure 5-18 and Figure 5-19.

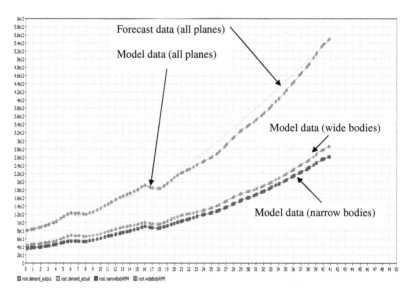

Figure 5-18 Comparison of composite airframer forecast data and model produced results for future demand. Historical and future demand from 1984 – 2025 is shown in the figure.

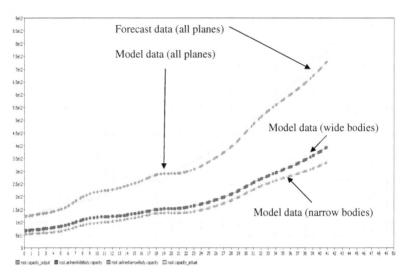

Figure 5-19 Comparison of composite airframer forecast data and model produced results for future capacity. Historical and future capacity from 1984 – 2025 is shown in the figure.

The future projects from the model and the airframer forecasts also matched well, within an error range of close to 10%. Finally, the model structure and results were also validated with expert opinion, with the modeling being developed and presented to experts in the field at MIT.

The following section presents the results obtained from using the system dynamics model to better understand "complex" real options in complex systems, using the BWB case study to illustrate.

5.3 RESULTS

The objective of the quantitative analysis was to better understand if a blended wing body type of aircraft would improve the flexibility already inherent in tube and wing type aircraft. As discussed previously, BWB technical architectures are seen as having inherent benefits and flexibility benefits. The inherent benefits of a BWB 250 and BWB 450 are examined briefly in the following section, with the remainder of the sections devoted to better understanding the benefits of flexibility.

180

5.3.1 INHERENT BENEFITS

BWB technical architectures create improved fuel efficiencies compared with conventional tube and wing planes of the same size. The size of the fuel efficiency varies as function of the size of the plane. Comparing BWB planes to comparably sized tube and wing planes, the larger the plane the larger the fuel efficiency that a BWB technical architecture provides.

It is estimated that a BWB seating 800 passengers would have about 27% great fuel-efficiency than a conventional plane seating 800 passengers (Liebeck 1998). Interviewees familiar with the program have stated that the fuel-efficiency gained from the BWB architecture goes to zero at smaller sized planes, such as the 150 passenger class planes like the 737 or A320. Since data is only available for relative fuel-efficiency of the BWB at the 800 passenger level (27%) and through discussions with interviewees at the 150 passenger level (0%), it is assumed for this analysis that the fuel-efficiency benefits of the BWB decrease linearly as a function of passenger size. Assuming that the fuel-efficiency varies linearly as a function of passengers, efficiencies of 4.2% and 12.5% are created for the BWB 250 and BWB 450, respectively, compared to conventional planes of the same size.

Comparing the BWB 250 and 450 to similar sized conventional planes, the fuel-efficiency benefits from the BWB planes causes the relative difference in net present value to be higher for the BWB planes, over the conventional planes. However, this is assuming that the BWB plane is competing against an optimized conventional plane. In practice, as seen in the practice of competition between Boeing and Airbus, often the Boeing plane is optimized for performance and the Airbus plane share commonality across families, decreasing performance but also decreasing costs. For example, the A330 and A340 share common fuselages, wings and cockpits and have a substantially lower price than the 777, which has a better fuel-efficiency but a high price tag as well. So comparing the BWB 250 both an optimized conventional plane as well as a conventional plane that has commonality across families (the BWB 450 was only compared with an optimized conventional 450 passenger plane, as currently only Boeing offers a plane in that class), it is determined that the inherent benefits of the BWB 250 are greater than the conventional plane only when the conventional plane is optimized as a single family. When the conventional plane share commonality across families, resulting in a lower cost, it out performs the BWB 250 in sales.

181

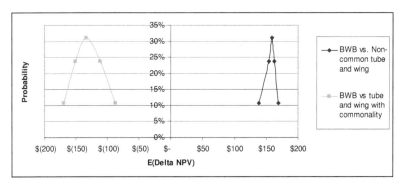

Figure 5-20 Comparison of BWB 250 and a conventional 250 passenger plane, with and without commonality.

This means that the inherent benefit of the BWB of providing increased fuel-efficiency can be overcome, at least on smaller sized planes where the benefit is smaller, by increased commonality on conventional planes, where the commonality across families lowers costs. The decision to proceed with commonality, or multi-family optimization, as opposed to single family optimization, is a decision that reflects corporate strategy and culture and is included in the model.

5.3.2 FLEXIBILITY BENEFITS

As described in the Chapter 4, flexibility is enabled from the ability to create derivative aircraft. Two major types of derivative aircraft are identified. The first is the ability to build a derivative plane and create a family of aircraft and the second is the ability to leverage knowledge, design work and tooling from a prior family to launch a new family, called cross-family derivatives. Both of these flexibilities are made possible, or improved, with the use of commonality.

The cost savings come from the commonality in components and tooling. This reduces the need to redesign components and develop new tooling and manufacturing processes, which can then increase scale of economies by increasing ordering rates for common parts. Additionally, derivatives can take advantage of learning curves started on prior planes in the family, instead of re-starting the learning curve.

The two types of derivatives are described below.

- **Same-family derivatives** - Derivative aircraft in a family are very similar, typically having about 40% of the plane in common with other aircraft in the family (Ferreri 2003). This commonality is relatively easy to accomplish, and is standard for all aircraft families that Airbus and Boeing offer, due to the relatively minor differences between aircraft due to similarities in the market niches they serve. For example, a 737 may be stretched (and has been) to create a larger plane, but it can not be stretched enough to cause it to move into a market niche served by the 747 for example. Instead, the 737 would serve market needs for planes ranging in size between 100-200 passengers.

- **Cross-family derivatives** - The second type of derivative aircraft, cross-family derivatives, is more challenging than the derivatives just described. While derivatives within families serve similar markets, commonality across families is more challenging because the market niches served by different families of aircraft can be significantly different. Still there are numerous examples of commonality across families in both Airbus and Boeing. For example, the Boeing 757 and 767 share a common cockpit while the A330 and A340 share common fuselages, wings and cockpits. While both Airbus and Boeing have included commonalty across families in the past, Airbus planes have utilized a strategy of commonality across families. Commonality in cockpits across almost all Airbus families is consistently maintained for new planes. And increased leveraging of existing technologies for new planes, to reduce development costs and speed time to market, has also been a design philosophy for Airbus. In effect, the increased usage of commonality across families creates a similar set of flexibility benefits that derivatives within families provide – namely the ability to produce a follow on plane in the future for a lower cost.

However, the major difference between these two derivatives is that the costs needed to complete development of them are substantially different. For a derivative within a family costs normally run around $1-3B in development costs; up to 90% less than producing the first of a new airplane family (Harrigan 2006). Since the commonality across families can not be leveraged to as great an extent without suffering larger performance penalties, cross-family "derivatives" cost more to develop. For example, the A350 as originally envisioned as a derivative of the A330-200 was estimated to cost €3.5B, or $4.7B (Answers 2006). Additionally, the performance penalty for cross-family derivatives also increases. For example, comparing the A350 as a A330-200 derivative and the clean sheet design for the A350 XWB that Airbus announced later, the development cost estimates about doubled (Wikipedia 2007a), the time until delivery increased by two years (Wikipedia 2007a), but the performance increased from being about 8% less efficient than the 787[4] to about 7% more fuel-efficient, per seat mile (Wikipedia 2007a)[5]. This example demonstrates the trade-offs that airframers must make in choosing greater commonality across families and its benefits of lower costs and faster development times, or optimization of a single family with higher costs, slower development times but higher performance.

---

[4] Based on calculations performed by author from data obtained from (Steinke 2005) and (Wikipedia 2007b).
[5] This number depends on which planes to compare. Boeing asserts that for the A350 XWB derivative used to make this comparison, it is more appropriate to compare this craft to a 787-9, rather than a 787-9, as the seat differential is smaller in that comparison (Baseler 2006).

The BWB has also been estimated at providing "unusual level of commonality", with studies being done on BWB families ranging from 250 - 450 passengers. (Liebeck 2004). Since past studies have mainly looked at commonality benefits in the BWB in ranges from 250 – 450 passengers, it is not known if the commonality benefits extend down to planes in the 150 passenger or up to the 800 passenger range, in addition to the 250-450 range looked at in past studies. This research will then only look at the 250-450 range for BWB.

The results provided in the remainder of this section provide an evaluation of flexibility in the BWB technical architecture. The purpose was to better identify flexibility, what the flexibility is and if a BWB type plane adds to that flexibility to make it more valuable.

Further exploring the concept of flexibility created through the use of same-family and cross-family derivatives, three types of flexibility can be created for each type of derivative.
1. The option to decide if a plane should or should not be built (this flexibility is also present in the first aircraft, even without derivatives).
2. The option to alter the timing of the derivative.
3. The option to change the design of the derivative to respond (or anticipate) changes in the environment or as a competitive response.

The first option allows the option holder to determine if they want to exercise the option to build a derivative or not, based on current conditions and expected future conditions. The second option allows the option holder to exercise the option at a variety of times in the future. And the third option allows the option holder to change the design of the derivative based on new information. All of these flexibilities are available to both conventional and BWB type aircraft, but BWB aircraft have the potential to improve on them.

As an example with the third option, for same-family derivatives, past derivatives offered have covered a range of performance and cost points. For example, Boeing currently offers four 737 derivatives; the 737-600, -700, -800 and -900ER. Prices vary from $47M for the 737-600 up to $80.5M for the 737-900ER. Passenger seating also varies from 132 for the 737-600 up to 215 for the 737-900ER. Fuel-efficiency also varies by up to 14% on a seat mile basis, between the 737-700 and 737-900ER, with the -900ER being the more efficient plane.[6] This is used as an assumption in the model; namely that airframers have some choice over how to design a future derivative that does not have to be made until some future uncertainty is resolved.

In a similar manner, with commonality, planes in a new family can be designed either as a cross-family derivative or as a clean sheet plane optimized for a particular market niche. The designs presented in 2005 and 2006 by Airbus for the A350 demonstrate this. Initially, Airbus planned to offer the A350 as a derivative on the A330-200, but then responding to customer demand, decided to offer it instead as a clean sheet design, billing it the A350 XWB.

---

[6] Based on calculations done by the author.

The remainder of this section looks at these three options. Because the first two options, the option to offer a derivative and the choice of timing of when to offer the derivative are tightly coupled, they are discussed together in the next section. The third option, the ability to postpone choosing the design of the derivative is then presented in the following section.

5.3.2.1 Options on Offering a Derivative and Timing of Derivatives

In analyzing the value of flexibility for these options, it seems evident that these options are not completely uncoupled. For example, when deciding on a derivate design choice to respond to a changed environment, the timing of when to offer the new derivative needs to be determined.

In addition to realizing that these options are linked, two other factors need to be taken into account. The first is the competitor's business strategy; is the competitor trying to be a first-mover or a second-mover in the market, and is the competitor trying to dominate the market, win in the market, maintain the market share or abandon the market. The second consideration is the competitor's product line strategy, simplified in the model as either a plane that is optimized for a particular market niche or a plane that takes advantage of commonality to create cross-family derivatives. For this model, it is assumed that optimized planes still posses the ability to create derivatives within families, but not across families. As a simplification, optimized planes are assumed to be high-cost but offer high efficiency. Planes with commonality are assumed to have lower costs but lower efficiency, as well as the ability to create cross-family derivatives.

Below, the following two sections discuss the options for offering a derivative and the option on the timing of the derivatives. The discussion centers around the benefits from offering a derivative in the first section and the different timing choices for offering the option in the second section.

5.3.2.1.1 *Option of Offering a Derivative*

To better understand the potential value of derivatives, using same-family derivatives as an example, consider the two following situations. In the first situation, Company A and Company B offer identical planes to the market and as a result, the airlines respond by purchasing each in equal numbers. In this situation neither airframer produces another derivative and therefore split the market indefinitely.

In the second situation, one company sees an opportunity to achieve a gain in market share at the expense of the other company by offering a derivative plane at a later date that performs slightly better than the original plane. In this case, after it is introduced, the derivative garners more sales than the original competing plane. However, while the additional marginal gain at the expense of the competitor will be enough to pull ahead in profits relative to the competitor, the building of the derivative does not necessarily have to be profitable enough by itself to create an absolute increase in net present value for the company. Instead, the absolute net present value could decrease, while the relative net present value increases. These trends are shown in Figure 5-21 and Figure 5-22.

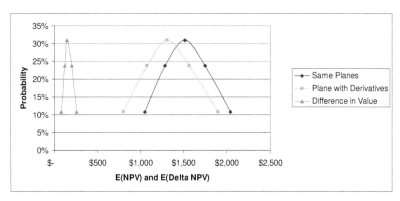

Figure 5-21 E(Delta NPV) in two situations; both competitors offering the same plane indefinitely and one competitor offering a derivative.

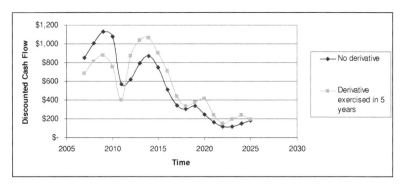

Figure 5-22 Discounted cash flows for two competing planes; one optimized and the other common with a derivative offered after five years.

This is important for multiple reasons. This demonstrates that exercise of a derivative can harm the absolute E(NPV) of a company, if the marginal increase in revenue is not enough to offset the additional development costs for the derivative. However, the derivative is likely to offer an improvement over a competitor's plane and steal market share, increasing the E(Delta NPV). The decision on whether to proceed with such a

186

derivative depends on corporate strategy and belief in competitor strategy. In the short-term, investing in the derivative in this case is the loser, because it results in a loss of NPv. However, over the long-term, in a duopoly market condition, even if the absolute NPV is a loss, the relative NPV gain will allow continued reinvestment of funds into more and better planes, sustaining the advantage. Further, since neither company can trust the other company not to invest in a derivative and steal market share, both companies must prepare to invest in derivatives to respond to the other companies' derivative, least they lose market share.

Note that in this case study five points were sampled from the input function, yielding a five point sample for the output distribution. Technically, the data originally presented in Figure 5-21 should instead be presented as a discrete probability distribution, as shown in Figure 5-23. However, as this becomes difficult to differentiate the different sets of data, the data will continue to be presented with a curve-fit, as done in Figure 5-21, for presentation purposes. This should not be taken to mean that the data represents a continuous probability distribution, as the probability values would change.

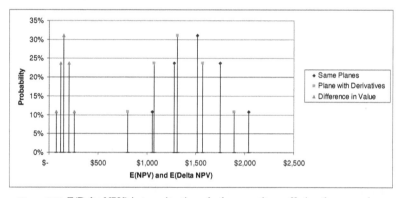

Figure 5-23 E(Delta NPV) in two situations; both competitors offering the same plane indefinitely and one competitor offering a derivative. This chart re-presents the data originally displayed in Figure 5-21, but as a discrete, rather than continuous, probability distribution.

5.3.2.1.2 *Timing of Derivatives and Company Objectives*

How many derivatives to produce is also a question. The number of derivatives is further determined by the match-up of the competing companies' objectives. Dividing company objectives for market share into dominate (vast majority of market share desired), win (majority of market share desired), maintain (some market share desired) and abandon (refrain from entering market), the match-up of different objectives can create different numbers of derivatives, as hypothesized in Table 5-1. This is important in determining

187

whether or not derivatives are important, and hence whether or not the company wants to spend the costs of designing derivatives into the plane. In states where there are likely to be fewer derivatives, it may not make sense for companies to invest in commonality as derivatives may not be exercised.

The need for derivatives seems to be tied closely to competitor intentions. In market niches with strong competition, such as the single aisle narrow-body market characterized by the competition between the 737 and A320, multiple derivatives exist. For example, since the 737 was introduced in the late 1960's, at least 12 different types of derivatives have been produced (Boeing 2007). However, this is compared with the 747, which was also produced around the same time in the 1960's. Early in the 747's life, it had direct competitors with the Douglas DC-10 and the Lockheed 1011. During this time, multiple 747 passenger derivatives were created, the 747-200, 747-300 and 747-400, with the 747-400 entering service in 1985. By 1989, both of the 747 competitors had left the market, leaving Boeing a monopoly with the 747-400. For about 20 years Boeing did not bring to market a single passenger derivative for the 747. It was not until Airbus began developing the A380, a larger competitor threatening the 747-400 monopoly, that Boeing has offered a new derivative, the 747-8. From this example, it seems obvious that without a competitor, Boeing did not see any need to invest in new derivatives for the 747, as sales would have cannibalized existing 747 sales. It is unlikely that the marginal gains of offering a new 747 derivative when there was no competition would have overcome the additional costs for developing a 747 derivative.

In this example, the relative business objectives are important, with Boeing maintaining the 747 market and no competitor willing to contest the market for decades after 1989. In this case, developing derivatives is unlikely. This contradicts other research on derivatives, such as that performed by Miller (Miller 2005), which have not considered some of these additional factors, such as relative business objectives, and have instead determined that because of the low-cost of exercising an option for a derivative, it will always be exercised and hence there is no flexibility value in the option. This may be true in many market niches that are actively being contested by both airframers, but it is not necessarily true across all market niches. Hence, in some markets, the same commonality designed into a plane will have some value of flexibility and in some it will not.
The valuation of flexibility as a relative measure related to its context has not received much attention to date in the literature but seems to affect option value.

Hence, for options in complex systems that operate in complex environments, it seems there is a need for increased sophistication in analysis methodology, over existing "standard" real option evaluation processes.

Table 5-1 Number of derivatives likely to be produced in market under different competing business objectives.

Company Objectives	Dominate	Win	Maintain	Abandon
Dominate	Lots of derivatives	Lots of derivatives	Lots of derivatives	No derivatives
Win	Lots of derivatives	Lots of derivatives	One derivative	No derivatives
Maintain	Lots of derivatives	One derivative	No derivatives	No derivatives
Abandon	No derivatives	No derivatives	No derivatives	No derivatives

A summary of results of options for offering a derivative and the timing of derivative offerings are presented in Table 5-2.

Table 5-2 Summary of results of options for offering a derivative and the timing of derivative offerings.

Option to Offer a Derivative
Derivatives can offer value, but do not under all circumstances
• A derivative has value when updating a plane when there is a competitor plane
• A derivative does not seem to have value when there is no competition
How a derivative's value is measured is critical for deciding to offer a derivative or not
• A derivative's value can be measured relative to the change in profits from the derivative relative to the company's performance before offering the derivative
• A derivative's value can be measured relative to the difference in profitability compared with a competitor's plane
Corporate Strategy and Derivative Timing
The comparison of both airframer's corporate strategies will determine the possibility and frequency of derivative offerings.

The following section discusses the option for postponing the design of the derivative plane until the future.

5.3.2.2 Option to Delay Design of Derivative

This section examines the option to delay the design of a derivative aircraft until some time in the future. This allows the derivative design to be chosen after information on either changes in the environment or competitor offerings have been revealed, rather than chosen at a time before this information is available. The remainder of the section is organized around the evaluation of the option to respond to changes in the environment and competitor offerings.

5.3.2.2.1 *Option to Delay Design of Derivative to Respond to Changes in the Environment*

In the model, changes in future fuel prices represents the uncertainty faced by airframers in deciding what type of plane to build. Should it be high-cost/high efficiency or low-cost/low efficiency? In this case, airframers can project future fuel prices and build the plane that would best maximize profits. However, if the environment changes, expected sales may not materialize. The ability to create derivatives creates the flexibility to respond with a derivative at a future date if fuel price trends start to change from the original forecast. This section examines two aspects of the option to respond to changes in the environment; the ability to choose a plane's technical performance specifications depending on the expected environment and the need to respond faster.

5.3.2.2.1.1 *Ability to Delay Choice of Aircraft Technical Design Performance Specifications*

In the following example, the flexibility value is calculated for options to create derivatives to respond to future fuel price uncertainty. In this example, two planes exist in the market, one supplied by Company A and the other by Company B. Company A has a plane optimized for a particular future baseline price for fuel and can not create derivatives, while Company B has a plane designed with commonality in mind that can create a derivative five years in the future if fuel prices change from their current state. Because of the design decisions to support commonality in Plane B, it initially suffers a performance penalty compared to Plane A and hence experiences some loss in sales relative to Plane A. The derivatives that can be created are high-cost / high efficiency or a low-cost / low efficiency plane.

Figure 5-24 and Figure 5-25 show the probability distribution function for both the high-cost and low-costs derivatives. These figures represent the distribution of values that Company B could expect to obtain if it committed in year zero to building either of these derivatives in year five – i.e. a situation in which there is no flexibility, as the commitment has been made in year zero.

These figures, as are several presented in the remainder of the chapter, are presented in terms of expected delta net present value, which is the expected difference in net present value between the competing planes. Negative number means that Plane A is outselling Plane B and a positive number indicates the opposite relative sales. E(Delta NPV) is presented on the x-axis, while the probability of the value occurring is plotted on the y-axis.

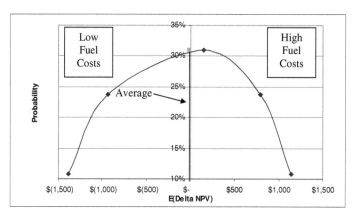

Figure 5-24 E(Delta NPV) for Plane A and the high-cost/high efficiency derivative for Plane B, committing in year zero to build this derivative in year 5. Values expressed in millions.

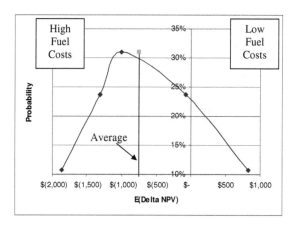

Figure 5-25 E(Delta NPV) for Plane A and the low-cost/low efficiency derivative for Plane B, committing in year zero to build this derivative in year 5. Values expressed in millions.

From Figure 5-24 and Figure 5-24, the average E(delta NPV) value for committing to either plane in year zero is negative, meaning neither plane is a winner against the optimized Plane A, though each plane is a winner against Plane A in some future states. However, since Company B does not have to commit in year zero to choosing which

191

derivative to build, it can wait until year five when it sees what fuel prices are doing. In year five if fuel prices rise and are expected to stay high, then the high-cost/high efficiency plane can be built. The opposite can be done if fuel prices fall.

Figure 5-26 displays the probability distribution function for considering the derivatives as options, with the plane design selection postponed until year five. *Delaying the decision on which derivative to build, Company B can better respond to changes in the environment with the appropriate plane.* In only a few cases in this example was it better to have committed to the baseline, highly optimized design at time zero.

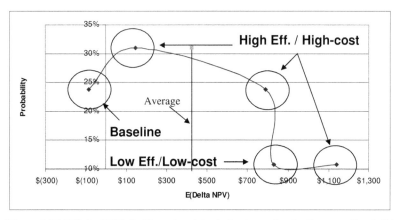

Figure 5-26 E(Delta NPV) for Plane A and the derivative option for Company B to build either the high-cost/high efficiency or low-cost/low efficiency derivative, delaying a commitment until year 5 after observing uncertainty. Values expressed in millions.

In this example, the value of the flexibility is found by the following equation:

Eq.1 : Value of flexibility = Average value of options − Max(value of derivatives)

where,
$$\$447M = \$442M - Max(-\$5M, -\$753M)$$

In this example, the value of the flexibility created with the commonality shifts the value of the expected delta net present value of either derivative from negative to positive, meaning instead of the derivatives being expected losers against the optimized Plane A, it is expected that the delayed selection of a derivative until year five will create expected winners against Plane A, as the appropriate plane can be decided upon in the future.

The results presented can be interpreted either for two competing conventional planes, two competing BWB type planes or a conventional and BWB plane, since the BWB and conventional plane at the 250 passenger size are similar in fuel-efficiency. Hence, the design choices of the BWB and the conventional plane can be enough to surpass the competing plane – i.e. there are only slight advantages to offering a BWB type plane at this size, where the advantages could be overcome with an appropriate tube and wing plane. Instead, there is more benefit in the flexibility afforded by commonality to choose an appropriate plane as future conditions unfold.

5.3.2.2.1.2 Timing of Bringing the Plane to Market
Once a decision has been made on the derivative to be built, the airframer should try and minimize the development time. Minimizing the development time will speed the time to market when the plane can be sold and revenues obtained. As an example, consider the difference between offering a derivative in five years compared to ten years, with the relative E(NPV) shown in Figure 5-27. In this case, it is assumed that the original plane has a penalty imposed because of the commonality designed into the plane but that the derivatives offered later have improved performance over the competitor's original optimized plane. Further, it is assumed that the derivative offered in year 10 is an improvement over the derivative offered in year 5 because of improvements available that would occur over a five year period. Even while the number of planes relative to the competitor increases for the derivative in year 10 compared to year 5, the E(Delta NPV) is still lower for the derivative in year 10. This is because the benefits from the year 10 derivative are pushed further out, meaning the time value decreases due to the discount rate, while the length of time that the original plane is losing market share compared to the competitor's optimized plane increases. While both the year 5 and 10 derivatives have positive E(NPV), only the year 5 E(Delta NPV) is positive. However, offering both the year 5 and the year 10 derivative can be beneficial, especially if the competitor responds with a derivative, say in year 7.

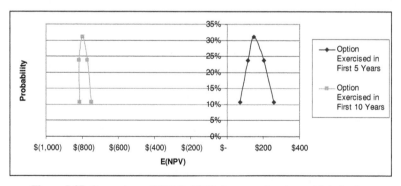

Figure 5-27 Comparison of E(Delta NPV) for a year 5 and year 10 derivative.

The value for being able to respond to changes faster, which is enabled with commonality, is also of importance when responding to a competitor's plane.

The following section discusses the option to delay by responding to a competitor's plane.

5.3.2.2.2 *Option to Delay Design of Derivative to Respond to Competitor's Plane*
In the model, an airframer must not only respond to changes in the environment, such as changes in fuel prices, but must also respond to competitor's offerings. As seen in Figure 5-21 and Figure 5-22 above, a superior Plane A will take the majority of the market share for Company A, but if competing Company B follows that plane with an improved derivative, Plane B, the market share shifts in the favor of Company B. *Without a counter-response, the originally best selling Plane A is consistently outsold. This means that each competitor tries not only to provide airlines with a plane that is matched to the needs of the airlines, but also performs at least slightly better than the competing plane.*

While moving first with a plane or a derivative can garner market share and increase revenues because discounted cash flows are moved forward in time, if a competitor follows this plane soon after with a slightly better plane, much of this benefit can disappear. This constant offering of both new families and new derivatives in families is an attempt to keep product offerings relevant and competitive against the planes offered by the other airframer. This section looks at the following examples; response to competitor's plane, decision whether or not to enter a market, decision rules and consequences for entering or not entering a market, choice of commonality or optimization, and the decision rules revisited.

5.3.2.2.2.1 *Competitive Response*
Historically, in most plane categories, airframers have mostly avoided direct competition, both technically and temporally for a variety of reasons. Technically, planes often have different enough performance criteria so to make them appeal to slightly different needs in the market, though they are similar enough to act as substitutes for one another. Temporally, new plane families have often been staggered. For example, the A330 family by Airbus competes most closely with the Boeing 757. The A330 "killed" the 757, though it was offered over a decade later. The Boeing 787 could be seen as a competitor for the A330 and itself was offered about 10-15 years after the A330. This temporal offsetting has allowed airframers to dominate the market with their new offering, as it is often competing against a plane many years older. However, there are multiple times when the airframers have matched up directly, the most recent being between the Boeing 787 and Airbus A350/A350 XWB. In this matchup, the 787 was garnering large orders against the A330, which prompted the A350 offering, which would be a cross-family derivative of the A330-200. The original planned A350 offering was to have extensive commonality with A330-200 and as such had low development costs.

Compared to the Boeing 787, the development costs were planned to be about half. And because of the commonality, even though the program was started after Airbus had seen the market response to the 787, the A350 was still scheduled to enter the market within a year or two of the scheduled 787 entrance date. If the 787 ran into development challenges that forced a delay, it was thought that the A350 could possibly even enter the market at the same time as the 787.

This commonality gave Airbus the option of responding quickly to the competing 787, more quickly than could be done with a clean sheet design plane, and at lower costs. In the end, airline customers wanted a new plane and Airbus scrapped the plans to offer the A350 as an A330-200 cross-family derivative and instead offered a clean sheet design, the A350 XWB. The increase to time and costs were substantial, increasing development time by two years and doubling development costs, though the performance did increase.

The following example compares the effect from commonality on a faster response. In Figure 5-28, the competitive response is assumed to take four years, while in Figure 5-29 the competitive response is assumed to take two years.

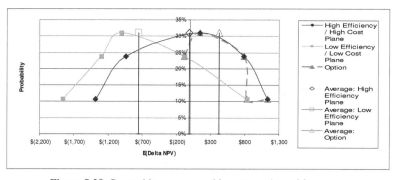

Figure 5-28 Competitive response with response time of four years.

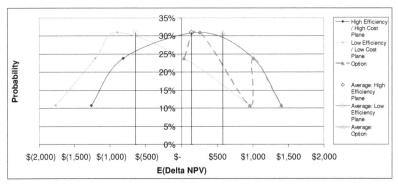

Figure 5-29 Competitive response with response time of two years.

Comparing the two different response times, the faster response time has the higher E(Delta NPV), with $570M, compared to $424M for the four year response. However, the flexibility value for the shorter response time plane is $430M compared with $440M for the longer response time plane.

The shorter response time creates the ability to respond faster to a competitor's plane, moving forward in time the revenue stream, which increases the net present value due to lowered effects of discount rates. However, the faster response time also forces a decision earlier, when waiting could help resolve additional uncertainty.

In this example, there is a trade-off between higher value obtained from moving faster with a lower value of flexibility. As the response time moves to zero, the value of flexibility should also decrease toward zero, as less uncertainty is resolved. A response time of zero would represent a first-mover, who would have no flexibility to respond to a competitor and would also likely have an inferior product, given the second-mover could design a slightly superior product, as described above.

However, the flexibility of the faster response time should also take into account the ability to choose whether the response will occur sooner or later. Taking this into account, the flexibility for the faster response time is the difference in average E(Delta NPV) between the faster response time flexible value and the slower response time flexible value, or $570M - $424M yielding $136M that should be added to the total value of flexibility. This "additional" flexibility creates a total flexibility of $566M for the faster response time plane, compared with $440M for the slower response time plane.

The flexibility value to the fast response time plane comes from the ability to exercise the flexibility before or any time up to the same time as the slower response time plane. In effect, this is similar to comparing an American option (which can be exercised at any point up to a expiration date) and a European option (which can only be exercised on the expiration date), where American options are always worth at least as much if not more

196

than a European option, because of the additional "flexibility" given to the option holder in the actual exercise timing.

In this case, it is not clear whether the BWB offers an advantage or not over a conventional plane. This is because a conventional plane could be designed with commonality that offers this speed to market advantage, as described above with the A350/A350 XWB example to illustrate. Two effects of the commonality are important here. The first is the amount of commonality between planes. It is not clear if a BWB type plane with commonality would have more inter-family commonality than a conventional plane. BWB literature shows about a 39% commonality estimate with another 33% cousins, which are similar parts but are differentially sized or have minor changes between planes (Liebeck 2005). Common subsystems in BWB type aircraft include common cockpits, common wings and some identical bays. However, conventional aircraft seem to have similar levels of commonality, if optimized across multiple families, like the A330 and A340 families, which share wings, fuselages and cockpits. The level of commonality between planes seems to be similar and is assumed in this model to be similar.

The second consideration for commonality though is over the range of families that can share the commonality. Here it is seems the BWB type aircraft has an advantage, with estimates of commonality across-family sizes at least from 250-450 passengers. This is a larger range of aircraft that has been seen at least to date in conventional aircraft. Ideally, while this commonality may not greatly reduce prices within a family, it extends the number of families that could benefit from the reduced commonality.

5.3.2.2.2.2 Decision to Enter Market

The above example assumes that a company can match or exceed the technical performance of their competitor's product. However, the incumbent plane may be too technically advanced to match. For example, the original A350 was deemed not technically advanced enough by customers to challenge the 787, resulting in pressure from customers to come up with a completely new design, with Airbus responding with the A350 XWB. A BWB type plane as an incumbent could also pose such a challenge, given its greater inherent benefits of fuel-efficiency. Figure 5-30 and Figure 5-31 show a hypothetical match-up between a BWB 250 and BWB 450 and comparably sized conventional planes.

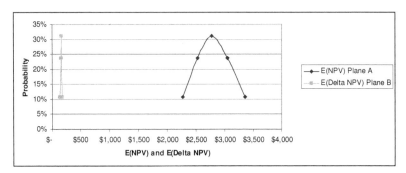

Figure 5-30 BWB 250 vs. conventional 250 passenger aircraft.

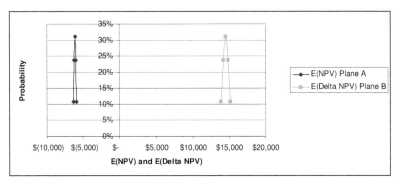

Figure 5-31 BWB 450 vs. conventional 450 passenger aircraft.

The matchup shown in Figure 5-30 shows that because of the slight advantage the BWB 250 has over a comparable 250 conventional plane, it would likely have a greater E(Delta NPV), though the challenging Plane A would still have a positive E(NPV). The matchup depicted in Figure 5-31 shows that the much larger fuel-efficiency of the BWB 450 would likely not only result in an E(Delta NPV) highly favorable to the BWB 450, but that the conventional 450 Plane A E(NPV) may not even have enough sales to break even.

In these cases, the expected challenger would need to make a decision on whether or not to enter the market against a technically superior plane, where they are expecting to lose a matchup either relatively (as in the 250 passenger case) or absolutely (as in the 450 passenger case). The challenging Company A has the option in this case to enter the market or not.

In the opposite case where the BWB is the challenger to an incumbent conventional plane, it should expect to have a greater advantage, so the decision on whether or not to enter may not be difficult to make. As discussed above, since a BWB 250 type plane and a conventional 250 plane are similar in performance, the BWB 250 is not guaranteed to outperform the incumbent conventional plane. *However, unless a significantly different plane emerges, such as an ultra-low fuel burn plane or a supersonic plane for example, BWB as a challenger against an incumbent is less likely to produce a difficult entry decision based on technical performance considerations, given the inherent advantage that a BWB type plane has over a conventional plane of a similar size, in the 250+ seat ranges.*

5.3.2.2.2.3 Decision Rules and Consequences for Entering or Not Entering a Market

Looking closer at the decision process Company A faces when entering the 250 market, Company A could craft decision rules to enter when the relative value of Plane A is higher than the BWB or it could decide to enter as long as the Plane A program did not have negative E(NPV). With either decision rule, Company A could choose not to enter if these criteria were not met, as shown in Figure 5-32 and Figure 5-33.

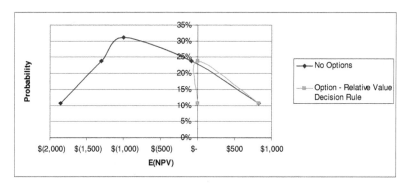

Figure 5-32 Option to enter market if relative value of Plane A is higher than BWB 250 competitor.

199

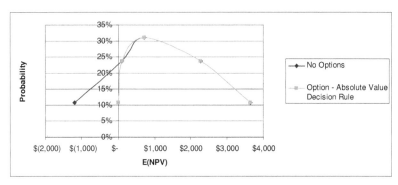

Figure 5-33 Option to enter market if absolute E(NPV) is greater than zero.

In both cases, Company A has flexibility to not enter the market and avoid the losses, either relative losses to their competitor or absolute losses. In general, Plane A wins when fuel costs are very low, but loses when fuel costs are high or at expected values. When fuel costs are very high, Plane A can not break even, due to lack of sales. The results of the option value for both decision rules is summarized in Table 5-3.

Table 5-3 Summary of option values and consequences for two different decision rules.

Option Decision Rule	Option Value	Competitor's Increase in Value with Option Exercise
Exercise if Absolute Loss	$128	$1,021
Exercise if Relative Loss	$841	$10,205

As shown in Table 5-3, the option to avoid relative loss is much greater than the option to avoid absolute loss, as most of the time Plane A will not experience an absolute loss (and hence will be exercised) but will experience a relative loss.

However, by not entering the market, it is assumed in this example that there is no competitor for the BWB plane, which takes the entire market. *The resulting expected gain in the competitor's plane (the BWB) can be quite large, especially with the decision rule based on exercising only if Plane A has a higher relative value.* With that rule, Company B would have an increase in expected value almost equal to the costs of developing an entirely new family!

200

Because of the consequences of exercising the option not to compete in a market, it is unclear that this option would ever be exercised, if only to keep the competitor from the increase in market share gain. This could explain the current moves by Boeing to bring the 747-8 to market. The 747-8 is a stretched and more efficient plane than the 747-400, but it is not nearly as large as the A380. However, even if the 747-8 only sells a few planes, each plane it sells will be one fewer plane sold for the A380, as the 747-8 is the closest competitor to the A380. Since the 747-8 is a derivative and the A380 is the start of a new family, the 747-8 needs many fewer planes to break even, and even if it does not, the investment loss will be much less than the A380 if it does not break even.

Because a BWB type plane as a challenger to a conventional incumbent plane has an inherent advantage in performance, this question on whether to enter becomes much less of a problem. This is because the BWB type plane has the inherent technical advantage and could be designed to match or come close to the incumbent. This eliminates the possible choice between bad alternatives of entering a market that is expected to never break even or cede the market uncontested to the competitor and let them extract monopoly profits from that market niche.

5.3.2.2.2.4 Commonality or Optimization of Plane

Instead of choosing not to exercise the option to enter the market with a low-cost / low efficiency plane, it is more likely that the challenging airframer will seek to enter with an optimized plane. For example, this is what Airbus recently decided on when the market reacted negatively to its A350 cross-family derivative. Instead of ceding the market for small wide-body planes to Boeing, it chose to redesign the A350 as the clean sheet design A350 XWB. In this manner, the airframer can choose to enter with the low-cost / low efficiency plane made possible with commonality, or with a newly designed and optimized plane that will have improved performance but at a higher price. Figure 5-34 shows this option.

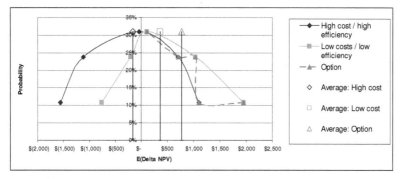

Figure 5-34 Option for choosing high or low-cost conventional aircraft as competitive response, comparing conventional to conventional planes.

201

For this choice, the challenger Plane A with commonality is expected to outperform the incumbent plane B unless fuel prices are higher than expected. If that is the case, Company B can choose to enter the market with a clean sheet plane. The option average value is $775M with a value for flexibility of $415M.

Figure 5-35 shows the same situation, but comparing a competition between BWB planes, where the incumbent BWB Plane B is optimized and the challenger BWB Plane A has been designed with commonality. In this case, the total option value increases to $1453M while the value of flexibility decreases to $93M.

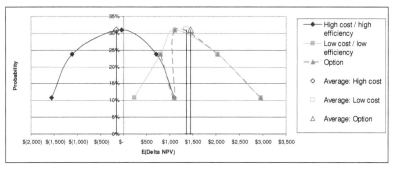

Figure 5-35 Option for choosing high or low-cost conventional aircraft as competitive response, comparing BWB to BWB planes.

In this case the BWB with commonality outperforms the optimized BWB in almost all situations, except when fuel prices are very high, meaning it almost always makes sense to exercise the option to proceed with the BWB with commonality. This is the case because the relative comparison between the BWB and conventional aircrafts, both with flexibility, is that the performance penalty that the BWB with commonality bears is much less than that for the conventional plane.

5.3.2.2.2.5 Decision Rules, Revisited

Revisiting the decision rules again, this time using a BWB as a challenger instead of a conventional plane as the challenger, the relatively small penalty that the BWB bears for commonality means that the absolute expected value will always be positive and the relative value will almost always be positive. Figure 5-36 and Figure 5-37 shows the decision rule for a BWB 450 with commonality matched against a BWB 450 optimized.

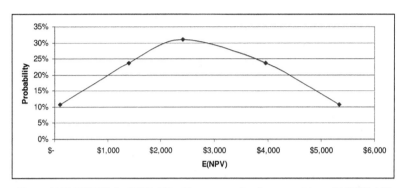

Figure 5-36 E(NPV) for BWB 450 with commonality, in competition with BWB 450 optimized.

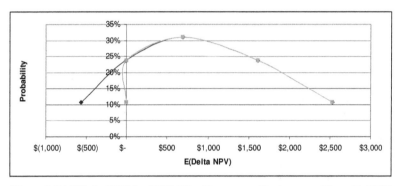

Figure 5-37 E(Delta NPV) for BWB 450 with commonality, in competition with BWB 450 optimized, showing option not to proceed with common BWB 450.

With the same two decision rules, using the absolute decision rule, entering the market with the common BWB would always be feasible, giving an option value of zero, as the difference in performance between an optimized and common BWB 450 is not enough to make the common BWB investment less than a positive NPv. Using the relative decision rule, there is some option value, as the challenging company can choose to enter with a common BWB or an optimized BWB if fuel prices are very high.

203

Table 5-4 Option values for two different decision rules for competing BWB 450's, one common and the other optimized.

Option Decision Rule	Option Value
Exercise if Absolute Loss	$0
Exercise if Relative Loss	$93

A summary of the results from the analysis of the option to delay the design of a derivative to allow response to environmental changes or a competitive response are presented in Table 5-5.

Table 5-5 Summary of results for option to delay design.

Option to respond to changes in environment
Delaying making decision on aircraft design allows the design of the plane to better match needs of environment; i.e. if fuel prices are high design a fuel efficient plane, and if fuel prices are low design a cheaper, less fuel efficient plane
Commonality provides ability to have a short response time. However, a short response time has trade-off associated with it: • Allows movement to market faster, starting the revenue flow earlier in time • Reduces value of flexibility, as decision is made earlier and uncertainty may not be resolved
Once decision has been made on design choice, plane should enter market as fast as possible
Commonality can reduce time needed to enter market
Option for competitive response
Offering a derivative allows airframer to offer a plane superior to current competitor plane
BWB inherent benefits in fuel efficiency would enable: • Improved performance compared with a tube and wing aircraft for absolute and relative metrics for 250 and 450 passenger sized planes • Decrease the possibility that competitor would be able to field a profitable 450 seat tube and wing plane
Option value differs depending on decision rule: • Option value measured on absolute value yields higher value • Option value measured on relative value yields lower value
Consequences of not exercising option depend on decision rule: • Magnitude of consequences from absolute value decision rule are higher • Magnitude of consequences from relative value decision rule are lower
Unclear that option not to enter market can ever be exercised, due to possibility of granting competitor a monopoly in a segment. Instead of not entering market with cross-family derivative (if it is not competitive to the incumbent plane) optimized plane should be considered in some cases
BWB increases value of commonality by decreasing the performance penalty from using BWB cross-family derivatives.

BWB does not seem to offer advantages over conventional plane in terms of flexibility in following dimensions:
• BWB does not create flexibility through commonality; both tube and wing and BWB technical architectures have this possibility
• BWB does not seem to improve flexibility through improved commonality in same-family derivatives, BWB and tube and wing seem to have similar same-family derivative benefits
BWB technical architecture impact on flexibility is mixed:
• Increases value of commonality by reducing performance penalty costs
• Decreases flexibility as cross-family derivatives are worthwhile most of the time

The following section provides an analysis of the results presented in this chapter.

5.3.3   ANALYSIS OF RESULTS

The following section synthesizes the results presented above to better understand the benefits that a BWB type aircraft can provide as a Dual Value Design, i.e. with inherent benefits and flexibility benefits. Also, the lessons learned while doing the analysis are discussed in terms of processes needs.

5.3.3.1   BWB Inherent Benefits

The BWB 250 and BWB 450 aircraft possess a significant inherent benefit over conventional aircraft, due to the increased fuel-efficiency brought about by the change in technical architecture. However, while the BWB 250 and 450 both possess this inherent performance benefit, it may not be enough to lead to higher sales over a competing tube and wing plane.

While comparing both 250 and 450 class BWB and conventional planes that are optimized to perform well in a specific market niche leads to improved sales for the BWB type planes, this matchup does not describe how the competition between Boeing and Airbus has emerged in the last decade and a half. Rather than competing against two planes optimized for a market niche, Airbus has relied on optimizing its planes over multiple market niches, creating cross-family commonality between planes to lower prices, even though it is at the expense of performance. In a BWB 250 matchup with a conventional tube and wing architecture plane with lower costs due to commonality, it is not a given that the BWB will outperform the conventional plane in sales. Because the performance differential in fuel efficiency is not that much higher for the BWB 250, the lower cost of the airplane due to commonality may offset the fuel efficiency, unless fuel prices are high.

The BWB 450 has a more pronounced advantage over a conventional tube and wing plane, so cost savings from commonality are less beneficial in overcoming the BWB 450 benefits. However, the margin of sales for the BWB 450 are less than would be expected from the increased performance due to lower prices in the conventional plane.

This analysis shows the inherent benefit of the BWB when compared with conventional planes. However, the analysis shows that the BWB inherent benefit is limited if the conventional plane can reduce costs due to commonality. The ability to reduce costs by designing in commonality across families reflects corporate goals and cultures. An airframer that has a very strong program relative to corporate management structure or a culture that emphasizes maximizing performance will likely find it difficult to embrace a strategy of commonality. This may even make it difficult to recognize the challenge posed by a competing plane with commonality, as the competing plane is being optimized on a different metric than single family performance.

For analysis purposes, this example shows the necessity of recognizing competing technical objectives. Without this recognition, it is difficult to properly assess the benefits of the plane in question, as the relative value of the plane's benefits, inherent or flexible, will change relative to the competing plane's performance and cost values. This requires alignment between the technical design of the airplane, the enterprise architecture and the evaluation metrics used. This interaction of various technical, organizational and processes characteristics is typical of a "complex" real option in a complex system. Because of the presence and interaction of these characteristics, there is a need for the Life-Cycle Flexibility Framework, which is designed to addresses these in a comprehensive manner.

5.3.3.2 BWB and Flexibility

A BWB type plane does not appear to contain additional flexibilities compared with a tube and wing conventional architecture plane. The flexibility that was identified came through the use of commonality in the planes. Both a BWB type and conventional type plane have the ability to create substantial commonalties across families and hence enable the set of flexibilities discussed above: 1) option to build a derivative, 2) option to determine when to build the derivative, and 3) option to delay the design of derivative to the future.

However, the BWB does have an effect on flexibility primarily in the reduction of performance penalty costs for commonality. From prior work done by Wilcox and Wakayama (Wilcox and Wakayama 2003), the performance penalty due to commonality in take off-weight (which was estimated for this model to directly translate into fuel-efficiency) for a BWB type plane is modest, only about 0.5% for a BWB 250 and 2% for a BWB 450. This is less than that calculated for a tube and wing plane using commonality, which was calculated by the author using the A350/A350 XWB as an example at around 10%.

The lower performance penalty due to commonality means that more of the time the BWB can "have its cake and eat it too", meaning that the BWB could enjoy have the cost effects of commonality without suffering the larger negative performance effects that a tube and wing plane architecture experiences. This increases the total value of the BWB type plane, relative to conventional or single family optimized BWB type planes, as the common BWB performs better over most future states.

However, the total effect on the value of flexibility is not clear. The value of flexibility is increased in terms of providing the ability to choose an appropriate plane quickly in response to environmental changes or as a competitor response. However, since the commonality solution is the higher value choice most of the time compared to a single family optimized BWB, the value of flexibility in this case decreases, as the common BWB plane value become more robust – i.e. offering the better value almost all of the time, meaning the common solution could be committed to without much loss of expected value.

5.3.3.3 Evaluation Methodology

The results presented above show the need to perform the evaluation with respect to multiple factors. These include technical factors, economics factors, corporate goals, decision making rules, and product strategies. Considering the performance of the flexibility in question over a range of these factors is necessary, as the value of the plane changes depending on these factors. For example, if a company that has optimized their products over a single family assumes that offering a BWB type product also optimized over a single family will have an advantage over competing conventional aircraft because of the inherent benefits due to the BWB technical architecture, this is only true if the competing company behaves in a similar manner, i.e. also optimizing their products over a single family. However, if the competitor has chosen a different product strategy, such as commonality across families, the BWB inherent benefits could be overcome, especially at the smaller range of the BWB offering, where the performance benefits seem to be lower.

Taking these factors fully into account would seem to require a multitude of analysis techniques. While this research primarily used system dynamics as a modeling approach to capture these effects, other techniques seem necessary, such as the use of game theory to try and understand competitor responses to design decisions. Additional consideration of "bigger picture" considerations also seems needed. For example, if the analysis points to including commonality across families as a product strategy that is expected to be successful, the analysis by itself may not be necessary to convince an organization that has relied on single family optimization to move toward multifamily optimization.

The following chapter explores these types of challenges in greater detail for the BWB case study.

A summary of the major results for the BWB case study quantitative analysis are presented in Table 5-6.

207

Table 5-6 Summary of main results for BWB case study quantitative analysis chapter.

BWB inherent value
A BWB type plane has greater fuel efficiency than a tube and wing plane and hence lower operating costs
The magnitude of the fuel efficiency varies as a function of the size of the plane, with larger BWB having significant savings over a tube and wing and smaller plane having a much more modest savings over tube and wing planes
The BWB fuel efficiency at lower plane sizes can be overcome by savings achieved with commonality. This means that while a BWB 250 would be more fuel efficient than a tube and wing 250 seat plane, if the tube and wing plane was designed with commonality, its lower cost could off-set the higher fuel efficiency of the BWB plane. This is not possible with a larger BWB 450 plane though.
This points to the need to properly choose metrics that adequately compare the benefits of planes and anticipate competitor product strategy.
BWB flexibility value
The BWB technical architecture reduces commonality costs
However, flexibility value is uncertain due to offsetting trends: • Commonality is more valuable in BWB • But cross-family derivatives are used more often • Against tube and wing plane, cross-family derivatives are always used, reducing flexibility value to zero
Evaluation needs
The evaluation conducted required explicit consideration of technical, organizational, process aspects of system
Results were sensitive to the technical, organizational and process aspects of the system; results differed greatly based on the different assumptions for metrics and corporate strategy

The following chapter expands on the quantitative evaluation conducted for the BWB case study. A qualitative analysis was performed, relying heavily on interviews with professionals with knowledge of the aircraft manufacturing industry. The purpose of the following qualitative analysis is to better understand the practical challenges associated with "complex" real options in complex systems.

5.4 REFERENCES

Airbus. (2006) Annual Global Market Forecast: The Future of Flying, 2006-2025, Airbus Industries, www.airbus.com.

Answers. (2006) http://www.answers.com/topic/airbus-a350

Baseler, R. (2006) Boeing Commercial Airplane Company Blog. http://boeingblogs.com/randy/archives/2006/11/talkin_turkey.html

Boeing. (2006) Current Market Outlook Report, Boeing Commercial Aircraft Company, www.boeing.com.

Boeing. (2007) 737 family website, www.boeing.com.

Capell, K. and D. Foust. (2006) Wal-Mart with Wings, Business Week, Nov. 27, n. 4011.

Clemons, E. and B. Gu. (2003). Justifying Information Technology Investments: Balancing the Need for Speed of Action with Certainty Before Action, Proceedings of the 36th Hawaii International Conference on System Sciences, Hawaii.

Ferreri, D. (2003) Marketing and Management in the High-Technology Sector: Strategies and Tactics in the Commercial Airplane Industry, Praeger, New York.

Greden, L., L. Glicksman, and G. Lopez-Betanzos. (2005). A Real Options Methodology for Evaluating Risk and Opportunity of Natural Ventilation. Proceedings of 2005 International Solar Energy Conference. August 6-12, 2005, Florida.

Harrigan, F. (2006) Integrating Theories of Boundary Choice: A Case from the Global Aviation industry, International Conference on Coordination and Cooperation across Organizational Boundaries, Milan, Italy.

Inflation Data. (2006) http://inflationdata.com/inflation/Inflation_Rate/Historical_Oil_Prices_Table.asp

Jiang, H. and R. Hansman (2004). An Analysis of Profit Cycles In the Airline Industry. M. Massachusetts Institute of Technology Cambridge, MIT International Center for Air Transportation. Report No. ICAT-2004-7.

Liebeck, R.. M. Page, B. Rawdon (1998) Blended Wing Body Subsonic Commercial Transport, 36th Aerospace Science Meeting and Exhibit, Reno, NV, January 12-15.

Liebeck, R. (2004) Design of the Blended Wing Body Subsonic Transport, Journal of Aircraft, v. 41 n. 1.

Liebeck, R. (2005) Design of Subsonic Transports, Presentation to MIT ESD.34 System Architecture, Massachusetts.

Lin, J., J. McConnell, S. Sgouridis. (2007) System Dynamics Model Overview for the Commercial Aviation Enterprise of Enterprises. Working paper.

Lyneis, J. (2000). System dynamics for market forecasting and structural analysis, System Dynamics Review v. 16 No. 1.

Mak, v. and M. Enright. (2002) The Airline Industry and the World Trade Center Disaster, Centre for Asian Business Cases, School of Business, The University of Hong Kong, HKI 189.

Miller, B. (2005) A Generalized Real Options Methodology for Evaluating Investments Under Uncertainty with Application to Air Transportation, MIT Doctoral Dissertation, Massachusetts.

Steinke, S. (2005) Overview of A350 Performance Specifications. http://www.flug-revue.rotor.com/frheft/FRHeft05/FRH0502/FR0502a.htm

Tufano, P. and A. Moel (1997). Bidding for Antamina, Harvard Business School Case No. 9-297-054. Rev. Sept. 15, Massachusetts.

Weil, H. B. (1996). Commoditization of Technology-Based Products and Services: A Generic Model for Market Dynamics. Cambridge MA, Sloan School of Management. Massachusetts Institute of Technology.

Wikipedia. (2007b) A350.

Wikipedia. (2007b) Boeing 787.

Willcox, K. and S. Wakayama. (2003) Simultaneous Optimization of a Multiple Aircraft Family, Journal of Aircraft, v. 40 n. 4.

World Bank. (2006) Real Historical Gross Rates of GDP for Baseline Countries/Regions 1969-2007, World Bank.

6 CHALLENGES OF FLEXIBILITY IN BLENDED WING BODY

This chapter continues the analysis of the case study of using the technical architecture of the Blended Wing Body aircraft to create or improve flexibility in a commercial aircraft company. The previous chapter quantitatively analyzed the options being considered for this system, evaluating the benefits and costs of each of the options. This chapter continues the analysis by looking at the second research question, namely **"What are the practical challenges associated with "complex" real options in complex systems?"**

To answer this question, multiple people in and related to the Boeing Company were interviewed. Interviewees were selected to try and gain a broad understanding of the aircraft enterprise. Combining the interview responses with Boeing and aircraft manufacturing industry specific data, information sources (such as newspaper articles) and various academic literatures, a qualitative evaluation was conducted to better understand the challenges associated with "complex" real options in complex systems. An emphasis was placed on trying to understand what new challenges would be created with flexibility and what existing challenges would be made even more difficult because of flexibility.

The chapter starts with a qualitative research methodology that is introduced in the first section. An inventory is then made of relevant stakeholders in the aircraft manufacturing industry to better understand the stakeholders involved in the system. An overview of the current situation in the aviation industry is then presented to illustrate the environment that the stakeholders are operating within. Each of the major questions that were posed to the stakeholders is then addressed. These included;

- What are specific instances of flexibility currently being pursued at Boeing or in the aviation industry?
- What are the processes used for designing, evaluating and managing flexibility used by your organization?
- What are your general views on flexibility and its challenges?
- What practical considerations related to the enterprise architecture exist in designing, evaluating and managing an aircraft system?

6.1 QUALITATIVE ANALYSIS PROCESS

Previously in Chapter 4, two sets of BWB real options were introduced. In Chapter 5, these real options were then evaluated in a quantitative manner, to better understand the costs and benefits associated with each set of BWB options. In keeping with the central theme of this research, because the options of interest in the BWB case study are "complex" real options in complex systems, quantitative analysis methodologies alone are not deemed not sufficient in the evaluation of the options. Rather, additional machinery in the LCF Framework needs to be employed to more completely evaluate these "complex" real options in complex systems.

In order to better understand the challenges associated with "complex" real options in complex system, a qualitative analysis of a BWB type aircraft in an aircraft manufacturer enterprise was conducted. The qualitative analysis performed here was general in scope and did not deal specifically with the options presented in Chapters 4 and 5 for two reasons. First, the options in Chapter 4 and 5 do not actually exist, but were instead used as a construct to illustrate feasible BWB real options that could be designed. In this manner, the options were used to demonstrate the BWB real option concept, the concept of dual value design, and to test out the quantitative analysis portion of the Life-Cycle Flexibility (LCF) Framework. Second, this research was exploratory in nature, regarding "complex" real options in complex systems. As exploratory research, it was deemed more valuable to perform a qualitative analysis on flexibility as it exists in an aircraft manufacturing enterprise. From this analysis, generalities and lessons learned could be obtained that would be useful for future attempts at designing, evaluating and managing "complex" real options in complex systems. This type of analysis was deemed sufficient, as the research serves as a proof of concept for the analysis of "complex" real options in complex systems.

The qualitative analysis consisted primarily of conducting interviews with stakeholders associated with aircraft manufacturing enterprises in general or the Boeing Company in specific. Figure 6-1 displays the analysis procedures used in this research.

Note, that as a convenience to the reader, the case studies were written to stand alone. The case study analysis procedure described here is parallel to that described for the ITS case study in Section 9.2.

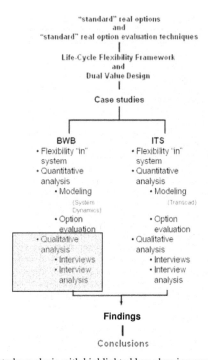

"standard" real options
and
"standard" real option evaluation techniques
|
Life-Cycle Flexibility Framework
and
Dual Value Design
|
Case studies
|

BWB	ITS
• Flexibility "in" system	• Flexibility "in" system
• Quantitative analysis	• Quantitative analysis
• Modeling	• Modeling
(System Dynamics)	(Transcad)
• Option evaluation	• Option evaluation
• Qualitative analysis	• Qualitative analysis
• Interviews	• Interviews
• Interview analysis	• Interview analysis

Findings
|
Conclusions

Figure 6-1 Case study analysis with highlighted box showing current stage of analysis.

Since very little to no literature is available on "complex" real options in complex systems, the purpose of this qualitative analysis was to identify and better understand critical challenges that exist in practice. The qualitative analysis was used to help determine what types of practical challenges associated with "complex" real options in complex systems would be significant enough that they should be taken into account during the design and management of flexible systems. In essence, this portion of the case study sought to answer the first research question, applied to the BWB case study: **How do "complex" real options and "standard" real options differ across the life-cycle of an option, including design, evaluation and management activities?** Specifically, this portion of the research deals with better understanding the management of "complex" options.

The remainder of this section discusses how this question was answered.

The qualitative research methodology is discussed immediately below. Following this discussion, the objectives of the interviews conducted and how interviewees were

213

selected is presented. The general set of questions used during the interviews is then presented, along with an overview of how the data was collected. The limitations associated with the qualitative analysis is then discussed.

6.1.1 QUALITATIVE RESEARCH METHODOLOGY

The results discussed in this chapter of the BWB case study were generated through the use of a case study analysis methodology. For this research, a variety of data sources were used to provide the necessary detail. While interviews were the primary source of data used, other sources including material on the BWB aircraft provided from the Boeing Company, the popular press, and information on the BWB and the Boeing Company that was found in the academic literature.

The selection of the BWB aircraft as a case study topic was a fundamental choice for this research, which was driven by several factors. First, as the technical architecture of the BWB aircraft provides higher levels of commonality across aircraft families compared to tube and wing aircraft, the BWB seemed suited to the study of flexibility. Second, early discussions with people knowledgeable about technical performance of aircraft seemed to indicate that the BWB technical architecture would be more suitable for study that the prior aerospace application that was of interest, the use of composites on the Boeing 787 Dreamliner. Third, a private sector enterprise was desired to complement the public sector enterprises found in the ITS case study. Finally, due to the affiliation with the MIT Lean Aerospace Initiative (LAI), an aerospace case study was desired.

The two case studies looked at in this research, BWB aircraft and Intelligent Transportation Systems (ITS), were chosen to allow contrast between case studies. While the two case studies both involve "complex" real options in complex systems, the technologies, technical architectures and enterprise architectures for each case study is different. For the ITS case study flexibility is created with a technology, ITS. For the BWB case study flexibility is created with a technical architecture, the use of blending the wing and the body of the aircraft together. For the ITS case study an extended enterprise architecture is of interest, consisting of multiple public and private enterprises. For the BWB case study the primary enterprise of interest is a single private enterprise, primarily an aircraft manufacturer. These differences are summarized in Figure 6-2. The differences between case study technologies, technical architectures and enterprise architectures allows the LCF Flexibility concept to be tested on very different systems to more effectively exercise it and probe its limitations.

214

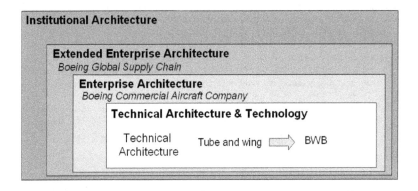

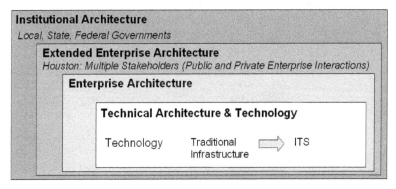

Figure 6-2 Characteristics of case studies on the dimensions of: technical architecture and technology, enterprise architecture, extended enterprise architecture and institutional architecture.

The next section discusses the objectives of the interviews.

6.1.2   INTERVIEW OBJECTIVES

The purpose of the interviews was to obtain information to better answer the research question of determining what practical challenges were associated with "complex" real options in complex systems. Interviews were chosen as the primary vehicle to do this for two reasons. First, the information available via interviews very often could not be found through any other means. While some information and prior study on BWB aircraft, the Boeing Company and the aircraft manufacturing industry in general were available, there was not enough found to be able to answer the research question. Second, the people interviewed had a range of practical experience with either the BWB aircraft, the Boeing Company, or with some aspect of commercial aircraft manufacturing enterprises in general. The practical experience that they had could be tapped to better understand the practical challenges associated with "complex" real options in complex systems.

The data that was desired from the interviews covered practical challenges associated with the entire life-cycle of the option as well as the different types of drivers that influence the steps in the LCF Framework. A reminder of the phases in an option's life-cycle re-appears in Figure 6-3. The specific steps of the LCF Framework that played a role in the interview process are highlighted in Figure 6-4.

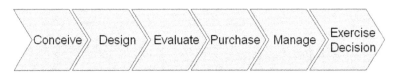

Figure 6-3 Life-cycle of an option.

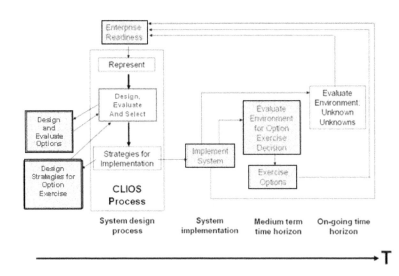

Figure 6-4 LCF Framework steps of interest for BWB case study.

The following section discusses the interviewee selection.

216

6.1.3 INTERVIEWEE SELECTION

As the interviews formed the primary data source for the BWB case study, the selection of the interviewees was important. The ideal set of interviewees would satisfy two objectives. The first objective was to have a set of interviewees that would facilitate collection of data on challenges facing "complex" real options in complex systems. Ideally, the interviewees would represent the breadth of stakeholders involved in commercial aircraft manufacturing enterprises. The second objective was to have depth in the set of interviewees, which would allow cross-checking of data provided by individual interviewees.

Due to time limitations and difficulty in arranging interviewees the first objective was given priority. While breadth was the priority in selecting interviewees, during the course of the interviews there was some overlap in the discussions held. This allowed interviewee statements to be cross-checked against one another. The cross-checking facilitated follow-up questions during interviews to better understand issues and interviewee's perspectives.

Selecting the interviewees occurred in three steps. First, in order to satisfy the breadth of stakeholder perspectives that was desired for the research, organizations internal to Boeing that were deemed important to either the BWB or to commercial aircraft manufacturing in general were identified. Second, the types of people that were thought to have the most relevant perspectives related to understanding challenges associated with "complex" real options in complex systems were identified. As a general rule, it was believed that people higher in the organization's hierarchy would be the best to interview. This was because the people higher in the organization often have a wider range of concerns, including financial, managerial and political. As the LCF Framework attempts to address these types of challenges in flexible systems, the perspectives of this level of people was desired. Finally, a snowball sampling technique was employed. This means that after an interview was completed, the interviewee was asked to provide the names of other people they felt would also be good to interview. Having just completed the interview process themselves, the interviewee's had an increased familiarity of the research topics of interest, and the snow ball technique provided additional high-quality interviewees that otherwise would not have been contacted.

The stakeholders that were contacted for this case study fell into two broad categories, as shown in Table 6-1. The first category consisted of stakeholders directly involved with an aircraft manufacturer, specifically in this case the Boeing Company. Stakeholders within the Boeing Company representing a variety of functions were interviewed, as shown in the table. The second category consisted of interviews of people currently primarily in academia. All of the people contacted in this category either had explicit prior or current first hand experience with the Boeing Company.

Table 6-1 Functional activities performed by interviewees for each case study.

BWB Case Study
• Large aircraft manufacturer
○ BWB program
○ Financial functions
○ Supply chain functions
○ New programs
• Academic

To accomplish the first objective of creating breadth in the interview data, a stakeholder map was created (presented in Section 6.2). The stakeholders identified represented a range of interests in the aircraft manufacturing industry and served as a backdrop to the qualitative analysis.

In general, people associated directly with the BWB program, either currently or in the past, were expected to have a good understanding of the technical and enterprise challenges associated with a BWB type aircraft. The people associated with financial functions were expected to have a good understanding of the financial analysis associated with aircraft design and evaluation. The people in supply chain functions were expected to have a good understanding of the issues associated with the Boeing Company extended enterprise, primarily the relationship between Boeing and its suppliers. The people associated with new programs were assumed to have a good understanding of the processes, priorities and challenges associated with launching a new commercial aircraft. While the BWB is not yet ready to be launched as a commercial product, it was assumed that the same processes, priorities and challenges would apply if the BWB were to be launched as a product.

Finally, the interviewees in the academic category had extensive experience with either the Boeing Company or with the aviation industry in general. It was expected that these people would be able to provide both a broad picture of both the Boeing Company and the aircraft manufacturing industry, as well as potentially less guarded information.

In total, ten interviews were conducted for the BWB case study. The majority of the interviews were conducted in one-on-one sessions, either in person or via telephone. One of the contacts was in the context of a question and answer format at a workshop.

A complete list of the organizations (either internal to Boeing or non-Boeing organizations) and positions of the interviewees is provided in Table 6-2. The selection of the organizations was done in a manner to try and best represent the range of stakeholders that were of interest. Within the organizations, interviewees at managerial levels were sought out. In many cases the leader of the organization was interviewed.

Table 6-2 ITS case study organizations and roles of interviewees. .

Organization	Role	Interviewees
Commercial Aircraft Integrator		
Blended Wing Body	Program Manager	Bob Liebeck
Computational Finance and Modeling	Technical Lead	Scott Mathews
Boeing Replacement Plane Study	Regional Director for Marketing, Commercial Airplanes	Reginald Able
Global Partners	Team Lead	Steven Patneaude
Product Development, Advanced Concepts and Product Evaluation	Product Development Chief	Mithra Sankrithi
Boeing Replacement Plane Study	VP Business Development	A. Kent Fisher
Academic		
MIT	Current Faculty Member	Debbie Nightingale
MIT	Current Faculty Member	Karen Wilcox
MIT	Former Faculty Member	Earl Murman
MIT	Current Doctoral Student	Ted Piepenbrock

The following section discusses the interview questions that were used for this research.

6.1.4 INTERVIEW QUESTIONS

A series of questions was crafted to better understand the challenges associated with "complex" real options in complex systems. The interviews were semi-structured and constructed around an open-ended question format. The semi-structured nature of the interviews was deemed appropriate for two reasons. First, the research was exploratory. As such, the research questions evolved not only between interviews but in the process of the interviews as well. As new information was uncovered, the interview questions were modified to take it into account. Second, given the wide range of organizations represented by the interviewees, semi-structured questions that could be modified where needed so that they would be appropriate for each interviewee's perspective.

Six general questions were asked for each of the interviewees. The six questions appear below along with a brief discussion on the type of information being sought for each one. It is emphasized that these six questions are not the only questions that were asked. Follow-up or more detail questions were also asked to get further detail on specific topics. These follow-up and detailed questions varied from interviewee to interviewee, though the six general questions remained constant across interviewees.

1. How does your organization fit into the aircraft design process?

> The purpose of the first question was to gain a better understanding of the role that the interviewee's organization played in the design process. Also, a better understanding of the organization's objectives and positions was sought out.
>
> In a similar manner, interviewees were also often asked to answer this question about other stakeholders. This allowed comparison of responses across stakeholders and also uncovered additional information concerning relationships between stakeholders.

2. Can you provide examples where flexibility is currently being used by your organization or by other organizations?

> For interviewees related to design functions, examples where the interviewee's organization was using flexibility were initially sought out. For interviewee's not directly related to a design function, their perspective on the flexibility examples raised by other interviewees was desired.
>
> In general, an understanding of whether flexibility is being used in practice was desired. If so, an understanding of how it was being used was the subject of the follow-up questions. The objective of this question was to better understand how flexibility was being used, what were its perceived benefits and costs, and what challenges were being experienced when using the flexibility.

3. If flexibility is used, can you provide examples of processes used by your organization to identify, design, evaluate or manage flexibility?

> For interviewees belonging to organizations using flexibility, a better understanding of what types of processes were being used to identify, design, evaluate and manage the flexibility was desired. If the interviewee's organization had a process, a better understanding of the successes and challenges associated with using the process were was of interest.

4. What is your organization's position on the benefits and costs associated with flexibility?

> The interviewee's general thoughts about the utility and feasibility of using flexibility were of interest. This question allowed general views on flexibility to be explored, independent of the flexibility that was actually used. This question was deemed important to try and understand what stakeholders felt

about flexibility, i.e. is it a good idea or not, without the pre-conceived notions associated with the performance of current systems using flexibility.

5. What are the critical enterprise and institutional architecture challenges that have been encountered by your organization?

In relation to flexible systems, interviewees were asked about practical challenges that were faced during the life-cycle of the flexibility. Any type of challenges was of interest.

This question also expanded the interview beyond a discussion on flexibility. Independent of flexibility, interviewees were asked to discuss the critical practical challenges that their organization regularly faced. This question was then used to try and determine if any of these challenges would affect flexible systems, and if so, would these challenges increase or decrease in magnitude due to the presence of flexibility.

6. Are there other critical points that should be discussed?

Finally, at the end of the interview, once interviewees had a better understanding of the topics of interest, they were asked to identify any other points that they felt would be of importance.

The following section discusses data collection from the interviews.

6.1.5   INTERVIEW DATA COLLECTION

During interviews, extensive hand written notes were taken. No recording devices were used in an attempt to not inhibit interviewee responses. The handwritten interview notes were then typed up and analyzed for major points.

In some cases follow-up questions concerning the interviewee response was asked at a later date. In other instances, follow-up with questions were posed to other interviewees. No full follow-up interview with the same interviewee was deemed necessary or practical.

While interviews were the primary source of data used for this part of the case study analysis, additional data sources were also used. These included publicly available information from the Boeing Company on the BWB, academic literature pertaining to the BWB, the Boeing Company or the commercial aircraft manufacturing industry, and articles appearing in the popular press.

In a few cases material was provided from interviewees. In most cases these additional data sources were found independent of the interviewees.

6.1.6 LIMITATIONS

Several limitations to this research are present, as noted below.

- **Case selection** – Two case studies were selected for this research; the ITS and BWB case studies. Including only two case studies from a much larger space of complex systems raises questions on the generalizability of the findings from this research. The large differences in technologies, technical architectures, and enterprise architectures between the two case studies was an attempt to address this limitation. As a result it is felt that the findings from this research are generalizable, but this should be further verified with additional case studies. However, the research provided here can create a framework in which additional case studies can be conducted.
- **Number of interviews** – The topic of interest for this research was "complex" real options in complex systems. One of the characteristics of the complex nature of the system is the large number of stakeholders involved in the system. To determine all of the stakeholder's perspectives requires a large number of interviews. Interviews with a diverse range of stakeholders were conducted to meet this research need. Of course, additional interviews that further expanded the range of stakeholders interviewed would have been worthwhile. For example, no interviews were able to be conducted with stakeholders representing the freight industry, which is an important stakeholder in any transportation system, but especially so for Houston, given the large amount of freight moving through the region from either the Port of Houston or from Mexico. Additionally, more interviews of people in the same organization would have been beneficial to cross-check information provided. Also, in some cases follow-up interviews with earlier interviewees would have been helpful, after a better understanding of the system was obtained during the entire interview process.
- **Increased data sources** – The non-interview data sources were very helpful in providing details to several of the points being made by interviewees. Additional access to data sources, such as organizational memos or agreements, as well as first observation, would have also been very helpful.

Much of the rest of this chapter focuses on the data obtained from the interviews and then a synthesis of that data in the final section. The data found from the interviews is organized according to the high-level interview questions previously presented. Data specifically addressing the first and last questions are not presented in its own section. Rather, the results for these questions; relating to the background of the organization and follow-on comments made by interviewees, is incorporated directly into the results presented for the other four questions.

As a reminder, the four general questions that will be addressed following the stakeholder map are as follows:

1. Can you provide examples where flexibility is currently being used by your organization or by other organizations?

2. If flexibility is used, can you provide examples of processes used by your organization to identify, design, evaluate or manage flexibility?

3. What is your organization's position on the benefits and costs associated with flexibility?

4. What are the critical enterprise and institutional architecture challenges that have been encountered by your organization?

A map of the major stakeholders associated with the aircraft manufacturing industry are presented in the next section.

6.2 STAKEHOLDERS RELATED TO THE AIRCRAFT MANUFACTURING ENTERPRISE

The aircraft manufacturing industry is a multibillion industry with a host of companies that span the globe. The size of the industry, the relative high price of the products, the strategic importance placed on maintaining a domestic aircraft manufacturing capability (Krugman 1986) and the prestige associated with aircraft manufacturing have drawn in governments and various financial market stakeholders into close contact with the aviation industry. Because of this, the following stakeholder inventory will cover aircraft manufacturing, airline, financial, and government stakeholders. The various stakeholders are organized and discussed according to these groupings, below.

6.2.1 PRIME INTEGRATOR AND MANUFACTURER

In the large commercial aircraft market, there are currently only two major companies that design, manufacture, market and support large commercial aircraft (i.e. over 100+ passengers); Airbus Industries (AI) and Boeing Commercial Aircraft Company (BCA). AI is a partnership of several European countries, primarily lead by the French and Germans, while BCA is an American based company; both of which are publicly traded companies.

BCA is the older of the two, getting its start in 1917. After WWII, Boeing concentrated on producing commercial jet aircraft and becoming the largest aircraft company of the three large U.S. companies; Boeing, Lockheed and Douglas (later McDonnell-Douglas). After Lockheed left the commercial aircraft market and McDonnell-Douglas was acquired by Boeing, BCA was by far the dominant worldwide aircraft company, with about 70% of aircraft orders and about 90% of the existing aircraft market. With the acquisition of McDonnell-Douglas in the mid-1990's Boeing substantially increased its defense business, making the defense and commercial business units near parity in terms of revenues.

An organizational chart of Boeing is provided in Figure 6-5. Interviewee organizations are highlighted.

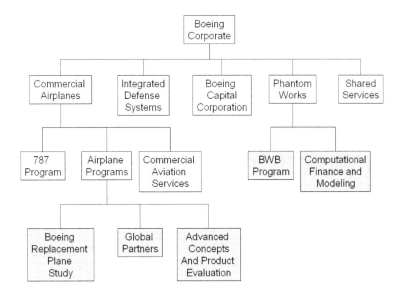

Figure 6-5 Boeing Company organizational chart showing interviewee organizations.

AI is a relative newcomer to the aviation industry, certifying its first commercial aircraft in 1974. AI has undergone a number of changes over its lifetime, both in its business classification and in its membership. Airbus was originally a consortium between the French and Germans, with other members joining and in some cases leaving and joining multiple times. Only recently has Airbus restructured and become a publicly traded company, though still with close ties to the original consortium governments.

6.2.2 SUPPLY CHAIN

Both AI and BAC use an extensive supply chain for their aircraft manufacturing operations. In general, some major subsystems, such as engines and avionics, are handled by only a handful of dedicated companies. The remainder of subsystems are generally designed and manufactured by some combination of the prime manufacturer or a supplier. Over time, the amount of work, both in manufacturing but also design, has been increasingly pushed to suppliers, away from the prime. This has been especially the case with BCA, which has embraced a prime integrator business model for its newest plane, the 787. In this model, BCA acts as the primary design lead, final integrator, supply chain manager, and interface with customers, both in determining design requirements and also in working to market and sell the finished planes. Under this model, BCA has pushed substantial design work, manufacturing and assembly work down to its supply chain, with the top tier called "partners". BCA then accepts only finished and pre-loaded assemblies from suppliers for final integration. AI still considers itself a prime manufacturer, keeping more of the detailed design, manufacturing and assembly work for itself.

There have been open statements by some of the largest supply chain partners working with AI and BCA, such as the Japanese and Chinese, on the desire to become prime integrators and manufacturers themselves in the future. This open acknowledgement of the desire to become direct competitors with AI and BCA has caused some to question the long-term wisdom of using foreign companies to participate in ever increasingly sophisticated design and assembly work, as it is seen as giving away knowledge that could eventually be used against AI or BCA (Pritchard and MacPherson 2004).

6.2.3 CUSTOMERS

Large commercial aircraft companies have three major sources of customers; commercial airlines, leasing companies and cargo carriers. For this research the concentration is on passenger planes, so cargo carriers will not be discussed. Additionally, commercial aircraft have been used in the past in commercial / military programs, such as the Boeing KC-135 / 707, KC-767 / 767 and A330 MRTT / A330 programs. Again, as the focus of this research is on commercial aircraft, military customers will not be dealt with in detail for this research.

6.2.3.1 Airlines

Commercial airlines have historically been the largest purchaser of aircraft from AI and BCA. As globalization continues and formerly underdeveloped countries industrialize, the global airline market continues to increase. Market liberalization in some countries, primarily the United States, has caused increased competition on price. This has resulted in pressure on AI and BCA to hold down costs, changing the dynamics of manufacturer's competition away from performance. The appearance of low-cost carriers and many new startups in undeveloped countries has also helped change aircraft purchasing trends over the years, with characteristics such as commonality and operating costs becoming increasing relevant as well as growth in the secondary market for used planes.

6.2.3.2 Leasing Companies

Leasing companies have been around for decades but play an increasingly important role in aircraft markets today. Leasing companies own large fleets of aircraft that they then lease out, typically in a relatively short-term basis of a few years, to airlines. By leasing, the airlines can keep the large capital purchases off their balance sheet and can make a shorter-term commitment to individual planes. This shorter-term commitment gives the airline an increased ability to add or subtract aircraft from its fleet at a faster rate to better meet changing market conditions and company objectives. Currently, leasing companies account for about 20% of AI and BCA aircraft order backlogs (AWAS 2005).

6.2.4   COMPETITORS

Besides the competition between Airbus and Boeing in the large commercial aircraft segment of the industry, other companies offer alternative products that compete either indirectly or directly with some of the products offered by Airbus and Boeing.

6.2.4.1   Large Commercial Aircraft Competition

AI and BCA essentially compete against one another in a duopoly, since the exit of Lockheed from the commercial aircraft market and the acquisition of McDonnell-Douglas by BCA in 1997. At the time of the acquisition, BCA had about a 70% market share of orders, with the balance being made up primarily by AI. In the intervening 10 years since, the market share split has been about a 50-50 split, with each company posting individual years of higher order and delivery rates.

6.2.4.2   Regional Jets

Regional jet manufacturers of smaller than the 100+ passenger sizes that AI and BCA compete over continue to pose a threat to AI and BCA products. As the regional jet manufacturers have gained experience, their offerings have steadily increased to the point where AI and BCA have withdrawn from the low end of the market, ceding their smallest plane niches to the regional jet manufacturers. It is not known if the regional jet manufacturers will enter larger plane markets in the future, but the threat is present.

6.2.4.3   Corporate / Fractional / Very Light Jets

Smaller jets used for corporate, fractional and air taxi services are starting to increase in popularity, due to advancing technologies bringing down prices for these smaller planes. While these planes do not directly pose a threat to AI and BCA, they do threaten to take the highest paying customers from airlines, directly threatening their current business model, which could have an effect on future aircraft order rates.

6.2.5   GOVERNMENTS

Due to the perceived value of aircraft design, manufacturing and integration capabilities, governments have become actively involved to varying degrees in the aviation industry. Besides serving as the conduit for making international regulations and solving trade disputes, governments have also created conditions to help or hinder domestic and foreign manufacturers. Involvement of European Union governments takes the form of direct launch subsidies to AI, while the U.S. national government interacts with BCA primarily through military and NASA contracts. However, state and foreign governments, notably the government of Japan, have recently provided direct subsidies to BCA as well during the 787 program.

6.2.6 FINANCIAL LENDERS AND MARKETS

Due to the high-costs of aircraft, financial lenders and markets are important in determining the feasibly of specific aircraft.

6.2.6.1 Financial Lenders

Financial lenders play a role primarily in the aviation industry, providing the financing needed to purchase planes. Recently, the concerns of financial lenders have been more directly taken into account by the aircraft manufacturers, with these concerns appearing in aircraft design decisions, such as the decision of the BCA 787 program to have multiple engines that could be easily switched out or more standardized avionics, making the plane easier to resell (.Mecham 2005).

6.2.6.2 Financial Markets

Since both AI and BCA are publicly traded companies, financial markets exert some pull over corporate decision making. As AI receives a greater share of its funding for new aircraft from government subsidies and has historically embraced government involvement to a greater extent than BCA, financial markets tend to play a greater role in BCA decision making, with a BCA emphasis on providing short-term shareholder value, sometimes at the expense of long-term value (Lawrence and Thornton 2005).

The following section provides and overview of the current situation faced by the aircraft manufacturing industry.

6.3 CURRENT SITUATION

The following section presents an overview of the current situation in the aircraft market, with respect to AI and BCA. Broad, general trends that were found from the literature and from the interview process are presented to create a backdrop to help understand the current transportation situation in the large commercial aviation industry. An overview of the future market outlook is presented, followed by the competitive situation between the AI and BCA.

6.3.1 STATE OF THE LARGE COMMERCIAL AIRCRAFT MARKET

The large commercial aircraft market is expected to continue to grow at a pace faster than the rate of global GDP (Boeing 2006). Fueled by increased growth in world GDP and industrialization in underdeveloped economies, especially in Asia, both AI and Boeing project large commercial aircraft needs to more than double the size of the current world large commercial aircraft fleet in the next 20 years (Airbus 2006, Boeing 2006). Much of this growth is caused by expected Asian orders, with both AI and BCA projecting the total percentage of orders in Asia to surpass Europe in the next 20 years and AI expects Asian orders to surpass orders in the United States as well (Airbus 2006, Boeing 2006). Boeing and Airbus forecasts are shown in Figure 6-6 and Figure 6-7.

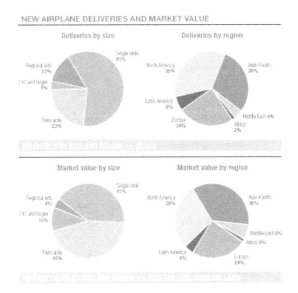

Figure 6-6 Delivery and market trend forecasts for Boeing Company. Figure from (Boeing 2006).

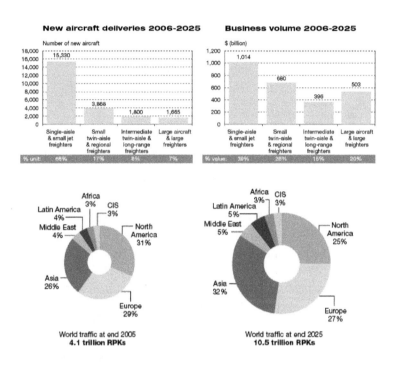

Figure 6-7 Delivery and market forecast for Airbus. Figure from (Airbus 2006).

The break-down in types of planes ordered differs between AI and Boeing. Both AI and BCA have made public statements that propose different world views on the future of airline operations. AI has forecasted an increasing reliance on hub and spoke operations as congested routes seek to increase passenger throughput with the use of larger planes. BCA has forecasted more point-to-point travel to link an increasing number of city pairs to by-pass congested hub cities and shorten travel times, requiring an increasing number of mid-sized aircraft (Pilling 2005).

However, while AI and BCA are sticking with their official forecasts and new entrants to meet these forecasts, the A380 and 787, respectively, both are moving forward with new entrants to compete in alternative operating conditions. AI is moving forward with a 787 competitor, the A350 XWB and BCA is moving forward with a stretched replacement for the 747-400, the 787-8. While both AI and BCA move forward with entries in the mid- and large-sized aircraft segments, both continue to forecast that the single-aisle segment

229

will continue to dominate in total aircraft sold and either surpass or rival the total value sold of twin aisle aircraft (Airbus 2006, Boeing 2006).

6.3.2 COMPETITIVE SITUATION IN LARGE COMMERCIAL AVIATION INDUSTRY

BCA, as the incumbent in the industry, has seen a loss in market share from a high of nearly 70% of orders after the acquisition of McDonnell-Douglas in 1997 to a near parity with AI currently. Currently, both AI and BCA have a family of aircraft that have a variety of payloads and range capabilities. The AI family starts around 107 passengers with the A318, an A320 derivative, and extends up to the forthcoming A380 with 555 passengers. The BCA family starts around 110 passengers with the 737-600 and extends up to around 467 passengers with the forthcoming 747-8. A summary of the families is presented in Table 6-3. The shaded entries are planes sizes that a BWB type aircraft could compete with effectively.

Table 6-3 AI and BCA Product Offerings, matched by closest competing products. Data from (Airbus 2007, Boeing 2007).

Airbus Product Offerings			Boeing Product Offerings		
Aircraft Family	Passengers	Range (km)	Aircraft Family	Passengers	Range (km)
A320	107-185	5600-6800	737	110-215	5648-10,200
A310	220	8050	767	245	10,454
A330	253-295	10,500-12,500	757 (discontinued)		
A350	253-300	13,900-16,300	787	220-300	5650-15,750
A340	239-380	13,350-16,100	777	301-365	14,594-17,556
A380	555	15,000	747	467	14,815

From the mid-1970's to the late 1980's AI developed and marketed a family of planes, including all of those listed above with the exception of the A350 and A380, which are currently at some phase in development, and began to erode BCA market share. In the 1990's BCA was determined to maintain a 60% market share and priced its planes accordingly to achieve this goal (Hartley 2004). As a result, BCA reduced prices over 20% off list prices (Biddle and Helyar 1998), which created future problems, as BCA did not have a lower cost production advantage over AI (Hartley 2004). In the competitive aircraft sales market, the low prices that BCA was offering, matched by AI, combined with good economic conditions occurring before the Asian financial crisis in 1997 caused a large surge in orders for both AI and BCA. While BCA was a leading provider of technically advanced products, its internal processes for such activities as design commonality, parts management and supplies created large inefficiencies in production. Because of these inefficiencies, as BCA attempted to ramp up its production capabilities to meet rising demand, the overall manufacturing system within BCA melted down, eventually resulting in a one month shut down of production to sort out the situation (Hartley 2004). The resulting delivery delay, combined with canceled and reduced orders resulting from the Asian financial crisis and the 9/11 terrorist attacks resulted in a reduced number of orders, making the remaining orders even more competitive between AI and BCA. To continue to win orders, AI offered deep discounts, but BCA refused to follow AI into unprofitable territory, resulting in AI winning a greater percentage of orders for the first time (Hartley 2004).

The competition between AI and BCA has also been driven by changes in the airline industry, especially deregulation of the US airline industry that has resulted in creating greater cost competition and increased sensitivity to costs, including aircraft purchase and operating costs. The resulting increase in competition for orders has caused AI and BCA to reassess their own business models, with an increased focus on customer requirements and focus on driving costs out of the supply chain (Harrigan 2006).

AI has continued its reliance on derivative aircraft for blending continuity and innovation (Thorton 1995) to continue to sell high quality aircraft at competitive prices. This is done by offering a range of aircraft that have multiple features in common, such as identical cockpits or identical fuselages and wings, which allow airlines to reduce maintenance and training costs or allow AI to reduce tooling and design costs. AI has also continued it reliance on designing and manufacturing critical components internally, especially for new models, reserving outsourcing for older models that are nearing the end of their lifecycle, allowing AI to keep its leadership role in manufacturing (Harrigan 2006).

BCA has chosen to take a different route, as demonstrated with the move towards recasting itself as a prime integrator with the new 787 Dreamliner, in a similar manner as that embraced earlier by the auto industry (A.T. Kearney 2003). Traditionally in the design and manufacturing process, BCA would do most of the design work itself, retain a high share of manufacturing in house and do most assembly in house as well, using the same manufacturing techniques that it had used for decades (Laudon 2000). Specialized subassemblies, such as engines or avionics would be provided by specialists. The remaining components would be designed by BCA and built to design by suppliers, without much real interaction between BCA and the supplier. Additionally, BCA would provide all the investment needed for the program (Harrigan 2006). With the 777 program in the mid-1990's BCA relied more heavily on several Japanese suppliers to take a larger role in some design and manufacturing tasks, though BCA still provided the bulk of the capital investments.

Focusing on systems integration, BCA is trying to reduce unit costs and potentially shift some of the non-recurring design and development costs and risks down the supply chain to suppliers (Pritchard and MacPherson 2004). The system integrator forms an integrated network of suppliers, in which each partner has a core competency in some area, with the system integrator ensuring that the entire system fits together in the end. This responsibility includes technical responsibilities for the overall design and production processes, program management responsibilities for costs, timings, and uncertainties, and customer interface responsibilities for determining the design requirements and selling and supporting the final product. A key responsibility is risk management, as customers have become more price conscious and as airlines have increasingly gone to a leasing over buying strategy, can exert greater pressure in aircraft purchase negotiations. Additionally, customer demand patterns have caused development times to become shorter, with increased requests for customization. The purpose of the systems integration business model is to divest BCA of low value-added component manufacturing tasks (Graham and Ahmed 2000) and to instead focus on improving the design, customer service and supply chain. BCA has adopted this business model starting with the 787, where its first tier suppliers, or "partners", will ship completed assemblies to BCA facilities for final assembly. Whether BCA will continue to utilize this business model in the future is uncertain, as is the effect it will have on BCA future operations.

The following section addresses the four questions that were used during the interview process. As a reminder, these four questions are:

1. Can you provide examples where flexibility is currently being used by your organization or by other organizations?

2. If flexibility is used, can you provide examples of processes used by your organization to identify, design, evaluate or manage flexibility?

3. What is your organization's position on the benefits and costs associated with flexibility?

4. What are the critical enterprise and institutional architecture challenges that have been encountered by your organization?

6.4   EXAMPLES OF FLEXIBILITY IN THE LARGE COMMERCIAL AVIATION INDUSTRY

This section presents the results from the first of the four questions: **Can you provide examples where flexibility is currently being used by your organization or by other organizations?**   An overview of multiple examples where flexibility is used or considered is presented below.

Real options in the aviation industry are a common occurrence. One of the most common real options that is mentioned in the popular press are options that airlines and leasing companies take out on future aircraft orders. This allows airlines to buy options on purchasing aircraft at a particular date. *This option allows airlines to reserve the right to a particular spot in the production queue to ensure that a future need for an aircraft can be meet at a particular date, rather than entering at the end of the queue, which can add years to the delivery date of the aircraft.*

Another option widespread in the aircraft manufacturing industry is the option "in" aircraft designs that allow for future derivatives to be designed and manufactured at a reduced price in the future. Modern aircraft are no longer optimized to a point design; rather the technical characteristics are set so that multiple derivatives can be designed around the initial baseline aircraft. As multiple interviewees stated, the first aircraft in a new aircraft family never makes a profit. The reason for this is that the first plane is not optimized or targeted for the profit maximizing point in the family. For example, if it is determined that airlines want a 150 passenger plane, the initial plane will likely be designed for 130 passengers. Subsequent planes in the family will then be stretched making the next plane a closer match to customer needs. Additionally, initial conservative can be removed from the plane, once the design is better understood, so that the performance of the plane is improved with subsequent planes. The initial plane's technical design can therefore be considered an option. This option allows the production of follow-on derivative planes in the family that have better technical performance characteristics and sizing that more closely matches customer needs. Pricing of these options has been looked at in the literature (Miller and Clarke 2005, Miller 2005).

In general, derivative aircraft have a commonalty index of about 40% (Ferreri 2003), meaning about 40% of the derivative is common with the baseline plane. Historically, this results in derivative aircraft having a development cost of about $1-3B compared to around $10B for the first plane in a new family (Harrigan 2006). *The cost savings come from the commonality in components and tooling. This reduces the need to redesign components and develop new tooling and manufacturing processes, which can then increase scale of economies by increasing ordering rates for common parts. Additionally, derivatives can take advantage of learning curves started on prior planes in the family, instead of re-starting the learning curve.*

The commonality used to reduce design and development prices between planes in a family can also be applied to planes across a company's product range. At a large-scale, common fuselages, wings and cockpits have been shared across families, as well as within families. AI takes the most advantage of this strategy of commonality, with the A300, A310, A330 and A340 all sharing a common fuselage, the A330 and A340 sharing a common wing and the A320, A330 and A340 sharing a common cockpit. BCA also has taken advantage of this cross-family commonality in the past, with the 707 and 757 sharing a common fuselage and the 757 and 767 sharing a common cockpit. This type of commonality called a "cross-family" derivative, a term introduced for this research.

Recently, BCA has not utilized such commonality between families, with the 777 and forthcoming 787 having unique fuselages and wings. Multiple interviewees characterized BCA's current strategy as optimizing each family, forgoing cross-family commonality, to improve the performance of individual planes in individual families. Even AI has been forced away from relying on commonality recently. For example, the initial A350 offering, which was offered as a competing product to the 787, was characterized as a modified A330 (Wallace 2005), and in response to pressure from customers, AI abandoned the design in favor of a completely new plane, the A350 XWB (Wikipedia 2007).

While the commonality between aircraft in a family enables the savings between planes and creates the option for new planes in the family, multiple interviewees attested that designing the commonality into a single family, much less across families, was not a trivial undertaking. For example, the difficulty in designing in commonality can manifest itself in small examples, such as offering 747 customers 38 different types of pilot clipboards and 109 shades of white paint (Greenwald 1998), to designing different tools to open wing access hatches on the same plane (Banks 1998), to larger examples such as having a wing design group for each plane family, redesigning wings from scratch for each new plane (Hartley 2004).

From the interviews and literature, it was apparent that real options in aircraft are commonly used, with several examples present. Some of the options, such as options on buying new planes or options in the design that allow for derivates to be produced, were common occurrences. Other options, such as commonality across families were less common. Further, with recent activities by Boeing and Airbus, it was unclear if the options created by commonality across families was being reduced.

A summary of the flexibility found in current aircraft manufacturing enterprises is listed in Table 6-4.

Table 6-4 Summary of flexibility examples found in current aircraft manufacturing enterprises

Flexibility found in aircraft manufacturing enterprises
Real options "on" systems were common: airline purchase options for new planes

Real options "in" systems were also common, with multiple examples
  • Option through commonality for building a derivative in the same aircraft family
  • Option through commonality for building "cross-family" derivatives

Both Boeing and Airbus make extensive use of options to build derivatives
Airbus has historically made extensive use of options for "cross-family" derivatives

While these examples illustrate the use of flexibility in aircraft manufacturing enterprises, the next section looks at the process that stakeholders use to recognize, design and evaluate flexibility in systems.

6.5   PROCESSES FOR IDENTIFYING, DESIGNING AND EVALUATING FLEXIBILITY IN SYSTEMS

This section presents the results from the second of the four questions: **If flexibility is used, can you provide examples of processes used by your organization to identify,**

design, evaluate or manage flexibility? An overview of interviewee experience with processes associated with flexibility is presented below.

Both AI and BCA have processes in place for using real option evaluation techniques in various aspects of their business. For example, AI uses option analysis techniques extensively when valuing the options that it sells to airlines for new plane purchases (Copeland and Antikarov 2001, Hanley 2001). The BCA division of Phantom Works also uses option evaluation techniques to help in evaluating research and development funding decisions (Stevens 2000).

For designing real options "in" planes, both AI and BCA appear to have processes to facilitate this. For example, BCA has developed the patented Datar-Mathews options evaluation methodology (Datar and Methews 2004). This process is designed to create an easy to work with tool, specifically targeted towards program managers and engineers, to allow explicit and quantitative evaluation of design choices to better understand the costs and benefits associated with the choices. The process has been designed with both the direct user in mind as well as the decision maker. By making the process more transparent and intuitive to the world view and decision making process for upper level management, the process is designed to help facilitate trade-offs and better understand cost and value streams in program design decisions. The result is a tool that can be used in an iterative process between management and program designers to converge on a design that maximizes value.

However, as one interviewee stated, in practice the process has not been widely adopted, despite the tailoring of the process to meet the needs of multiple users. The reasoning for this is two-fold. *First, the consideration and quantitative evaluation of real options "in" designs is not standard operating procedure in aircraft programs.* As another interviewee stated, their program is aware of the real options methods available within the company. However, the program chooses not to use them for a variety of reasons, such as little prior experience with the method and skepticism over the need for such complex pricing mechanisms to make program decisions.

Second, as another interviewee stated, in an aircraft development program, decision making on major aspects of the program are done by senior management, who are advised on the financial impacts of the decision by various people, including people from the corporate finance department. As an interviewee stated, the corporate finance department is strongly rooted in net present value evaluation techniques, as opposed to real option evaluation techniques. As such, they do not support evaluations using non-NPV techniques in discussions with management.

Because the corporate finance department will have at least one person assigned to a program to help the program manager understand the financial impact of decisions, the program manager can be presented with a difficult situation when making design decisions or preparing major decisions for review with senior management. Due to the different evaluation techniques of real options and NPV, the program manager can see two different versions of financial reality, but only one of these is supported by the corporate finance department, which also advises senior management. As a result, program managers typically opts to use the financial evaluation techniques that have historic corporate support.

Another interviewee stated that one of finance's functions was to ensure that internal accounting could be properly stated in external government filings. Since options are only listed as notes in government filings, they are not treated with the same serious effort as other metrics that are of more central importance in the filings.

A summary of the results found from the interviewee responses to question about process for identifying, designing and managing flexibility are presented in Table 6-5.

Table 6-5 Summary of interview results for process for identifying, designing and evaluating flexibility

Processes for Flexibility
Both Airbus and Boeing have multiple processes for evaluating flexibility
Boeing has a process for identifying, deigning and evaluating flexibility "in" systems, called the Datar –Mathews Process
Despite being designed to support engineers and program managers, the Datar-Mathews methods has not been adopted in programs. Reasons for this include: • Program managers unconvinced of benefits or need of new process • Corporate finance function uses NPV and not real options analysis processes. As corporate finance advises corporate managerial decision making concerning program decisions, program manager end up using NPV as real options analysis is not supported

The following section discusses general stakeholder views on flexibility and its challenges.

6.6 SUMMARY OF INTERVIEWEE VIEWS ON FLEXIBILITY

This section presents the results from the third of the four questions: **What is your organization's position on the benefits and costs associated with flexibility?** An overview of interviewee general views on flexibility are presented below.

In general, interviewees were mixed on the idea of flexibility "in" systems. While interviewees thought the idea of flexibility was good and that Boeing actively tried to make systems flexibility, most of the interviewee responses instead indicated that the costs associated with flexibility "in" aircraft was too high to be worthwhile.

Interviewee views on flexibility centered primarily around two costs associated with flexibility "in" aircraft. The first related to the difficult incorporating flexibility in a design, due to high design complexity. The second related to the performance penalty associated with the flexibility. Each are discussed below.

6.6.1 TECHNICAL CHALLENGES

Commercial aircraft are among of the most complex pieces of technology mass produced. For example, the 747 alone has over six million parts (Boeing 2007). Because of the technical complexity in aircraft designs, according to one interviewee, it is often a challenge to get the first aircraft flying at all in a manner that still meets at least most, or is close to meeting, the technical specifications that have already been released to customers. *To meet these technical challenges, any additional features that have not been deemed critical to the first flight of the plane, such as features creating options, are often dropped.* Weight is a large driver for aircraft performance, and as it is almost always the case in the aerospace industry, the first aircraft has weight issues that must be resolved. As almost all features on the plane have some weight penalty attached to them, in order to get the weight down and performance up, features that are not immediately necessary for the plane are given a low priority and often dropped from the design.

Another interviewee described adding flexibility "in" a system design as a weight penalty. Even for the blended wing body aircraft, which has been shown to have a large degree of commonality capability (Liebeck 2003), the penalty for commonality across families has been shown to be as great as 2% (Willcox and Wakayama 2003), which is not insignificant when comparing it to the airline industry which typically with low profitability. Since an option in the initial aircraft for a latter aircraft will depend on the success of the initial aircraft, i.e. if the initial aircraft does not fly no derivates will be built, to ensure that the initial aircraft can fly may require dropping the option for the later aircraft. In this case, the need to reduce the technical complexity and weight for the initial aircraft makes an option an ideal initial target to drop, as it is a weight penalty that adds nothing to the initial aircraft, as all the benefits are realized in later aircraft.

6.6.2 PERFORMANCE PENALTY

Multiple interviewees felt that flexibility in systems would be too expensive in terms of the performance penalty that the flexibility would require of the system. Examples such as the common wing in the A330 and A340 were discounted as causing huge performance penalties and creating an inferior product, though until recently the A340 has considerably outsold the 777, its closest competitor. Several interviewees felt this was due more to subsidies, rather than any savings granted from the commonality, though some interviewees felt that the entire strategy of crating commonality across families had merit and the potential to create considerable value for customers.

A summary of interviewee's views on flexibility are provided in Table 6-6.

Table 6-6 Summary of interviewee views on flexibility.

Stakeholder views on flexibility
Interviewees were mixed on the idea of flexibility "in" systems
• In general, the idea was favorably received
• However, when discussing specifics, interviewees generally thought that there were too many challenges and costs associated with flexibility "in" systems to be worthwhile
Challenges and costs identified centered on the technical
• Technical complexity in aircraft design makes it difficult to add flexibility to the system, which is seen as adding complexity
• The performance penalty from the flexibility is not worth the benefit

The following section discusses interviewee responses to limitations to option use due to various practical concerns that must be taken into account during the life-cycle of the option. Various challenges that appear throughout the option's life-cycle are identified and discussed.

6.7 ENTERPRISE AND INSTITUTIONAL CHALLENGES RELATED TO FLEXIBILITY

This section presents the results from the last of the four questions: **What are the critical enterprise and institutional architecture challenges that have been encountered by your organization?** An overview of critical enterprise issues raised by interviewees is discussed.

The enterprise architecture challenges arise along multiple dimensions, including: enterprise goals and evaluations, design process for aircraft and corporate culture, and financial evaluation. How each of these creates barriers at different stages in the life-cycle of an option is discussed below.

6.7.1 ENTERPRISE GOALS AND DECISIONS MAKING PROCESSES

Options assume that the goal of the option holder is to maximize the net value of the system over the life-cycle of the option, which for real options can be a relatively long time period. However, as multiple interviewees stated, this is not always the case. *Rather, there can be a strong need to show that a plane maximizes value immediately.* This need to maximize immediate value can come from several sources.

First, the enterprise architecture of aerospace enterprises has historically been very driven by individual programs, both on the military and commercial sides of the business. As one interviewee characterized the situation, the program is "king". *Hence most metrics and evaluations are based around the performance of the program.* Corporate performance is then the sum of the performance of individual programs. This emphasis on programs empowers program managers to have the authority to make decisions without needing to constantly consult with corporate or functional leadership. *However, the downside is that it also has the effect of reducing the potential for cross-program synergies and increases duplication between programs.* While enterprise architectures, such as the deployment of a matrix organizational structure by BCA, are meant to overcome these issues and integrate programs, in practice substantial difficulties prevent this.

One interviewee described functional management as having the responsibility to ensure that cross-program synergies were being exploited and cross-program duplications minimized. However, this often has not happened, as the example of multiple wing design teams illustrates (as first mentioned in Section 6.4), though progress along this dimensions has been made, as this example shows, since BCA now only has one common wing design group across-programs (Hartley 2004).

Another interviewee stated that since BCA has a strong corporate culture that is aligned with programs, while functional managers may have responsibility over cross-program decisions, they are often not regularly "invited to the table" during decision-making at higher levels. Instead, major decisions are made by groups with direct profit and loss responsibility, such as sales and marketing functions. As BCA has historically been an engineering driven company interested in offering customers products that push the technological envelope (Collins and Porras 2004), functions such as sales and marketing have evolved to sell planes based on performance. Performance can best be obtained by optimizing the plane in a single program, rather than making performance reducing trades for a single program, such as options may require, to improve value across multiple and future programs.

An interviewee also mentioned that the BCA relationship with the markets prevents long-term planning across product families, as is more commonly done with AI products. Instead, BCA attempts to please the market and maximize shareholder value. This short-term maximization can lead to behaviors that boost share prices in the short-term, but not for the long-term. For example, in the early 2000's BCA announced a major stock buyback program, to return value to shareholders. At the same time, the stable of BCA products, with the exception of the 777 consisted of planes that had been designed in the 1960's and 1970's. Instead of a longer term perspective of investing in new programs or R&D, increased earnings were used to provide a short-term boost to share prices (Lawrence and Thornton 2005). As one interviewee described, the only metric that the finance industry uses to evaluate the company are current orders and order backlog. Therefore, as the interviewee continued, to maximize share price, a flashy new product is needed that makes a big splash and creates a short-term increase in orders. A constant need to generate products, each generating a home run, is often at odds with the requirements generated by building in flexibility in a system, where incremental steps are taken over time as uncertainty resolves, rather than committing to a product design before uncertainty has been resolved.

A summary of the challenges related to the enterprise goals and decision making process are presented in Figure 6-8.

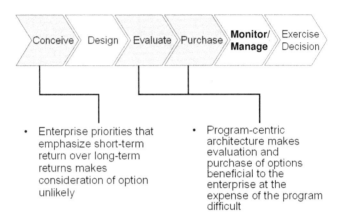

• Enterprise priorities that emphasize short-term return over long-term returns makes consideration of option unlikely

• Program-centric architecture makes evaluation and purchase of options beneficial to the enterprise at the expense of the program difficult

Figure 6-8 Summary of challenges related to enterprise goals and decision making process

6.7.2 DESIGN PROCESS FOR AIRCRAFT AND CORPORATE CULTURE

The decision making process for technical decisions has increased the difficulty in designing flexibility in systems. Multiple interviewees described the design process for including new technologies in planes as a bottom-up decision making process. During the course of a program, if a new technology is seen as being beneficial to a program, the decision can then be made to add it into the program. If other programs then find the technology of use, it could also find its way into other programs, either new programs or ongoing programs. If not, the new technology may not be used for other programs in the future. For example, the change to a two-person forward-facing cockpit design was made on the 767 and 757 programs. Due to the perceived benefits of this layout, other programs latter adopted a similar concept of two-person forward-facing cockpits for their programs. However, unlike in AI planes where cockpits are shared across families to reduce the training and operating costs for airlines, only the 767 and 757 shared a similar cockpit layout in the BCA families.

An example of where technologies may not be adopted across-programs are between the 787 and forthcoming 737 programs. While a large investment in composite technologies were made for the 787 program, its benefit to a new 737 program are not likely to be immediately realized. This is because many 737 operators are low-cost carriers, such as Southwest Airlines, who maintain a low-cost business model in part by reducing operating and maintenance costs by only operating one type of plane. For these customers who buy in bulk because they only operate a limited number of plane models, a switchover to a new technology such as composites replacing aluminum, creates additional costs that should be postponed for as long as possible. As a result, pressure is applied to forgo the use of composites in the plane, despite the large buildup of costs necessary to build the 787 out of composites.

This illustrates a problem with respect to flexibility in the bottom-up design process. *While this process creates increased opportunity to innovate at the program level, it can create unnecessary duplication and waste between programs.* This is because similar technologies and designs have to be redone to fit other programs, such as the need to redesign the two person cockpit for the 737 program. *Without increased top down guidance, it is difficult to make good judgments about what options to include in a plane.* In some cases, such as the forward-facing cockpit, the technology was picked up in other programs and it would have been worthwhile to have designed a cockpit that could be transferred to other planes without the need for redesign. This would have entailed additional design costs up-front for the initial plane, but would have reduced overall costs for design as the cockpit could be used in subsequent planes. In other cases, such as the use of composites on the 787, with additional top-down direction the large increase in use of composites may not have occurred, as looking out to the next program it could have been seen that there was significant customer pushback over such a large switch in technologies.

The culture of the decision making process and goals for programs has not aligned well with the constraints posed by real options. Designing real options into a system requires that critical uncertainties be identified early in the design process and design solutions identified for the system that can be exercised in the future, dependant on the resolution of the uncertainty. In practice, a range of potential outcomes for the system can be realized, depending on if and when the option is exercised, but this range may be constrained early in the process. While the presence of options may present future program managers the opportunity to take advantage of previous option purchases, these options can also present a constraint. For a company whose culture is pushing the performance enveloped to offer the latest technology, the constraint from options envisioned in the past with older technology may present a design constrain that is undesirable. As one interviewee put it, the result is that the option may be purchased, but then never exercised in the future, as some new technology consistently is available that makes the prior option obsolete.

A summary of the enterprise architecture and culture challenges are presented in Figure 6-9.

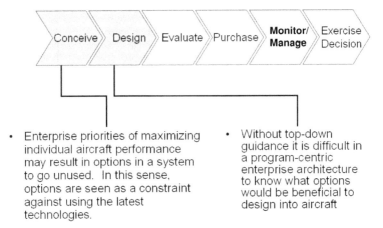

| Conceive | Design | Evaluate | Purchase | **Monitor/ Manage** | Exercise Decision |

- Enterprise priorities of maximizing individual aircraft performance may result in options in a system to go unused. In this sense, options are seen as a constraint against using the latest technologies.

- Without top-down guidance it is difficult in a program-centric enterprise architecture to know what options would be beneficial to design into aircraft

Figure 6-9 Summary of enterprise architecture and culture challenges.

6.7.3 FINANCIAL EVALUATION

The financial evaluation of programs and options also create difficulties in purchasing options "in" aircraft programs. Continuing with the theme above, programs are financed on a program by program basis. Benefits and costs are attributed to individual programs. For an option "in" a system, this may translate into options being built into an initial aircraft and then being exercised in other future aircraft.

This means that the initial aircraft would be required to "purchase" the option, taking the performance penalty and additional design costs to create the option, so that future programs could exercise the option and realize reduced costs by using common components and assemblies that had been previously designed by the original aircraft program.

From a financial evaluation perspective, the initial program that is designing the option in the system may experience higher development costs and lower sales than if it was optimized to just meet its own needs. However, as one member of a product line consisting of multiple families, spreading these costs over each family could result in lower costs for the entire product line.

For example, the A330 and A340 share a common wing, which is one of the most complex assemblies on the aircraft. The design challenges in creating a common wing were substantial, as the A330 has two engine pods, while the A340 has four. The performance of the plane suffered, as comparing the A340 with its closest competitor the 777, the 777 has improved performance being a point design. However, until recently when fuel costs increased substantially, the lower costs of the A340, due in part to the commonality it shared with the A330, resulted in significant increased sales over the 777.

A summary of the challenge of using a cross-program option with current program based accounting practices is shown in Figure 6-10

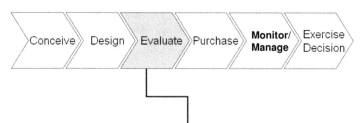

- Financial accounting is on a program basis and does not take into account cross-program costs. Cross-family derivatives have costs charged to one program and benefits experienced by different program with this financial accounting system. As a result, it is not worthwhile for the first aircraft program to include options in the system.

Figure 6-10 Summary of challenges associated with cross-program options and current program based financial accounting.

The following section synthesizes the results presented above. More generalized lessons concerning the limitations on options due to practical considerations are presented.

6.8 LESSONS LEARNED ABOUT "COMPLEX" REAL OPTIONS IN COMPLEX SYSTEMS: THE BWB CASE STUDY

The sections above present the results for each of the interview questions that were discussed with interviewees. This section synthesizes the above results and presents the set of generalized lessons learned about "complex" real options in complex systems.

Two major lessons learned are presented below; the challenge with design and evaluation processes in enterprises, and the conflict between option design and enterprise architecture. Each are discussed in below.

6.8.1 REAL OPTION DESIGN AND EVALUATION PROCESSES

Design and evaluation techniques used to create and evaluate flexibility "in" systems were not widely embraced, even though effort has been made to create a process that is tailored to the needs and paradigms of the large commercial aviation industry. Multiple reasons were found for this, including not understanding the new valuation techniques or their benefits, skepticism on the need for new valuation techniques, and lack of support from corporate finance functions.

Two lessons learned were drawn from this discussion. First, a real options process that is tailored to a specific organization is needed; a generic real options process that does not take into account enterprise specific viewpoints and needs will not be used. Two, even with an enterprise specific process, fragmentation within the enterprise on decision making processes may still result in a real options process not be adopted by decision makers.

6.8.2 ALIGNMENT BETWEEN ENTERPRISE ARCHITECTURE AND OPTION DESIGN AND EVALUATION

A common assumption in the option literature is that options will be created to maximize enterprise value. This assumes active oversight and management across the entire enterprise and over the life-cycle of programs. As multiple interviewees stated, the enterprise architecture of large commercial aircraft producers is very program-centric, with little integration between programs; either concurrently existing or over time. One interviewee also stated that life-cycle considerations for programs were just starting to be better understood, but that this has not been the case historically. *Looking at commonality as a means of creating flexibility across families may require that some foresight into future needs is taken into account early and more centralized decision making enacted to ensure that decision decisions are made that increase enterprise value.* For example, increased commonality in cockpit design from a three person to two person crew could have created a common cockpit across the range of BCA aircraft families. Instead, most aircraft have unique layouts that increase operating, maintenance and training costs for airline customers. Because there was not a greater influence by central or functional decision makers to create capabilities in the initial program, the 757 and 767, latter programs adopting the two person forward facing cockpit had to design a unique cockpit.

The blended wing body aircraft architecture creates flexibility through the increased commonality that is created across what is now a range of multiple aircraft families, from 250 to 450 passengers, which would translate into the 787, 777 and 747 families for BCA. While the BWB has the potential for increased flexibility, design decisions must still be taken early to create the flexibility in the aircraft, as there are differences in a point optimized BWB and a BWB optimized to share commonalities with other BWB over the 250-450 range of passenger loads. These design decisions will impose penalties on the early BWB that would not exist without the need for commonality. So to create this commonality, increased decision making that optimizes over the enterprise and life-cycle are needed, instead of decision making that optimizes over the program.

The lesson learned from this discussion was that enterprise architecture and option design and evaluation must be aligned if an option is to be included in a system. Certain

options, such as cross-program derivatives, may create value but will never be purchased
or exercised if they create value in a way that is not aligned with the enterprise
architecture.

6.8.3   COMPLEX DECISION METRICS

A common assumption in the option literature is that options will be created to maximize
enterprise value. Rationality in pure enterprise value maximization is not absolute, as
evidenced by multiple examples. In the early 2000's BCA unveiled the Sonic Cruiser, a
commercial aircraft that could cruise just below the sound barrier, as the aircraft it had
decided to produce after the 777 in the 1990's. One interviewee described the internal
decision process occurring in the late 1990's and early 2000's over the path the next BCA
program would take. Describing the choice as one being debated between pursuing either
the Sonic Cruiser or the BWB, the decision process was presented as one that was
primarily political. Continuing, the interviewee described a clash in cultures between the
two proposed programs, where the Sonic Cruiser came from within BCA, while the BWB
concept originated from personnel at BCA that had arrived from the McDonnell-Douglas
acquisition. Describing the culture clash as an "us against them" mentality, the political
aspect of the decision process creates doubt that future choices could be based purely on
rational enterprise value maximization.

Creating further complications, aircraft design choices are not based solely on expected
returns for a particular program. Rather, the aircraft program and the resulting aircraft
design can play a role in larger strategic decisions, whose value is difficult to quantify.
For example, the 757 was originally conceptualized as a replacement for the 727, which
carried between 148-189 passengers. However, the eventual 757 ended up much larger,
being capable of carrying up to 243 passengers. For most airlines, this was a much larger
plane than they had originally stated was needed, and as a result 757 sales were slow,
until much later in the production run when airlines had no choice but to replace their
time expired 727's. The rationale for creating the 757 at the larger size was as part of a
larger strategy to try and destabilize the AI partnership. Prior, the British aerospace firm
British Aerospace (BAe), had left the then Airbus Consortium, but was considering
rejoining, bringing with it the expertise needed by the consortium in wing design to move
forward with its second plane, the A310. The larger design for the 757 was favored by
British Airways and Rolls Royce, both British companies. The hope was that by creating
a plane specifically tailored to the needs of British Airlines, using a Rolls Royce engine at
launch on the 757, and offering BAe the chance to become a risk sharing partner on the
757 project, enough pressure would be created to entice BAe into joining the 757
program, which would substantially delay design efforts on the A310. In this example,
the design choice made for the 757 show that value maximization on a purely competitive
basis may be too narrow a metric, that BCA was aiming to maximize long-term value by
trying to delay the competing A310 aircraft, which would increase market share for their
own planes. Without additional evaluation techniques, such as game theory, it is difficult
to capture the valuation presented by these types of decisions, which impacts the decision
process and evaluation process for designing flexibility in an aircraft.

245

The major lesson learned from this discussion is that the metrics used to evaluated programs in practice are themselves complex and changing. Politics and strategic considerations that are not easily quantifiable seem to dominate design decisions at multiple levels in an aircraft program. These complex evaluation metrics add to the challenge of designing and evaluating an appropriate real option.

A summary of the lessons learned from the BWB case study are presented in Table 6-7.

Table 6-7 Summary of lessons learned for BWB case study.

Real Option Process in Enterprises
Real option processes need to be tailored to the specific needs and viewpoints of enterprises; generic real option processes will not likely be adopted
Even tailored real options processes may not be adopted due to fragmentation in the enterprise on the view of appropriate evaluation processes
Alignment of Enterprise Architecture and Design and Evaluation of Option
An option will never be purchased or exercised if it creates value in a way that is not aligned with the enterprise architecture
Options and Enterprise Decision Metrics
Enterprise decision metrics are complex. Designing option exercise rules capable of being useful in practical considerations and still allowing the option to be evaluated is non-trivial

The following chapter introduces the ITS case study.

6.9 REFERENCES

Airbus. (2007) Product Technical Overview website,
http://www.airbus.com/en/aircraftfamilies/productcompare/

Airbus. (2006) Annual Global Market Forecast: The Future of Flying, 2006-2025,
Airbus Industries, airbus.com.

A.T. Kearney. (2003) Restructuring the Global Aerospace Industry: Shifting the Roles
of Suppliers, A.T. Kearney Consulting Company.

AWAS. (2005) A Lessor's Perspective, Presentation at 4th Annual EASA Industry
Meeting, Cologne, Germany.

Banks, H. (1998) Slow Learner, Forbes Mary 4, 1998.

Biddle, F. and J. Helyar. (1998) Behind Boeing's Woes: Clunky Assembly Line, Price
War with Airbus, Wall Street Journal, April 24, 1998, A1, A16

Boeing. (2007) Product Technical Overview website,
http://boeing.com/commercial/products.html

Boeing. (2006) Current Market Outlook Report, Boeing Commercial Aircraft Company,
boeing.com.

Collins, J. and J. Porras. (2004) Built to Last, Harper Collins, New York.

Copeland, T. and v. Antikarov. (2001) Real Options: A Practitioner's Guide, Texere,
New York.

Datar, v. and S. Mathews. (2004) European Real Options: An Intuitive Algorithm for
the Black-Scholes Formula, Journal of Applied Finance, Spring/Summer 2004.

Ferreri, D. (2003) Marketing and Management in the High-Technology Sector:
Strategies and Tactics in the Commercial Airplane Industry, Praeger, Connecticut.

Graham, B. and P. Ahmed. (2000) Buyer-Supplier Management in the Aerospace Value
Chain, Integrated Manufacturing Systems, v. 11, no. 7.

Greenwald, J. (1998) Is Boeing out of its Spin?, Time Magazine, July 13, 1998.

Hanley, M. (2001) Reality Bites, CFO.com, July/August 2001.

Harrigan, F. (2006) Integrating Theories of Boundary Choice: A Case from the Global Aviation industry, International Conference on Coordination and Cooperation across Organizational Boundaries, Milan, Italy, April 20-21.

Hartley, R. (2004) Marketing Mistakes and Successes, 9th ed., Wiley, New York.

Krugman, P. (1986) Strategic Trade Policy and the New International Economics, MIT Press, Boston.

Laudon, R. (2004) Can Boeing Fly High Again? Case Study, University of Maryland.

Lawrence, P. and D. Thornton. (2005) Deep Stall: The Turbulent Story of Boeing Commercial Airplanes, Ashgate, New York.

Liebeck, R. (2003) Blended Wing Body Design Challenges, AIAA/ICAS International Air and Space Symposium and Exposition, Ohio.

Mecham, M. (2005) Evolution and Revolution, Aviation Week and Space Technology, March 27, 2005.

Miller, B. (2005) A Generalized Real Options Methodology for Evaluating Investments Under Uncertainty with Application to Air Transportation, MIT Doctoral Dissertation, Boston.

Miller, B. and J. Clarke. (2004) Application of Real Options to Evaluate the Development Process of New Aircraft Models, 4th AIAA ATIO Forum, Illinois.

Pilling, M. (2005) On a Roll, New Aircraft, April.

Pritchard, D. and A. MacPherson. (2004) Industrial Subsidies and the Politics of World Trade: The Case of the Boeing 7e7, The Industrial Geographer, v. 1 No. 2.

Stevens, T. (2000) Picking the Winners, IndustryWeek.com, March 6, 2000.

Thorton, D. (1995) Airbus Industrie: The politics of an International Industrial Collaboration, St. Martin's Press, New York.

Wallace, J. (2005) With Airbus Sputtering, Boeing Talks of New Jet, Seattlepi.com, April 19, 2005.

Wikipedia. (2007) A350 History, http://en.wikipedia.org/wiki/Airbus_A350, accessed on February 2007.

Willcox, K. and Wakayama, S. (2003) Simultaneous Optimization of a Multiple-Aircraft Family, Journal of Aircraft v. 40 n. 4.

7 FLEXIBILITY IN HOUSTON GROUND TRANSPORTATION SYSTEM USING ITS

This chapter presents an introduction to the ITS (Intelligent Transportation Systems) in managed lanes option case study. The ITS in managed lanes option is the second "complex" real option in complex systems that is examined in this research, the first being the Blended Wing Body (BWB) aircraft discussed in the previous three chapters. The purpose of the ITS case study is to provide a platform to test the Life-Cycle Flexibility (LCF) Framework and demonstrate the concept of Dual Value Design (DVD). The relationship of the two case studies is shown in Figure 7-1.

249

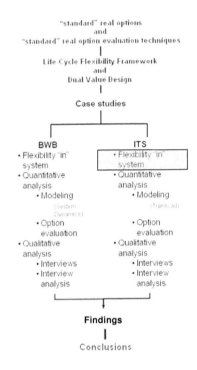

"standard" real options
and
"standard" real option evaluation techniques

Life-Cycle Flexibility Framework
and
Dual Value Design

Case studies

BWB
• Flexibility "in"
  system
• Quantitative
  analysis
  • Modeling
    [System
    Dynamics]
  • Option
    evaluation
• Qualitative
  analysis
  • Interviews
  • Interview
    analysis

ITS
• Flexibility "in"
  system
• Quantitative
  analysis
  • Modeling
    [Transcad]
  • Option
    evaluation
• Qualitative
  analysis
  • Interviews
  • Interview
    analysis

Findings

Conclusions

Figure 7-1 Case study analysis with highlighted box showing current stage of analysis.

The two case studies looked at in this research, ITS and the blended wing body (BWB) aircraft, were chosen to allow contrast between case studies. While the two case studies both involve "complex" real options in complex systems, the technologies, technical architectures and enterprise architectures for each case study is different. For the ITS case study flexibility is created with a technology, ITS. For the BWB case study flexibility is created with a technical architecture, the use of blending the wing and the body of the aircraft together. For the ITS case study an extended enterprise architecture is of interest, consisting of multiple public and private enterprises. Specifically, the extended enterprise architecture of interest is for the Houston, Texas metropolitan region. For the BWB case study the primary enterprise of interest is a single private enterprise, primarily an aircraft manufacturer. These differences are summarized in Figure 7-2. The differences between case study technologies, technical architectures and enterprise architectures allows the LCF Flexibility concept to be tested on very different systems to help prevent the possibility that a case study was chosen to generate pre-defined outcomes.

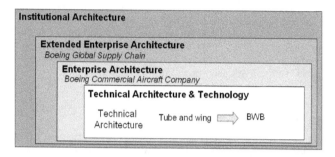

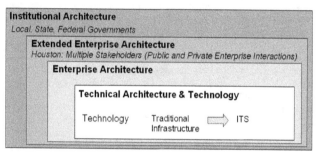

Figure 7-2 Characteristics of case studies on the dimensions of: technical architecture and technology, enterprise architecture, extended enterprise architecture and institutional architecture.

This chapter is the first of three chapters that discuss the ITS case study. This chapter presents the background on transportation systems and ITS capabilities and ends with the presentation of the three options that will be analyzed in the following chapter. Chapter 8 provides the quantitative analysis of the options to that a better understanding of the costs and benefits associated with ITS in managed lane options can be understood. Finally, Chapter 9 provides a qualitative analysis of ITS in managed lane options, to better understand the challenges associated with using "complex" real options in a complex system. In Chapter 9, to better understand these challenges, stakeholders involved in an actual regional transportation system were contacted, to provide a practical perspective to the research. For the ITS case study, the region centered on Houston, Texas was selected for study.

The content of this chapter is as follows. At the start, the concept of regional architecture as an organizing framework for regional transportation systems is presented. ITS technologies are then introduced, with an overview of costs and benefits associated with ITS as well as the various types of ITS capabilities. A more in-depth look at technologies, architectures and pricing strategies are then examined for several different managed lane concepts that are enabled by ITS. The types of managed lanes that are examined are: High Occupancy Toll (HOT) lanes, Bus Rapid Transit (BRT) lanes and Truck Only Toll (TOT) lanes. Three ITS in managed lane options are then introduced and discussed. Finally, the concept of DVD is applied to the ITS in managed lane option, where inherent and flexibility values are identified.

7.1   REGIONAL ARCHITECTURE DESCRIPTION

A regional architecture can be described as a framework for deploying a transportation system in a particular region (Chowdhury 2003). The region is typically composed of several jurisdictions and stakeholders that must plan and operate the transportation system together, with various levels of coordination necessary. The architecture specifies how the different aspects of the technical system will interact with one another to address the regional transportation issues. The architecture provides a basic framework to plan, design, deploy and integrate the systems in the region to accomplish specific objectives. This idea of regional architecture focuses mainly on the physical system regional architecture. This notion of architecture can be expanded to also encompass the enterprise level (organizational structure, information flows, business plans, etc.) architectures and the institutional level (laws, mandates, relationships/jurisdictions between public and private roles, etc.) architectures. Considering the physical system, enterprise architecture and institutional architecture in tandem facilities two objectives. First, it allows the regional architecture to address both the socio-technical aspects of the transportation system. Second, it provides a tool that can be used by the various applicable organizations to coordinate and interface with one another during the planning and operations of the transportation system.

7.1.1   ASPECTS OF ARCHITECTURE

The regional architecture is composed of the physical architecture, information architecture, enterprise / institutional level interfaces, and interfaces with users.

- **Physical architecture** – The physical architecture is the most visible aspect of the regional architecture that is envisioned. The physical architecture encompasses all aspects of the physical system. This includes the choice of technologies (types of ITS technologies, types of traditional infrastructures, types of rolling stock), the interfaces between the technologies, and the interfaces between the physical system and the larger social system and larger environment. Historically, traditional infrastructure has dominated the portfolio of design decisions used to address problems in the transportation system – "building our way out of congestion", for instance. ITS technologies, relatively new, present another alternative to building new traditional infrastructure in some cases and in many cases can be added to existing or new traditional infrastructure to better manage the investment.

- **Information architecture** – The information architecture denotes how the information that is gathered from the transportation system is used within the physical architecture, flows between the physical architecture to the enterprise / institutional level organizations and stakeholders, and flows to the transportation system users (travelers, commercial vehicles, emergency vehicles, etc.). Information flows and information architectures are especially relevant with the introduction of ITS technologies into the transportation system and can be used to greatly enhance efficiency and effectiveness, as well as introduce entirely new capabilities. With ITS, additional information architectures can be constructed entirely between enterprise level organizations to better share information, coordinate operations and manage the transportation system. The information architecture can also be used to gather increased information, which aids in the understanding of how the transportation system is being used and can facilitate improved planning and system management.
- **Enterprise / institutional level interfaces** – The various organizations at the enterprise and institutional levels interface in many ways with the physical and information architecture. Additionally, there are many interfaces between enterprises. With the introduction of ITS capabilities, these enterprise and institutional architecture interfaces will need to become more explicit (with increased needs such as technology and information standardization) and will likely become stronger (with increased opportunities and requirements for interacting across a larger range of issues).
- **Interface with users** – The architectural interfaces with the users are of great importance to the design and operation of a transportation system that meets the needs of the users. Users can include private travelers, commercial operators, emergency vehicles, etc. Additionally, with the advent of ITS capabilities, the transportation system users can include a whole new range of users. For example, telecommuters that do not use the physical transportation architecture can be important to consider, as well as non-traditional transportation private firms that offer services to travelers, such as information or related services.

7.1.2 CHANGES TO REGIONAL ARCHITECTURE PROCESS WITH THE INCLUSION OF ITS

ITS capabilities added into the architecture change the technologies, organizational focus, skills and opportunities that are present in the regional architecture.

- **Technologies** – The shift from traditional infrastructure to ITS technologies is a large change. Planning processes, operations, contractor familiarity, and new opportunities and relationships between organizations and between users and the transportation architecture can change dramatically.
- **Organizational Focus** – With traditional infrastructure, the organizational focus has been on building and maintenance. With ITS the focus changes to operations and management. This will require a shift in how funding is obtained also.

- **Skill Sets** – With traditional infrastructure, organizations can specialize in planning and building. ITS adds the additional aspects of operation management to this focus.
- **Opportunities** – ITS adds additional opportunities for private enterprise to become involved in the transportation system. These private enterprises can include transportation related and non-transportation related firms.

Historically, ground transportation networks have been conceived and implemented on a project-by-project basis, with even the federal Interstate system being constructed in small project sized pieces. The factors that have lead to this are many and include funding guidelines that de-emphasize overall system planning, procurement practices of minimizing project costs rather than system costs, focus on individual modes and low interaction between projects (Parson 2000). There is an increased need for considering ITS as part of a regional transportation architecture. This is because of (Bunch 2000, Parsons 2000, Chowdhury and Sadek 2003):

- technical sub-system compatibility,
- regional scale deployment of capabilities,
- shift in emphasis to increased operations management and operations / infrastructure integration over just infrastructure construction,
- increased need for cooperation between public agencies,
- increased opportunities for involvement of private industry in deployment, operations and ownership

The following section provides a discussion on the uses, benefits and costs associated with ITS capabilities.

7.2 ITS Technologies

ITS (Intelligent Transportation System) technologies add a new dimension to transportation systems. This section provides a brief description of ITS in general, presents an overview of standard ITS types and uses and discusses some benefits and drawbacks to using ITS.

7.2.1 DESCRIPTION OF ITS

ITS technologies create several new opportunities for architecting transportation systems. First, ITS technologies make use of a blend of information and communication technologies, computers, software, and modeling tools. These technologies allow transportation system operations to be actively managed in a way not previously possible. Second, the use of these various technologies enables the collection, evaluation and sharing of unprecedented amounts of information concerning the transportation system usage and status. Third, ITS capabilities often entail significantly lower capital outlays than comparable improvements in traditional infrastructure. The new opportunities that ITS capabilities create, coupled with their relatively low-cost, will permit transportation systems and enterprises to be architected in very different ways in the future.

7.2.2 STANDARD ITS TECHNOLOGIES AND USES

ITS technologies can be used in almost all aspects of the transportation system and can even aid in the transportation system planning process. Table 7-1 presents the common ITS bundles that are considered, along with the user services that these bundles provide. As can be seen from this table, ITS can be used in a variety of applications, including: improved travel/traffic management capabilities for private autos, improved public transit operation management, enabling new pricing schemes for tolling, improved commercial vehicle operations, and improved emergency vehicle management.

ITS capabilities can be used to not only improve the transportation system along traditional metrics (such as congestion relief or safety), but can offer improvements in directions that are not the primary focus of traditional infrastructure improvements (such as operations or increased information collection).

Table 7-1 Traditional set of ITS bundles and user services. Taken directly from FHWA [FHWA 1995].

Bundle	User Services
Travel and Traffic Management	• Pre-trip Travel Information • En Route Driver Information • Route Guidance • Ride Matching and Reservation • Traveler Services Information • Traffic Control • Incident Management • Travel Demand Management • Emissions Testing and Mitigation • Highway – Rail Intersection
Public Transportation Operations	• Public Transportation Management • En Route Transit Information • Personalized Public Transit • Public Travel Security
Electronic Payment	• Electronic Payment Services
Commercial Vehicle Operations	• Commercial Vehicle Electronic Clearance • Automatic Roadside Safety Inspection • Onboard Safety Monitoring • Commercial Vehicle Admin. Processes • Hazardous Material Incident Response

255

	• Commercial Fleet Management
Emergency Management	• Emergency Notification and Personal Security
	• Emergency Vehicle Management
Advanced Vehicle Safety Systems	• Longitudinal Collision Avoidance
	• Lateral Collision Avoidance
	• Intersections Collision Avoidance
	• Vision Enhancement for Crash Avoidance
	• Safety Readiness
	• Pre-crash Restraint Deployment
	• Automated Vehicle Operation
Information Management	• Archived Data Function
Maintenance and Construction Management	• Maintenance and Construction Operations

7.2.3 BENEFITS AND DRAWBACK TO ITS

The use of ITS offers several benefits compared with only using traditional infrastructure investments. These benefits include;

- **increased level of service** – ITS capabilities offer the means of improving traveler level of service in ways not possible with traditional infrastructure improvements. These increased level of service improvements can include such things as the provision of additional information to travelers so that they can better manage their travel time and schedule and increased options for safety.
- **improved operations** – ITS allows the existing infrastructure to be managed. Previously, infrastructure was built and was not actively managed to the extent possible with ITS. ITS capabilities can improved operations through: active management of highways, improved coordination between inter- and intra- mode connections (rail and buses, or rail to rail connections), and improved coordination of commercial vehicle fleets.
- **increased amount of information collected** – ITS capabilities allow for additional information to be collected on the operation of the transportation system. This can be used in real time to improve operations (such as improved emergency vehicle routing to speed accident removals) or longer term (to increase information collection on long-term trends and transportation system usage trends to improve future planning and decision making)
- **lower capital costs** – ITS capabilities often come with a lower price tag than traditional transportation infrastructure investments, often an order of magnitude lower. ITS can be used to delay expensive traditional infrastructure improvements.
- **ease of upgradeability** – ITS capabilities consist of IT technologies, computers and software. Upgrades through software applications can be made easier and cheaper than traditional infrastructure upgrades.

- **increased opportunities for private investment** – ITS capabilities offer new avenues for private investment monies to be brought into the transportation system. These additional investments can increase the rate of improvement of the transportation system or enable new improvements that were previously impossible just using limited public funds.

While ITS capabilities have several benefits associated with them, there are also several drawback. These include:

- **new standard operating procedures for transportation agencies** – The use of ITS will require a major shift in how transportation agencies design and manage transportation systems. Traditionally, transportation agencies have been involved in building and maintenance of infrastructure. ITS capabilities require a greater emphasis on operations.
- **need for increased coordination between organizations** – Previously, transportation agencies could easily operate almost independently of one another. Agencies were fragmented along geographical, functional and political jurisdiction lines. Effective use of ITS will require that the technologies used by different organizations be compatible, which will require greater coordination in the planning and operation stages.
- **shift of funds needed to different part of life-cycle** – Traditional infrastructure investments required funds at the beginning of the life-cycle and then only modest funds later in the life-cycle. ITS by contrast will require more modest funds for construction, but will require more funding for operations. Securing continual funding from government sources is much more difficult than securing funding a single time for construction.
- **resistance from entrenched interests** – ITS capabilities that replace traditional infrastructure investments will encounter resistance from stakeholders that already have vested interests in maintaining the status quo. For example, construction companies have little incentive to embrace ITS capabilities that will reduce the need for traditional infrastructure and hence will reduce their business.

The following section discusses ITS capabilities on managed lanes in more detail.

7.3 MANAGED LANES

One set of ITS capabilities that are currently the focus of much research interest is managed lanes. As defined by Texas Department of Transportation, a managed lane is any lane that:

> *Increases freeway efficiency by packaging various operational and designations into the facility. Lane management operation may be adjusted at any time to better match regional goals.* (TxDOT 2000)

Essentially, a managed lane differs from a general purpose lane in that its operations are actively managed, possibly in a dynamic manner over time. Typically, managed lanes run parallel to general purpose lanes, but are separated from the rest of the roadway in some manner, either physically with concrete barriers or plastic pylons, with a painted designation, increased spacing or some combination. This separation, along with proper signage, rules and enforcement, allows roadway traffic to be segregated between the general purpose and managed lanes. The vehicles allowed onto the managed lane may vary with the objectives set out for the managed lane, but typically are some combination of the following:

- **High Occupancy Vehicles (HOV)** – travel is restricted to vehicles with multiple travelers, where the minimum number of travelers vary by local choice. HOV 2+ and HOV 3+, requiring at least two or three travelers, respectively, are typical. Historically, HOV lanes have accounted for by far the majority of managed lane miles, though the managed lane types discussed next are slowly gaining in popularity, enabled by newer ITS capabilities.
- **High Occupancy Toll (HOT) lanes** – similar to HOV lanes, but allows automobiles that would not normally be eligible to use the lane access after paying a toll. For example, in an HOV 3+ lane, cars with one or two passengers could not use the lane. With an HOT lane, depending on the strategy, the one and two passenger autos could have access to the lane by paying a toll. The automobiles eligible for access and the fee structure of the tolls vary by HOT lane, but the primary purpose is to keep the lane uncongested at all times.
- **Bus Rapid Transit (BRT) lane** - travel is restricted to public transit vehicles, allowing less congested and lower travel times for high density public transit. BRT has gained in popularity because of the ability to provide a continuum of service, from upgraded local bus to rail like service, often at costs lower than light rail (Hess et al. 2005). Often, BRT lanes are combined with HOV or HOT lanes, allowing both public transit and high occupancy vehicles simultaneous access to the lane. This combination takes advantage of several synergies, such as; increase in effectiveness by providing travelers with additional travel choices, use of road pricing tolls to cross fund transit investments such as stations, parking facilities and rolling stock, and increase in political support due to affordable toll rates and viable travel alternatives (DeCorla-Souza and Barker 2005).
- **Truck Only Toll (TOT) lanes** – travel is restricted to large commercial vehicles after paying a toll. The purpose is both to allow uncongested movement for high value commercial vehicles and to improve the safety of the general purpose lanes by segregating large truck and automobile traffic. While the amount of truck traffic is usually smaller in total numbers of vehicles, the economic impact is often greater for reduced truck travel times, as time savings for truck are assumed to be used for productive purposes while personal travel is split between work and leisure related activities (Haning and McFarland 1963, Kawamura 2000). Often, TOT and BRT lanes are combined to allow simultaneous truck and bus traffic to the lane.

Other managed lane concepts with different strategies for selecting which vehicles gain access have been proposed. Some of these other managed lane concepts include: lanes for Inherently Low Emitting Vehicles (ILEV), taxis, shuttles, emergency vehicles, motorcycles (Kuhn 2004).

HOV lanes were some of the first types of managed lanes to be deployed. HOV lanes work by restricting access to multi-passenger vehicles. Originally vehicles eligible for access was limited to commuter vans and buses. Later, access was expanded to include multi-passenger vehicle access. Due to low utilization of many HOV facilities, passenger limits have been reduced on many HOV lanes to allow vehicles with 2 or more travelers (2+) to use the lane, down from 3 or 4 travelers per vehicle (3+ and 4+). However, in some cases, HOV lane restrictions have been tightened, from 2+ passengers to 3+ passengers. This has occurred because of the high volume of 2+ passenger usage (Goodin 2005).

In general, HOV lanes reduce travel time for a small set of travelers. As a total share of travelers, multi-passenger vehicles are a percentage of mode share; a 16% decrease from 1990 to 2000 (Poole and Orski 2003). The need to utilize unused capacity available on many HOV facilities is a driving motivator behind the HOT, BRT and TOT managed lane concepts.

Below is an examination of the different objectives and attributes of managed lanes.

7.3.1 LANE OBJECTIVES
The HOV, HOT, BRT and TOT lane concepts all share some common goals such as reducing congestion, improving travel reliability and creating new sources of funding. Some considerations on making the operational strategy of the lane dynamic over time have also been considered.

7.3.1.1 Reducing Congestion
Congestion is reduced for travelers using the managed lane (as they get access to a congestion free lane) and for users of the general purpose lanes.

Improved travel conditions for managed lane users are achieved by separating the managed lane user out from the remainder of traffic and proving a facility that is kept congestion free.

Congestion relief on general purpose lanes is typically obtained in two ways. First, some subset of road users are removed from the GP lanes and re-routed onto the managed lanes. In all of the above cases except for TOT, these lanes typically emphasize the diverting of vehicles with higher number of passengers. This increases traveler throughput on the overall system. In the HOT lane tolling concept, any additional capacity on the HOT lane not used by high occupancy vehicles is then sold to low occupancy vehicles, such as single passenger vehicles. The vehicles that pay the toll for access to the HOT lane are removed from the general purpose lane flow, freeing up capacity.

While the absolute number of vehicles removed from the GP lanes will vary with the number of managed lanes available and the operational strategy selected, even the removal of a small number of vehicles can greatly enhance traffic volumes on the GP lanes. This is because traffic conditions on roadways have been shown to have a step, non-linear drop-off in flow if the number of vehicles attempting to use the road pass a certain critical value. Making matters worse, traffic flow improvements can take hours to be restored (Chen and Varaiya 2002). It has been observed that even the removal of a few vehicles can vastly improve traffic conditions. Examples include observed traffic flows in Massachusetts during Jewish holidays and California during state employee holidays (Wachs 2003).

The other means of relieving congestion is through a change in driver behavior. By the provision of lanes reserved for high occupancy vehicles, a change in travel behavior to favor these travel patterns is encouraged.

7.3.1.2 Travel reliability

In addition to improved traffic flows, travel reliability is another goal of the system. Increases in travel reliability are desirable even if average travel time remains unchanged, as it reduces planning margins travelers must engage in to ensure timely arrival at a destination. The increase in travel reliability has been found to be a main reason why people choose to travel on HOT lanes, with the combination of travel time reductions and reliability accounting for up to 66% of a service quality differential compared to travel on GP lanes (Brownstone and Small 2005). However, quantifying the value of reliability is not done by transportation planners or transportation modeling packages, making it difficult to fully quantify the benefits associated with managed lanes (Endsor 2006).

7.3.1.3 New Funding Mechanisms

A common goal for HOT and TOT lanes is to increase the number of funding alternatives available for the deployment and operation of these types of managed lanes. Typically, new capacity construction must compete with other funding priorities. This competition for funds can increase the time needed to secure funding, which then increases the time until the facility is deployed (Sorenson and Taylor 2005, TTI 2002).

Tolls assessed on the managed lanes can be used to help fund the construction of new lanes or the conversion of existing HOV lanes to HOT lanes. It has been estimated that the tolls collected from a network of such lanes in most major U.S. cities could fund the majority of costs associated with construction, conversion and operations of a regional managed lane network (Poole and Orski 2003). Additionally, it has been advocated that the tolls collected could also be used to expand or provide public transit, like BRT, simultaneously on the managed lanes, where the funds could be used for new stations, park and ride facilities and rolling stock (Poole and Orski 2003, DeCorla-Souza and

Marker 2005). This type of cross funding, from private autos to public transit, also helps meet equity concerns that tolled lanes can pose (Poole and Orski 2003, Decorla-Souza 2004).

While the objectives described above are the most common associated with managed lanes, other objectives are possible. These could include: charging users for marginal social cost of transportation facility use, charging external transportation system users access to regional facilities, streamlining the tolling process, reducing road wear, improving the environment and reducing both accident occurrence and fatality rates by separating autos and heavy trucks (Sorenson and Taylor 2005, Middleton and Venglar 2006).

7.3.1.4 Dynamic Operating Strategies

A benefit of managed lanes relative to GP lanes is the ability to change operating conditions over time, both over the short- and long-term. In the short-term, access rules can be changed relative to a variety of conditions. A common condition is more stringent access rules during peak hour usage, while increased access is granted on off-peak travel hours. Over the long-term, access rules can be modified as macro trends change or emerge. For example, if the excess capacity being sold on a HOT lane diminishes over time due to a growth in high occupancy vehicles, SOV access can be either tolled at a higher rate or eliminated completely.

The next section discusses the attributes of managed lanes.

7.3.2 ATTRIBUTES OF MANAGED LANES

The following section will describe different attributes necessary for managed lane facilities, including pricing strategies, physical infrastructure and ITS equipment.

7.3.2.1 Pricing Strategies

The tolling scheme implemented can be constructed to accomplish a number of objectives. Typically, the most common objective is to toll at a rate that maintains a congestion free lane. This can be done with a variety of methods, such as static pricing, variable pricing or congestion pricing.

As the name suggests, static pricing does not change over time. While it is the easiest pricing strategy to implement, it offers the crudest ability to control traffic levels on the managed lane. Dynamic, or congestion, pricing is the opposite of static pricing in that toll rates are continuously updated based on current traffic conditions so that traffic is always free-flowing. Variable pricing falls between static and congestion pricing. While prices may change, they do so less often than in congestion pricing. Time of day pricing is a typical example of variable pricing, where prices are higher during peak hours and are then reduced or eliminated during off-peak hours. During these hours, the pricing is static.

7.3.2.2 Physical Infrastructure

At a minimum, the physical lane and some means of restricting access to the lane is required for a managed lane facility.

The physical infrastructure of managed lanes typically consists of one or more lanes that run adjacent to a larger number of general purpose lanes. Typically, managed lanes are first introduced through the conversion of existing HOV lanes. The addition of ITS to the HOV lanes enables new operating strategies for managing the lanes.

Managed lanes are typically at grade and are limited access lanes to the far right (inside lane). However, exceptions exist where the managed lane is elevated or runs in a parallel but separate location to the GP lanes. Access to the lanes is limited in some manner, either through physical barriers, such as concrete or plastic pylons, or painted markings showing the separation between the managed and GP lanes, as shown in Figure 7-3, Figure 7-4, and Figure 7-5.

Figure 7-3 Concrete barrier separated managed lane. Figure from www.FHWA.gov

Figure 7-4 Plastic pylon separated managed lane. Figure from www.tfhrc.gov

Figure 7-5 Managed lane separate by paint stripe. Figure from www.its.dot.gov

7.3.2.3 ITS Equipment

To enable a HOT, BRT or TOT lane, some set of ITS capabilities are needed. In the past, access, enforcement and tolling technologies, have either been unavailable, cumbersome or highly dependant on manned applications. For example, tolls have been collected either with manned toll booths or automated coin baskets. Manned toll booths can process up to 450 vehicles per hour per lane and coin baskets can process up to 600 vehicles an hour per lane (NCHRP 1993). The use of ITS transponders in toll lanes has achieved vehicle processing rates as high as 1200 vehicles per lane per hour in Miami and new open toll road concepts, similar to HOT lanes, are expected to process up to 2200 vehicles per lane per hour (MDX 2006).

There are many ITS technologies related to managed lanes. Typically, managed lanes can only be effective when these technologies are bundled together. For example, in the London congestion pricing system, vehicles are charged a toll when passing through the cordon around the central business district. This is done by cameras mounted on the roadside that capture an image of the license plate number of each vehicle passing through the cordon. This image is processed using automatic number recognition software and checked against a database of user tolls paid. In this case, the system requires both the camera and the number recognition software; either alone can not be used to enable system management.

Below is a description of several typical ITS technology bundles that could be used to create managed lane facilities. The bundles presented are those used for HOT, BRT and TOT lanes. Not emphasized in this discussion are supporting technologies, such as traveler information systems or enforcement systems, though some are mentioned briefly where applicable.

7.3.2.3.1 *HOT Lanes*

For a HOT lane, several types of ITS capabilities can be used to create the desired operational and pricing strategy. In general, dedicated short range communication (DSRC) systems, wide-range communication systems and video based systems have been used in the past. DSRC and wide-range systems are shown in Figure 7-6 and a video based system is shown in Figure 7-7.

As both figures show, several pieces of ITS equipment are necessary to enable a HOT lane. These include equipment in the vehicle, roadside equipment and enforcement equipment. A centralized traffic control center may also be needed, depending on how the ITS capabilities are designed.

In general, the DSRC and wide-range communication technologies are very similar, differing primarily in the specific pieces of equipment and some of the specific performance characteristics between them. Both DSRC and wide-range communication systems require equipment in the auto, such as some type of transponder or On-Board Unit (OBU), which is essentially a simple computer. The principal of both systems is that the vehicles movements can be tracked by signals sent from the vehicle based equipment to a network of sensors. In DSRC systems the communication range is short and the sensors must be placed roadside. For wide-range communication systems the communication range is longer and can either be ground based, such as a series of cell phone-like towers or even GPS satellites.

Vehicles on the HOT lane are tracked via the wireless communication interface between the vehicle based sensor and the network of sensors. For the basic tolling schemes of static, variable and dynamic tolls, the vehicle transponder is interrogated at each tolling station. For more sophisticated tolling schemes, such as distance-based tolling, the vehicle is tracked along the entire length of the HOT lane and the final toll that is charged is a function of the distance traveled. Both DSRC and wide-area communication technologies can enable the basic tolling schemes. However, wide-area communication systems are typically needed to enable the more sophisticated tolling schemes. This is

264

because the network of sensors can track the vehicle over a much longer range than can the DSRC sensors. This enables many fewer sensors needed for wide-range communication based systems.

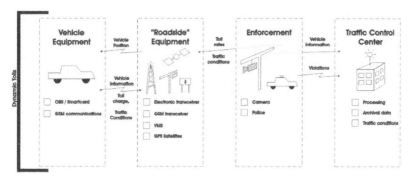

Figure 7-6 Needed ITS equipment for a HOT lane utilizing DSRC or wide-range communication equipment.

A set of equipment necessary for HOT lanes employing video equipment to charge tolls is shown in Figure 7-7. For HOT lanes utilizing video systems, an image of the vehicle is captured at certain points on the HOT lane. The image of the vehicle, typically the license plate, is sent to a facility for image recognition so the license plate number can be read and a toll accessed. The primary difference between these systems, aside from the obvious differences in technologies, is that with a video based system no vehicle based equipment is necessary. However, the video based system is the most limited of the three.

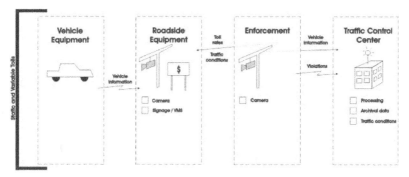

Figure 7-7 Needed ITS equipment for a HOT lane utilizing video-based equipment.

265

7.3.2.3.2 *BRT lanes*

Strictly speaking, BRT lanes do not need ITS capabilities. Instead, a restricted access lane is all that is necessary. However, ITS capabilities can be used to improve the efficiency and effectiveness of the BRT lane.

In general, BRT lanes make use of either DSRC or wide-range communication systems. The purpose of the systems is different than for HOT lanes. While for HOT lanes the purpose is to access tolls, for BRT lanes the purpose is to track the position to allow for better management of the bus fleet and improved information to passengers. While the information is used in different manners between HOT and BRT lanes, the way in which the information is collected is the same.

Another difference between BRT lanes and HOT lanes is the lack of need for enforcement. However, in practice enforcement will likely be needed as BRT lanes may not be dedicated and may be shared with autos, such as a BRT / HOT lane.

The needed ITS equipment for a BRT lane is shown in Figure 7-8.

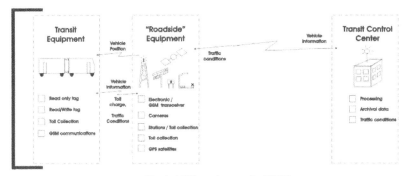

Figure 7-8 Needed ITS equipment for BRT lane.

7.3.2.3.3 *TOT Lane*

TOT lanes use a combination of the functionality of the HOT and TOT lanes. TOT lanes combine the tolling of a HOT lane along with the information for fleet planning purposes of a BRT lane. The equipment needed for TOT lanes are similar to that needed for HOT and BRT lanes.

Typically, the equipment in the truck is more sophisticated and tracks additional pieces of information than that found on autos or buses. On the truck, the inclusion of additional technologies, such as tachographs, which can be used to sense vehicle speed, times, distance traveled, etc. are useful to collect increased amounts of data concerning vehicle

266

operating conditions. Additional roadside sensors, such as weight sensors, can also be used to collect current vehicle operating conditions as well.

Related to the equipment needed for tolling on a TOT managed lane is equipment that is of interest to the commercial vehicle operator. Equipment that can sense in real time vehicle operating conditions, such as cargo temperature, improved vehicle tracking and cargo logistics are all of interest. Much of this equipment can have dual benefits. For example, logistic equipment can help the commercial operator improve supply chain efficiency while also increase cargo monitoring, which could have potential security benefits.

Needed ITS equipment for TOT lanes are shown in Figure 7-9.

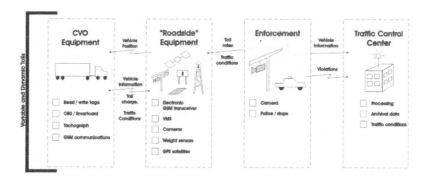

Figure 7-9 Needed ITS equipment for TOT lanes.

The following section discusses regional congestion pricing.

7.4   REGIONAL CONGESTION PRICING

Related to the concept of managed lanes is that of regional congestion pricing. While managed lanes apply toll schemes to a subset of all lanes on a particular facility, regional congestion pricing applies a tolling scheme to all lanes on a facility or in an entire metropolitan area. The purpose of regional congestion pricing also differs somewhat from managed lanes. While a prime objective of managed lanes, such as HOT lanes, is to increase the effective capacity of a lane by implementing a toll scheme to keep traffic at free flow conditions at all times, the objective of regional congestion pricing is to reduce travel demand during peak periods, at least for single occupancy vehicles. By tolling all lanes on a facility or in a region, congestion pricing systems have the objective of reducing demand by increasing the costs associated with traveling, especially during peak hours.

267

Congestion pricing systems utilize similar technologies to those described above in the managed lane section. The major difference is the scope of deployment for the technologies involved and the pricing schemes possible. The scope of deployment covers the entire area where the congestion pricing system is to be deployed, leaving either no non-tolled routes available or forcing non-tolled travel onto secondary routes. The schemes possible for regional congestion pricing fall into three categories; facility pricing, cordon pricing and area pricing.

Facility pricing – Facility pricing is an expansion of the HOT lane concept presented above, but where all lanes on a facility are priced. The available ITS equipments are similar to the ones previously presented. The lanes that are priced may be all highway lanes along a certain route or all lanes along a certain route, including local roads.

Cordon pricing – Cordon pricing typically creates concentric rings around a congested area, typically a central business district (CBD). Vehicle crossing the cordon are charged a toll. The actual tolls levied are a function of the particular system, but can vary with travel direction, number of times the cordon is crossed, time of day, day of travel, vehicle types, residency status, etc. Performance of the pricing scheme is critically dependant on the location chosen for the cordon and the toll imposed (Sumalee et al 2005). Cordon tolls have been used in London and Singapore. The London based congestion pricing system utilizes video cameras and automated number plate recognition software, while the Singapore congestion pricing system utilizes on-board units and smart cards installed in vehicles and a series of electronic transceivers mounted on overhead gantries that interrogate the OBUs through dedicated short-range communication technologies.

Compared to area pricing, described next, cordon pricing has several advantages, including the transparency of the toll scheme, ease of implementation and proven technologies. However, several disadvantages also exist, including; difficulty in changing location of cordon over time, inefficient tolling from charging vehicles same rate regardless of distance traveled, and potential increase in congestion just outside of cordoned area (Safirova et al 2005). Typically, cordon pricing has been used outside of the US, while facility pricing is more common in the US (Safirova et al 2005).

Area pricing – Area pricing tolls travelers for travel within a certain area. An example of this is distance based pricing. With this toll scheme, vehicles are charged based on the distance traveled, with toll rates dependant on the area of travel (i.e. CBD more expensive than rural travel), time of day, etc. Other factors can also be added to the toll scheme, such as vehicle type, vehicle weight, emissions, etc. An example of an area based pricing scheme is a commercial pricing scheme deployed in Switzerland, the Switzerland Heavy Vehicle Fee System, that accesses tolls on all commercial vehicles over 3.5 tons, based on distance traveled and vehicle emissions. The Swiss system utilizes a combination of OBUs, GPS receivers, DSRC interfaces and driver declarations of data for toll purposes. Also, Germany has experimented with GPS based distance tolling for heavy commercial vehicles over 12 tons with mixed results (Porter et al. 2004). Typically, area based pricing requires the use of GPS and GSM technologies, as a

DSRC based system would require a large investment in transceiver sensors if the area was larger than a modest size. .

A wide range of other congestion pricing schemes have also been forwarded, such as; point pricing, zone pricing, parking charges, time spent in area, and a combination of time and distance traveled (Gomez-Ibanez and Small 2004).

The following section introduces the concept of ITS capabilities having the potential to provide flexibility.

7.5 FLEXIBILTY IN ITS

ITS capabilities can also be used to help increase the transportation system's ability to cope with uncertainty. A proposed way of doing this is through the creation of a concept of ITS as a real option.

ITS capabilities can be deployed in such a manner that they introduce flexibility in a transportation system. There are multiple ways in which ITS capabilities can be used as real options. It is straightforward to identify different ITS capabilities that match with each of the six basic types of real options. Examples of these are presented in Table 7-2.

Table 7-2 Examples of ITS real options.

Option Type	ITS Example
Postpone/Defer/Wait	The use of ITS capabilities to defer infrastructure investments until additional information is gathered on future transportation system conditions (Leviäkangas, 1999, 2002).
Abandon	End of service for most types of ITS capabilities is possible and is easier to accomplish than with fixed infrastructure. For example, ending service to customers is simple, compared with removing infrastructure.
Expand / Contract	Variable Message Signs can be used to expand the types of information available to travelers or Electronic Toll Collection technologies can have their use expanded upon, first as dedicated ETC and then to help monitor congestion. Similarly, ITS capabilities can then be contracted after an expansion.
Growth	ITS infrastructure, such as fiber optic cable or embedded roadside sensors, can be invested in during routine construction, before there is an identified need for full ITS capabilities. This can

269

	result in new capabilities being added at a later date. The addition of non-transportation capabilities is discussed in more detail later in the paper.
Switch	Variable message sign information can be switched between types of information, such as level of service information, safety information, congestion information, etc.
Compound	ITS capabilities that enhance user operations can be deployed sequentially – including GPS onto trucks first, then tracking equipment, then two way communications, then centralize scheduling capabilities, etc.

These examples serve to demonstrate that there are a large number of possibilities available for using ITS as real options. The ITS as real options that are studied for this case study are presented in Section 7.7.

Options have been identified for transportation systems in the past and include examples such as, moveable barriers for reversible lanes, strengthened road and bridge construction to support future conversion to rail (FHWA 2006) and flexible transport service to be demand responsive to needs to non-conventional travelers (Mageen and Nelson 2003).

Managed lanes have also been identified as offering potential flexibilities; a managed lane "facility could operate as HOV or HOT lanes during peak periods, toll express lanes during off-peak periods and potentially a truck only facility during certain times of the day" (Goodin 2005). However, "little is known about the complexities of designing a practical, flexible, safe and efficient facility that may have multiple operating strategies throughout the course of a day, week, a year or beyond" (Kuhn and Lopez 2005).

The following section introduces the current situation in Houston. From this situation, ITS as real options are then presented in Section 7.7.

7.6 CURRENT SITUATION IN HOUSTON , TX

The Houston metropolitan area is one of the national leaders in the use of ITS and managed lanes. As the population of Texas has grown at a far faster pace than road capacity, the transportation network in Texas has become strained. With a growing realization that construction of sufficient freeway capacity to maintain free-flowing traffic in urban areas will be difficult due to costs, land use, neighborhood impacts and environmental concerns, the Texas Department of Transportation has been examining managed lanes as one method to fight the growing traffic congestion problem (TTI 2001).

Houston has already deployed one of the largest networks of HOV lanes in the country. Currently, Metro operates 112.5 lane miles of HOV and Diamond[7] lanes on six different freeways serving eight counties. Houston's HOV lanes are reserved for buses, vanpools, high occupancy vehicles and motorcycles. In most cases, single occupant vehicles, vehicles with any towed load and large trucks are never allowed on the HOV lanes. With the exception of two segments of two-way HOV lanes on US 290 (Northwest Freeway) and I-10 (Katy Freeway), all other HOV lanes in Houston are reversible single lanes, changing direction to match rush hour flows (Houston Metro 2006). A map of Houston's HOV network is shown in Figure 7-10

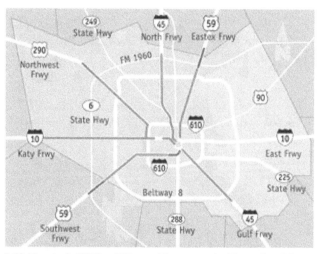

Figure 7-10 Houston's HOV and Diamond lane network. Figure from Metro website.

Houston Metro runs bus service on the HOV lanes and has built several park and ride facilities and transit facilities throughout the Houston area, as shown on the maps in Figure 7-10 and Figure 7-11. Park and ride facilities allow commuters to park their car in the lot for the day and use Metro buses to journey the rest of the way to work. A picture of a park and ride facility is shown below in Figure 7-12. Transit centers are covered facilities that act as hubs, providing a sheltered waiting area for travelers and nodes in the network for route to route transfers and express bus service stops. A map of the Metro transit centers is in Figure 7-13. A picture of a typical Metro transit center is shown below in Figure 7-14.

---

[7] Diamond lanes are operated in the same manner as HOV lanes, but are differentiated in Houston by the type of separation used; HOV lanes are separated by physical barriers and Diamond lanes are only separated by a wide dual paint stripe. The Diamond lanes currently are only operational on the Katy (I-10 West) Freeway.

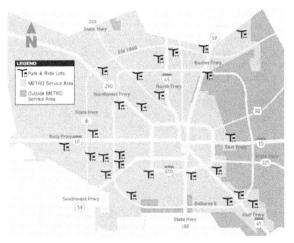

Figure 7-11 Park and ride map of Houston. Figure from Metro website.

Figure 7-12 Park and ride facility. Figure from Metro website.

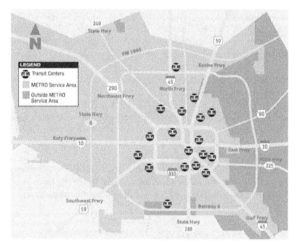

Figure 7-13 Transit center location map. Figure from Metro website.

Figure 7-14 Transit center picture. Figure from Metro website.

In addition to HOV lanes for high occupancy vehicles and bus service, Houston operates two of only four existing HOT lanes in the country, called QuickRide; one on the Katy Freeway (I-10 W) and the other on the Northwest Freeway (US 290). The QuickRide lane on the Katy Freeway was opened in 1998 and the Northwest Freeway HOT lane opened in 2000. Both of the HOT lanes utilized existing HOV lane facilities, which are still one-way reversible lanes, operated in the direction of peak traffic flow. Both lanes are about 13 miles long and have entrance and exit points along their entire length.

The QuickRide program, managed by Metro, operates the HOT lanes as a 3+ passenger facility during peak hours, but as a 2+ facility during non-peak hours. During peak hours, 2+ vehicles are allowed to use the lane for a flat $2.00 fee. Previously, the lane was switched from a 2+ to a 3+ passenger HOV lane, due to heavy 2+ passenger vehicle traffic. The lane was upgraded to a HOT lane to help fill the unused capacity that resulted after the switch to 3+ passenger access rules (Goodin 2005).

The equipment used on both QuickRide lanes utilizes DSRC equipment. To pay for access during rush hour, each 2+ passenger vehicle must have an account and transponder, which is interrogated by overhead electronic transceivers, charging the driver the $2.00 toll (Goodin 2005).

A map of Houston's road network showing all existing managed lanes is presented in Figure 7-15.

Figure 7-15 Houston's managed lane network.

Currently, no truck only lanes are operated in the Houston area. However, the Texas Department of Transportation currently has plans for construction of the Trans-Texas Corridor, a tolled highway with separated auto and truck lanes, along with right-of-ways for rail and utility lines. The Trans-Texas Corridor is planned to crisscross the state, running through mostly rural areas, rather than in urban areas. (Keep Texas Moving 2006).

7.7   ITS AS A REAL OPTION IN HOUSTON

Three uses of ITS as a real option have been identified by the author as potentially having value in the regional transportation network of Houston. To bound the ITS case study research, all three options are ITS in managed lane options. A description of the three options and the manner that they cope with specific types of uncertainty are presented below.

275

1. Managed lanes as a means to delay traditional infrastructure investment.
Traditionally, when traffic demand approaches maximum roadway capacity and congestion becomes an issue, additional capacity is added by expanding the roadway or building another facility, increasing the capacity of the network. Typically, this involves the addition of new lanes in a variety of manners. Most expensive is the widening of the roadway by adding one or more lanes, to increase the total number of lanes available for travelers. In urban areas especially, this can be an expensive and time consuming alternative, as new right-of-ways need to be obtained and road configurations may need to be modified, such as removing and then redesigning entrance and exit ramps. Even in non-urban areas, capacity expansion through the addition of new lanes or facilities can be expensive and time consuming because of environmental concerns and resistance from property owners that will either lose land or are worried about the effects of an expanded roadway and the resulting increase in traffic near their property.

Other potential strategies for expanding capacity through traditional infrastructure can be through the remarking of existing lanes. In some cases, it may be possible to increase the number of lanes by reducing the width of existing lanes. Often this is a temporary measure used to maintain the number of lanes on a roadway if the roadway is being narrowed to make room for construction equipment.

Operational changes can also be used to increase capacity with strategies such as using shoulders or breakdown lanes as general purpose lanes during peak hours, effectively increasing the road capacity, at least during peak hours.

The use of managed lanes is another potential solution for increasing capacity or changing traveler's habits. High occupancy vehicle (HOV) lanes have been added to many highly congested roadways since the 1970's. These lanes have typically created new lanes and reserved these lanes for vehicles carrying multiple people, such as computer vans, buses or carpools. The purpose has been to offer increased travel speeds for travelers willing to share a ride in the hopes that the improved travel speed and reliability will act to change travel behaviors away from single occupancy vehicle travel. To date, HOV lanes have had mixed results. As HOT lanes are a relatively new concept, it is not yet known whether HOT lanes will reduce single occupancy vehicle usage.

Often related to HOV lanes is the use of reversible, or zipper lanes, which is usually a middle lane in a two-way highway. The reversible lane is typically physically separated from traffic flow, usually with concrete barriers or plastic pylons, but possibly only with painted strips. Traffic on the lane is run on different directions during different periods of the day, usually inbound during the morning and outbound during the afternoon.

By adding ITS equipment and changing the lane operating strategies, existing HOV lanes can be converted into HOT lanes or TOT lanes. The effect of including the ITS capabilities serves to increase the capacity carrying potential for a managed lane, increasing the overall capacity for the entire highway facility, as additional traffic is diverted from the general purpose lanes onto the managed lane. In effect, capacity that is not being utilized in a HOV lane can be better utilized with and ITS managed lane, such as HOT or TOT lanes. This can be especially effective as many cities, including Houston, have an extensive network of HOV lanes already deployed. Houston's HOV network is shown in Figure 7-16. By using ITS technologies in conjunction with the operational goal of maintaining free flow traffic on the managed lane at all times, a significant increase in highway capacity may be obtainable. For example, on California's Orange County I-91 highway, two HOT lanes that operate during peak hours carry more than 40% of total traffic, even though the lane capacity is only 1/3 of total capacity, i.e. two out of six lanes (Poole and Orski 2003).

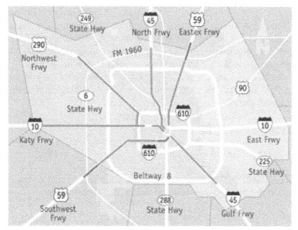

Figure 7-16 Houston HOV and Diamond lane network, existing and under construction. In Houston, Diamond lanes are HOV lanes separated by only dual paint stripes, rather than physical barriers.

It should be noted that the use of HOT lanes does not actually increase the capacity of a particular road segment. Rather, it allows the road segment to operate closer to its theoretical maximum capacity. This is done by selling capacity that would have been excess capacity if the lane had been operated as an HOV lane. It has been shown that as traffic increases, flows breakdown and both speed and throughput decrease to reduce capacity to a state lower than the theoretical maximum, which can then take hours to clear (Chen and Varaiya 2002). Deploying ITS technologies on the managed lane that enables congestion pricing helps prevent this breakdown in flow from ever occurring and maintains the effective road capacity.

Since the managed lane can only increase the utilization of the network, future demand increases may still require the addition of new traditional infrastructure or change in travel habits, such as increased use of transit or off-peak travel. In this case, the use of

ITS technologies on managed lanes may only delay, as oppose to replace the need for, traditional infrastructure expansion.

The use of managed lanes as an option to delay the need for new traditional infrastructure construction is useful for a variety of reasons. First, future traffic demand is uncertain, both in terms of level of demand (total number of vehicles) and the timing of the demand (when the capacity will increase). Second, traditional infrastructure expansion is typically more expensive than the use of ITS on managed lanes. As many states and metropolitan areas throughout the U.S., including Texas and Houston, are facing budget shortfalls for transportation systems, it is uncertain when, or even if, funding would become available for new infrastructure expansion. Third, increased environmental and stakeholder concerns have made it more difficult to build new or wider roads. The ability to add new capacity in a timely manner, even if the funds were available, is uncertain, especially in metropolitan areas. Fourth, the level of political pressure for enacting a solution to growing congestion problems is uncertain. An increased level of political pressure for a solution for alleviating congestion in the near term may be great enough to threaten politicians who can not enact new road widening construction projects in enough time to placate constituents.

The deployment of managed lanes with the option to delay has two sources of value; an inherent value associated with the ITS managed lane and a flexibility value associated using the ITS managed lane as an option.

- **Inherent value** - The managed lane can provide two sets of inherent benefits; benefits directly to the user and benefits to users in the GP lanes.

- **Flexibility value** – The need to fund expensive traditional infrastructure may be delayed to a future date, or even potentially postponed indefinitely.

The use of ITS capabilities on managed lanes to create the option to delay infrastructure expansion can be configured in a variety of ways. The exact characteristics of the ITS managed lane and potential traditional infrastructure expansion will vary from facility to facility. For the purpose of this research, it is assumed decision makers can always add one or more lanes to a facility, though at a large construction cost. It is also assumed that either a HOT/BRT or TOT/BRT managed lane could be converted from an existing HOV lane. As transit ridership is not great enough in Houston to warrant a dedicated BRT lane, a dual HOT/BRT or TOT/BRT managed lane is instead considered.

The decision path of this option is presented in Figure 7-17.

278

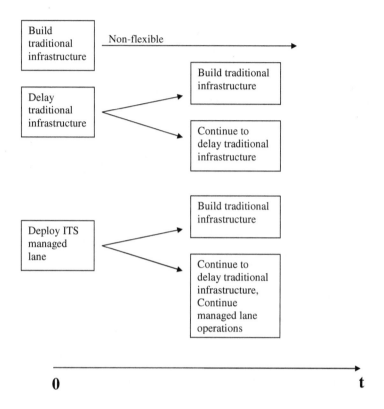

Figure 7-17 Decision path for ITS managed lane option to delay infrastructure

As shown in Figure 7-17, decision makers can chose between three alternatives at time = 0. The non-flexible solution is to build the traditional infrastructure immediately. The decision maker also has a choice of two options. The first is simply a delay option; do nothing at time = 0 and delay making the decision to build until a future time. The second is the ITS managed lane option. The ITS managed lane option deploys the ITS managed lane at time = 0 and delays a build decision to some time in the future.

While the simple delay option creates flexibility benefits, the ITS managed lane option creates both flexibility benefits (from the possibility of construction delay) and inherent benefits (from the ITS managed lane itself). Additionally, there is the possibility that the ITS managed lane inherent benefits can influence the flexibility benefits; namely the

279

more efficient utilization on the managed lane could further delay the need to build the traditional infrastructure.

This option is discussed and analyzed in Section 8.3.1.

The second option is presented below.

2. Managed lanes as option to switch operations.
Current managed lane implementations have been of a single application variety to date, meaning that managed lanes have been of only one type, HOT, BRT, or TOT, or at most a combination of types, such as HOT/BRT or TOT/BRT. While the ability to switch a managed lane from one type to another has been identified, such as switching from a HOT lane to a TOT lane, this has not been applied in practice. While this practice has the benefit of decreasing the complexity of the managed lane, both through reduced ITS technology needs and operational configurations, the benefits associated with switching operational states have not been pursued.

The potential exists to switch the managed lane operations over multiple time-scales. For example, in the long-term, the lane could be switched from a HOT lane to a TOT lane if the growth in truck traffic outpaced the growth in auto traffic. The switch option could also be designed for use in the short-term. For example, during rush hour the lane could be a HOT lane and during mid-day could be switched to a TOT lane. To bound this research, only long-term switching is considered.

The primary benefit associated with the option to switch between managed lane operational states comes from coping with the uncertainty associated with relative growths in different traffic mode shares. While both passenger and commercial vehicle mode shares have been growing over time, the relative growth between these mode shares has been different. In general, commercial vehicle mode share has increased at a faster rate than passenger vehicle mode share. Compounding the uncertainty of relative growth rates, the location of the highest growth rates is often uncertain. Local changes, such as a new logistics facility, or national changes, such as increased international commercial traffic from treaties such as NAFTA, can both increase commercial traffic in unforeseen ways on various facilities. The ability to re-configure or change operational conditions on a managed lane to cope with changes in mode share is the benefit of using ITS as an option to switch between different managed lane configurations.

The decision path for this option is shown in Figure 7-18.

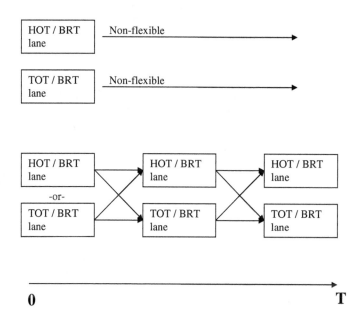

Figure 7-18 Decision path for ITS managed lane switch option

As shown in Figure 7-18, a decision maker has the choice of two non-flexible alternatives at time = 0, deploying either a HOT/BRT or TOT/BRT lane and keeping the chosen operating strategy in the future. The ITS managed lane option could also be chosen. This would entail choosing either the HOT/BRT or TOT/BRT lane operating strategy in time = 0 and the having the potential to maintain or switch strategies at some time in the future. The time frames considered for this research were measured in years, so switches can only occur at a minimum of one year apart from one another.

The ITS managed lane option creates benefits from the inherent benefits of the ITS managed lane, as well as the flexibility benefits from switching modes to best meet uncertain future mode share demand.

This option is discussed and analyzed in Section 8.3.2.

The final option is presented next.

281

3. Option to expand to a congestion pricing system.

The ITS managed lane concepts considered in this research help relieve traffic congestion by increasing the capacity of the ITS managed lane facility through a tolling scheme. Once this additional effective capacity has been reached, the first option considered above looks at the construction of new traditional infrastructure to supply the capacity. Another choice is to help manage the demand on the road network through the introduction of a regional congestion pricing system. The regional congestion pricing system can be considered as an expansion of the technologies and operations deployed on the ITS managed lane to all lanes on a facility or a regional network. The deployment of a regional congestion pricing system can act to manage demand during peak periods and eliminate or delay the need for additional traditional infrastructure expansion. Additional benefits include the possibility of reduced emissions, as traffic conditions improve and high emissions resulting from acceleration / de-acceleration profiles are reduced.

The option decision path is presented in Figure 7-19.

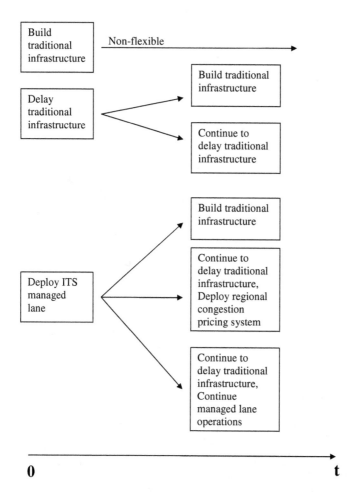

Figure 7-19 Decision path for ITS managed lane option to expand to regional congestion pricing system.

As shown in Figure 7-19, the decision maker has several alternatives to chose from at time = 0. In the same manner as presented in the ITS managed lane option to delay, the decision maker can either build the new capacity immediately or delay. However, the ITS managed lane with the option to expand could also be deployed. This option is similar to the original ITS managed option to delay traditional infrastructure expansion. However, an additional outcome is added, which is the ability to expand the ITS managed lane pricing functions across the entire region, creating a regional congestion pricing system.

The flexibility benefits provided would be further the possibility of further delay in construction of the traditional infrastructure expansion, perhaps permanently. The inherent benefits from this option come from the benefits associated with operating the ITS managed lane.

The benefits associated with these three options are presented in the next section, which discusses ITS managed lanes in the context of the dual value design concept.

7.7.1 ITS MANAGED LANES AS A DVD

The ITS managed lane options presented above can be expressed in terms of the dual value design concept. As a reminder, dual value designs provide two benefits streams, one from the inherent value of the technology or technical architecture used and the second from the flexibility in the system. For the ITS managed lane concept, the ITS technology is the enabler for the DVD concept. That is, the ITS capabilities on the managed lane provide both inherent value and flexibility value.

The inherent value of using ITS managed lanes comes from several sources. These include:

- Increased number of travelers able to use the managed lane facility. Without ITS the managed lane concept could still be used, such as a HOV lane. However, to keep the managed lane uncongested, without ITS the capacity of the managed lane can not be fully utilized without risking congested flow. Deploying ITS enables excess capacity to be efficiently utilized, allowing more travelers access to the facility.
- Improved travel conditions for the managed lane users. Improved travel conditions could include reduced travel time and increased reliability, measured as a decrease in the variability of travel times.
- Improved travel conditions for GP lane users. The ITS managed lane enables more travelers from the GP lane to switch over to the ITS managed lane facility than would have been possible without ITS. This reduction in travelers on the GP lane reduces congestion and benefits all users for the facility and possibly the network.
- Additional funding source. ITS managed lanes allow more effective tolling of the managed lane facility, creating a new revenue source. This revenue can be used for a variety of purposes, such as funding other transportation priorities around the network or improving mode shares, such as transit.
- Continued ability to provide uncongested facility for transit vehicles.
- Other inherent benefits are possible, depending on the design and operation of the ITS. For example, increased information collection and dissemination to travelers

284

or improved safety functions could be possible. However, these types of benefits are not considered in this case study.

The three ITS managed lane options presented above also appear to possess value from flexibility. The flexibility values that the ITS managed lane possesses are described below.

- The ITS managed lanes can be used to delay traditional infrastructure expansion. Strictly speaking, the ITS managed lanes do not create this flexibility, as the option to delay is always available. However, it is thought that the ITS managed lanes improve the value of the option to delay. This is because of the interaction between the inherent benefit of the ITS managed lane to remove vehicles from the GP lane to the managed lane and the value of delay. By reducing traffic on the GP lanes, the ITS managed lanes option can increase the time of delay that is possible for building the traditional infrastructure. This delay is longer than what would have been possible without the ITS managed lane.
- The ITS managed lane allows operating strategies to be switched over time. By allowing access to the lane to switch over time, such as between autos and trucks, the ITS managed lane can constantly allow the road network to better service the mode type whose access to the managed lane would best improve the network flow.
- The ITS managed lane can allow an expansion of capabilities over time. By expanding the ITS managed lane capabilities for congestion pricing from a single lane to a regional network, the ITS managed lane option to expand creates additional value by providing the ability to continue to delay traditional infrastructure construction for even longer periods of time.

The above discussion lists multiple ways in which ITS managed lanes possess both inherent and flexibility benefits. Without the ITS technology on the managed lane, most of the inherent and flexibility benefits would be either reduced or entirely eliminated. Because of this the ITS managed lane is a DVD.

Note, that the DVD concept is not itself a separate contribution to this research apart from the LCF Framework. Rather, the DVD concept is another way to describe flexible systems.

The following chapter continues the ITS managed lane case study by providing a quantitative analysis of the three options presented above.

7.8 REFERENCES

Blythe, P. (2004) Road User Charging in the UK: Where will we be 10 Years from Now?, 12th IEE International Conference on Road Transport Information and Control, London, England.

Brownstone, D and K Small. (2005) Valuing Time and Reliability: Assessing the Evidence from Road Pricing Demonstrations, Transportation Research Part A, Washington DC, pg 279-293.

Chen, C. and P. Varaiya. (2002) The Freeway-Congestion Paradox, Access, N. 20 Spring.

DeCorla-Souza, P. (2004) An Evaluation of High Occupancy Toll and Fast and Intertwined Regular Networks, TRB Annual Meeting, Washington DC.

DeCorla-Souza, P. and W. Barker. (2005) Innovative Public-Private Partnership Models for Road Pricing/BRT Initiatives, Journal of Public Transportation, v. 8, n. 1.

DeCorla-Souza, P. (2006) FAST Miles: A Multimodal Strategy Integrated with Credit Based Pricing, TRB Annual Meeting, Washington DC

Endsor, J. (2006) Key Challenges in Estimating the Impacts of Road Pricing with State of the Practice Transportation Models, TRB Annual Meeting, Washington DC.

Feldstein, D. (1998) Taken for a Ride?: The Ranks of HOV Naysayers are Increasing, but Even Critics Praise Houston's System as One of the Best While Proponents Say its Function is Often Misunderstood, Houston Chronicle, Nov. 8.

FHWA. (2006) Managed Lanes: A Primer, found at : www.fwha.dot.gov/publications

Goodin, G. (2005) Managed Lanes: The Future of Freeway Travel, ITE Journal, February.

Gomez-Ibanez, J. and K. Small. (1994) NCHRP synthesis 210 of highway practice: road pricing for congestion management: a survey of international practice. Report, National Research Council, Washington, D.C.

Gulipalli, P., S. Kalmanje, K. Kockelman. (2005) Credit Based Congestion Pricing: Expert Expectations and Guidelines for Application, TRB Annual Meeting, Washington DC.

Hamdar, S., S. Eisenman, and H. Mahmassani. (2006) Evaluation of Operational Strategies for Integrated Corridor Management, TRB Annual Meeting, Washington DC.

Haning, C. and W. McFarland. (1963) Value of Time Saved to Commercial Motor Vehicles Through Use of Improved Highways, TTI Bulletin no 23, Texas.

Hess, D., B. Taylor, and A. Yoh. (2005) Light Rail Lite or Cost Effective Improvements to Bus Service? Evaluating the Costs of Implementing Bus Rapid Transit, TRB Annual Meeting, Washington DC

Kawamura, K. (2000) Perceived Value of Time for Truck Operators, Transportation Research Record 1725, TRB, Washington DC.

Keep Texas Moving. (2006) www.keeptexasmoving.com

Kuhn, B. and C. Lopez. (2005) Managed Lanes Research in Texas, ITE Journal, February.

Kushner, M. (2000) Transit Technologies, Chapter16 in Intelligent Transportation Primer, Institute of Transportation Engineers, Washington DC.

Mageean, J. and J. Nelson. (2003) The Evaluation of Demand Responsive Transport Service in Europe, Journal of Transport Geography, v. 11.

MDX (2006) Miami-Dade Expressway Authority Website, http://www.mdx-way.com/tolls/faqsORT.htm.

Middleton, D. and S. Venglar. (2006) Operational Aspects of Exclusive Truck Roadways, TRB Annual Meeting, Washington DC.

Mitretek Systems (1999) NCHRP 8-35: Incorporating ITS into the Transportation Planning Process Interm Report, National Cooperative Highway Research Council of the Transportation Research Board, Washington DC.

MnDOT. (1997) Field Test of Monitoring of Urban Vehicle Operations Using Non-Intrusive Technologies, Federal Highway Administration Report, FHWA-PL-97-018.

(NCHRP) National Cooperative Highway Research Program. 1993. Electronic Toll and Traffic Management (ETTM) Systems - A Synthesis of Highway Practice, Transportation Research Board, National Research Council, Washington, D.C.

Poole, R. and C. Orski. (2003). HOT Networks: A New Plan for Congestion Relief and Better Transit, Reason Foundation, Los Angeles.

Porter, J., D. Kim and H. Vergara. (2004) Electronic Road Pricing Systems: Capabilities and Existing and Needed Technology Solutions, TRB Annual Meeting, Washington DC.

Rakha, H., A. Flintsch, K. Ahn, I. El-Shawarby, and M. Arafeh. (2005) Evaluating Alternative Truck Management Strategies Along I-81, TRB Annual Meeting, Washington DC

Richeson, K. and v. Barnes. (2000) Commercial Vehicle Operations and Freight Movement, Chapter 9 in Intelligent Transportation Primer, Institute of Transportation Engineers, Washington DC.

Safirova, E., K. Gillingham, W. Harrington, P. Nelson, A. Lipman. (2005) Choosing Congestion Pricing Policy: Cordon Tolls vs Link Based Tolls, TRB Annual Meeting, Washington DC

Sorenson, P. and B. Taylor. (2005) Innovations in Road Finance: Examining the Growth in Electronic Tolling, TRB Annual Meeting, Washington, DC.

Sumalee, A., A. May, and S. Shepherd. (2005) Specifying Optimal Road Pricing Cordons for Different Objectives, TRB Annual Meeting, Washington DC

Thorpe, C. (2000) Vehicle Based Technologies, Chapter 15 in Intelligent Transportation Primer, Institute of Transportation Engineers, Washington DC.

TTI. (2001) Current State of the Practice for Managed Lanes, Appendix A in Year 1 Annual Report of Progress: Operating Freeways with Managed Lanes, Report 4160-2, Texas.

TTI. (2002) Managed Lanes: More Efficient use of the Freeway System, Texas Transportation Institute TxDOT report 4160-5-P1.

Wachs, M. (2003) Congestion in Cities: Where, When, What Kind, How Much, Traffic Congestion: Issues and Options, Report on Conference held in Washington DC.

Wood, E., D. Shelton, M. Shelden. (2006) Designing BRT for LRT Convertibility: An Introduction for Planners and Decision Makers, TRB Annual Meeting, Washington DC

8 VALUE OF FLEXIBILITY IN HOUSTON GROUND TRANSPORTATION SYSTEM USING INTELLIGENT TRANSPORTATION SYSTEMS (ITS) IN MANAGED LANES

Previously in Chapter 7, three ITS in managed lane real options were introduced. In Chapter 8, these real options are evaluated in a quantitative manner, to better understand the costs and benefits associated with each ITS in managed lane real option. Instead of trying to calculate a definitive value for flexibility with ITS managed lane options, this chapter presents results that look at the various aspects of flexibility and the factors that can affect it. The resulting analysis presented here demonstrates that the quantitative analysis of flexibility with ITS managed lane real options is not a simple process, as it depends on a variety of factors including technical, organizational and strategic, as well as the underlying uncertainty in question.

Because the ITS in managed lane real options are "complex" real options in complex systems, a more sophisticated quantitative analysis technique was used in the evaluation process, compared with "standard" evaluation techniques for real options discussed in the literature. As a reminder, these "standard" real option evaluation techniques are described in Section 2.5. Figure 8-1 displays the analysis procedure for the current phase of the ITS case study research. The following chapter, Chapter 9, expands on the quantitative evaluation conducted here with a qualitative analysis of the ITS case study, to better understand the practical challenges associated with "complex" real options in complex systems.

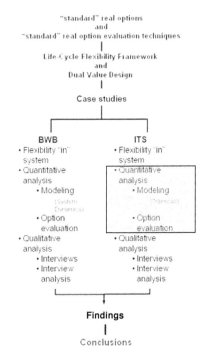

"standard" real options
and
"standard" real option evaluation techniques

Life-Cycle Flexibility Framework
and
Dual Value Design

Case studies

BWB	ITS
• Flexibility "in" system	• Flexibility "in" system
• Quantitative analysis	• Quantitative analysis
• Modeling (System Dynamics)	• Modeling (Transcad)
• Option evaluation	• Option evaluation
• Qualitative analysis	• Qualitative analysis
• Interviews	• Interviews
• Interview analysis	• Interview analysis

Findings

Conclusions

Figure 8-1 Case study analysis with highlighted box showing current stage of analysis.

The purpose of the quantitative analysis was to help better understand the flexibility associated with "complex" real options in complex systems, using the ITS case study as an example. For this purpose, a better understanding of where flexibility occurs and what its value is for ITS in managed lanes was sought. Also, the process that was used to obtain the results is central to this thesis, where the process refers to both the LCF Framework and the quantitative evaluation process used to value flexibility. In essence, this portion of the case study addresses the first research question, applied to the ITS case study: **How do "complex" real options and "standard" real options differ across the life-cycle of an option, including design, evaluation and management activities?** Specifically, this chapter seeks to better understand the design and evaluation portion of this research question.

To accomplish this purpose a quantitative analysis centered on the building and use of a traffic demand model for the Houston, Texas regional transportation network was conducted. The traffic demand model built was based on the network and travel demand data obtained from the Houston region metropolitan planning organization. However, no

290

attempt was made to completely reproduce all aspects of the traffic demand model used in actual planning activities in Houston, as this was deemed unnecessary. Rather, the model was used to be representative of traffic conditions in Houston. In this way, the quantitative analysis can serve as a "proof of concept" for studying "complex" real options in complex systems.

This chapter is composed of three main parts. The first part describes the quantitative evaluation process that was used for the quantitative evaluation. The second part describes the traffic demand model that was used in the quantitative evaluation. As will be described, this model is the main engine used in the evaluation process to generate quantitative results for the ITS "complex" real options in complex system. The third part of this chapter presents the results and what we learned from them.

8.1 CASE STUDY ANALYSIS PROCESS

The analysis process used for the case studies is based on a portion of the Life-Cycle Flexibility (LCF) Framework, specifically the part involved in quantitatively evaluating real options, as shown in Figure 8-2. As a reminder, a discussion of the entire LCF Framework is presented in Chapter 3.

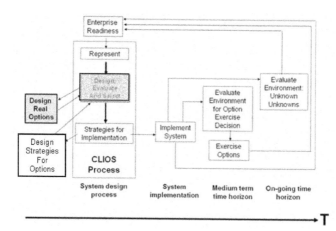

Figure 8-2 High level overview of LCF Framework, with components used in the research highlighted.

Note, that as a convenience to the reader, the case studies were written to stand alone. The case study analysis procedure described here is parallel to that described for the BWB case study in Section 5.1.

The quantitative analysis used for this research builds on prior real options analysis work. An emphasis in this dissertation that has not received much attention in the real options literature is in the evaluation of "complex" real options in complex system. As previously discussed in Chapter 3, "complex" real options in complex systems have technical, organizational and process characteristics that are interconnected with one another. This differs from "standard" real options, which are characterized as a single relatively simple change or addition to a system that creates flexibility. Also, "standard" real options in "standard" system do not take into account organizational and process issues associated with the flexibility. "Standard" real options analysis techniques, as discussed in Chapter 2, are not therefore not adequate for taking into account the complexities associated with the option and the system.

To better analyze "complex" real options in complex systems, a new analysis procedure was used to quantitatively evaluate flexibility, and applied to the BWB and ITS case studies. In general, the analysis procedure developed for this research utilizes at its core more sophisticated modeling techniques to better simulate the options and system of interest. For the ITS case study, a regional traffic demand model was built to better characterize travel behaviors on individual facilities and on a regional scale. The more sophisticated modeling techniques used in this research were deemed necessary to adequately capture the full richness of the issues surrounding the analysis of "complex" real options in complex systems.

As shown in Figure 8-3 and Figure 8-4, the quantitative evaluation process that was used for the ITS case study consisted of three main parts; generation of inputs, the travel demand model, and the quantification of option value. An overview of the activities and purpose of these three main parts are described below.

Note, that as part of the LCF Framework, the quantitative evaluation of the flexibility is not the only evaluation that needs to be conducted. Rather, a qualitative evaluation of the "complex" real options in complex systems is conducted to better understand the practical challenges that exist. This qualitative analysis for the ITS case study is described in the next chapter.

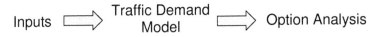

Figure 8-3 Overview of three steps in ITS case study quantitative analysis.

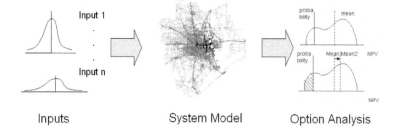

| Inputs | System Model | Option Analysis |

Figure 8-4 Quantitative analysis process for ITS case study, using Transcad traffic demand model as system model.

- **Inputs** – The inputs for the ITS case study that are important to the modeling need to be determined. These inputs can describe network characteristics (such as numbers of lanes for facilities), traffic characteristics (such as modes and mode split), and environmental characteristics (such as travel demand growth). A few of these inputs whose uncertainty may affect systems decisions are then determined, such as uncertainty surrounds future travel demand growth. A probability distribution is then assigned to represent the uncertainty associated with these inputs. As shown in Figure 8-4, multiple inputs, each with a separate probability distribution can be used.
- **Traffic Demand Model** – A traffic demand model, using the Transcad travel demand modeling software package, was created to allow facility and network level analysis of traffic flows and speeds. The traffic demand model allows a better quantitative understanding of how different decisions relating to the ITS real options being considered affect specific facilities or the entire regional transportation system. The model can be run multiple times using the probability distributions generated from the above discussion on inputs to understand how the system reacts under the input uncertainty. The outputs of interest from the model are flows and speeds on specific facilities under different input conditions.
- **Real Options Analysis** – Results from the traffic demand model with the input uncertainty are used to create probability distributions of the benefits associated with specific choices of ITS and traditional infrastructure. Benefits of interest for this research are value of time savings and toll revenues. The choice of these two benefit streams are discussed in more detail in 8.2.3.

Comparing the probability distribution function averages for systems with flexibility and without flexibility yields the value of flexibility. For example, the NPV distribution for addressing congestion problems with non-flexible and flexible solutions are generated. A non-flexible solution could be building traditional infrastructure capacity in year zero, while a flexible solution could be building ITS managed lane capabilities that would delay construction of

293

additional traditional infrastructure until it was needed in the future. Comparing the average of the two NPV distributions would provide the value of flexibility. A more detailed discussion of this calculation is presented in the option analysis in 8.3.

Note that the valuation of flexibility through the comparison of the NPV distribution averages follows previous work (Tufano and Moel 1997, Clemons and Gu 2003, Greden et al. 2005, and Miller 2006). However, it is noted that other means of valuing the options could be considered, or that additional constraints in the valuation process could be added to make the evaluation more sophisticated. However, for this research, the comparison of averages is used. As this research serves as a proof of concept for the analysis of "complex" real options in complex systems, this means of valuing flexibility was deemed sufficient.

More detailed discussion of the traffic demand model used for this case study is presented in the following discussion.

8.2 TRANSPORTATION DEMAND MODELING

The following section presents the modeling techniques that were used in this research to generate quantitative values for the inherent benefits and flexibility benefits associated with using ITS in managed lanes. A general discussion of travel demand modeling is first presented, along with an overview of the Transcad software package used for this modeling. Specific details on the traffic demand model built to represent the Houston regional transportation network is then presented. Inputs and outputs of interest for the ITS case study are then discussed. Finally, a brief discussion on model validation is then presented.

8.2.1 TRAVEL DEMAND MODELING AND TRANSCAD

Traffic flow analysis forms the basis for designing operating strategies and physical infrastructure construction decisions for transportation systems (Banks 2002). To aid in better understanding the inter-relationship between traffic flow and speed, a variety of transportation analysis techniques are possible, such as queuing analysis and network analysis. The scope of the analysis techniques also varies from the micro to the macro, where micro-simulations are used to understand interactions between individual vehicles and macro-simulations allow increased understanding of conditions over the entire network.

This research made use of network traffic demand modeling at a macro-scale, to better understand traffic conditions on the Houston, Texas regional network. The remainder of this section describes some of the basics of network travel demand modeling in general and the modeling package, called Transcad, which was used to obtain the results.

8.2.1.1 Travel Demand Modeling

The travel demand model used for this research was based on the common four-step model, which has been a basis for transportation forecasts since the 1950's (Wikipedia 2007). The four-step model, as shown in Figure 8-5, has, as the name would suggest, four main steps in the process, though over time additional activities have been added (without referring to these additional activities as "steps").

The four steps in the model are as follows:

1. **Trip generation** – The output of trip generation is the total numbers of trips created and trips attracted to each centroid (the points where trips start and end) in the model. These are called productions and attractions. Centroids are the representation of the center of the traffic analysis zone (TAZ). The TAZ is an area that is defined by a transportation agency for the purposes of "book-keeping" of traffic-related data. The size of the TAZs will be specific to an urban area.

2. **Trip distribution** – The output of trip distribution is the prediction of trips taken between each pair of nodes, or the origins and destinations. The Origin-Destination (OD) Matrix is the output that creates a record of the total number of trips made between each centroid in the system. Essentially, the OD matrix differs from productions and attractions by explicitly detailing the trips that start from specific productions and go to specific attractions. Multiple methods exist for changing the production and attraction data generated in the previous trip generation step into origins and destinations, including the gravity model, which was used in this research. The gravity model, similar to Newton's theoretical model of actual gravity, is based on the premise that the further two centroids are from one another, the fewer trips that will occur between the two centroids, while centroids that are closer together will generate more trips between one another.

3. **Mode choice** – The output of the mode choice step is the determination of what types of modes will be used by travelers. These will be limited, of course, to modes that are available to travelers; i.e. if there are no rail networks, no rail trips will be used in the model.

4. **Route assignment** – The route, or trip or traffic, assignment, is the most computationally intensive step, where the output is generation of the actual routes followed for each trip that is undertaken. Different procedures exist for calculating the route assignment, but most involve the simultaneous calculations of traffic flows and speeds on each link in the network (where links represent the roads or rail lines available for travel).

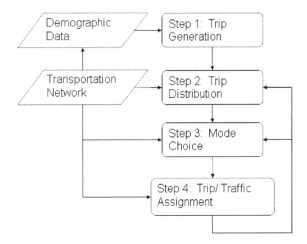

Figure 8-5 Four-step model.

Also shown in Figure 8-5 are the two "extra" steps. The first pertains to obtaining projections of socioeconomic conditions and land use. This is used to anticipate future demographic data, such as mode preference, number of travelers, value of time, etc. The second pertains to building the transportation network available for travelers. This could be limited to current network conditions, or could include future proposed changes to the network, to better understand the effect that proposed changes would have on traffic conditions.

For the model used in this research, data and network conditions were obtained from the Houston area Metropolitan Planning Organization (MPO), the Houston-Galveston Area Council (H-GAC). The data and network that were obtained were from the actual transportation demand model used by H-GAC to support planning activities and are based on the 2025 Regional Transportation Plan (HGAC 2005). A 2025 proposed network, partial OD matrix data, and mode share splits were obtained from H-GAC. The data and network obtained allowed steps 1-3 and the two extra "steps" to be skipped, as the OD matrix, mode share data and a network were provided, leaving only the route assignment step to be completed in this research.

8.2.1.2 Transcad

The modeling package used to generate route assignment results for this research was Transcad. Transcad is a "full-featured geographic information system designed specifically for planning, managing, and analyzing the characteristics of transportation systems and facilities" (Caliper 2000). Transcad has multiple components, allowing a

296

range of traffic analysis studies to be performed. The geographic information system (GIS) and route assignment analysis procedures were the only components used for this research.

As travel demand models are inherently dependant on spatial and temporal data, Transcad GIS capabilities were used to re-create the Houston regional transportation network from network data obtained from H-GAC. OD matrix data and mode choice data, also obtained from H-GAC, was used to create route assignments for trips. Then, using the GIS component, the location of traffic conditions, such as speed and flows, on the network was obtained.

8.2.2 HOUSTON MODEL

The following section discusses the specific characteristics of the Houston model used to generate results for this research. The discussion centers on how current and proposed future conditions for the Houston network are represented in the model. This section contains discussion on the Houston regional network, available travel modes, OD data, facility types and modeling assumptions.

8.2.2.1 Houston Transportation Network

The Houston metropolitan region has an extensive transportation network, as shown in Figure 8-6. Currently, Houston is very road-centric, having only a single rail line, shown in Figure 8-7. The lack of rail constrains almost all travel to trips made via the road network. Therefore, for this model, all trips are assumed to take place via the road network.

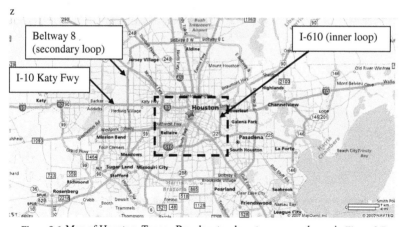

Figure 8-6 Map of Houston, Texas. Box denotes downtown area, shown in **Figure 8-7**
Figure from Mapquest.

297

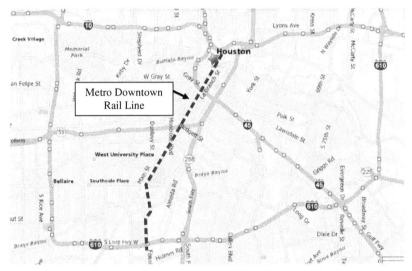

Figure 8-7 Downtown Houston, showing rail line. Map from MapQuest.

The Houston area transportation network used for the research is a detailed representation of all the roads in the Houston area, including freeways, arterials, frontage roads, local roads and toll roads. Figure 8-8 shows the network obtained from H-GAC and used in the ITS case study for traffic demand modeling.

298

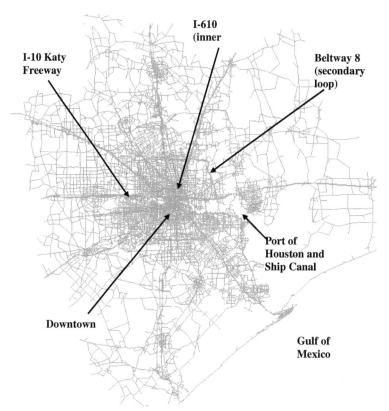

I-610
(inner

I-10 Katy
Freeway

Beltway 8
(secondary
loop)

Port of
Houston and
Ship Canal

Downtown

Gulf of
Mexico

Figure 8-8 Houston road network in Transcad. Callouts presented to orientate the reader with the network.

Network data obtained from H-GAC includes road information, such as directionality (one way or two way), number of lanes, and road type (freeway, frontage, local, toll).

The network data available from H-GAC was for a proposed 2025 Houston road network. No network data was available for the current 2007 network. As using the 2007 network as a baseline starting point was desired, this means that changes had to be made to the 2025 network to re-create the 2007 network.

The H-GAC 2025 network includes planned and approved changes, such as road capacity expansions that do not currently exist. For example, on the I-10 West Katy Freeway, current plans are for a major expansion, with additional general purpose freeway, managed lanes and frontage road lanes to be added to the existing set of lanes. For this research, a better understanding of the traffic benefits created with ITS, rather than physical infrastructure addition, were of interest. To create a representation of the current 2007 network, a comparison between the 2025 network and current actual network conditions was conducted. The purpose was to change selected facilities on the 2025 network model to create network conditions representative of the current network. Specifically, the number of lanes available on certain facilities was changed in the model to better represent current conditions. For example, on the Katy Freeway, the extra lanes currently being planned for and appearing in the 2025 network were removed from the 2025 model and replaced with the number of lanes currently in use. Current numbers of lanes were determined from examining satellite photos of selected facilities in the Houston network, available through Google maps. An example is shown in Figure 8-9 and Figure 8-10.

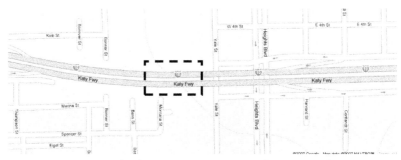

Figure 8-9 Closeup map of I-10 West Katy Freeway. Boxed area appears in **Figure 8-10** as a satellite photograph.

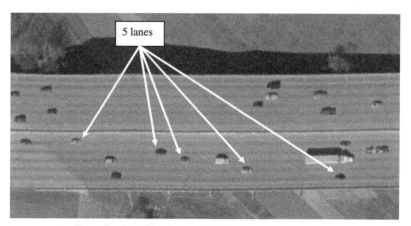

Figure 8-10 Example of satellite photograph of section of I-10 West Katy Freeway, showing umber of lanes inbound on a particular segment.

Due to the size of the network, which contains over 100,000 links, no attempt was made to change the number of lanes on all links in the network. Rather, effort was placed only on facilities of immediate interest for the research. As a result, network effects will likely differ from expected results for running current data, as it is likely that additional 2025 network characteristics were still embedded in the network on facilities not of immediate interest. However, since only specific facilities were of interest for this research, and those facilities were changed to match current conditions, the model output on those facilities should be a reasonable representation of current day conditions.

8.2.2.2 Available Travel Modes

Data on available travel modes was obtained from H-GAC. However, a complete set of data for all available travel modes could not be obtained from H-GAC. The travel mode data that was obtained was limited to the following modes:

- Autos with a single passenger
- Autos with 2 passengers
- Autos with 3 passengers
- Truck and taxis (as Houston has few taxis outside downtown, this was assumed to be 100% trucks)

No transit data was obtained from H-GAC, limiting the analysis to auto modes and trucks.

The mode data obtained from H-GAC was available only in aggregate form, with no differentiation between mode type travelers. For example, no value of time differentiation was available for each mode share, which is important for determining traveler response to road pricing and tolls. As a result, a two single values of time were assigned; one to all passengers and one to all trucks, based on prior studies.

8.2.2.3 Origin and Destinations

Data for origins and destinations, in the form of OD matrices, was provided from H-GAC. In total, 20 matrices were made available, with matrices for each mode share (the four presented above, plus matrices for trips originating from outside the network, which for the purposes of this research were combined with single passenger trips) at four times of day; AM, mid-day, PM and overnight.

The origins and destinations depict trips between the model centroids, which were also provided as part of the network data from H-GAC. In total, 2954 centroids appear over the region. As shown in Figure 8-11 the centroids show possible trip origins and destinations that cover the entire Houston region, as would be expected.

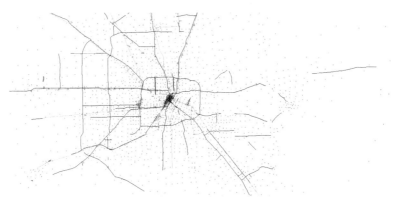

Figure 8-11 Centroids on the Houston network model. Centroids appear as points, while major roads appear as lines.

The OD matrices provided by H-GAC create the underlying demand on the transportation model, which is then assigned to specific routes by Transcad.

The origins and destinations from the H-GAC data are presented in Figure 8-12 and Figure 8-13. Figures are centered on downtown, where most of the trips occur. The OD data presented is for AM trips, and as expected, the destinations are primarily in major employment areas, such as downtown, while the origins are spread through the Houston region.

302

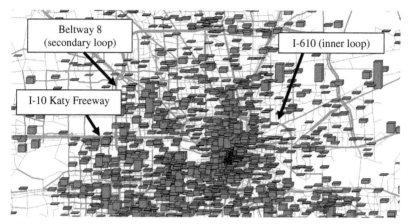

Figure 8-12 Origins, as provided from H-GAC data. Taller bars indicate larger numbers of trips.

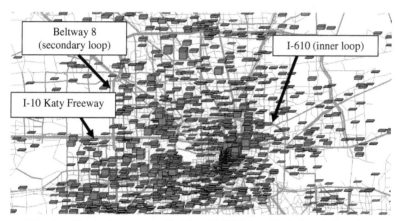

Figure 8-13 Destinations, as provided from H-GAC data. Taller bars indicate larger numbers of trips.

8.2.2.4 Facility Types

Transcad has the ability to assign specific conditions to different facility types, to better model the traffic flow characteristics that would be created due to differences in facility types. For this research four basic facility types were of interest; general purpose lanes, HOV lanes, HOT lanes and TOT lanes, as defined below.

- **General Purpose Lanes** – General purpose (GP) lanes cover the vast majority of the network. The GP lanes are open access to all mode types and are available to all vehicles free of charge. Travel conditions depend on the type of GP lane. For example, a GP lane on a freeway can carry a greater capacity at higher speeds than a local GP lane. In general, the conditions shown in Table 8-1 were set for different GP lanes. These setting were set after consulting modeling experts at MIT.

Table 8-1 GP lane characteristics.

Lane Type	Maximum Capacity	Maximum Speed
Freeway	2000 cars / lane / hour	65 mph
Arterial	1600 cars / lane / hour	40 mph
Local	800 cars / lane / hour	25 mph

- **HOV lanes** – HOV lanes are limited access managed lanes. HOV3+ and HOV2+ lanes were of interest. Currently, congested facilities in Houston, such as the Katy Freeway, have too many two-passenger vehicles to allow the HOV lanes to operate at the HOV2+ level. Therefore, HOV3+ operations were the baseline used for this case study as an HOV operating strategy.
- **HOT lanes** – HOT lanes are also limited access lanes. Currently Houston Metro operates two HOT lanes, called QuickRide, on the west side of the city on the Katy Freeway and US 290, the Northwest Freeway. QuickRide is operated as a HOT2+, where 3+ passenger vehicles and transit vehicles are permitted free access and passenger vehicles with two people are permitted access for a flat $2 fee. Note, a static toll is a single, constant toll assessed to vehicles. Single occupancy vehicles are never allowed on the QuickRide lanes. The HOT managed lane concept is enabled by ITS. For this research HOT2+ and HOT1+ were of interest. Also of interest were the toll schemes possible on the HOT lane. Specifically, static tolling and congestion pricing, which variably changes toll rates to utilize all available capacity but to also maintain free-flow speed. Trucks can never utilize the HOT lane facility.
- **TOT lanes** – TOT lanes are similar to HOT lanes, but limited to trucks and transit vehicles. TOT lanes were modeled as being operated in a congestion pricing manner, to maintain free-flow conditions for trucks and transit vehicles.

Note, that while transit data was not available for this research, it was assumed that transit vehicles would occupy 200 passenger car equivalents (PCE) per hour on all managed lane types.

8.2.2.5 Major Modeling Assumptions

Due to the data available, several major assumptions were made in the creation of the Transcad transportation model used for the ITS case study.

- **Scaled data** – OD data was only available from H-GAC for 2025. As the analysis needed for this research involved understanding how traffic would be impacted with the addition of ITS capabilities over time, time series OD data was needed. Aggregate traffic data for 2005 was also made available from H-GAC. Using the 2005 aggregate data and the detailed 2025 OD matrices, a linear growth rate in trips was assumed. As a result, a 2.1% constant annual growth rate was calculated as necessary to achieve projected 2025 levels from 2005 levels. This constant growth rate was used as the baseline growth estimate for travel demand for a 20 year period lasting from 2005 to 2025.
- **Mode split** – A mode split between the four modes presented in 8.2.2.2 were given for the 2025 data. As no 2005 mode split data was available, as a baseline it was assumed that the mode split would remain constant throughout the 20 year period of interest for the ITS case study.
- **No new mode shares** – No rail transit data was available from H-GAC. While the Houston rail system is currently limited to a single line, future plans entail a vast expansion of rail and bus rapid transit systems throughout the regions. Since no data was available for this at all, the appearance of new travel modes in the future was not considered.
- **Constant OD matrix structure** – OD data for 2025 was made available by H-GAC. As no data was made available for other time periods, it was assumed that the structure of the OD matrices would remain constant over time. This means that the origins and destinations in the 2025 matrix are the same for all 20 years examined in this research, with only the magnitudes of the OD data changing over time. This means that no new origins and destinations appear over time and the relative magnitude between OD data across time remain the same.

To relax the above assumptions, considerable additional data would need to be obtained. However, even without the additional data, it was felt that the above assumptions still allowed for a general understanding of how ITS affected traffic behaviors.

8.2.3 INPUT UNCERTAINTY AND OUTPUTS OF INTEREST

The Transcad model requires numerous input variables in order to generate the traffic behavior for the road network. Four of these in particular were of interest for the analysis of better understanding the impact that ITS managed lane flexibility would have on the road system. These inputs are presented below. Following the discussion on inputs are the primary outputs of interest from the model.

- **Overall demand growth** – The overall demand growth determines the level of travel demand for passengers and commercial trucks over time. For the facilities of interest in this research, which are those experiencing congestion problems (facilities with no or low congestion problems were not considered for this research), demand growth rates help determine the urgency that either new capacity or new operating strategies are needed. In general, lower demand growth rates make for a less compelling case for new capacity addition via new physical infrastructure expansion, given the high-costs of construction and the low levels of travel demand growth for utilizing the capacity in the future.

- **Mode split** – The relative mode split between autos and commercial trucks was of interest for determining the relative value between HOT and TOT managed lane strategies. In general, low truck mode share, relative to autos, makes TOT less compelling, while higher truck mode share, relative to autos, makes TOT more compelling.

- **Exercise decisions for new physical infrastructure** – The decision rules for when new physical infrastructure should be build as opposed to deploying ITS managed lane solutions was examined. Three types of decision rules were considered; build new capacity when net present value for the project is positive, build new capacity when Benefit-Cost Ratio for new capacity is higher than ITS solutions, or build new capacity when congestion reaches a threshold level (i.e. irregular traffic flow conditions are experienced).

- **Operator stakeholder type** – Two different system benefits were considered; increases in societal benefits from time savings and toll revenue collected. The relative benefits generated from both vary depending on operating condition. As decisions for when to build physical infrastructure or when to change ITS managed lane operations are based on the anticipated returns, how to measure return is of interest. Each type of return, societal returns and pure monetary returns from tolls, could appeal to different stakeholders, where public stakeholders are swayed by mandate to consider societal returns, and private stakeholders may only be interested in monetary returns. The stakeholder operating the system will therefore help determine the relative benefits of importance between physical infrastructure and ITS managed lane strategies.

The two outputs of interest for this research were value of time savings and revenue generated from tolls. Many other benefits could be considered, such as: environmental improvements and reduced fuel usage from smoother traffic flows, decreased vehicle costs resulting from lower congestion levels, decreased accident rates from lower traffic levels, increased reliability of travel times, etc. Travel time savings was chosen over these other possible metrics as the "majority of transportation improvements are dominated by travel time savings" (Burris and Sullivan 2006). Additionally, no data was available from some of these other types of savings (such as environmental effects) and other benefits (such as those stemming from increased reliability) are still an open research topic on how to best quantify the benefits.

Toll revenues were also considered. Tolls are not a benefit generated from the system; rather they are simply a transfer from one stakeholder to another. However, inclusion of tolls is important given enterprise architecture considerations. For example, private enterprises running toll facilities see toll revenue as a benefits stream and may not be as interested in societal benefits (unless the private tolling authority gathers shadow tolls from a public agency that is interested in societal benefits). Without considering tolls as a benefit stream, the difference in operating agency strategies can not fully be explored.

8.2.4 MODEL VALIDATION

The Transcad model was judged as valid in three ways. First, the structure of the model and the data used for mode splits and OD matrices came from the Houston area MPO, which uses the model as part of planning activities and decision making. As the network and data originated with the MPO and are used professionally, the quality of the network and data were deemed to be high.

Second, the results that are generated from the Transcad model are what would be expected. As shown in Figure 8-12 and Figure 8-13 the origins and destinations seem to, at least in general, match up with expected travel patterns, with AM trip origins covering a large number of points (homes) and converging to a relatively fewer number of points (primarily places of work). Additionally, the traffic flow patterns follow expected behaviors, with the majority of travel taking place on highways, as shown in Figure 8-14.

Finally, extensive consultations on building, calibrating and running the model were had with researchers at MIT who are experts in the field of using transportation models in general and Transcad in particular[1].

---

[1] Very special thanks to Mikel Murga at M.I.T. for the extensive help in building, calibrating and analyzing the model. Any errors or omissions are the author's alone.

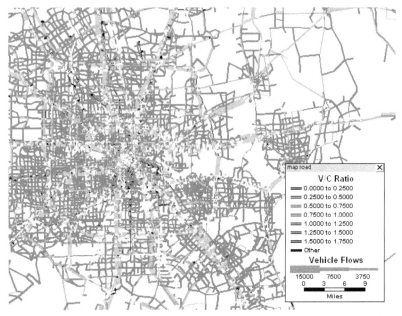

Figure 8-14 Transcad model results for AM peak hour flow. Traffic volume to road capacity ratios are shown, with lighter colors on highways indicating higher volumes.

8.3   RESULTS

The objective of the quantitative analysis was to better understand the benefits associated with using ITS in the context of managed lanes. Specifically, the inherent benefits and the flexibility benefits that are enabled by the use of ITS capabilities on managed lanes were of interest. Each of the three options considered in the previous chapter; option to use HOT lanes to delay traditional infrastructure expansion, option to switch managed lane operating strategy between HOT and TOT lanes, and the option to expand ITS capabilities across all lanes to create a regional congestion pricing system; are discussed below.

For the remainder of the analysis, the focus of each of the options is on facilities that are already congested, as opposed to facilities that are not experiencing or expected to experience, substantial congestion. Congested facilities were chosen as being of greater interest that non-congested facilities. This is because it is anticipated that TxDOT will be significantly short of resources for infrastructure improvements for the foreseeable future. Therefore, it is assumed that funding priorities will be geared towards facilities already experiencing congestion or have utilizations near 100% of capacity. This is opposed to funding improvements that would prevent future congestion on facilities that have a lower current utilization.

As congested facilities are of interest, the analysis conducted below is for the I-10 West Katy Freeway, a major east-west Interstate that is currently experiencing significant congestion. Currently, there are plans for major expansion of the Katy Freeway corridor, adding five lanes of capacity in some places for a total of 18-20 lanes. Current plans are for four managed lanes (two each direction), up from the one reversible HOT2+ QuickRide lane, and additional general purpose lanes added to the freeway and the frontage roads.

This analysis looks at the Katy Freeway corridor and applies the three options to better understand the benefits from using ITS in the three options of interest.

8.3.1 OPTION TO DELAY TRADITIONAL INFRASTRUCTURE EXPANSION

Current plans for the Katy Freeway call for significant addition of new lane capacity. In total, about 25 miles of the Katy Freeway corridor are slated for construction of additional capacity and re-construction, at a total estimated cost of $1.446 billion (Katyfreeway.org 2007). The number of lanes planned for construction vary along the 25 mile construction length, with costs per lane miles also varying between $2 million and $14 million[2].

As a contrast, the QuickRide program, which converted the existing reversible HOV3+ lane on the Katy Freeway to a HOT2+ lane, had total start-up costs of $447,900 with annual operating costs of approximately $100,000 (Burris and Sullivan 2006). In the past, the Katy HOV lane had been operated as a HOV2+ lane. Due to heavy lane usage that degraded travel speeds, operating conditions were changed to HOV3+ access conditions. However, the result was excess capacity on the HOV lane. This excess capacity was to be sold under the QuickRide program to two-passenger vehicles for a flat $2 fee. While the QuickRide program has been around for close to 10 years, access by two passenger vehicles willing to pay the $2 fee has been modest, with only about 400 passengers (200 vehicles) per day accessing the lane (Burris and Sullivan 2006). It is estimated by the author that about 900 3+ passenger vehicles an hour access the Katy managed lane currently during peak hours, leaving excess capacity available from about 500 additional two passenger vehicles[3]. This means that additional capacity of several hundred vehicles per hour, capable of carrying an extra 1000 passengers an hour (for two passenger vehicles), exists during peak hours for the Katy Freeway corridor.

The analysis of the option to use ITS on managed lanes to delay capacity construction had the purpose to determine if more efficient utilization of the Katy managed lane could add value. Value was defined in terms of increasing passenger travel time savings

---

[2] Calculated from author, based on figures from (Katyfreeway.org 2007).
[3] Calculated from author, based on figures from (FHWA 2003). This assumes about 200 passenger car equivalents are utilized by transit vehicles.

(inherent value) and perhaps increasing the amount of time that capacity construction could be delayed (flexibility value).

The remainder of Section 8.3.1 is presented in four parts. The first part, Section 8.3.1.1, conducts an analysis of the current QuickRide operating conditions and examines societal travel time savings benefits and toll revenues. The second part, Section 8.3.1.2, examines the benefits and costs associated with adding the additional lane capacity through traditional infrastructure expansion. The third part, Section 8.3.1.3, re-visits the managed lane facility and compares the operating strategies of charging a static toll and operating the lane as a congestion priced facility, where tolls are changed to use all available capacity but always maintain free-flow conditions. The final part, Section 8.3.1.4, makes use of the preceding three parts to evaluate the option to delay infrastructure. How the option value changes with and without the use of ITS capabilities is examined in this section.

8.3.1.1 Current QuickRide Operation

As a first step, the benefits associated with utilizing the existing managed lane under the current operating strategy was conducted. As a reminder, the current QuickRide operating strategy allows 3+ passenger vehicles free access and charges a flat $2 toll to two-passenger vehicles. Single occupancy and trucks are never allowed access to the HOT lane. A summary of the inputs and results for the analysis are presented in Table 8-2.

Table 8-2 Inputs and Results for Existing Katy QuickRide.

Costs		
	Startup	$500,000
	Yearly operating	$100,000
	Total operating over 10 years	$1,000,000
Speed improvement benefits		
	Average increased speeds for 2 passenger cars using HOT2+ over GP lanes	14 mph
	Hourly benefits per passenger	$18 / hour
	Total annual value of time savings	$220,000
	Total value of time savings over 10 years	$2,200,000
Benefit/Cost Ratio		1.5

Even though the Katy managed lane under the QuickRide program does not fully utilize the existing capacity on the lane, the benefit to cost ratio is still greater than 1.

This is because of the low-cost of converting and operating the existing HOV lane to a HOT lane.

The results obtained here, of a Benefit-Cost Ratio (Benefit-Cost Ratio) of 1.5, are comparable to previous research on benefit-cost analysis for the Katy QuickRide. Prior work done by Burris and Sullivan calculated a Benefit-Cost Ratio for the Katy QuickRide at 1.61 (Burris and Sullivan 2006).

The results presented above were calculated in a similar manner to those presented in the Burris and Sullivan work, to allow direct comparison. However, for the remainder of this research the calculations of benefits and costs will be different than that presented above in the following ways.

1. The results calculated above were taken from non-discounted future benefits and costs. For the remainder of the research, only discounted benefits and costs, discounted at a standard 7% discount rate for government projects (OMB 1992), will be used to take into account discounting revenue and cost streams over time.

2. The above calculations assume the operating strategy and the number of two passenger vehicles remain constant over the 10-year period studied. This research also looks at the strategy of operating the HOT lane as a congestion priced facility, lowering prices when needed to utilize additional capacity and raising prices when needed to ensure free flow conditions are always maintained.

3. Only the time savings for the vehicles using the managed lane are calculated above. However, enough excess capacity exists on the managed lane to impact congestion on the general purpose lanes, if the managed lane capacity is fully utilized. Therefore, further results will take into account time savings from vehicles switching to the HOT lane from the GP lanes AND the time savings that the remainder of vehicles on the GP lanes experience when some vehicles switch to the HOT lane.

4. Toll revenues are not considered as benefits in the above calculation. This is because only societal benefits are considered above and tolls are a transfer from one group to another, as opposed to generation of benefits. However, this does not take into account two considerations. First, if a private actor will be operating the HOT lane and collecting tolls, the revenue stream generated by the tolls will be seen as benefits in their benefit-cost analysis. This is especially true if the lane is completely privatized and the tolls are the only benefit stream realized by the operator. If the facility is some type of public-private partnership (PPP), a private operator may see additional revenue streams derived from shadow tolls paid to them by a public entity that is more concerned with societal benefits and hence pays the private operator accordingly. Second, even if a public actor is operating the managed lane and collects the tolls, it is assumed that these revenues will be re-invested in some other project that will also generate comparable societal

311

benefits. Therefore, counting the toll revenues as a benefit seems not only viable, but also necessary when considering different enterprise architecture strategies for building and operating a managed lane facility.

5. Prior benefit-cost analysis conducted by Burris and Sullivan take into account vehicle ownership costs, vehicle operating costs and emission changes when operating the QuickRide. As their research showed that these additional benefits were between two to three orders of magnitude smaller than travel time savings, only travel time savings and toll revenues were considered here as the main benefits produced by the HOT lane.

The above analysis is re-visited in Table 8-3, taking into account discounting of future revenue streams and operating costs and toll revenues. As the QuickRide operating strategy of charging a flat $2 toll is maintained in the analysis presented in Table 8-3, the effect on traffic in the GP lanes is minor and is not included.

Table 8-3 QuickRide analysis re-visited with discount rates and toll revenues.

Costs		
	Startup	$500,000
	Yearly operating	$100,000
	Total operating over 10 years, discounted at 7%	$750,000
Speed improvement benefits		
	Average increased speeds for 2 passenger cars on HOT2+	14 mph
	Hourly benefits per passenger	$18 / hour
	Total annual value of time savings	$220,000
	Total value of time savings over 10 years, discounted at 7%	$1,600,000
	Tolls per vehicle	$2
	Total annual toll revenue	$100,000
	Total value of toll revenue over 10 years, discounted at 7%	$800,000
Benefit/Cost Ratio (time savings + tolls)		1.9
NPV (time savings + tolls)		$1,150,000
Benefit/Cost Ratio (tolls)		0.6
NPV (tolls)		-$450,000

From the analysis above, with the discounting of future revenues and costs and the addition of societal and toll revenues as the total benefit stream, the QuickRide operating strategy still has a favorable Benefit-Cost Ratio. However, when just considering the toll revenues, the Benefit-Cost Ratio drops below 1, indicating a non-favorable investment for a fully private operator.

While the analysis indicates that this project as conceived would not be beneficial for a private operator to undertake by themselves, the analysis also points to additional possibilities for public-private partnerships. First, shadow tolls could be paid directly to a private operator, based on the societal benefits generated. Alternatively, if the startup costs are covered by a public agency, management could be turned over to a private operator. In this analysis, even if the private operator covers the operating expenses, the toll revenues exceed the expenses, making the investment viable for a private operator. Additionally, the private operator would have incentives to reduce operating costs, which would increase their profitability. Since this result was found from the limited utilization created with the current QuickRide operating strategy, increased utilization of the lane will likely increase toll revenues and make the investment more attractive to a private operator. This increases the possibility that multiple enterprise architectures for building and operating managed lanes can be found for future managed lane projects.

8.3.1.2 New general purpose lanes

To better understand the benefits from deploying ITS in a managed lane setting with the potential to delay future traditional infrastructure construction on congested corridors, the benefits and costs from simply deploying the traditional infrastructure rather than the ITS need to be examined.

For this purpose, the Katy Freeway were of interest, due to its congested nature, current HOT lane operations, and future planned capacity expansions. A length of approximately 25 miles was considered, starting near I-610, the inner loop, and running west to the Grand Parkway, the planned third loop, as shown in Figure 8-15. This is the same portion of the corridor currently being planned for expansion by TxDOT.

313

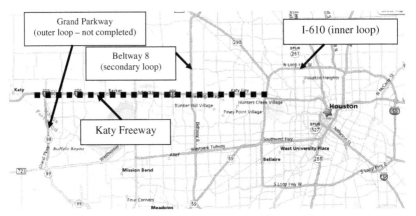

Figure 8-15 Katy Freeway corridor planned for expansion.

The number of lanes on the Katy Freeway varies along the entire length, with the widest point being between Beltway 8 and I-610 (with 3 to 4 lanes in each direction, depending on location) and the narrowest point further west near the Grand Parkway (two lanes each way). Planned construction has the addition of two GP lanes (one in each direction) along the total length of the Katy Freeway marked in Figure 8-15. For simplicity in analysis, it is assumed that there are three lanes for the length of the freeway (in each direction), with new construction adding a fourth lane.

Using the Transcad model, average peak hour speeds were determined for the Katy Freeway during morning rush hours. It was assumed afternoon rush hour traffic would be comparable, but in the opposite direction. Average peak hour speeds are presented in Figure 8-16 assuming baseline traffic growth conditions for the next 20 years and no additional lane construction. A constant speed of 35 mph was assumed as the average speed once volume exceeded capacity by the amount capable of causing irregular traffic flows – i.e. stop and go traffic conditions or onset of irregular traffic flow, or traffic breakdown speeds.

Because the Katy Freeway is already near maximum capacity, the Transcad model results indicate that average peak speeds drop from about 42 mph in 2005 to consistent breakdown speeds by 2008, where they remain for the rest of the 20 year model run.

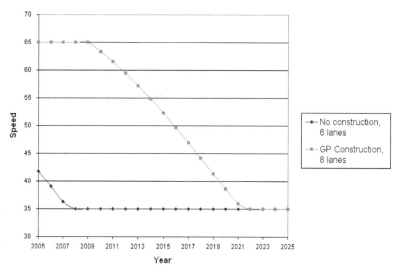

Figure 8-16 Addition of two general purpose lanes on Katy Freeway in year 0 increases average peak travel speeds.

As shown in Table 8-4, re-running the Transcad model with the additional planned capacity expansion of an additional GP lane in each direction significantly improves travel speeds, both immediately and for several years into the future.

However, even with the additional capacity added, there is not enough capacity to prevent a return to breakdown speeds during the 20 year period of interest, as irregular traffic conditions would be projected to return in 2021. Note that these conditions could occur sooner, as any induced demand generated from the new capacity expansion was not considered in this analysis.

Converting these increased speeds into time savings, the results are presented in Table 8-4.

Table 8-4 Summary of results for additional GP lane construction on Katy Freeway corridor.

Costs		
	Construction costs per lane mile	$8,000,000
	Lane miles	2 * 25 = 50
	Total construction costs for 2 additional GP lanes over 25 mile Katy Corridor	$400,000,000
Speed improvement benefits		
	Hourly benefits per passenger	$18 / hour
	Hourly benefits per truck	$100 / hour
	Total value of time savings	$735,000,000
Benefit/Cost Ratio		1.8
NPV		$335,000,000

As shown in Table 8-4, the addition of the two GP lanes is a worthwhile project, based on the costs and benefits involved.

As a first order comparison of the benefit-cost analysis for the GP lanes and the QuickRide program from the previous section, two points are immediately apparent. First, while the Benefit-Cost Ratio for both projects are comparable, the total benefits provided from the two new GP lanes dominates those provided from the HOT lane. Even when including toll revenue and societal benefits in the calculation, the GP lane benefits are two orders of magnitude greater than those for the HOT lane.

The second point is that the costs involved with both projects are also vastly different, with the GP lane additions costing over two orders of magnitude more than the HOV to HOT lane conversion and operations. Furthermore, the HOT lane costs are spread out over time, given that a large portion of the costs come from operating expenses. In contrast, the GP lane conversion has to be paid initial before the extra capacity can be utilized[4].

This means that even while new GP lane construction would create more benefits from time savings than HOT lanes, the costs involved are much higher. *If obtaining the needed funding for the GP lane capacity expansion is anticipated to be a problem, HOT lanes using ITS may be a solution.* This is because the HOT lane generates benefits and requires a much lower amount of funding. In this manner, deploying the HOT lanes could be seen as a temporary fix for the congestion problems. Additionally, ITS

---

[4] In reality, under pay as you go funding systems, the funding is not all initial, but is distributed over a number of years. However, it can still be considered "initial" funding as the funding has to be provided before the benefits can be realized.

capabilities are typically deployable faster than new capacity construction, meaning the benefits could be available sooner as well.

The HOT lane analysis is now re-considered below, where a congestion pricing strategy is assumed, instead of a static toll. Employing congestion pricing, instead of static tolls, is expected to more fully utilize the existing HOT lane capacity.

8.3.1.3   HOT Lane with Congestion Pricing

As was previously noted in 8.3.1.1, the current operation of the QuickRide lane does not fully utilize the available capacity. It was calculated that about 500 more passenger vehicles could be added to the lane during peak hours, while currently only about 200 two-passenger vehicles a day are utilizing the lane. It is assumed that either decreased tolls or increased congestion on the GP lanes would facilitate the use of the remainder of this capacity. Either way, implementing a congestion pricing scheme, instead of flat pricing, would allow the lane to be fully utilized.

As total GP lane capacity is about 6000 vehicles / hour for the three lanes (2000 vehicles / hour / lane), the availability of an additional 500 vehicle / hour capacity is significant, as it is about 8% of total GP lane capacity.

Assuming these vehicles would have otherwise been on the GP lanes, the decreased traffic flow on the GP lanes creates a substantial improvement to average peak speeds, as shown in Figure 8-17. *Additionally, the transfer of these vehicles from the GP lanes to the HOT lane also delays by three years the onset of consistent irregular traffic flows.*

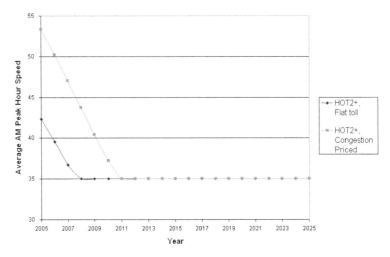

Figure 8-17 Average peak hour speeds on GP lanes by changing operating strategy of
HOT lane from static tolling to congestion pricing.

While the speed increase and the delay in congestion is not as much as that generated by
the addition of new GP lane capacity, the costs of implementing a congestion pricing are
considerably lower than the construction of additional lane capacity. Additionally, the
cost differential between a static tolling system and a congestion pricing system are
estimated to be not significantly higher than the original conversion costs for the existing
QuickRide.

As the exact cost differential between the existing QuickRide static toll system and a
system capable of congestion pricing is not known, two cost points are presented to better
understand the HOT lane sensitivity to deployment and operating costs. On the low end,
it was assumed that the costs for a congestion pricing system were twice the costs
incurred in the QuickRide program for static tolling. On the high end, cost estimates
from prior studies on other HOT lanes were incorporated, which placed the cost per lane
mile at $0.12 million to convert to a congestion priced system (Poole and Orski 2003).
This compares with the $0.03 million per lane mile costs for deploying the QuickRide
program (or the $0.06 million estimate assumed as the low-cost point). A summary of
the Benefit-Cost Ratio generated from the HOT lane employing flat pricing and
congestion pricing, using costs numbers scaled from the QuickRide program and from
the Poole research, are presented in Table 8-5.

318

Table 8-5 Benefit-Cost Ratios for Katy HOT lanes under flat and congestion pricing strategies, using two different cost assumptions.

Deployment Costs	HOT2+ Static tolls	HOT2+ Congestion Priced
Based on existing Katy QuickRide (assume costs are twice existing costs for congestion pricing capability)	1.9	4.0
Based on numbers generated by Poole	0.6	1.8

Table 8-5 demonstrates that under both high and low-cost assumptions, the congestion priced HOT lane is economically worthwhile. For the higher cost estimates, the static tolled HOT lane is not economically worthwhile.

The following section combines the analysis from the preceding three sections, and discusses the inherent and flexibility benefits from using ITS managed lanes to delay traditional infrastructure investments.

8.3.1.4 Benefits of using ITS Managed Lanes to Delay Traditional Infrastructure Investment

ITS investments in managed lanes, such as the conversion from HOV to HOT lanes, can help more efficiently utilize existing capacity and delay investments in traditional infrastructure. However, the ITS investments do not *create* the ability to delay, as the option to delay is always present. Below is an analysis of the flexibility value for the option to delay infrastructure investments, without considering ITS at all. Immediately following that analysis is additional analysis for determining how ITS investments change the value of the traditional infrastructure investment delay option, as well as an analysis of the inherent value of the ITS capabilities.

8.3.1.4.1 *Evaluation of Option to Delay, with no ITS Investments*

Under the baseline growth projections of 2.1% annual growth for traffic on the Katy Freeway, as presented in the assumptions, there is a need for additional infrastructure by year three, 2008, in the analysis. This assumes that the decision on building new capacity is based on the need to relieve irregular traffic flow conditions. However, due to uncertainty in traffic growth projections, the actual traffic growth could be higher or lower than the baseline, which either decreases or increases, respectively, the amount of time needed before new capacity is added. For uncertainty ranging from 0.5 to 1.5 times the projected growth rate (1% and 3.2% annual growth rates, respectively), the projected NPV distribution for traditional infrastructure expansion is shown in Figure 8-18

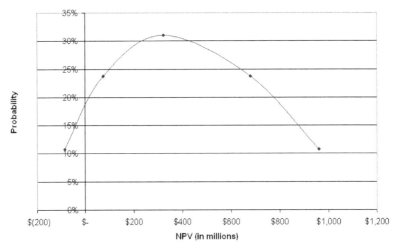

Figure 8-18 Probability distribution for expected NPV associated with new traditional infrastructure construction.

As seen in Figure 8-18, under most conditions, building additional GP lane capacity makes economic sense, as the NPV is greater than zero. However, under conditions of slower growth, the case for construction of additional capacity in year zero can not be justified. The option to delay infrastructure investments until they are needed, which for slow growth may be many years in the future, would seem to have value compared with the always build in year zero solution.

Note that in this case study five points were sampled from the input function, yielding a five point sample for the output distribution. Technically, the data originally presented in Figure 8-18 should instead be presented as a discrete probability distribution, as shown in Figure 8-19Figure 5-23. However, as this becomes difficult to differentiate the different sets of data, the data will continue to be presented with a curve-fit, as done in Figure 8-18, for presentation purposes. This should not be taken to mean that the data represents a continuous probability distribution, as the probability values would change.

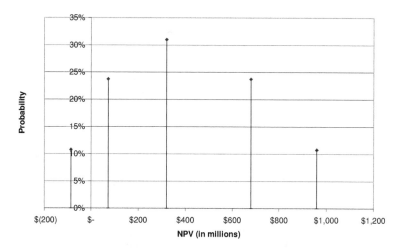

Figure 8-19 Probability distribution for expected NPV associated with new traditional infrastructure construction, shown discreetly. This chart re-presents the data originally displayed in **Figure 8-18**, but as a discrete, rather than continuous, probability distribution.

Figure 8-20 shows the shift in NPV if the option to delay is present. With the option to delay, it is assumed that the traditional infrastructure is not built until irregular traffic flows are experienced sometime in the future. It is then assumed that new capacity is added immediately to the system, with no delay time.

Additionally, it is assumed that the funds that would have been invested in the traditional infrastructure had it been build in year zero are re-invested in some other project if the capacity expansion is delayed. Considering the entire state of Texas for a moment as the scope of the possible transportation system space of possible investments, re-investing in an alternative project makes sense, as TxDOT is only projected to have funds to cover 35% of future investment needs (TTI 2002). This means that funds not spent on one project can be freed to spend on another project. Alternatively, even if there are no additional projects to spend the funds on in the transportation system, the money raised through taxes could instead be re-invested somewhere else or taxes could be lowered, allowing re-investment or consumption from the tax-base. In all cases, the delay in infrastructure expansion allows some other opportunity to be pursued.

In any of these alternative project cases, three different sets of alternative investments can be envisioned. First, alternative investments could offer a similar NPV as that projected for the project to be delayed. In that case, the returns are constant across project in terms of the benefits that are expected for society as a whole and only differ in terms of which segments of society benefit. For example, delaying investments for facilities on the west side of town to allow for re-investment in facilities on the east side of town may benefit the region as a whole equally, but will benefits travelers using the east-side facilities more than travelers using the west side facilities.

Second, the alternative investment could offer a rate of return higher than the initial proposed investment in expanding the traditional infrastructure. Under this condition, the alternative investment would always provide returns at least as high, if not higher, than the proposed capacity expansion. In this case, delaying the capacity expansion frees up the funds for a better investment and increases societal returns. In this case, using a purely rational investment prioritization methodology, the alternative investment should have been the top choice for investing anyway. However, even with higher returns, there is the potential that the capacity expansion being considered was needed more by travelers than the higher return alternative investment. Having the ability to delay the capacity expansion would then allow investment in this alternative higher return project.

Finally, the alternative investment could offer a lower rate of return than the initial proposed investment in expanding the traditional infrastructure. In this case, delaying the capacity expansion so that the funds could be re-invested in an investment with lower returns would actually destroy societal value, as a higher return project is being traded for lower return project. However, the case may be that the lower return investment is needed more urgently than the initial capacity expansion. Or, alternative metrics could be the reason why the lower return investment is desired. For example, for political reasons or equity reasons, it may be that some stakeholders prefer one investment over another because it benefits them more than the original capacity expansion, even if it benefits society as a whole less. This type of trade-off, where the capacity expansion is delayed to instead invest in a lower returning project is not considered further. This is because this type of project would not be selected on a value maximization methodology, but rather would be selected more because of political motivation. This is not to say investment using this type of criteria is wrong, but quantitative analysis is less useful for making these types of political decisions.

Figure 8-20 presents the shift in the NPV density function, comparing the build immediately case, delay with re-investment in an alternative project with projected returns equal to the baseline projected return, and delay with re-investment in an alternative project with projected returns greater than the projected return for capacity expansion.

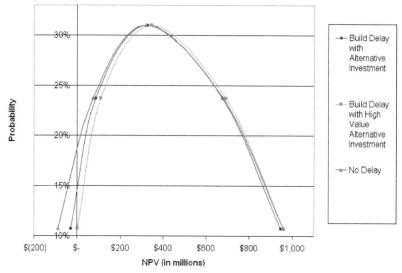

Figure 8-20 NPV density function, with two types of alternative investments if capacity expansion is delayed, along with original build now alternative for capacity expansion.

With both types of alternative investments, the NPV density function experiences changes primarily at the lower end of NPV values. This is because the capacity expansion under slow growth creates lower NPV estimates for the capacity expansion project, and the delay time allows for re-investment in a project at higher rates of return. When the alternative investment is high enough, the negative NPV experienced from slow growth can actually be off-set from the alternative investment and the NPV can turn positive. Alternatively, the NPV density function at the higher end actually decreases slightly, as the immediate capacity expansion under higher than expected traffic growth rates would have given better returns if the project would have been built sooner rather than delayed. Finally, Figure 8-20 shows that if there is an alternative investment with high enough expected returns, it makes sense to always delay the capacity expansion, as returns from the alternative investment will always exceed the capacity expansion under all growth scenarios.

Figure 8-21 shows the expected NPV when there is a commitment in year zero to delay the project. While the overall value of the project may increase, as alternative projects could be invested in, committing to the delay initial does not add value from flexibility. Flexibility value is added when the decision maker has the choice of whether to delay the project and invest in an alternative project, or proceed with the original capacity expansion. Figure 8-21 shows the difference in the value for committing in year zero to a delay, or having the flexibility to determine whether or not the project should be delayed.

323

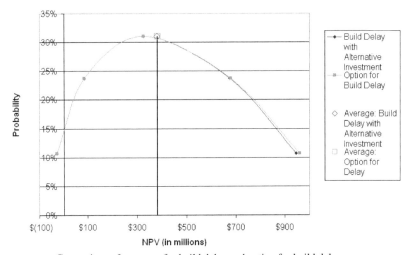

Figure 8-21 Comparison of averages for build delay and option for build delay.

Figure 8-21 *shows that the flexibility to choose when to delay has some value, compared with committing to delay at time zero.*

In this case, the higher than expected levels of traffic growth make it beneficial to begin immediately with capacity expansion, while baseline and lower levels of growth make it beneficial to delay. While the average value shown in Figure 8-21 for the flexible and non-flexible systems are too close to resolve from the figure, the difference in value is $2 million. When the alternative investment is higher than the baseline capacity expansion, the total value of the delay increases, but the value of flexibility goes to zero. This means that there would be no flexibility; it always makes sense to delay if such a high return investment is available.

The action sequence for the option to delay would be to delay the projects under lower than expected growth rates and build immediately for higher than expected growth rates. The NPV is the same for delay or immediate building for the baseline growth case.

Results from the analysis are summarized in Table 8-6.

Table 8-6 Summary of flexibility to delay or proceed with traditional infrastructure capacity expansion.

Alternative	NPV (in millions)
Non-Flexible Alternatives	
Build at year 0 (no flexibility)	$372
Delay Build Until Congested with Alternative Investment	$380
Delay Build Until Congested with High Value Alternative Investment	$401
Flexible Alternatives	
Option to Delay Build with Alternative Investment	$382
Option to Delay Build with High Value Alternative Investment	$401
Delay Valuation	
Value of Delay with Alternative Investment	$380 – 372 = $8
Value of Delay with High Value Alternative Investment	$401 – 372 = $29
Option Valuation	
Value of Flexibility with Alternative Investment	$382 – 380 = $2
Value of Flexibility with High Value Alternative Investment	$401 – 401 = $0 (always delay)

8.3.1.4.2 *Evaluation of Option to Delay with ITS Managed Lane*

The use of ITS capabilities to create a HOT lane enables the transfer of vehicles from the GP lanes to the HOT lanes, beyond the vehicles that would be traveling on the HOV lane, which has unused capacity.

If the HOT lane operates with a congestion pricing scheme, this allows for the HOT lane travelers to travel at free-flow speeds. This creates value from the increased time savings for the HOT lane users as well as time savings from users of the GP lanes. Additionally, toll revenues from the HOT lane users can be collected and re-invested in other projects.

Figure 8-22 presents the NPV distribution created from the deployment of a HOT lane. The benefits come from the time savings (HOT lane users and GP lane users) and toll revenues. Figure 8-22 then presents a comparison of the option to delay capacity expansion construction with and without ITS. The delay option with ITS NPV includes the additional years of delay made possible with deploying the HOT lane operating with a congestion pricing scheme. The delay option without ITS assumes the current static toll pricing scheme for the HOT lane, which leaves excess capacity under-utilized. Additionally, the NPV curve for the option to delay with the ITS includes the inherent benefits from the ITS system, which are the benefits derived from the time savings and the tolls collected. Table 8-7 summaries the results.

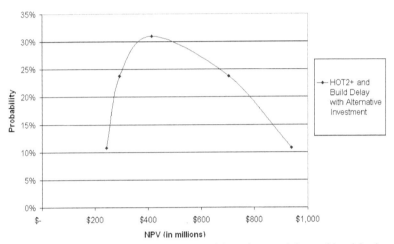

Figure 8-22 ITS HOT lane using a congestion pricing scheme and the resulting delay in traditional infrastructure expansion made possible with the ITS capabilities.

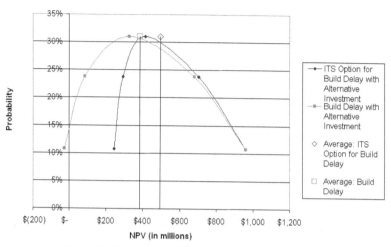

Figure 8-23 Comparison of ITS/delay option and delay option.

Table 8-7 Summary of results for ITS option to delay infrastructure expansion.

Alternative	NPV (in millions)
Inherent ITS value: HOT 2+ using congestion pricing, with benefits in excess of using managed lane as HOV 3+ facility	$80
HOT 2+ and Build Delay with Alternative Investment	$493
Option to Delay Build with Alternative Investment	$382
Option value: Value of HOT 2+ Option	$493 – 80 – 382 = $31

As shown in Table 8-7, the option to delay capacity expansion with ITS creates significant value, both through inherent ITS benefits and flexibility, applied to the Katy Freeway. This underscores the notion of Dual Value Design considerations in ITS in managed lanes.

The inherent ITS benefits, from time savings for HOT lane and GP lane users and tolls generated, are significantly larger when compared to the benefits generated when operating the managed lane with static tolls. This is due to the excess capacity that is more fully utilized and the resulting time savings on the GP lanes that is realized. This points not only to the assertion that ITS capabilities generate inherent benefits compared to operating the managed lane as an HOV3+ without ITS capabilities, but that the ITS should be deployed or operated in a manner to maximize these inherent benefits. In the case of the managed lane with a static tolling structure, significant excess capacity is not being utilized on the managed lane facility. In that case, the ITS capabilities are present, and adding inherent value, but do not add as much value as when the managed lane is operated with a congestion pricing scheme.

The delay option with using ITS is also greater than the delay option by itself. This is because the use of ITS-enabled congestion pricing allows for delay of expensive capacity expansion for an even longer period of time than what could have occurred without deploying ITS. This creates value at the lower end of growth rates, as it allows more time for alternative projects to be invested in.

In this case, the relative benefit streams from the inherent value and from flexibility are both substantial. In the case of inherent value, the ITS creates value around $80 million, while it creates about $30 million in value from flexibility. In this case, the inherent value is worth more, but the flexibility is a significant source of value. *Without considering the ITS capabilities as a dual value design, if only a single benefit stream is considered, significant value is not accounted for.*

The value from flexibility in this analysis is dependant on the current traffic levels of the facility and the decision rules that go into making the build decision. For this analysis, the Katy Freeway was used, where traffic levels make irregular traffic flows a consistent problem after just a few years for baseline growth and even sooner for higher growth rates. When high growth is experienced, there is only so much that can be done with the remaining capacity on the HOT lane before traffic conditions are again irregular. The decision rule used here assumes that irregular traffic flow is to be avoided and that new capacity construction begins when consistent irregular flow is experienced. However, the decision rule could be changed so that it is based on economic conditions or maintaining a higher level of service, which would mean building additional capacity when average traffic speeds dropped past a certain point, which would result in construction at an earlier date.

In the following section, the second option intended to provide flexibility is discussed. This option involves switching operating schemes on a managed lane. Additional discussion on decision rules is also presented.

8.3.2 OPTION TO SWITCH MANAGED LANE OPERATIONS

The option to switch the operating state of the managed lane was examined and presented in this section. Two operating states were considered; allowing passenger cars access to the managed lane and allowing trucks access to the managed lane. In both situations it was assumed that transit vehicles would continue to have access to the managed lane. For the first state, all autos were assumed to be granted access to the lane. The toll structure was also assumed to be an extension of that used today. Namely, 3+ passenger

328

vehicles would continue to gain free access to the HOT lane, and two-passenger and single occupancy vehicles (SOV) would pay tolls based on the level of congestion and the vehicle occupancy rate, with SOVs paying a higher toll than two person vehicles. For the second state, a truck only toll (TOT) lane was considered, also based on congestion pricing to maintain free flow conditions.

A summary of the both operating states is presented below in Table 8-8.

Table 8-8 Summary of existing mode share, passenger car equivalents for each mode share and value of time.

Modes	
Modes	**Current Peak Flows (vehicles / hour)**
3 passenger autos	900
2 passenger autos	1400
1 passenger autos	4500
Trucks	1200
Existing HOV Lane Capacity (minus transit vehicles)	1400
Passenger Car Equivalents	
Modes	**Passenger Car Equivalents**
3 passenger autos	1
2 passenger autos	1
Trucks	2.5
Value of Time	
Modes	**Value of time ($/hour)**
3 passenger autos	$54 ($18 per person)
2 passenger autos	$36 ($18 per person)
Trucks	$100 (per truck)

For the existing single, reversible HOV lane determining the relative value of operating the managed lane as either a HOT or TOT lane is relatively straightforward. This is because traffic conditions are currently already high enough under either operating strategy to more than use all the available capacity.

Under a TOT operating strategy, there is room for only about 560 trucks. At a value of time of $100, this yields time savings of $56,000 / hour. Under the HOT lane operating strategy, there is capacity for all 900 three passenger vehicles and 500 two passenger vehicles, for a time savings value of 900 * $54 + 500 * $36 = $66,600 / hour. For the current conditions and value of time, the lane is more valuable operating as a HOT lane. While the relative time savings per vehicle favor using the managed lane as a TOT lane, the relative size of the vehicles means more passenger vehicles can utilize the lane. As 2.5 vehicles can utilize the lane for every one truck, it is likely that the number of vehicles occupying the same space as a single truck would generate more time savings.

This is because 2.5 three-passenger vehicles have a greater time savings than a single truck, though 2.5 two-passenger vehicles have a lower time savings than a single truck. If the relative proportion of three-person to two-person passenger vehicles change, the relative value of a single managed lane under the TOT and HOT lane operating strategies could change. However, it was assumed that the ratio of three/two/one-passenger vehicles remained the same over time.

While the vast majority of the Houston HOV network is composed of reversible single lanes, additional managed lane capacity is planned for construction on the Katy Freeway. The single reversible lane is planned to be expanded to a four lane (two in each direction) facility. The question of flexibility from switching between HOT and TOT lanes is revisited under these new conditions of expanded managed lane capacity. With the additional capacity, there is currently not enough three- and two-person vehicles and trucks to fill the managed lane facility. For the HOT lane operating strategy, this additional capacity could be filled by SOVs, while for the TOT lane, no additional vehicles could initially fill this excess capacity, as it is assumed on a TOT lane that only trucks and transit vehicles will be allowed access.

Figure 8-24 presents the time savings value for operating the expanded four lane facility as either a HOT or a TOT lane. The ability to switch between these operating states is also presented. As can be seen, the relative values of each operating state changes over time. Due to the lack of trucks on the Katy Freeway capable of utilizing the available TOT lane capacity, significant capacity goes un-used and the managed lanes create more value of time savings as HOT lanes. However, as truck volume increases, the value of the TOT lane surpasses the HOT lane, as trucks generate more savings than single and two-passenger vehicles. Over time, because of the larger size of trucks, the TOT lane capacity is reached and the value of operating the facility as a TOT facility plateaus. While the TOT operating strategy plateaus over time, for the 10-year time frame considered here, the HOT lane value continues to increase. This is because, while the HOT lane capacity can always be filled with SOV, the number of three- and two-passenger vehicles continues to increase. Overtime, these three and two-passenger vehicles can displace the SOVs on the HOT lane, which allows the time savings of the HOT lane to continue to increase. This is because while the utilization in terms of vehicles is constant, the utilization in terms of passengers continues to increase.

330

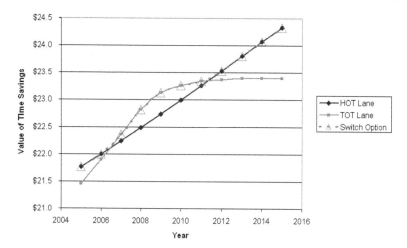

Figure 8-24 Value of time savings from operating the managed lane facility as a HOT lane or TOT lane. The ability to switch between operating states is also presented.

Since the relative value of the two operating states changes over time, there is value in the ability to switch between operating states.

Using a value of time metric, initially the managed lane facility should be operated as a HOT lane, then switched to a TOT and finally switched back to a HOT lane. This would ensure that the maximum value is extracted from the facility.

Re-visiting the idea of appropriate benefit metrics, the analysis above addressed only HOT and TOT benefits derived from travel time savings; toll revenues were not considered. *Adding in toll revenues to the analysis changes the outcome substantially, as shown in* Figure 8-25.

331

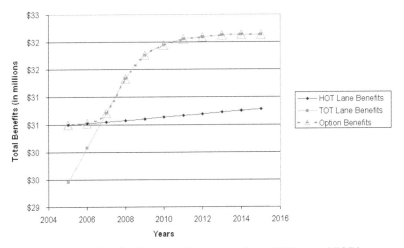

Figure 8-25 Total benefits of managed lane, operated as a HOT lane and TOT lane. Benefits from ability to switch are also shown.

As shown in Figure 8-25 the operating state of the managed lanes should again be started as a HOT lane and then over time switched to a TOT lane. While the preceding analysis using only time savings indicated that the operating strategy would be changed for a second time in the future back to a HOT lane, when considering both tolls and time savings, this changes. Instead of switching back to a HOT lane, the value of maintaining TOT lane operations are apparent.

While the usage of the lane is identical to that previously discussed, the value extracted is not. Here, while trucks reach capacity limits and the total benefits generated, it does so at a much faster rate than a HOT lane would. This is because for HOT lane operations there are two counteracting trends occurring. As a reminder, the HOT lane capacity is always filled, as SOVs can be allowed access for a fee, and there are more than enough SOVs to fill the HOT lane. The first trend is that over time the number of vehicles with two or more passengers increases, increasing the total number of passengers riding on the HOT lane. This trend increases the time savings from the HOT lane, as shown in Figure 8-24. The second trend however, dampens returns. While total passengers and total time savings increase, toll revenues decrease. This is because SOVs, which are assumed to pay a higher toll to gain access to the HOT lane, are reduced in number to make room for two and three-passenger vehicles. Under current conditions, three-passenger vehicles ride free. If this is maintained, total toll revenues will decline over time. While the total value of the facility increases, it does so at a slower rate due to the loss of toll revenues from SOVs.

This illustrates the importance of selecting the benefit metric in determining the operating mode for the managed lane facility. A purely public enterprise interested in maximizing societal gains may operate the facility as shown in Figure 8-24 while a purely private enterprise would operate the facility as shown in Figure 8-25. A public-private partnership could create tensions, as each partner would desire to operate the facility in different ways. A compromise could be created, such as transferring shadow tolls from the public enterprise to the private enterprise, *but the inherent conflict of interests between them may persist and could create externalities beyond the single facility.*

An example of the conflict between public and private partners in the operation of a HOT lane, and the externalities created, can be found on the SR 91 managed lane in California. SR 91 operates as a HOT lane utilizing congestion pricing and is operated by a private enterprise in a public-private partnership. This has created conflicts in operating strategies, as the private enterprise has exerted pressure through political channels on the public enterprise concerning improvements on nearby facilities. The private enterprise has been opposed to the public partner investing in improvements of nearby facilities. This is because nearby facilities would experience an increase in capacity, which would decrease congestion and hence decrease the demand for the tolled, congestion priced facility (FHWA 2003). *Here, the inherent conflict between the public and private partners have created externalities that have affected other parts of the network beyond the facility where the partnership is applied.*

The option values for the switch option are summarized below in Table 8-9.

Table 8-9 Summary of switch option benefits.

Operating Strategy	NPV (in millions)
Time savings value	
TOT lane *only*	$182
HOT lane *only*	$183
Switch option	$184
Switch option value	$184 – 183 = $1
Time savings value + toll revenue	
TOT lane *only*	$346
HOT lane *only*	$337
Switch option	$347
Switch option value	$347 – 346 = $1

From Table 8-9, the relative value between the inherent ITS value and the flexibility value is large, two orders of magnitude different for the analysis performed on the Katy Freeway.

While the delay option had inherent and flexibility benefits, magnitudes that were relatively comparable, this option shows that the same ITS capabilities utilized in a different manner produce different relative inherent and flexibility value.

333

In the delay option, considering ITS as a dual value design was worthwhile, as significant value was created in both inherent and flexibility values. For the switch option however, while flexibility value is still created, the flexibility value created is minimal when compared to the inherent value. In this case, the flexibility value added to the system is minimal and the dual value design concept did not add to the total benefits associated with the switch option.

However, even while the dual value design concept does not add value in every case, in general the importance of dual value design extends beyond the immediate value gained from the system. The recognition that some designs may produce a dual value is important, because otherwise the full value of the design may not be consistently investigated. This means that without recognizing that the design *may* have dual value, and then checking to determine if it does, either the flexibility value or the inherent value may not be recognized. As was seen in the delay option, the value from both sources was substantial, and the dual value design thinking was useful.

The final option, expanding the managed lane concept to congestion pricing across an entire facility or regional network was not analyzed quantitatively, due to a lack of necessary data. Data that could not be obtained included: travel types and the associated time value and elasticities (home to work, home non-work, non-home based) and transit ridership. Without this data we could not determine how congestion pricing would affect traveler behavior. For example, facing a toll travelers could elect to pay the toll, car-pool, take public transit, switch travel to off-peak hours or avoid the trip all-together. Without additional data, it was unknown how the resulting travel behaviors would effect flows and travel speeds, preventing the evaluation of the congestion pricing option. We leave the analysis of this option for future work.

8.3.3 ANALYSIS OF RESULTS

The following section summaries and synthesizes the results presented above to better understand the benefits that ITS provides with respect to flexibility. Also, the lessons learned while doing the analysis are discussed in terms of the analysis process.

Results presented above are summarized in Table 8-10.

Table 8-10 Summary of ITS case study quantitative results.

Option to Delay Capacity Expansion
Uncertainty of interest is in future traffic demand
Current QuickRide HOT lane Operating Strategy (Static tolls)
HOT lane has favorable Benefit-Cost Ratio > 1
When just considering toll revenues, HOT lane has an unfavorable Benefit-Cost Ratio < 1 • QuickRide static toll operating strategy not suitable for private operator without public agency support • Benefits indicate multiple PPP strategies could exist; shadow tolls, public actor deploys system and public actor operates system
Capacity Expansion through GP Lane Construction
GP lane investment is favorable with Benefit-Cost Ratio > 1
GP lanes have both greater NPV and greater costs than ITS HOT lanes • Lower ITS HOT lane costs may make it favorable to delay higher traditional infrastructure construction costs
HOT Lane operated with Congestion Pricing Strategy
Congestion pricing more fully utilizes facility
Significant speed benefits on the GP lanes are achieved with congestion pricing strategy, compared to static toll facility
Use of congestion pricing strategy, compared with static toll strategy, could delay irregular traffic flows by multiple years
Option to Delay Capacity Expansion Construction
Option to delay without ITS is worthwhile
Delay of capacity expansion construction allows opportunity to re-invest construction costs in other projects • Three general types of alternative investments exist; higher, lower and same returns as construction project • If alternative investment provides higher returns, then always delay and re-invest • Lower return investments denote political returns in addition to economic returns
Option to delay with ITS is more valuable than option to delay without ITS
Less value in option to delay when high growth is experienced on a facility with initial congestion
Using ITS in delay option creates significant dual value – the option has comparable inherent and flexibility values
Option to Switch Operating Strategies between HOT and TOT Lanes
Uncertainty of interest is relative share of mode growth
Option to switch is worthwhile
Selection of benefit metrics changes operating strategy
Enterprise architecture can affect the benefit metrics and hence the operating strategy
Enterprise architecture can create externalities that affect other facilities on the network, beyond the managed lane
Using ITS in the switching option does not create significant dual value – the inherent value of ITS is substantially greater than the flexibility value

Option to Delay Capacity Expansion – The option to delay capacity expansion construction on a congested facility is always present and has value, assuming that some alternative investment that provides comparable returns is available. The use of ITS on a managed lane facility does not create flexibility in this context, as this option already exists, but it does increase the value of the option. Using ITS on the managed lane to enable a congestion pricing operating strategy allows all of the remaining capacity to be utilized. By utilizing the existing capacity, additional vehicles can be removed from the GP lanes, which creates value not only for the vehicles using the HOT lane, but for the vehicles on the GP lanes as well, in the form of time savings. As seen from this analysis, using ITS in a more limited way, such as charging a static toll, as is being done with the QuickRide program, creates benefits, but not as much as a HOT lane using congestion pricing does. This is because the existing capacity is not being fully utilized.

The value of the option to delay capacity expansion construction is increased compared with an option to delay capacity expansion construction without using ITS because the increased capacity utilization on the HOT lane delays the onset of irregular traffic flow conditions on the GP lanes, possibly by years. This delay in investing in the capacity expansion construction allows other opportunities to be pursued, which otherwise may not have been possible as the funds would be used in the construction of additional capacity.

The operational strategy of the managed lane not only affects the benefits generated, but also helps determine the feasible enterprise architectures that could pursue deployment and operation of a managed lane facility. In all cases studied, the managed lane facility produced positive benefits that exceeded costs, making it a worthwhile investment for a government agency. However, when differentiating the benefits into societal and toll revenues, the benefit stream showed that deployment and operation of a managed lane facility would not be worthwhile for a private company acting alone. However, public-private partnerships seemed feasible from the analysis, with multiple strategies being apparent. For example, shadow tolls from societal time savings gains could be paid to a private operator from a public agency. Or, a public agency could fund the deployment of the managed lane facility and grant a concession to a private company to operate the HOT lane, as revenues exceeded operating expenses.

Option to Switch Operating Strategies - The option to switch operating strategies between HOT and TOT lanes was examined and found to have value. Further, ITS capabilities are needed to create this option. The manner in which the lane would be operated over time, either as a HOT lane or as a TOT lane, was found to depend on the benefit metric chosen. Considering just societal time savings benefits or considering both societal time savings benefits and toll revenues changed the relative value of the lane when operating as a HOT or TOT lane. In general, for the ten year period of interest, the managed lane facility is most valuable when used as a HOT lane, if just considering societal time savings benefits. However, when considering toll revenue as well as time savings benefits, the managed lane facility becomes more valuable when operated as a TOT lane.

Similar to the above discussion of the delay option, the choice of benefit metrics affects the enterprise architecture of the organization that would deploy and operate the managed lane facility. Additionally, the enterprise architecture affects the benefits that are of interest. Which perspective to use depends on the specific situation. The difference in perceived benefits and the resulting desire to operate the managed lane with different strategies could create conflict in a public-private partnership. Further, the conflict stemming from a public-private partnership would not need to be limited to the managed lane facility only. Instead, because the demand for the managed lane facility is partially dependant on the state of other nearby facilities, an operator of a managed lane facility interested primarily in toll revenues would maximize revenues when surrounding facilities were continuously congested. This creates externalities, as a private operator may seek, through political means, constraints on public agency investment in the transportation network that could negatively affect the managed lane revenues, even if it benefits society as a whole.

Finally, the consideration of options as dual value designs was shown to be of value in the delay option, but not the switch option. While the actual values generated in the switch option point to low flexibility values, and hence less of a need to consider the system as a source of dual value, the thinking behind dual value design seems sound. That is, without the thinking of dual value design, determining whether or not the system possess dual sources of value may not be done in a consistent manner. Further, dual value design considerations may lead to iteration within the design process, in an attempt to create additional value, either in the inherent value stream or the flexibility value stream, from a baseline state. This means that if a design is seen to provide benefits in only one stream, a design iteration may be called for to determine if benefits in the other stream could also be obtained.

Analysis Methodology - The results presented above show the need to perform the real options analysis with respect to multiple factors that may not be present in a "standard" real options analysis. In the ITS case study these additional factors included technical factors related to the ITS managed lane and the GP lanes, decision rules concerning when to exercise options, and choice of valuation metrics, which reflect the needs and effect the selection of stakeholders involved in the system, such as public or private enterprises.

The following chapter examines in more detail the practical challenges involved with using ITS in managed lanes in a flexible manner. The question is whether the flexibility benefits discussed here are achievable in practice. Challenges related to embedding "complex" real options "in" a complex system are identified and discussed.

337

8.4 REFERENCES

Banks, J. (2002) Introduction to Transportation Engineering, 2nd ed. McGraw Hill, New York.

Burris, M. and E. Sullivan. (2006) Benefit-Cost Analysis of Variable Pricing Projects: QuickRide HOT lanes, Journal of Transportation Engineering, March 2006.

Clemons, E. and B. Gu. (2003). Justifying Information Technology Investments: Balancing the Need for Speed of Action With Certainty Before Action, Proceedings of the 36 th Hawaii International Conference on System Sciences. Honolulu, Hawaii.

FHWA. (2003) A Guide for HOT Lane Development, Federal Highway Administration.

Greden, L., L. Glicksman, and G. Lopez-Betanzos. (2005). A Real Options Methodology for Evaluating Risk and Opportunity of Natural Ventilation. Proceedings of 2005 International Solar Energy Conference. August 6-12, 2005, Orlando, Florida.

H-GAC (2005) 2025 Regional Transportation Plan, Houston-Galveston Area

Katyfreeway.org. (2007) Katy Freeway construction information website at www.katyfreeway.org.

Miller, B. (2005) A Generalized Real Options Methodology for Evaluating Investments Under Uncertainty with Application to Air Transportation, MIT Doctoral Dissertation, Boston.

OMB. (1992) Office of Management and Budget Circular No. A-94: Guidelines and Discount Rates for Benefit-Cost Analysis of Federal Programs.

Poole, R. and C. Orski. (2003). HOT Networks: A New Plan for Congestion Relief and Better Transit, Reason Foundation, Los Angeles.

Transcad. (2000). Transcad user's Guide, Caliper.

TTI. (2002) Managed Lanes: More Efficient use of the Freeway System, Texas Transportation Institute TxDOT report 4160-5-P1.

Tufano, P. and A. Moel (1997). Bidding for Antamina, Harvard Business School Case No. 9-297-054. Rev. Sept. 15.

Wikipedia. (2007) Entry for Transportation forecasting.

9 CHALLENGES OF FLEXIBILITY IN HOUSTON GROUND TRANSPORTATION SYSTEM USING ITS

This chapter continues the analysis of the case study of using Intelligent Transportation Systems (ITS) and managed lanes to create flexibility in the Houston, Texas regional transportation network. The previous chapter quantitatively analyzed the options being considered, evaluating the benefits and costs of each of the options. This chapter continues the analysis by looking at the second research question, namely **"What are the practical challenges associated with "complex" real options in complex systems?"**

To answer this question, multiple people in Houston, representing a variety of stakeholders were interviewed. Combining the interview responses with Houston specific data, information sources (such as newspaper articles) and various academic literatures, a qualitative evaluation was conducted to better understand the challenges associated with "complex" real options in complex systems. An emphasis was placed on trying to understand what new challenges would be created with flexibility and what existing challenges would be made even more difficult because of flexibility.

The chapter first grounds this question in existing transportation planning processes. The qualitative research methodology used is then introduced. An inventory is then made of relevant stakeholders in the Houston transportation system to better understand the stakeholders involved in the system. An overview of the current situation in Houston is then presented to illustrate the environment that the stakeholders are operating within. Each of the major questions that were posed to the stakeholders are then addressed. These included;
- What are specific instances of flexibility currently being pursued in Houston?
- What are the processes used for designing, evaluating and managing flexibility used by your organization?
- What are your general views on flexibility and its challenges?
- What practical considerations related to institutional and enterprise architecture exist in designing, evaluating and managing the transportation system?

At the end of the chapter, the results collected from the stakeholder interviews are synthesized and five major lessons learned concerning challenges associated with "complex" real options in complex systems are presented.

9.1 TRANSPORTATION PLANNING PROCESS: RATIONAL VS PRAGMATIC

The transportation planning is conceptualized as a rational process that seeks to guide an orderly set of activities used to help systematically identify and solve transportation issues. Typically, these activities move through early stages of goal definition, identification of needs, development of alternative solutions, evaluation of alternatives and finally a decision process where a particular alternative is selected for implementation.

Incorporated into this view is that politics enters the process primarily at two points: political leaders, representing the public interest, help set goals for the transportation system and then the decision concerning system choices is resolved by input from elected officials, or leaders representing them. This process assumes a coherent set of goals across stakeholders in the transportation system (especially those directly involved in the planning process), that alternatives are developed to maximize system value (where the definition of system value is coherent), and finally that decision makers are primarily influenced by the goal to maximize system value (Banks 2002). Houston itself has such a rationale transportation planning process, summarized in 17 steps, shown below in Figure 9-1.

While this rational planning process was developed early in the professional history of planning, and is still used today by most planning organizations (Johnson 1997), it is widely recognized that practical considerations intrudes on this rationale planning process. Multiple other planning process ideologies have been developed to explicitly take political considerations into account (Johnson 1997). Instead of the planning process being purely rationale, the following departures are found:

- There is a fragmentation of organizations and stakeholders involved in the planning process, each pursuing their own priorities.
- Alternatives may not be designed to maximize value with respect to the system.
- Decision making may be primarily political instead of value maximizing for the system.

These departures from the rational planning process can greatly affect the transportation system compared to what would have been expected if all stakeholders had conformed to a rational planning process. While these departures from the rationale planning processes are known and create challenges in many transportation systems, these departures from the rational planning process can have increased importance when trying to design flexibility in the system. Practical considerations such as politics, institutional fragmentation, funding constraints, culture, legal and liability issues all can both create new challenges as well as increase the already present challenges that arise when developing and deploying a transportation system. Because of this, a qualitative analysis of "complex" real options in complex systems is deemed necessary.

The following section presents the research methodology that was used to perform the qualitative analysis in the ITS case study.

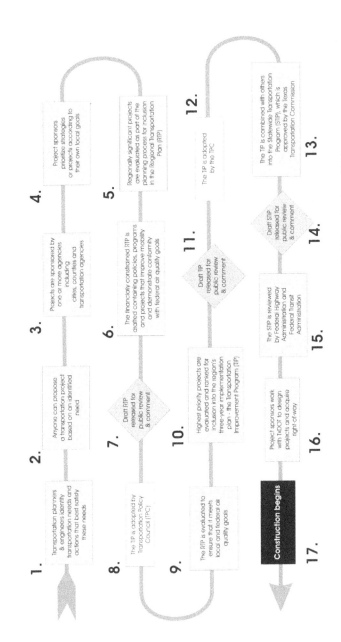

1. Transportation planners & engineers identify transportation needs and actions that best satisfy these needs

2. Anyone can propose a transportation project based on an identified need

3. Projects are sponsored by one or more agencies including cities, counties and transportation agencies

4. Project sponsors prioritize strategies or projects according to their own local goals

5. Regionally significant projects are evaluated as part of the planning process for inclusion in the Regional Transportation Plan (RTP)

6. The financially constrained RTP is drafted containing policies, programs and projects that improve mobility and demonstrate conformity with federal air quality goals

7. Draft RTP released for public review & comment

8. The TIP is adopted by Transportation Policy Council (TPC)

9. The RTP is evaluated to ensure that it meets local and federal air quality goals

10. Highest priority projects are evaluated and ranked for inclusion into the region's three-year implementation plan - the Transportation Improvement Program (TIP)

11. Draft TIP released for public review & comment

12. The TIP is adopted by the TPC

13. The TIP is combined with others into the Statewide Transportation Program (STIP), which is approved by The Texas Transportation Commission

14. Draft STIP released for public review & comment

15. The STIP is reviewed by Federal Highway Administration and Federal Transit Administration

16. Project sponsors work with TxDOT to design projects and acquire right-of-way

17. Construction begins

Figure 9-1 17 step planning process for Houston (from Gulf Coast Institute 2006)

342

9.2 QUALITATIVE ANALYSIS PROCESS

Previously in Chapter 7, three ITS in managed lanes real options were introduced. In Chapter 8, these real options were then evaluated in a quantitative manner, to better understand the costs and benefits associated with each real option. In keeping with the central theme of this research, because the options of interest in the ITS case study are "complex" real options in complex systems, quantitative analysis methodologies alone are not deemed sufficient in the evaluation of the options. Rather, additional machinery in the LCF Framework needs to be employed to more completely evaluate these "complex" real options in complex systems.

In order to better understand the challenges associated with "complex" real options in complex system, a qualitative analysis of ITS in managed lane options was conducted. The qualitative analysis performed here was general in scope and did not deal specifically with the options presented in Chapters 7 and 8 for two reasons. First, the options in Chapter 7 and 8 do not actually exist, but were instead used as a construct to illustrate feasible ITS in managed lane options that could be designed. In this manner, the options were used to demonstrate the ITS in managed lane option concept, the concept of dual value design, and to test out the quantitative analysis portion of the Life-Cycle Flexibility (LCF) Framework. Second, this research was exploratory in nature, regarding "complex" real options in complex systems. As exploratory research, it was deemed more valuable to perform a qualitative analysis on flexibility as it exists in the Houston transportation system. From this analysis, generalities and lessons learned could be obtained that would be useful for future attempts at designing, evaluating and managing "complex" real options in complex systems. This type of analysis was deemed sufficient, as the research serves as a proof of concept for the analysis of "complex" real options in complex systems.

The qualitative analysis consisted primarily of conducting interviews with stakeholders associated with surface transportation systems in general or the Houston surface transportation system in specific. Figure 9-2 displays the analysis procedures used in this research.

Note, that as a convenience to the reader, the case studies were written to stand alone. The case study analysis procedure described here is parallel to that described for the BWB case study in Section 6.1.

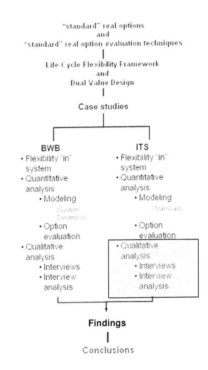

"standard" real options
and
"standard" real option evaluation techniques
|
Life-Cycle Flexibility Framework
and
Dual Value Design
|
Case studies
|

BWB
• Flexibility "in"
  system
• Quantitative
  analysis
  • Modeling
    (System
    Dynamics)
  • Option
    evaluation
• Qualitative
  analysis
  • Interviews
  • Interview
    analysis

ITS
• Flexibility "in"
  system
• Quantitative
  analysis
  • Modeling
    (Transcad)
  • Option
    evaluation
• Qualitative
  analysis
  • Interviews
  • Interview
    analysis

Findings
|
Conclusions

Figure 9-2 Case study analysis with highlighted box showing current stage of analysis.

The purpose of the analysis conducted for this research was not meant to directly update or change the quantitative analysis already performed, though in actual practice this should be the case. Since very little to no literature is available on "complex" real options in complex systems, the purpose of this qualitative analysis was to identify and better understand critical challenges that exist in practice. The qualitative analysis was used to help determine what types of practical challenges associated with "complex" real options in complex systems would be significant enough that they should be taken into account during the design and management of flexible systems. In essence, this portion of the case study sought to answer the first research question, applied to the ITS case study: **How do "complex" real options and "standard" real options differ across the life-cycle of an option, including design, evaluation and management activities?** Specifically, this portion of the research deals with better understanding the management of "complex" options.

The remainder of this section discusses how this question was answered.

344

The qualitative research methodology is discussed immediately below. Following this discussion, the objectives of the interviews conducted and how interviewees were selected is presented. The general set of questions used during the interviews is then presented, along with an overview of how the data was collected. The limitations associated with the qualitative analysis is then discussed.

9.2.1 QUALITATIVE RESEARCH METHODOLOGY

The results discussed in this chapter of the ITS case study were generated through the use of a case study analysis methodology. For this research, a variety of data sources were used to provide the necessary detail. While interviews were the primary source of data used, other sources included material on ITS capabilities, the popular press, organizational memos, official agreements / memorandums of understanding, legislation, and information on managed lanes and Houston that was found in the academic literature.

The selection of ITS capabilities as a case study topic was a fundamental choice for this research, which was driven by several factors. First, the technologies associated with ITS seemed suitable for the provision of flexibility. Second, ITS capabilities require involvement by public, and likely private, enterprises for deployment and management. Third, Houston was selected as the specific region of interest due to its leadership position in the deploying ITS capabilities. Fourth, prior research conducted by former graduate students covered ITS in Houston, which could then be built on (Dodder 2006). Finally, the primary research advisor for this dissertation has domain expertise in the field of ITS as well as contacts that were useful for beginning the ITS case study research.

The two case studies looked at in this research, ITS and the blended wing body (BWB) aircraft, were chosen to allow contrast between case studies. While the two case studies both involve "complex" real options in complex systems, the technologies, technical architectures and enterprise architectures for each case study is different. For the ITS case study flexibility is created with a technology, ITS. For the BWB case study flexibility is created with a technical architecture, the use of blending the wing and the body of the aircraft together. For the ITS case study an extended enterprise architecture is of interest, consisting of multiple public and private enterprises. For the BWB case study the primary enterprise of interest is a single private enterprise, primarily an aircraft manufacturer. These differences are summarized in Figure 9-3. The differences between case study technologies, technical architectures and enterprise architectures allows the LCF Flexibility concept to be tested on very different systems to more effectively exercise it and probe its limitations.

345

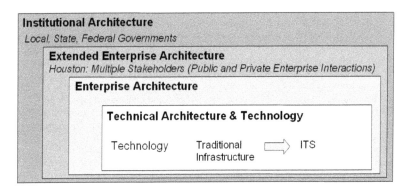

Figure 9-3 Characteristics of case studies on the dimensions of: technical architecture and technology, enterprise architecture, extended enterprise architecture and institutional architecture.

The next section discusses the objectives of the interviews.

9.2.2 INTERVIEW OBJECTIVES

The purpose of the interviews was to obtain information to better answer the research question of determining what practical challenges were associated with "complex" real options in complex systems. Interviews were chosen as the primary vehicle to do this for two reasons. First, the information available via interviews very often could not be found through any other means. While some information and prior study on ITS in managed lanes and the Houston transportation network were available, there was not enough found to be able to answer the research question. Second, the people interviewed had a range of practical experience with either ITS or with some aspect of the transportation system in general. The practical experience that they had could be tapped to better understand the practical challenges associated with "complex" real options in complex systems.

The data that was desired from the interviews covered practical challenges associated with the entire life-cycle of the option as well as the different types of drivers that influence the steps in the LCF Framework. A reminder of the phases in an option's life-cycle re-appears in Figure 9-4. The specific steps of the LCF Framework that played a role in the interview process are highlighted in Figure 9-5.

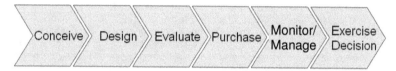

Figure 9-4 Life-cycle of an option.

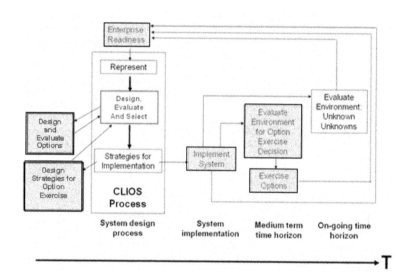

Figure 9-5 LCF Framework steps of interest for ITS case study.

The following section discusses the interviewee selection.

9.2.3 INTERVIEWEE SELECTION

As the interviews formed the primary data source for the ITS case study, the selection of the interviewees was important. The ideal set of interviewees would satisfy two objectives. The first objective was to have a set of interviewees that would facilitate collection of data on challenges facing "complex" real options in complex systems. Ideally, the interviewees would represent the breadth of stakeholders involved in a regional transportation system. The second objective was to have depth in the set of interviewees, which would allow cross-checking of data provided by individual interviewees.

Due to time limitations and difficulty in arranging interviewees the first objective was given priority. This priority on breadth of stakeholders was especially important for the ITS case study. This is because of the large number of stakeholders involved in any regional transportation system. While breadth was the priority in selecting interviewees, during the course of the interviews there was substantial overlap in the discussions held. This allowed interviewee statements to be cross-checked against one another. The cross-checking facilitated follow-up questions during interviews to better understand issues and interviewee's perspectives.

Selecting the interviewees occurred in three steps. First, in order to satisfy the breadth of stakeholder perspectives that was desired for the research, organizations that were deemed important to the Houston transportation system or to transportation systems in general were identified. Second, the types of people that were thought to have the most relevant perspectives related to understanding challenges associated with "complex" real options in complex systems were identified. As a general rule, it was believed that people higher in the organization's hierarchy would be the best to interview. This was because the people higher in the organization often have a wider range of concerns, including financial, managerial and political. As the LCF Framework attempts to address these types of challenges in flexible systems, the perspectives of this level of people was desired. Finally, a snowball sampling technique was employed. This means that after an interview was completed, the interviewee was asked to provide the names of other people they felt would also be good to interview. Having just completed the interview process themselves, the interviewee's had an increased familiarity of the research topics of interest, and the snow ball technique provided additional high-quality interviewees that otherwise would not have been contacted.

The stakeholders that were contacted for this case study fell into three broad categories, as shown in Table 9-1. The first category consisted of stakeholders in either a government transportation or urban planning agency. Stakeholders at the national, state, regional, county, city and sub-city levels were contacted. This first category contained the largest number of interviewees of the three categories. The second category is essentially a catch-all category. Elected and appointed officials, business leaders, citizen group representatives and environmental group representatives were all interviewed. The final category involved stakeholders in academic and think tank positions. It should be noted that some of the interviewees in this third category were also actively involved in trying to influence the regional transportation system.

Table 9-1 Functional activities performed by interviewees for each case study.

ITS Case Study

• Transportation agency personnel
    • National level
    • State level
    • County / city / sub-city level
• State and Local stakeholders
    • Political leaders / appointees
    • Business / developers
    • Citizen
    • Environmental
• Academic and think tank

To accomplish the first objective of creating breadth in the interview data, a stakeholder map was created (presented in Section 9.3). The stakeholders identified represented a range of interests in the transportation system and served as a basis for selecting interviewees.

In general, it was expected that stakeholders from transportation agencies would have a good understanding of both the specifics concerning the ITS and managed lane systems, as well as an understanding of the considerations that went into decision making. The stakeholders representing political leaders were interviewed to better understand the concerns and influence on decisions that they exerted. Business leaders and land developers were expected to provide the perspectives of stakeholders that were pro-growth and favored expansion of the transportation network to accommodate and enable additional economic growth. Citizen and environmental groups were expected to provide the perspective of stakeholders that were generally opposed to growth in the transportation network and may prefer alternatives other than traditional capacity expansion.

Finally, academics and think tank stakeholders were expected to provide a "big picture" perspective as they were not involved in the day-to-day concerns of the transportation system, but instead had as their purpose the study of the system. Academics at MIT and Houston think tank personnel were contacted.

In total, thirty interviews were conducted for the ITS case study. The majority of the interviews were conducted in one-on-one sessions, either in person or via telephone. One of the interviews was conducted via email.

A complete list of the organizations and positions of the interviewees is provided in Table 9-2. The selection of the organizations was done in a manner to try and best represent the range of stakeholders that were of interest. Within the organizations, interviewees at managerial levels were sought out. In many cases the leader of the organization was interviewed.

Table 9-2 ITS case study organizations and roles of interviewees. .

Organization	Role	Interviewees
Transportation and Planning		
Houston Galveston Area Council (MPO)	Director	Alan Clark
METRO	Director Traffic Management	Loyd Smith
Transtar	Director	John Whaley
TxDOT, Houston District	Director Transportation Operations for Houston District (retired Oct. 2006)	Sally Wegmann
TxDOT, Houston District	Deputy District Engineer	Delvin Dennis
Harris County Public Infrastructure Department	Manager of Traffic and Transportation	Andy Mao
Grand Parkway Association	Executive Director	David Gornet
Houston Downtown Management District	Director, Planning, Urban Design and Development	Patrick Hood-Daniel
Greater Greenspoint Management District	President	Jack Drake
USDOT, FHWA, Office of Transportation Management, Congestion Management and Pricing	Program Manager	Patrick DeCorla-Souza
USDOT, FHWA, Office of Transportation Management, Congestion Management and Pricing	Team Member	Angela Jacobs
USDOT, FHWA, ITS Joint Program Office, Integrated Corridor Management	Congestion Program Manager, formerly FTA Team Leader of Advanced Public Transportation Systems	Brian Cronin
USDOT, Volpe Center, Economic and Industry Analysis Division	Team Member	Jane Lappin
USDOT, Volpe Center, Economic and Industry Analysis Division	Project Manager	Alan DeBlasio

USDOT, Volpe Center, Office of System and Economic Assessment	Chief Economist	Don Pickrell
USDOT, Volpe Center	Surface Transportation Infrastructure and Operations Domain Expert	Gary Ritter
USDOT, Volpe Center, Service and Operations Planning Division	Team Member	Scott Smith
Political		
TX State Legislature	TX State Legislator	Rob Eissler
City of Houston	Executive Assistant to Mayor for Transportation Planning	Carol Lewis
Harris County Commissioners Court	Director of Transportation and Infrastructure Initiatives	Rose Hernandez
Land Developers		
West Houston Association	President and CEO	Roger Hord
North Houston Association	Executive Director	Paula Lenz
Commercial		
Greater Houston Partnership	Chair, Transit Planning Committee	Jack Drake
Citizen Groups		
Citizens Transportation Coalition	Chair	Robin Holzer
Houston Property Rights Association	Founder	B.J. Klein
Environmental		
Houston Regional Sierra Club	Group Conservation Chair	Frank Blake
Research / Think Tank		
Texas Transportation Institute, Center on Tolling Research	Director	Chris Poe
Texas Transportation Institute, Research and Implementation for ITS	Program Manager	Tony Voight
Gulf Coast Institute	President	David Crossley
MIT	Researcher staff	Fred Salvuci

The following section discusses the interview questions that were used for this research.

9.2.4 INTERVIEW QUESTIONS

A series of questions was crafted to better understand the challenges associated with "complex" real options in complex systems. The interviews were semi-structured and constructed around an open-ended question format. The semi-structured nature of the interviews was deemed appropriate for two reasons. First, the research was exploratory. As such, the research questions evolved not only between interviews but in the process of the interviews as well. As new information was uncovered, the interview questions were modified to take it into account. Second, given the wide range of organizations represented by the interviewees, semi-structured questions that could be modified where needed so that they would be appropriate for each interviewee's perspective.

Six general questions were asked for each of the interviewees. The six questions appear below along with a brief discussion on the type of information being sought for each one. It is emphasized that these six questions are not the only questions that were asked. Follow-up or more detail questions were also asked to get further detail on specific topics. These follow-up and detailed questions varied from interviewee to interviewee, though the six general questions remained constant across interviewees.

1. How does your organization fit into the transportation planning process?

    The purpose of the first question was to gain a better understanding of the role that the interviewee's organization played in the planning process. Also, a better understanding of the organization's objectives and positions was sought out.

    In a similar manner, interviewees were also often asked to answer this question about other stakeholders. This allowed comparison of responses across stakeholders and also uncovered additional information concerning relationships between stakeholders.

2. Can you provide examples where flexibility is currently being used by your organization or by other organizations?

    For interviewees in transportation agencies, examples where the interviewee's organization was using flexibility were initially sought out. Later in the interviewing process, after several examples had already been obtained, more information on these examples was sought out, as opposed to seeking new examples. For interviewee's not in transportation organizations, their perspective on the flexibility examples raised by other interviewees was desired.

    In general, an understanding of whether flexibility is being used in practice was desired. If so, an understanding of how it was being used was the subject of the follow-up questions. The objective of this question was to better understand how flexibility was being used, what were its perceived benefits and costs, and what challenges were being experienced when using the flexibility.

3. If flexibility is used, can you provide examples of processes used by your organization to identify, design, evaluate or manage flexibility?

>For interviewees belonging to organizations using flexibility, a better understanding of what types of processes were being used to identify, design, evaluate and manage the flexibility was desired. If the interviewee's organization had a process, a better understanding of the successes and challenges associated with using the process were was of interest.

4. What is your organization's position on the benefits and costs associated with flexibility?

>The interviewee's general thoughts about the utility and feasibility of using flexibility were of interest. This question allowed general views on flexibility to be explored, independent of the flexibility that was actually used. This question was deemed important to try and understand what stakeholders felt about flexibility, i.e. is it a good idea or not, without the pre-conceived notions associated with the performance of current systems using flexibility.

5. What are the critical enterprise and institutional architecture challenges that have been encountered by your organization?

>In relation to flexible systems, interviewees were asked about practical challenges that were faced during the life-cycle of the flexibility. Any type of challenges was of interest.

>This question also expanded the interview beyond a discussion on flexibility. Independent of flexibility, interviewees were asked to discuss the critical practical challenges that their organization regularly faced. This question was then used to try and determine if any of these challenges would affect flexible systems, and if so, would these challenges increase or decrease in magnitude due to the presence of flexibility.

6. Are there other critical points that should be discussed?

>Finally, at the end of the interview, once interviewees had a better understanding of the topics of interest, they were asked to identify any other points that they felt would be of importance.

The following section discusses data collection from the interviews.

353

9.2.5 Interview Data Collection

During interviews, extensive hand written notes were taken. No recording devices were used in an attempt to not inhibit interviewee responses. The handwritten interview notes were then typed up and analyzed for major points.

In some cases follow-up questions concerning the interviewee response was asked at a later date. In other instances, follow-up with questions were posed to other interviewees. No full follow-up interview with the same interviewee was deemed necessary or practical

While interviews were the primary source of data used for this part of the case study analysis, additional data sources were also used. These included information on ITS capabilities, managed lanes and Houston such as: academic literature, the popular press, organizational memos, official legal agreements / memorandums of understanding, and legislation.

In a few cases material was provided from interviewees. In most cases these additional data sources were found independent of the interviewees.

9.2.6 Limitations

Several limitations to this research are present, as noted below.

- **Case selection** – Two case studies were selected for this research; the ITS and BWB case studies. Including only two case studies from a much larger space of complex systems raises questions on the generalizability of the findings from this research. The large differences in technologies, technical architectures, and enterprise architectures between the two case studies was an attempt to address this limitation. As a result it is felt that the findings from this research are generalizable, but this should be further verified with additional case studies. However, the research provided here can create a framework in which additional case studies can be conducted.
- **Number of interviews** – The topic of interest for this research was "complex" real options in complex systems. One of the characteristics of the complex nature of the system is the large number of stakeholders involved in the system. To determine all of the stakeholder's perspectives requires a large number of interviews. Interviews with a diverse range of stakeholders were conducted to meet this research need. Of course, additional interviews that further expanded the range of stakeholders interviewed would have been worthwhile. For example, no interviews were able to be conducted with stakeholders representing the freight industry, which is an important stakeholder in any transportation system, but especially so for Houston, given the large amount of freight moving through the region from either the Port of Houston or from Mexico. Additionally, more interviews of people in the same organization would have been beneficial to cross-check information provided. Also, in some cases follow-up interviews with earlier interviewees would have been helpful, after a better understanding of the system was obtained during the entire interview process.

- **Increased data sources** – The non-interview data sources were very helpful in providing details to several of the points being made by interviewees. Additional access to data sources, such as organizational memos or agreements would have also been helpful.

Much of the rest of this chapter focuses on the data obtained from the interviews and then a synthesis of that data in the final section. The data found from the interviews is organized according to the high-level interview questions previously presented. Data specifically addressing the first and last questions are not presented in its own section. Rather, the results for these questions; relating to the background of the organization and follow-on comments made by interviewees, is incorporated directly into the results presented for the other four questions.

As a reminder, the four general questions that will be addressed following the stakeholder map are as follows:

1. Can you provide examples where flexibility is currently being used by your organization or by other organizations?

2. If flexibility is used, can you provide examples of processes used by your organization to identify, design, evaluate or manage flexibility?

3. What is your organization's position on the benefits and costs associated with flexibility?

4. What are the critical enterprise and institutional architecture challenges that have been encountered by your organization?

A map of the major stakeholders involved with the Houston transportation network are presented in the next section.

9.3 STAKEHOLDER INVENTORY

Much literature has been written that describes the fragmentation of local governments, starting in the 1930's (Studenski 1930), and the host of stakeholders that can play a pivotal role in urban decision processes, including transportation planning processes (Hunter 1953, Judd and Swanstrom. 2004). The result of this type of fragmentation is the lack of decision making that maximizes value for the region as a whole; instead creating benefits for specific stakeholders at the expense of the region.

Below is a short description of the primary stakeholders involved in the Houston transportation planning process. These organizations are grouped according to their affiliation, and presented in the following categories; government transportation agencies, elected officials, business related interests, and citizen / environmental interests.

9.3.1 GOVERNMENT AGENCIES

In the Houston metro area, government control of the transportation network is fragmented between several different agencies. The major stakeholders providing transportation services include: the City of Houston, Harris county (and the other seven counties surrounding Harris Country), Houston's transit agency Metro, the toll road operator Harris County Toll Road Authority (HCTRA), the metropolitan planning organization Houston-Galveston Area Council (H-GAC), and the ITS coordination and operations organization Greater Houston Transportation and Emergency Management Center (TranStar). At the state level, the Texas Department of Transportation (TxDOT) has twenty five local districts, one of which, the Houston District, is responsible for transportation activities within the Houston area. At the Federal level, the US Department of Transportation also is involved in transportation planning, usually through the Federal Highway Administration (FHWA) or the Federal Transit Authority (FTA). The following gives a brief overview of the role that each agency plays in Houston's transportation system.

Several organizational charts are included in the discussion below to help illustrate the relationship between the different stakeholders. Stakeholder organizations were an interview was conducted are highlighted in each chart.

9.3.1.1 City of Houston

The City of Houston's Public Works and Engineering Division is responsible for the "administration, planning, maintenance, construction management and technical engineering of the City's infrastructure" (City of Houston PW&E 2007). This includes, among other public utilities, the transportation infrastructure, such as local roads, with 16,000 lane miles (City of Houston PW&E 2007), and traffic control intersections.

An interview was conducted with the primary Mayoral political appointee for transportation policy issues, the Executive Assistant to Mayor for Transportation Planning. This is shown in the organizational chart in Figure 9-6.

9.3.1.2 Harris County

Harris County is the major county by population in the Houston metro area. The transportation responsibilities of Harris County for providing local road infrastructure and intersections are similar to those for the City of Houston, but extend outside of the city's borders.

Harris County has major transportation related responsibilities as about 1.7 of the 3.7 million Harris County residents live outside of Houston city limits. For these citizens, Harris County is the sole provider of transportation services. As an indicator of the importance that Harris County plays in the provision of transportation infrastructure, the size of Harris County is 1,778 square miles, compared to 1,214 square miles for the state of Rhode Island. The population of Harris County living outside of Houston City limits that rely solely on Harris County for transportation needs is about 1.7 million, compared with about 1 million for Rhode Island.

An interview was conducted with the Harris County Manager of Traffic and Transportation and the Harris County Director of Transportation and Infrastructure Initiatives, a political appointee of the county judge. This is shown in the organizational chart in Figure 9-6.

The Houston metropolitan region consists of seven other counties, with each of the surrounding counties providing similar services as Harris country, though at a smaller scale, reflecting their population sizes and travel needs. Figure 9-7 shows the counties in the Houston region.

9.3.1.3 Metro

The Metropolitan Transit Authority of Harris County, or Metro, is the transit service provider for the Houston region. Metro operates multiple transit modes, including light rail in downtown, local buses and commuter buses. In addition, Metro built, operates and enforces travel on the high occupancy vehicle (HOV) lanes in Houston, which is one of the most extensive networks in the country, at over 105 lane miles (Metro 2007). Metro provides a variety of other services, such as para-transit, ride matching, motorist assistance and park and ride operations.

9.3.1.4 HCTRA

The Harris Country Toll Road Authority (HCTRA) is a special authority created to build and manage toll roads in the Houston metro area. HCTRA has built a series of toll roads, 83 miles over multiple toll roads (HCTRA 2007), and substantial supporting infrastructure, such as bridges and ITS capabilities, to support the toll roads. HCTRA was formed in 1983 as a result of funding shortfalls in both TxDOT and, the now disbanded, Texas Turnpike Authority. These funding shortfalls prevented several major Houston area roads from being funded and built at the time. As the roads were left to be funded locally, and Harris County also could not fund the roads from its general budget, HCTRA was created via voter referendum to build two of these roads. Since then, HCTRA has expanded its system to include additional toll roads around the Houston area, with plans for more roads being actively pursued.

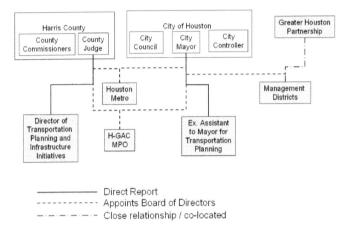

Figure 9-6 Organizational Chart showing city and local level stakeholders. Interviewees are highlighted.

9.3.1.5 H-GAC

The Houston-Galveston Area Council (H-GAC) is the MPO that is responsible for coordinating all urban and transportation planning in the Houston region, serving five additional counties plus the seven counties immediately adjacent to Harris County, for a total of 13 counties, shown in Figure 9-7. HGAC was originally organized by a local initiative in 1966 to serve the core eight counties, expanding to all 13 counties in 1971 (HGAC 2007). Transportation plans are approved by the Transportation Policy Council (TPC) before being recommended to H-GAC's governing Board of Directors, composed mostly of elected officials from the surrounding counties and cities.

Figure 9-7 H-GAC area of responsibility. Figure taken from H-GAC website (HGAC 2007).

The relationship between H-GAC and other regional stakeholders is shown in the organizational chart in Figure 9-6.

9.3.1.6 Transtar

Transtar, created in 1993 and opened in 1996, is a partnership for providing traffic and emergency management services to the Houston metro region. The four partner organizations are the City of Houston, Harris Country, Metro and TxDOT. Transtar operations are based heavily on the use of ITS capabilities, such as cameras, variable message signs and a traffic control center, which together provide services such as near real time traffic flow conditions and improved emergency management.

The relationship between Transtar and the four partner stakeholders is shown in Figure 9-8.

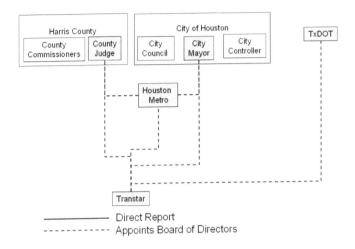

Figure 9-8 Relationship between Transtar and the City of Houston, Harris County, Metro and TxDOT.

9.3.1.7 TxDOT

Texas Department of Transportation (TxDOT) is the state transportation agency that "plans, designs, builds, operates and maintains the state transportation system" (TxDOT 2007). The TxDOT Houston District has responsibility for the six largest counties in the Houston metro region, excluding the more rural counties east of Harris County. Most of the major arterials in the Houston area, with the exception of HCTRA funded toll roads, are built on TxDOT right-of-ways. Most of these roads were built and are maintained with TxDOT disbursed funds, with the exception of the HOV lanes which were partially built with FTA funding distributed through Metro (though the HOV lanes are also on TxDOT right-of-way).

State level stakeholders are shown in the organization chart in Figure 9-9.

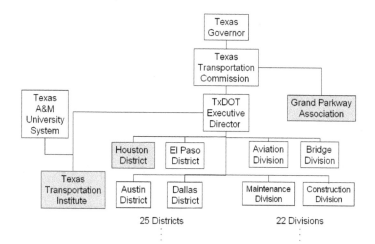

Figure 9-9 State level stakeholders.

9.3.1.8 USDOT

The U.S. Department of Transportation, starting operations in 1967, was created to help develop and coordinate policies to facilitate an efficient and economical transportation system (USDOT 2007). USDOT operates over multiple modes, only some of which pertain to the ground transportation system. For the ground transportation system, the Federal Highway Administration (FHWA) and the Federal Transit Administration (FTA) are the primary agencies responsible for funding the construction and maintenance of physical infrastructure. Additionally, through other programs the FHWA and FTA also offer funds for ITS projects.

National level stakeholders are shown in the organizational chart in Figure 9-10.

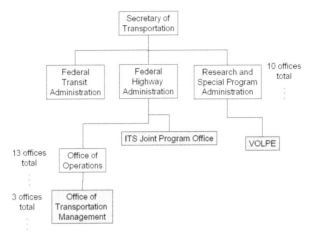

Figure 9-10 National level stakeholders.

9.3.2 POLITICAL ACTORS

The following section discusses the primary political stakeholders for the Houston regional transportation system.

9.3.2.1 Houston Mayor and City Council

The Mayor and City Council of Houston are together responsible for policy and funding decisions that relate to the transportation system. Houston has a strong mayor form of government, and as such, the Mayor has substantially more impact on the transportation system in the city than the city council, from goal setting, policy positions and funding decisions. Additionally, the Mayor is able to appoint five out of nine board members to the Metro Board of Directors, with the remainder being appointed by Harris County and other city's serviced by Metro, giving the Mayor effective influence over Metro priorities and funding decisions.

9.3.2.2 County Judge and Commission

The county judge is an elected position for Harris County with similar powers and responsibilities as the Mayor of Houston, but for Harris County. The County Commissioners Court has five members, including the country judge, and serves a similar role as the Houston City Council, but for the county. The county judge serves as the executive for a number of different transportation related offices, such HCTRA and the Harris County Office of Homeland Security and Emergency Management (Harris County 2007).

362

9.3.2.3 State Legislators and Governor

The governor and legislatures in tandem create transportation policy and help appropriate funds across the state of Texas, including the Houston metro area. In Texas, the governorship influences transportation policy at TxDOT indirectly by appointing all members to the five-member Texas Transportation Commission. The state legislature is bicameral, with both House and Senate transportation committees.

9.3.3 BUSINESS INTERESTS

Business leaders and land developers were two of the most important stakeholders in the Houston regional transportation system. Development districts, while strictly a government agency, are very closely aligned with private interests and receive funding from assessments placed on local businesses.

9.3.3.1 Greater Houston Partnership

The Greater Houston Partnership (GHP) is the premier business organization for the Houston area. Comprised primarily of executives from the largest corporations and business owners, the Houston Partnership advocates to represent the interests of Houston businesses. In the 1930's through 1960's the forerunner to the GHP was comprised primarily of representatives of the oil industry, though this began to diversify significantly in the 1970's (Parker and Feagin 1991). The GHP is an umbrella organization created in the late 1980's to coordinate the advocacy activities of multiple pro-business groups and continues to work closely with local government on transportation issues, among others.

9.3.3.2 Development Districts

Houston has a number of development districts that are, technically, special authorities created by the Texas State Legislature in the 1990's. The development districts are designed to leverage public funding by supplementing them with private resources. The development district activities are individually guided by a Board of Directors, which is primarily composed of members from the business community.

9.3.3.3 Land Developers

Stakeholders involved in land developing, including realtors, architects, construction firms, land speculators, as well as developers, comprise a large group of stakeholders in the Houston metro area. Multiple advocacy organizations that primarily represent land developer interests have been set up and are active in the Houston area.

9.3.4 CITIZEN GROUPS

Small groups of citizen coalitions and environmental groups were active in Houston.

9.3.4.1 Citizen coalitions and think tanks

Citizen groups in Houston are a relatively new phenomenon. Currently, only a few umbrella groups and think tanks representing citizen and neighborhood interests are active in the Houston area, though this is an increase from the past. Past trends, continuing today, have seen more citizen organization focused on specific projects, rather than sustaining organizations.

9.3.4.2 Environmental

A few environmental groups operate in Houston, representing a variety of environmental issues, from air quality to land use. Local chapters of national organizations are also present and active in transportation planning issues.

The stakeholder inventory shows the number of stakeholders involved in the Houston regional transportation system. As would be expected with such a wide variety of stakeholders in a transportation system, the goals and relative power between these stakeholders differs substantially. More detail on the individual stakeholders and their relationship with one another is presented, as needed, in the results for the remainder of the chapter.

The following section presents the current situation in Houston with respect to these stakeholders. After this, the four interview questions are addressed.

9.4 CURRENT SITUATION IN HOUSTON

The following section presents an overview of the current situation in Houston. Broad, general trends that were found from the literature and from the interview process are presented to create a backdrop to help understand the current transportation situation in Houston. An overview of the current long range plan and a proposed alternative, are presented next. Finally, a few recent key events that are changing the nature of transportation planning in Houston are presented.

9.4.1 GENERAL TRENDS

In most cities, a growth coalition committed to economic expansion presents the dominant ideology and greatly influences the planning process (Altshuler and Luberoff 2003). In this dimension, Houston may be even more dominated by growth politics than most cities, with its lack of any type of land use zoning (Parker and Feagin 1991), rapid expansion and growth of geography and road networks, dominant role of the business community (Parker and Feagin 1991) and the relative "invisibility" of citizen groups (Judd and Swanstrom 2004). This heavy preference towards growth is reinforced in both explicit institutional structural and informal arrangements in the city. For example, the Mayor of Houston has power to appoint all department heads in the city, with the exception of the City Controller. Typically, on major decisions, the mayor has already met with business interests before meeting with department heads (Parker and Feagin 1991) and since the department heads serve only at the discretion of the mayor, it becomes relatively easy to present a pro-business agenda. Another example is the relationship between government agencies such as Metro and the city and the Greater Houston Partnership. Major addresses on agency and city policy are typically announced at luncheons held by the GHP. Even management districts, created by the state legislature, are often either co-located with a local chamber of commerce or headed by a member of the GHP. The geography of Houston also facilitates a pro-growth agenda, as the Houston region is relatively unconstrained by natural barriers, save for the Gulf of Mexico on the south east side of the city. As a result, continual expansion, especially to the north and west sides of the city has occurred, as large amounts of undeveloped land still exist in those areas.

To support the growth plans of Houston, a large investment in infrastructure for roads has been made and investments continue. As Houston had been without any rail based transit until the 2000's, it has become an overwhelmingly auto-based city. Combined with suburban booms and large increases in population starting in the 1960's (Parker and Feagin 1991), Houston has built an extensive network of roads extending far from the central business district. The vast majority of these roads are large arterials built on TxDOT right-of-way, making TxDOT a significant player in any Houston transportation system issues, due to this ownership. Additionally, since the TxDOT Houston District is a single district covering the majority of the Houston metro region, compared to other cities like Dallas-Ft. Worth where multiple TxDOT districts exist, it has created, what one interviewee described as the "800 lb gorilla" in Houston transportation planning.

In general, multiple interviewees described relationships between the major transportation agencies in Houston as cordial and informal, with agencies routinely asking one another for, and receiving, day to day operational help when incidents arise. Also, interviewees indicated that their partnership with one another through Transtar helps facilitate more cooperation, and is growing as the partners become more involved with Transtar.

Metro has recently completed laying a light rail system in downtown Houston, the first segment of an ambitious regional transportation plan that expands multi-modal transportation access across the region (Metro Phase II 2003). As other researchers have noted (Dodder 2006), Metro is a relatively well funded agency, being partly funded with local sales taxes. However, due to political resistance from local and national political leaders opposing LRT in Houston and supporting increased road and ITS investments instead, Metro was forced to fund the $324M 7.5 mile LRT segment out of local funds, forgoing federal support (Metro Solutions 2007). As one interviewee noted, this has left Metro in a weaker financial position than it has been in the past, resulting in some question as to the timing for future rail and BRT expansion.

This weak financial position is contrasted with what several interviewees described as HCTRA's cash flush status. Increasing numbers of toll facilities and heavily increasing usage of these facilities have contributed to HCTRA's revenues rising steadily for the last several years, as shown in Table 9-3. The increasing revenues have helped contribute to HCTRA's ability to continue their expansion plans. A number of projects are currently being actively built, such as the I-10 Katy Freeway expansion, on the Westside of Houston, or are at various stages of consideration, such as US 290 Northwest Freeway expansion and re-alignment along Old Hempstead Road or the conversion of the HOV network to HOT lanes.

Table 9-3 HCTRA revenues (HCTRA Financial Statements 2003-2006)

Year	HCTRA Revenues
2003	$260M
2004	$277M
2005	$342M
2006	$370M

In general, the pro-growth climate and heavy involvement of business and developer interests in the transportation planning process, combined with a financially weakened Metro, financially strong HCTRA, TxDOT ownership of right-of-ways and relatively small citizen groups, contributes to a strong bias in pro-road infrastructure expansion to meet a growing and more dispersed regional population.

9.4.2 CURRENT LONG RANGE TRANSPORTATION PLANS

H-GAC currently has a long range plan; the 2025 Regional Transportation Plan for the Houston-Galveston Area. The 2025 plan projects continued population growth of over 65% from 2000 levels and continued decentralization of Houston living, working and travel patterns (HGAC 2005). Projecting major congestion with the current infrastructure and system operations in 2025, the plan proposes three major classes of solutions; expanded road and transit infrastructure, improved operations and demand management strategies, with a projected cost of around $77B (HGAC 2005). However, the plan relies heavily on expanded road infrastructure to meet much of the needs and is fuzzy on where transit funding would come from (Crossley 2004). The 2025 plan focuses primarily on the expansion of existing roads, with only 1,554 miles of new center lane capacity, but 13,271 miles of new lane mile capacity, compared with 2002 amounts (HGAC 2005).

In response to what has been viewed by citizen and environmental groups as a very road intense long-range plan that does not address the primary issues of urban planning, sprawl and environmental concerns, an alternative plan called Blueprint Houston has been developed. This alternative plan was developed in conjunction with H-GAC and a private land use planning firm, where a series of workshops entitled Envision Houston were opened up to a variety of stakeholders for input (HGAC 2006). The alternative plan differed greatly from the 2025 plan, in that an alternative urban planning paradigm was examined, concentrating less on low density development between major roadways and more on mixed residential, business and retail land use in clusters, rather than spread out.

The resulting plan forecasted more transit usage and lower vehicle miles traveled and lower congestion levels (HGAC 2006).

Currently, the Envision Houston process results are being used as an alternative scenario to the 2025 scenario, with HGAC now presenting both scenarios to decision makers. As one interviewee described it, prior to this exercise, HGAC was only presenting one scenario, the one laid out in the 2025, but they are now presenting two scenarios, the 2025 and Blueprint Houston plans. As another interviewee explained, the use of clustered and higher density developments was a threat to extant land development interests and the future of development similar to that presented in Blueprint Houston was still far from certain. This view was reinforced from an interviewee representing land developers, who felt that land use such as that proposed in Blueprint Houston would require government intervention and that such intervention would inherently favor one type of land use over another, disadvantaging current styles of land development.

As a result of the increased activity from citizen groups surrounding the Envision Houston process it is unclear what the future direction of Houston land use and transportation development will follow. It does seem apparent that invested interests in current urban and transportation planning forms will likely resist any change to the status quo.

9.4.3   KEY EVENTS

A key event that is changing and has the potential to further change many aspects of transportation planning in Houston is the recent passage of House Bills 3588 and 2702 from the 78th and 79th sessions of the Texas legislature, held in 2003 and 2005 respectively. House Bills 3588 and 2702 are both Omnibus transportation bills, covering multiple transportation issues. House Bill 3588 contains at least two issues of relevance to this research. First, H.B. 3588 authorized TxDOT to raise money for projects through debt financing, i.e. by floating a bond. Second, it allows TxDOT to engage in tolling, either for new facilities being designed or via conversion of existing facilities, subject to certain constraints (H.B. 3588 2003). These changes are substantial compared with the alternatives that were available to TxDOT and to the impact this is having on its relationship with other agencies, especially HCTRA.

Prior to H.B. 3588, TxDOT could only fund projects on a pay as you go basis, where transportation monies came primarily from taxes raised from state ($0.15/gallon) and federal ($0.184/gallon) gas taxes and motor vehicle registration fees (Governors Business Council 2006). Using tax sources for funding, projections indicate that TxDOT will face a $66B budget shortfall, of which about $44B would come from state funding sources, over the next 25 years, to pursue current transportation plans (Governors Business Council 2006). This means that multiple projects would either need to be canceled, delayed or have their construction period slowed in order to pay for the facility. Budget shortfalls from the 1980's and the resulting delays to building planned facilities were the primary reason for the creation of HCTRA, which was allowed to debt finance the construction of the original two toll roads in the HCTRA system; the Hardy Toll Road north of Houston and the Sam Houston Toll Road running primarily in the east-west portion of Beltway 8 corridor (the secondary ring road around Houston). Debt financing is estimated to save years in the construction of a facility, as it avoids the need to pace construction under a pay as you go scheme (Sallee and Brewer 2002).

Related to the debt financing portion of H.B. 3588 is the potential for TxDOT to convert gas tax roads or build new roads as tolled facilities. The potential to toll the facility can secure a revenue stream that can then be used to secure the debt financing. As HCTRA has shown, tolled facility revenue sources in Houston can be quite substantial.

As part of the tolling ability granted in H.B. 3588, TxDOT has multiple new alternatives in managing the tolled facility. TxDOT can operate the facility itself, engage in a partnership, such as a public private partnership (PPP) or divest itself from the facility to a third party.

H.B. 2702, passed two years after H.B. 3588 in the following legislative session (the Texas legislature only meets every other year), clarified and enhanced several perceived shortcomings in H.B. 3588. For example, while H.B. 3588 granted TxDOT authority to engage in tolling, it did not grant it authority to engage in all activities needed to operate a tolled facility, such as enforcement. H.B. 2702 enhanced TxDOT authority to make it a viable tolling operator.

Historically, TxDOT has been a very traditional state DOT. "Growing up" in the Eisenhower era of Interstate construction, multiple interviewees characterized TxDOT as being an agency focused on construction, not operations. Indeed, one interviewee with long standing experience with TxDOT continued by characterizing TxDOT as being resistant to the idea of tolling in general and the subsequent demands it would place on operations. Before H.B. 3588, TxDOT would often enter into agreements with local agencies regarding the use of its right-of-way, especially if they were not able to develop the right-of-way themselves. For example, the Sam Houston Toll Road was built and is tolled by HCTRA entirely on TxDOT right-of-way, which was simply turned over to HCTRA.

The era of simply turning over right-of-way to other agencies seems to be over with the passage of H.B. 3588 / 2702. TxDOT has realized the potential value that it can now directly exploit from the right-of-way and is determined to leverage that value to help make up its funding shortfall. For example, TxDOT is currently expanding the lanes on the Katy Freeway, as discussed in more detail below, in partnership with HCTRA. HCTRA is expanding the current two HOV lanes and converting them, plus additional right-of-way, into four high occupancy toll (HOT) lanes that it will operate and collect revenue on. To do this, HCTRA has entered into an agreement with TxDOT that pays TxDOT $250M outright and provides another $250M in loans (TxDOT/ HCTRA Memorandum of Agreement 2003). This agreement is much different than the free right-of-way 20 years earlier for the Sam Houston Toll Road right-of-way.

Discussions with interviewees with knowledge of both TxDOT and HCTRA have stated that the new ability of TxDOT to toll, and their subsequent desire to earn a return on their right-of-way, similar to the TxDOT/HCTRA agreement for the Katy Freeway expansion, has started to create friction between the two organizations. While TxDOT has the newfound powers of tolling, forces appear to be at work to limit the exercise of this power, at least in urban areas. The culture of TxDOT itself is firmly rooted in construction and not in operations. As one interviewee with knowledge of TxDOT responded, this culture of construction, combined with the difficulties TxDOT has encountered trying to expand or build new roads in the urban environment of Houston has made TxDOT and other political players start to look for other "playgrounds" for TxDOT. In support of this notion, H.B. 3588 also moves forward with the idea of the Trans-Texas Corridor, a massive multi-modal tolled facility running the north-south length of Texas. With support from local agencies and business groups for keeping toll revenues local (Great Houston Partnership 2006), TxDOT may be preparing, or forced, to exit major toll road construction in urban areas in the near future.

An effect of H.B. 3588 / 2702 appears to be the changing of relationships between TxDOT and other local agencies. As TxDOT can now directly price their right-of-way, all indications, and interviewees with knowledge on the subject agreed, appear to be that TxDOT will carefully value their right-of-way and require any agency wanting to use or convert use of that right-of-way in the future to pay a price. This may be further complicated by continuing disagreements on funding and distribution of revenue sources between state and local control. Overall, H.B. 3588 / 2702 appear to have added to the complexity, at least in the short-term, for an already fragmented local transportation system.

The following four sections present the results of the four questions asked during the interviews. As a reminder, the four questions considered were:

1. Can you provide examples where flexibility is currently being used by your organization or by other organizations?

2. If flexibility is used, can you provide examples of processes used by your organization to identify, design, evaluate or manage flexibility?

3. What is your organization's position on the benefits and costs associated with flexibility?

4. What are the critical enterprise and institutional architecture challenges that have been encountered by your organization?

9.5 EXAMPLES OF FLEXIBILITY IN THE HOUSTON TRANSPORTATION SYSTEM

This section presents the results from the first of the four questions: **Can you provide examples where flexibility is currently being used by your organization or by other organizations?**

This section focuses on current instances of where flexibility is being used in the surface transportation system in Houston. An overview of multiple systems where flexibility was explicitly designed into the system is presented, along with the current status of the flexibility.

9.5.1 KATY FREEWAY EXPANSION

The portion of Interstate-10 west of Houston, called the Katy Freeway and constructed in the 1960's, is now one of the most congested freeways in the United States. Designed initially for 60,000 vehicles per day, it now carries over four times that amount on typical weekdays (Katy Program 2004). As a solution to this congestion the Katy Freeway is currently undergoing significant widening, from 250 feet to 410 feet, over a length of about 12 miles (Katy Program 2004). The areas of expansion start just west of Texas State Highway 6 and ends near I-610 West, the inner ring road around Houston, as shown in Figure 9-11. At present, the construction is set to let in nine separate contracts, one for each proposed segment, with construction planning on being completed around 2009. Total estimated costs are about $1.45 B (Katy Freeway Organization 2007).

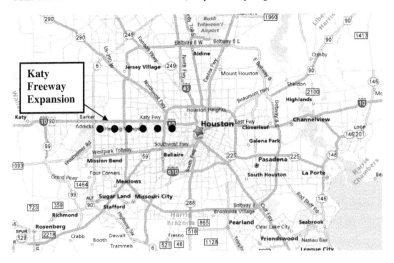

Figure 9-11 Map of Houston showing area of Katy Freeway expansion. Map from Mapquest.

Currently, the cross section of the Katy Freeway varies along the length of the corridor, but at a minimum has three general purpose lanes and two frontage lanes, in each direction, with five general purpose lanes at its widest. In addition to the general purpose and frontage roads, the Katy also currently has a combination of diamond or HOV lanes along most of the length being expanded. The diamond lanes are managed lane facilities on the inner left of the road, down the centerlane. The diamond lanes are separated from general traffic by a painted stripe, as shown in Figure 9-12. The HOV lane is barrier-separated from the general traffic flow and in some places is elevated above the general purpose lanes, as shown in Figure 9-13.

Previously, the diamond and HOV lanes were restricted to 2+ occupancy vehicles, but due to high usage, lane restrictions were changed several years ago to 3+ occupancy vehicles. However, starting in 1998 under the FHWA's Value Pricing Pilot Program, authorized by the Intermodal Surface Transportation Efficiency Act (ISTEA) as the Congestion Pricing Pilot Program, and then renewed with the Safe, Accountable, Flexible, Efficient Transportation Equity Act: A Legacy for Users (SAFETEA-LU), some amount of pricing was added to the operation of the managed lanes on the Katy Freeway. Under the pricing scheme administered by Metro, 3+ passenger vehicles could still use that facility for free, but at certain times of day 2+ passenger vehicles could gain access to the managed lane for a flat fee of $2. The purpose of the pricing was to use the excess capacity created by the shift in operations from 2+ to 3+ vehicles and to generate extra revenue.

Figure 9-12 Diamond lane separated by painted line only.

Figure 9-13 Limited access HOV lane in Houston. Picture from FHWA.

Under current construction plans, the entire Katy Freeway is to be widened, to different degrees along its length. At its maximum, the facility will be between 18-20 lanes wide, composed of, from the center, two managed lanes, four or five general purpose lanes and three frontage road lanes, running in each direction. Under the proposed plan, the four managed lanes will be a combination of diamond lanes and barrier-separated lanes. The new managed lane facilities will all be HOT lanes 24 hours a day, with free access continued to be reserved for 3+ passenger vehicles and transit vehicles. Tolls will be collected using open road tolling based on transponder / dedicated short range communication (DSRC) ITS capabilities. The managed lanes will also be equipped with operator-less booths that accept coins and credit cards for travelers without the required transponder. Additionally, the ITS infrastructure installed on the managed lanes will have the option to switch to full congestion pricing if traffic conditions drop below the goal of maintaining traffic levels at level C or better.

Another change to the Katy Freeway managed lanes is in operators, as HCTRA will be in charge of operations, as opposed to Metro. Under an agreement with TxDOT, HCTRA is responsible for upgrading the facility with the additional lane capacity, additional ITS capabilities and management of the lane (HCTRA . TxDOT 2003). Under a related Memorandum of Understanding (MOU) between HCTRA and Metro (HCTRA / Metro 2002) HCTRA will take over operation of the HOV lanes on the Katy Freeway. In the MOU between HCTRA and Metro, HCTRA further agrees to continue to provide free access to the facility for 3+ passenger vehicles, Metro transit vehicles and various Metro support vehicles. The total number of transit vehicles able to use the facility under the agreement is 65 per hour, in each direction, with an additional 300 tags provided for Metro support vehicles (HCTRA / Metro 2002).

Also of interest is another part of the agreement that creates the option for Metro to convert the HOT lanes to a LRT system at some point in the future. Part of Metro's long-term plan includes a LRT line along the Katy Freeway right-of-way. The most cost effective place to put it has been found to be in the same physical space as that occupied by the HOT lanes, as opposed to off to one side of the freeway, which would require an elevated track along the entire freeway length (Houston Chronicle 2002). However, proceeding with the LRT line would require the conversion of all of the right-of-way reserved for the HOT lanes to rail. Also, the LRT line requires additional physical support infrastructure on the bridges, due to the additional weight of the trains. The MOU between HCTRA and Metro explicitly covers the option to convert the HOT lanes to LRT. In this case, HCTRA and Metro are both paying portions of the option cost. HCTRA is funding the expansion of the current single diamond and HOV lane into four lanes. Metro's part is funding the cost difference in the upgrading of the bridges during construction to enable the bridge to support a future LRT line, if the option is exercised. The option terms are described in the MOU and allow Metro to reclaim the right-of-way from HCTRA at some point in the future, for a price.

As a summary of the optionality, the managed lanes on the Katy Freeway can be considered as having multiple options built "in" to the system design, as described below. Note that these options are the options that are actually in existence, as opposed to the proposed options discussed in the preceding two chapters.

1. **Operational option 1** - The building of the managed lanes, diamond and HOV, in the 1980's created an option in how the lane can be operated. Lane operations have been changed in the past, such as increasing the occupancy requirement from 2+ to 3+ passenger vehicles, once congestion on the managed lanes became too great. However, the 3+ passenger requirement created unused capacity. Without ITS capabilities, however, this was the best the lane could be operated. With the addition of ITS capabilities, the managed lane can be upgraded to a HOT lane, with a combination of free and priced travel. Here the option to manage the lane with ITS was exercised in 1998 with the deployment of ITS technologies that facilitated the pricing scheme used in the QuickRide program on the Katy Freeway. In this case, the construction of the managed lane would be the option price, the addition of the ITS would be the exercise price and the underlying uncertainty would be the level of traffic demand for the facility.

2. **Operational option 2** – The inclusion of the appropriate ITS equipment also creates another option, the option to switch the pricing strategy for the HOT lane. Currently, the HOT lanes are operated as free lanes for 3+ passenger vehicles and transit vehicles, and 2+ passenger vehicles must pay a flat fare at selected times of day. Once reconstruction is done the HOT lanes could be managed as 24 hour congestion pricing lanes, and the option to do so is being designed into the system. In this case, the option price is the additional cost needed to deploy ITS technologies that are capable of the more sophisticated congestion pricing

scheme, instead of flat fee tolling. As the ITS technologies are already deployed, the financial costs for exercising such an option are near zero.

Note that in the options considered in the previous chapters, an additional operating state was also considered; namely operating the lanes as truck only toll (TOT) lanes. However, TOT lane operations have not been seen on the Katy Freeway to date.

3. **Mode switch option** – Bridges along the Katy Freeway are being upgraded during reconstruction to allow a future conversion from auto / bus traffic on the HOT lanes to deploying an LRT line. Metro can exercise this option at some point in the future. Here, the option cost is the additional costs for the higher load bearing nature of the bridges. The exercise costs will be the conversion of the roadway into a LRT line, plus the difference in revenue that is expected between the HOT lane and the fare box from the LRT. Note, depending on the pricing scheme and demand for the HOT lanes and LRT line, it is possible that the LRT fare box revenues could exceed the HOT lane revenues, making this "cost" an additional benefit.

9.5.2   HOV TO HOT CONVERSION

Similar to the conversion of the diamond and HOV lanes on the Katy Freeway into HOT lanes, Metro is looking at the possibility of converting its entire HOV network into a HOT network. This option is at a very early stage, with meetings to address this topic starting in late 2006. Metro is currently considering upgrading the ITS capabilities on its HOV lanes to allow a future option exercise to congestion pricing if needed. In tandem, Metro is considering the expansion of the facilities along several corridors, which are now mostly single, reversible lanes and in many corridors the HOV lanes are already near capacity, leaving little excess capacity to sell under a HOT lane scheme. Metro is currently investigating different operating strategies, where either they operate the HOT lanes directly or turn over operations to HCTRA, in a similar manner as was done on the Katy managed lane facility.

9.5.3   WESTPARK TOLLWAY PRICING AND CONSTRUCTION

The Westpark Tollway is a new tolled facility that opened in 2004 in west Houston, as shown in **Figure 9-14**. The facility is mostly a four lane toll road, two lanes in each direction, that utilizes advanced ITS capabilities capable of open road tolling and congestion pricing. Both were designed into the system at its conception. To date, the option to change the pricing scheme from a static tolling charge, based on vehicle entrance location and number of axles, to a congestion based pricing scheme has not been exercised. This is even with current congestion levels that create a level F service.

The Westpark Tollway is a not only a new tollway, it is also new to the Houston transportation plan, as it does not appear on any plan before 2001 (TexasFreeway.com 2001). The tollway was built on existing commercial rail right-of-way previously owned by the Southern Pacific Railroad. In 1992, Metro purchased the 100 foot wide right-of-way from Southern Pacific. The original intention was to connect several Park and Ride facilities along that corridor with a reversible HOV lane. Also, in the future a potential rail line could be built.

However, due to interest in a tollway for that corridor by developer and business interests, and with the support of Harris County, considerable pressure was placed on Metro to reach a compromise to create a toll road. However, with a change in administration of the Houston mayoralty, the Metro right-of-way was not transferred to HCTRA. Where the previous Mayor had been anti-rail and pro-road, the new Mayor was pro-rail, resulting in appointment of a Metro board that supports rail based policies. A resulting compromise had Metro selling half of its right-of-way to HCTRA. HCTRA used the right-of-way, supplemented by additional right-of-way from adjacent Westpark Road and high voltage utility right-of-ways, to build Westpark Tollway. Metro maintains the other half of the right-of-way and has yet to develop it, though there is discussion on developing it either as an HOV lane or as a LRT line.

Two examples of options can be found in the Westpark Tollway.

1. **Operational option** – This option allows the pricing scheme of Westpark Tollway to be switched from a static toll to congestion pricing, similar to that described above in the Katy Freeway options discussion.
2. **Option to delay** – Metro sold half of its right-of-way but has kept the other half. While Metro has not decided what mode to support in the right-of-way, one interviewee described the situation as having an option that could be exercised in the future, depending on Metro's future needs and resources. In this case, purchasing the right-of-way from Southern Pacific represents the option cost, while the option exercise cost is represented by the sum of the build out costs and the forgone benefits lost from an earlier build out.

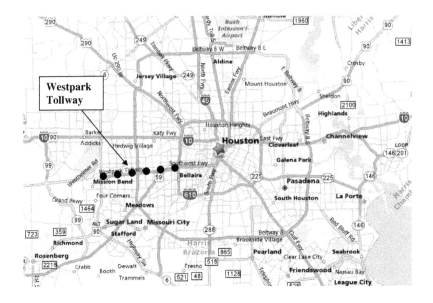

Figure 9-14 Map of Houston showing Westpark Tollway. Map from Mapquest.com.

The above examples clearly illustrate the desirability of flexibility in the use of managed lanes and ITS in Houston. In many of the cases presented above, the flexibility was enabled through the deployment of ITS capabilities. Without these ITS capabilities, the flexibility would be limited or would not exist at all.

Additionally, the above examples clearly show that flexibility "in" systems is considered by transportation planner and practitioners.

Later in this chapter, in Section 9.8, how the use of flexibility impacts the system and how the system impacts the use of flexibility will be discussed. The Katy Freeway and Westpark Tollway examples will be used to illustrate this discussion, along with some additional examples.

While these examples illustrate the desirability of flexibility in transportation systems, the next section looks at the process that stakeholders use to recognize, design and evaluate flexibility in systems.

9.6 PROCESSES FOR IDENTIFYING, DESIGNING AND EVALUATING FLEXIBILITY IN SYSTEMS

This section presents the results from the second of the four questions: **If flexibility is used, can you provide examples of processes used by your organization to identify, design, evaluate or manage flexibility?** An overview of interviewee experience with processes associated with flexibility is presented below.

As was found, the presence of a process for identifying, designing or evaluating flexibility was not evident for any stakeholder.

Without some sort of process, the concept of flexibility in systems is difficult to institutionalize into the standard practices of transportation organizations. As a result, it is unlikely that flexibility is being used as often as it could be in the surface transportation system.

As none of the stakeholders interviewed had a process in place, the need for a process was instead discussed.

9.6.1 PROCESSES TO SYSTEMATICALLY IDENTIFY AND DESIGN FLEXIBILITY IN SYSTEMS

The literature has several examples of processes for evaluating real options, as discussed in Section 2.5. However, it quickly became apparent from discussions with practitioners in the transportation field that there was currently no process for identifying, designing or evaluating flexibility in systems. While many interviewees recognized the benefits of flexibility, not one knew of any formalized or informal process that would aid in designing flexibility in systems, or evaluating it once it was in the design. A few of the interviewees were aware of generic tools, such as real options, but had not seen them applied by others and had no immediate plans for looking into these concepts.

Instead, the ability to recognize instances where flexibility would be useful and design it into systems was seen as more of a combination of luck, skill, experience and circumstances. If the conditions were right and someone with enough skill and experience was around, interviewee responses indicated someone may seize the opportunity to design flexibility in the system.

The good news from this behavior was that interviewees consistently recognized the value of flexibility and could act opportunistically to design flexibility in systems when appropriate. But the bad news from this behavior was that there was no process to institutionalize the consideration of flexibility as a way to cope with uncertainty. This means that it is unlikely that flexibility could be considered in a consistent manner.

The need for a process to help design and valuate flexibility in a system was seen differently by stakeholders at the local and national levels.

Locally, interviewees were less enthusiastic about the need or prospect for additional processes to follow during transportation planning. The reason for this could be because of the large number of processes that are required in the planning process currently, or it could be because of the need to conform with existing design standards, for legal and liability reasons. Additionally, local planners were not overly interested in being able to quantitatively evaluate the flexibility being designed in the system in terms of the value of flexibility itself.

This thinking differed sharply from program managers and analysts at the federal level. At this level, most of the interviewees believed that flexibility had the potential to increases the value of projects over their life-cycles. Several interviewees were actively studying how to include flexibility in systems that they had direct contact with, or were aware of research or other programs were this was of interest.

The difference in interests in processes to consistently and systematically design flexibility in systems between local and federal planners is possibly due to the different role in the transportation planning process that each plays. While many managers and analysts at the federal level have a very high level, long range view of particular systems and their life-cycle, local level planners are more detail oriented and concerned with implementation activities concerning day to day considerations. When asked about having to deal with considerations such as politics and legal issues, these practical considerations seemed to occupy more of the time of local level stakeholders than of federal level stakeholders.

9.6.2 PROCESSES TO EVALUATE FLEXIBILITY

Federal level interviewees also had a greater interest in evaluation techniques for flexibility than local level interviewees.

Part of the reason for this interest may be the more analytical and high level view of planning taken by federal level planners. But part of the explanation could be found in the response of one federal level interviewee who gave the following example of local initiatives for bus rapid transit systems (BRT). This interviewee had seen most of the proposals for federal funds that local regions around the country had submitted for BRT systems. It was pointed out that almost all of them had a common thread of flexibility in the proposals, where the BRT would have an option to be converted into a LRT system at some future date. It was noted, however, while the benefits of the flexibility were qualitatively described, there was no analysis comparing the benefits to the costs needed to proceed with the flexibility. The interviewee described the result as some proposal having a dubious cost associated with supporting the flexibility to convert the BRT lines.

An example of this type of dubious flexibility was brought up by multiple interviewees in Houston who mentioned plans to build managed lanes with an option for future LRT. The dubious flexibility came from the plan to lay the rail tracks during construction and then pave over them with asphalt, allowing the asphalt to be removed at a latter date if funds for the LRT could be obtained.

The federal level interviewee continued with hypothesizing that the localities were often submitting these types of dubious flexibilities in proposals as a way to engage in political and funding maneuvers. The interviewee mentioned that most of these localities had wanted LRT lines, but the current federal administration preferred funding BRT lines instead of LRT lines, due to the lower costs involved. Not to be deterred, the localities submitted proposals for BRT lines, but included flexibility for future conversion to LRT lines. Officially the flexibility would be exercised if demand warranted an LRT line. The interviewee however felt that realistically, if the political climate towards rail transit solutions changed with the next presidential administration the options would be exercised and the LRT lines would be built, regardless if that was justified by demand levels. In this way, the localities could move forward towards a LRT line, with the federal funding going towards a flexible BRT line, where the flexibility would get the localities as close to a LRT line as possible.

Because of these types of repeated requests, a means of quantitatively evaluating the costs AND benefits of flexibility in proposals was seen as worthwhile at the federal level.

The greater desire at the federal level to have a systematic means of evaluating flexibility does not seem surprising, given that localities were using flexibility as a means of getting the federal government to continue funding initiatives that diverged from its stated policy goals.

From the interviews, it quickly became apparent that while flexibility was appearing in multiple systems and was perceived to have value, there was no systematic process for recognizing, designing or evaluating flexibility. Furthermore, there was disagreement on the need for such processes, with local level interviewees seemingly less interested than their federal level counterparts.

A summary of the responses for the question concerning processes for identifying, designing and evaluating flexibility are listed in Table 9-4.

Table 9-4 Summary of interviewee responses to the use and need for a flexibility process.

Stakeholder Processes
No stakeholder had a process for systematically identifying, designing or evaluating flexibility
Stakeholder Positions on Need for Flexibility Process
Stakeholders had a different view on the need for a flexibility process
• Local level stakeholders did not see a need for a new process
• Federal level stakeholders saw a need for processes to aid in the design and evaluation of flexibility

The following section presents an overview of interviewee views of flexibility in general.

9.7 SUMMARY OF INTERVIEWEE VIEWS ON FLEXIBILITY

This section presents the results from the third of the four questions: **What is your organization's position on the benefits and costs associated with flexibility?** An overview of interviewee general views on flexibility are presented below.

In general, interviewees were mostly receptive to the idea of including flexibility in systems. This receptivity to flexibility, combined with the examples of flexibility currently in the Houston surface transportation system discussed in Section 9.5, indicate that flexibility in systems is not uncommon. For the most part, the concept of flexibility in systems was viewed in a good light. Contrary to the views held in academia, at least in the MIT Engineering Systems Division, the concept of flexibility in systems was not seen as novel, but as common sense and a common practice when feasible.

While interviewees were receptive to the idea of flexibility, they also pointed out challenges with flexibility in general and existing organizational characteristics that would make utilizing flexibility difficult.

9.7.1 STAKEHOLDER IDENTIFIED CHALLENGES WITH FLEXIBILITY

Most interviewees had an intrinsic understanding of the use of flexibility in systems, specifically, real options "in" a system's technical design. As many of the interviewees were relatively highly placed in their organizations, they also had a feel for several of the difficulties that would be created with using flexibility in systems. Four concerns cited by multiple stakeholders are described below.

1. Several interviewees saw flexibility as an attempt to look ahead into the future and try to understand possible solutions to problems whose status is currently unclear. To address these situations that may or may not occur in the future required some type of investment today. This investment today creates two problems.

   a. First, future problems are being addressed with today's dollars. Interviewees felt there was not enough money to deal with today's problems, let alone tomorrow's problems and that while it made sense and created lower life-cycle costs, it was difficult to justify the spending initial if there was not an immediate need for system change.

   b. Second, making the investment in options even more difficult was the feeling that the investment may or may not be used. It was felt that at least with investing in problems being faced today, there was certainty that the money would be used, while investing in tomorrow's problems, it was uncertain the money would ever be used.

2. A common problem identified with flexibility was how the value would be manifested in an easily understandable and presentable manner. As one interviewee stated, a politician "can't cut a ribbon on flexibility". While flexibility can have outcomes that allow ribbon cutting, the value of flexibility

may not be tied to a physical project, making it hard to present the benefit to others.

3. Real options were not seen as a way of providing, as one interviewee said, "real flexibility". Instead, options were seen as requiring plenty of foresight and skill in both determining what the important uncertainties would be and what solutions would be good in meeting various potential future outcomes. This was seen as too similar to predicting the future. Instead, "real flexibility" would entail the ability to quickly change to circumstances that you did not think of previously or had not already planned for.

The LCF Framework and the concept of DVD together provide solutions to all of the concerns raised above. In response to the first three concerns (1a, b, and 2) the use of a DVD technology or technical architecture provides inherent benefits in addition to flexibility benefits. These inherent benefits create immediate value that can be used in all circumstances. While the flexibility value stream may be difficult to present, the inherent value stream may provide a "ribbon-cutting" opportunity.

The last concern about "real flexibility" is analogous to the ability to address unknown unknowns, which is included in the LCF Framework. The LCF Framework focuses more on addressing unknown unknowns through enterprise or institutional architecture mechanisms, but the potential for a physical system architecture that is capable of addressing unknown unknowns deserves more attention.

9.7.2 ORGANIZATIONS AND FLEXIBILITY

Interviewees also favored some types of options over other types. Interviewees were systematically more interested in options that dealt with growth or expansion. This is in contrast to options that dealt with abandonment or even switching to some extent. Interviewees felt that growth options could make use of prior investments, while options to abandon or switch may waste prior investments. Culturally, the idea of waste seemed tied to the use of a specific physical investment rather than the impact that the investment had on the operation of the overall system. This type of cultural aversion to options that downsize or abandon prior investments has been discussed in Section 3.1.2.4.

Designing flexibility in a system requires some proactive thinking during the conceptualization of the system, identifying critical uncertainties and possible outcomes that would unfold if the option were exercised or not. *Several local interviewees noted that this type of proactive thinking was not uniform and often not commonly done within their organizations, or at least was not adhered to.* Rather, the organization often found itself making decisions more reactively, such as reacting to requests from political leaders or pressure from stakeholders that would then shape their decisions. This can create a problem when long-term plans include contingent actions that require organizations to act proactively, but they are only used to acting reactively.

Finally, one interviewee noted that the skills needed for designing and analyzing such options would mean additional training to understand the financial impact of the design decisions being made concerning flexibility. This state level interviewee noted that being trained as an engineer was no longer enough; "now people needed training in both engineering and finance".

Interviewees were able to point out fundamental shortcomings in their organizations, such as culture, standard operating procedures and training, which served as barriers to embracing processes to better add flexibility to systems. Interestingly, some of the lack of interest in developing such skills at the local levels may be because of the way that flexibility is being used, described here as less a matter of increasing system value and more as a means of political and funding request subterfuge to obtain funding for the project that is desired at the local levels, getting around the fact that local objectives are not aligned with federal policy goals.

A summary of the major findings for this section are listed in Table 9-5.

Table 9-5 Summary of findings for interviewee perspectives on flexibility.

Interviewee views on flexibility
In general, interviewees felt flexibility in systems was good
Several examples of flexibility in systems in the Houston surface transportation system were found
Flexibility did not appear to be considered consistently, rather only opportunistically, meaning it is likely opportunities are being overlooked.
Interviewees preferred options that dealt with growth or expansion, rather than abandonment or switching
Organizations and flexibility
Interviewees stated that organizations spent most of their time reacting instead of acting proactively.
Interviewees noted a lack of financial analysis skills among transportation personnel

The following section discusses interviewee responses to limitations to option use due to various practical concerns that must be taken into account during the life-cycle of the option. Various challenges that appear throughout the option's life-cycle are identified and discussed.

9.8 ENTERPRISE AND INSTITUTIONAL CHALLENGES RELATED TO FLEXIBILITY

This section presents the results from the last of the four questions: **What are the critical enterprise and institutional architecture challenges that have been encountered by your organization?**

382

During the interview process, several dimensions of the institutional architecture were identified as having the potential to create barriers at one or multiple points during the life-cycle of options. The following discussion looks at several of these barriers, drawing from multiple examples discussed with the interviewees. These institutional architecture barriers come from a variety of sources, including: institutional fragmentation of authority, responsibility, budgetary powers and interests, lack of political will, legal / liability reasons, and fundamental incompatibility of flexibility with stakeholder needs. How each of these create barriers at different stages in the life-cycle of an option are discussed below, with specific examples used to illustrate each.

9.8.1 INSTITUTIONAL FRAGMENTATION

The fragmentation of government at local levels has repeatedly been a source of consternation for local reform advocates and study in the urban and transportation planning literatures. Advocates for reform have advocated an end to government fragmentation, to be replaced with a single government that could represent the region (Judd and Swanstron 2004). Identified problems associated with fragmented governments include (Morgan and Pelissero 2007):

- Less efficient administration and planning because of overlapping jurisdictions, duplication of services and lack of economies of scale
- Low political accountability to citizens
- Lack of area wide planning and an increase in coordination costs
- Fiscal disparity between different areas
- Variation in services across region

In addition to government fragmentation, when taking into account all stakeholders that are involved in transportation planning, the fragmentation is even greater. This is because there are a variety of non-governmental stakeholders that are directly involved in or influence the transportation planning process.

The problems identified in the literature with fragmentation also pertain to flexible systems. In many of these cases the same issues apply to flexible systems as to non-flexible systems, but to a greater degree because of the flexibility included in the system. The remainder of this section provides three examples of the effect that stakeholder fragmentation has on flexibility.

9.8.1.1 Katy Freeway Expansion

Revisiting the example presented above on the Katy Freeway in Section 9.5.1, institutional fragmentation is evident in the need to involve TxDOT, HCTRA and Metro in multiple agreements. While an agreement was eventually reached to include the option for HOT lane to LRT conversion in the construction plans, there is much evidence that the conflicting goals of the stakeholders involved made this difficult. In this example, the conflict was between stakeholders supporting transit and those supporting roads and toll roads. For transit supporters, the first best alternative was to build the line now. A second best alternative was the option to build in the future, as this prevented the worst alternative, foreclosing the possibility of transit in the future, from occurring. For road and toll supporters, the opposite was true. The best alternative was the removal of rail construction from the managed lane right-of-way. The second best alternative was the delay of any rail construction to sometime in the future. As each set of stakeholders had their own preferences on how to use the right-of-way, the conflict over the option spilled over into the political arena, including political leaders at the local and state levels.

A few notable quotes from political leaders against the inclusion of the Metro HOT / LRT conversion option include;

> *Metro wants to come to the table with no money, no expertise, and claims they don't want to stall the project. If it takes legal action to keep them from sticking their fundless claws into this project, I (Harris County Commissioner Steve Radack) am prepared to ask Commissioners Court to pursue it. (Brewer and Sallee 2002)*

> *U.S. Rep. John Culberson boorishly threatened that Metro would 'rue the day they slow down one spade of dirt or one concrete pour.' (Houston Chronicle 2002)*

> *Culberson's ally, Harris County Commissioner Steve Radack, threatens to sue Metro to "keep it under control." (Houston Chronicle 2002)*

> *Radack and (Harris Country Judge Robert) Eckels said Metro lacks credibility with county officials and the public, especially compared with the toll road authority. While the latter generates revenue and gets things done efficiently, they said, taxpayer-subsidized Metro is mistrusted and viewed skeptically (Sallee, Brewer and Hindan 2002)*

One interviewee said that the local pressure against Metro to drop the option was overwhelming and would have succeeded if not for the intervention of another political leader, who they declined to name. According to the Houston Chronicle, Texas U.S. Senator Kay Bailey Hutchison asked Metro and TxDOT to "consider ways to incorporate light rail along I-10 from downtown Houston to Katy" (Houston Chronicle 2002).

The participation by Metro did not seem to be the issue. Suggestions from the same political leaders quoted above suggested that Metro could "spend some of their money on the project as we're planning it, that's fine" (Sallee, Brewer and Hindan 2002). The existence of rail in the corridor also was not entirely ruled out, as two political leaders quoted above suggested that Metro could build the rail line along the side of I-10, though that would require an entirely elevated track that would cost twice as much as running it down the middle of I-10 (Houston Chronicle 2002). A schematic of the two possible Katy corridor configurations are shown in **Figure 9-15**

Figure 9-15 Katy Freeway configurations, showing HOT lane conversion to a LRT line on the top and an elevated LRT lane on the bottom.

Rather, from the above quotes and discussions with interviewees, the existence of rail or the potential for rail to displace the managed lanes seems to be the primary issue. Since a rail line today is not a possibility, the *potential* of a rail line tomorrow is opposed. Since this potential is created with the HOT / LRT conversion option, the flexibility is opposed. The opposition to the flexibility to convert to light rail is because of the different goals that the various transportation agencies and stakeholders have for the design and operation of the transportation system, which is caused by institutional fragmentation.

If Metro were to exercise its option sometime in the future, even if this option exercise were needed to be approved through voter referendum as proposed by rail opponents (Brewer and Sallee 2002), HCTRA would lose out on a potentially lucrative revenue stream. The loss of this revenue stream would constitute a blow to HCTRA's revenue stream and future plans, which one interviewee described as "building an empire" and another interviewee as "crushing Metro".

The best way for HCTRA to secure the existence of the HOT lane revenue source is to build the HOT lanes now, instead of rail. This is currently happening and has strong support from HCTRA, political leaders and the business community. The easiest way to ensure that the HOT lane toll revenues will continue to be available in the future is to block the HOT to LRT conversion option from being purchased by Metro. Blocking of the purchase of this option almost succeed, but through the intervention of political support in favor of the option purchase.

The current strategy being pursued by the anti-rail stakeholders is two-fold. First, there is a suggestion that the option outcome should change, so that Metro could build an elevated LRT line to the side of the Katy Freeway. This would both save the HOT lanes as well as reduce the potential for the LRT line getting built, while still appearing not to overtly resist the construction of an LRT line in the Katy corridor. This would likely reduce the probability that the option would be exercised because of the doubling in costs due to the added construction costs of a entirely elevated rail line. Delaying or eliminating the exercise of the HOT to LRT conversion option would benefit HCTRA by reducing competing mode shares that could reduce demand for the HOT lanes, and hence reduce toll revenue.

The second part of the strategy being pursued by the anti-option group of stakeholders is to make the exercise of the option more difficult. As interviewees with knowledge of both sides of the MOU described, the MOU was left intentionally vague to facilitate its signing. While this facilitated the agreement on the purchase of the option, the language concerning option exercise was left vague. Multiple interviewees made mention that it would be very difficult for Metro to actually exercise the option, especially against the wishes of HCTRA. Reasons include:

- the need to win a voter referendum (which in the past has been difficult given active and well financed opposition to rail) (Canon 2002),
- uncertain financial obligations Metro would have to TxDOT and HCTRA (Canon 2002), and
- political opposition, at least from Rep. Culberson who has stated he "would fight the conversion of even one freeway lane to rail" (Brewer and Sallee 2002).

The Katy HOT to LRT conversion option shows how institutional fragmentation creates differing goals between different transportation agencies concerning how best to design and operate the transportation system. Because of this fragmentation, an option to convert managed lanes into a LRT line were viewed differently by the stakeholders involved. Rail supporters saw the option as keeping their hopes for a rail line on the Katy corridor alive, while rail opponents saw the option as a continued threat to their plans to operate and generate revenues from the HOT lane facility. The result is fighting between the stakeholders on how to structure the option and attempts by anti-rail stakeholders to delay option exercise or increase the cost of option exercise.

A summary of pragmatic concerns dealing with the Katy HOT to LRT option are listed in Figure 9-16.

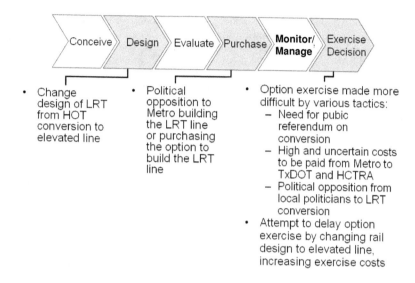

Conceive > Design > Evaluate > Purchase > **Monitor/ Manage** > Exercise Decision

- Change design of LRT from HOT conversion to elevated line

- Political opposition to Metro building the LRT line or purchasing the option to build the LRT line

- Option exercise made more difficult by various tactics:
  - Need for pubic referendum on conversion
  - High and uncertain costs to be paid from Metro to TxDOT and HCTRA
  - Political opposition from local politicians to LRT conversion
- Attempt to delay option exercise by changing rail design to elevated line, increasing exercise costs

Figure 9-16 Summary of pragmatic concerns deal with the Katy HOV to LRT conversion option.

The next example illustrating the effect of institutional fragmentation on options is the Westpark Tollway.

9.8.1.2 Westpark Tollway

Revisiting the Westpark Tollway example from Section 9.5.3, institutional fragmentation between the public and private sector and their effect on transportation system objectives and requirements are illustrated. In the Westpark Tollway, Metro purchased a 100 foot right-of-way from Southern Pacific Railroads, sold half to HCTRA and kept the other half of the right-of-way for themselves. The Metro right-of-way has not been developed and to date no decision has been made whether to develop the right-of-way as an HOV lane or as a rail line, as future needs along this corridor are uncertain. This decision to delay a decision until future uncertainties are resolved is a classic delay option.

However, while the option to delay a decision on which mode Metro will use on this corridor has created value for Metro, it has caused problems for other stakeholders.

On its western edge, the right-of-way cuts through land that is actively being developed by private land developers. As is a common practice in land developments, the developer will bear the burden of laying down roads in the development and roads to connect the development to the existing road infrastructure. Often, because of the sprawl of Houston developments, the road connections that are built by the developers can be of significant length and size. Even if the road connections are on the planning books as future roads that either the city or county plans to build, because of timing issues, the developer will often reach an agreement with the city, county or state to develop all or part of these roads themselves. As interviewees with knowledge of this process explained, developers and transportation agencies will usually come to some agreement on the breakdown work through informal agreements. Typically, the developer will pay for and build the road themselves, with the country, city or state often taking financial responsibility for more expensive portions of the facility, such as building a bridge. Also, the planned build time will often be moved up to build the facility sooner rather than later. In this manner, both stakeholders get something they want. The government gets a private developer to pay for the construction of a facility that was previously planned. And the developer gets the government to use public funds to build a facility that they need sooner than the government would have otherwise.

Because the private developer runs a private, for profit enterprise, the timing of these build decisions can be critical, to recoup the initial investment at a reasonable return. In the case of the Westpark Tollway, the developer is required to put in appropriate grade crossings at intersections. The appropriate crossing will be determined, from a technical standpoint, by the facility being crossed, with a road and a rail line requiring different technical solutions. Since Metro has essentially purchased an option to delay such a decision, the developer is faced with additional uncertainty. As one interviewee explained, the developer can live with either decision that Metro makes, building road or rail, but the developer can not easily live with no decision.

A delayed decision creates value for Metro, but creates greater uncertainty for the developer and potential problems at a latter date if the developer guesses as to what Metro will do in the future, guesses incorrectly that require additional changes. In this case, it creates further uncertainty as to who the responsible party is for making the necessary changes – Metro, the developer or the new community (or if the new community is within city limits, the city).

This example demonstrates that the existence of flexibility in a system that has fragmented stakeholders may create externalities. Here, Metro paid the option purchase price when buying the Southern Pacific rail line. In return, the ownership of the right-of-way creates flexibility for Metro to decide sometime in the future whether or not to build an HOV lane or an LRT line. This flexibility has some value for Metro. However, the costs associated with flexibility are not being paid entirely by Metro. The delay of a build decision by Metro has created uncertainty for other stakeholders that will be impacted by an eventual Metro decision. For the developer impacted, they do not see option benefits, rather they see Metro indecision that affects their own decision making on what types of facilities need to be built and when they should be built. For a private company on a schedule to complete their project, the time spent by Metro to make a decision is translated into schedule delay, which can be equated into increased costs.

A summary of pragmatic concerns dealing with the Westpark delay option are listed in Figure 9-17

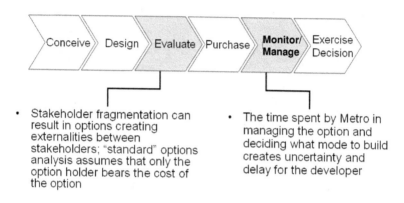

- Stakeholder fragmentation can result in options creating externalities between stakeholders; "standard" options analysis assumes that only the option holder bears the cost of the option

- The time spent by Metro in managing the option and deciding what mode to build creates uncertainty and delay for the developer

Figure 9-17 Summary of pragmatic concerns deal with the Westpark delay option.

The next example illustrating the effect of institutional fragmentation on options is the use of ITS for traffic management and emergency response.

9.8.1.3 ITS: Traffic Management and Emergency Response

Houston has one of the most sophisticated and extensive deployments of ITS of any city in the country. Much of this ITS infrastructure is operated and managed though the Transtar facility in Houston, which resembles a NASA control center, as shown in **Figure 9-18**. Through the control center, Transtar has access to multiple ITS resources in the city, such as video cameras, variable message signs and auto transponders. The control room currently acts not only as a source for gathering information, but also disseminating information back to the public and to other transportation related agencies. Many of the resources that Transtar controls or manages, while used for transportation purposes, could easily be used for other objectives as well, such as homeland security. If needed, the technology would facilitate relatively easy conversion to support homeland security functions. This could be classified as an option to switch operations, from transportation related to homeland security focused, if exercised. Such an option has been built in Chicago, where transportation and other agencies' relevant assets are being combined into a system that could be used in the event of a homeland security incident in Chicago (CTA 2004, Kirsner 2004, Chicago Tribune 2004, ABC7 2004).

Figure 9-18 Transtar control room in Houston. Figure from (Transtar 2003).

However, the ability to design, or purchase, such an option is severely limited by fragmentation in funding and culture. As one interviewee with knowledge of the situation described, overtures have been made in the past from Transtar to the local first responder community. The effort was to share in the design and funding of a system and management center that could be used both in a day to day transportation capacity, but to also perform extended emergency functions in the event of a homeland security crises.

According to the interviewee, these initiatives went nowhere because of a combination of funding and cultural differences. In order to make the necessary upgrades to the Transtar facility to enable both functions being supported, additional funding was needed, part of which was being asked for from the homeland security budget. Since the local homeland security funding is controlled by first responders for the most part, local first responders were contacted. These groups, being unfamiliar with the potential being proposed, were hesitant to part with any funding, especially without seeing some sort of demonstration of the proposed capabilities first.

As the interviewee continued to describe, when monies for a pilot program were requested through transportation sources from federal levels, funding was denied, due to lack of reciprocal funding from homeland security sources in the past, at both local and federal levels. Despite the potential benefit such an option would have, multiple interviewees commented on the ongoing hostility over funding between transportation and homeland security focused organizations.

In this example, because of the fragmentation over funding and cultural experience, the option was not purchased. Funding and cultural fragmentation affects flexible systems to a greater extent than non-flexible systems. As shown in this example, fragmentation prevented the proposed project from moving forward, even though there seem obvious synergies between the transportation and homeland security functionality of ITS. For a non-flexible system, the ability to craft an agreement over funding and system capabilities and bridge different cultures may only need to happen once. However, for a flexible system, there may need to be multiple such events. Typically, each decision to exercise an option may require an exercise cost be paid, which may provoke the same questions as to funding as shown here in paying for the option purchase cost.

Additionally, interviewees noted that the difference in culture and operating protocols had the potential to create friction that could result in each party reaching different outcomes on whether an option should be exercised or not. In this case, if each organization is only a partial owner of the option, there is the potential for concern that the option will not be exercised in a manner that is most beneficial for their own organization's needs. As one interviewee noted, this is an ongoing concern at Transtar, but over time experience and familiarity between member organizations has tended to reduce this concern.

A summary of pragmatic concerns dealing with the ITS option to switch between traffic management and homeland security functions are listed in **Figure 9-19**.

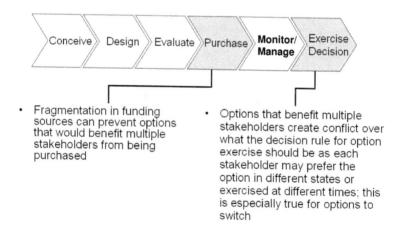

Figure 9-19 Summary of pragmatic concerns dealing with ITS option to switch between traffic management and homeland security.

391

The next section looks at pragmatic concerns dealing with political support or opposition to an option.

9.8.2 POLITICAL SUPPORT AND OPPOSITION

As seen in the Katy Freeway example, political resistance can be brought to bear to oppose the purchase of an option, force a change in the option, or resist option exercise. Real options can be created to address long-term uncertainty and require active management and multiple exercise decision points during the option's life-cycle. Whereas a non-flexible option may require only one implementation decision at the project's outset, a flexible system may require multiple exercise decisions, each encountering the same political support or opposition as that experienced during implementation. Given that resistance to option exercise may be present, there is a need for the will to exercise an option. The following example discussed the Westpark Tollway. .

The ITS technologies that enable congestion pricing are relatively new, and to date, only I-15 in San Diego has operated with full scale congestion pricing in the U.S. (Goodin 2005). So there is relatively little experience with these technologies.

Currently, HCTRA operates one of its toll roads on the south west side of Houston, the newly opened Westpark Tollway. Currently the Westpark Tollway charges a flat rate toll. However, this toll road is equipped with ITS capabilities that also would allow open road tolling and operation as a congestion priced facility. The planned driver for making this switch from static tolling to congestion pricing was the overall demand for the facility. If the traffic levels on Westpark Tollway degraded level of service past a certain point, the facility was planned to switch from a static tolling to a congestion pricing scheme. Technically, congestion pricing is much better more capable of managing demand and maintaining a desired level of service than is flat pricing.

While the Westpark Tollway is equipped with the necessary ITS capabilities to make the switch to congestion pricing HCTRA has continued to use a flat pricing scheme based only on entrance location and vehicle type by number of axles (HCTRA 2007). This option to switch to congestion pricing has not been exercised, even though one interviewee noted that current levels of service on the tollway are at level F just three years after the facility opened.

Here, the option exercise price to switch operating modes is near zero and conditions warrant the exercise of the option, yet when talking with interviewees, there are no plans to exercise this option in the foreseeable future. Several interviewees noted that a primary reason is the uncertainty in public response to changing the pricing scheme to congestion pricing, with some trepidation concerning any potential public backlash. This trepidation is well founded, as interviewees listed multiple of projects that experienced strong public backlash in the face of pricing changes. These past experiences on other facilities has created a lack of will for exercising the option to switch to congestion pricing, even though the exercise cost is near zero and the benefits would improve level of service for travelers and increase toll revenue for HCTRA.

This example helps illustrate that the exercise price of an option is not just about the price that has to be paid in monetary value, but also the political price. For Westpark, even the potential of a large public opposition has resulted in the option not being exercised. This phenomenon is not unique to Westpark or Houston. Recently, Chicago sold a 99-year lease on an eight mile long tollway, the Chicago Skyway. Immediately after the sale tolls were increased $0.50 to $2.50 and are expected to eventually reach around $5.00 (USA Today 2006). One reason for the sale was the lack of ability to exercise the option to raise tolls, as it is politically unpopular. Instead, revenue was extracted from the facility by selling it to private interests and allowing them to exercise the option to raise tolls. This demonstrates that different option holders will have different costs in exercising the same option. With private owners, exercising options such as raising or changing toll prices or schemes can be accomplished with a much lower political price than the exercise of the same option by public agency owners. In the Westpark example, even HCTRA, a special authority, is still headed by the Harris Country judge, an elected official, and thus feels some political pressure.

A summary of pragmatic concerns dealing with the option to switch pricing schemes on the Westpark Tollway are listed in Figure 9-20.

- Option exercise costs represent a broader array of costs than purely monetary costs; political costs are another potential option exercise cost
- Political will may be needed to exercise an option
- Different stakeholders may view the option exercise costs differently for the exact same option; i.e. a private enterprise may not have to worry about paying political exercise costs while a public agency may have to worry about the political costs

Figure 9-20 Summary of pragmatic concerns dealing with option to switch pricing schemes on the Westpark Tollway

The next section looks at pragmatic concerns dealing with legal and liability concerns.

9.8.3 LEGAL AND LIABILITY CONCERNS

Legal and liability issues and uncertainty concerning these issues consumes much of transportation decision maker's energy and concern about any transportation project (Mehndiratta et al. 2000). For flexible systems, the source of these concerns can often create barriers for purchasing or exercising options.

9.8.3.1 Legal Issues

Option design can be constrained by legal issues concerning the transportation system, which reduce the number of alternative options that can be considered. For example, some real options that have been shown to have value, such as the purchase and holding of right-of-way until future uncertainty has been resolved (Zhao et al. 2004), may not be legal in all cases. In discussing this type of option with planners in Houston, it was pointed out that it was not legal to purchase right-of-way with public monies prior to the successful completion of an environmental impact study (EIS). In many cases, completing an EIS is a major hurdle in getting a transportation project from a plan on paper to an actual completed facility; completing the EIS means that a substantial amount of resources have already been invested into the project. As interviewees also explained, the purchase of the right-of-way is often one of the most expensive parts of the project. For maximum benefit, an option that would purchase right-of-way and postpone the decision to develop it would need to purchase the right-of-way as soon as possible, when the land is still cheap. Delays, such as meeting legal requirements like completing an EIS, can substantially reduce the value of the option as the cost of the land in this example, and hence the purchase price of the option, increase.

Another example regarding the legality of options was the option to operate roads as toll roads. Prior to H.B. 3588 / 2702, TxDOT did not have the ability to act as a toll operator, constrained through law to only fund activities through tax revenues. Other entities, such as HCTRA or the former Texas Turnpike Authority, had the ability to operate toll roads. In this case, the option was legal, but the ability of the organization to purchase the option was constrained by law; some organizations could purchase the option and others could not.

9.8.3.2 Liability

Multiple interviewees noted that liability issues, along with funding, are one of the primary issues that they are concerned with when making decisions. Working out liability issues is one of the key concerns and stumbling blocks when working on transportation issues across organizations, which given the fragmented nature of road ownership and operation in the Houston area, occurs often. A concern of agencies is the dynamic nature of agreements or changes in the system that will affect liability. For example, one interviewee described an incident on the Houston HOV system. This incident involved Metro placing automatic gates at the entrance and exit points of the reversible HOV lanes as a safety precaution to keep drivers from entering from the wrong direction and to reduce the need to monitor all entry and exit points. Metro did this without consulting TxDOT on this plan (where TxDOT owns the HOV right-of-way). The incident involved a driver going the wrong way onto the HOV lane by bypassing a gate that subsequently caused an accident. Metro was sued and eventually TxDOT was pulled into the case as a defendant as well, and in the end was forced to pay a part of the settlement. In this case, TxDOT had a problem with Metro making a change to the system without consulting TxDOT, which eventually caused TxDOT to share in the liability. As a result, similar changes to the system are more difficult, as all parties want to avoid liability. With a flexible system, by design the system can change over time to meet changing conditions. This change in conditions can create problems, not because of opposition to the end state, but because of the change itself and the subsequent additional actions, such as vetting liability concerns, that such changes cause.

These examples show that legal and liability issues can affect a stakeholder's ability to purchase or exercise an option. In the first example, legal issues regarding when right-of-way could be purchased or who could access tolls limited the ability to purchase the option. In some cases the option could not be purchased at all and in others the option could only be purchase by some stakeholders but not others. Liability concerns also affect exercise decisions. As option exercise changes a system, fragmentation of stakeholder involvement in an option creates liability concerns that changes in the system will open up stakeholders to legal risks. This can create problems if one stakeholder is the option holder and wants to exercise the option, but the liability risk is shared with other stakeholders that were not involved in the exercise decision.

A summary of pragmatic concerns dealing with the legal and liability issues associated with options are listed in Figure 9-21.

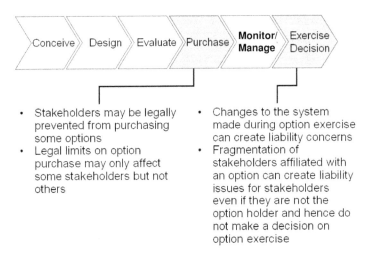

Conceive ⟩ Design ⟩ Evaluate ⟩ Purchase ⟩ **Monitor/ Manage** ⟩ Exercise Decision

- Stakeholders may be legally prevented from purchasing some options
- Legal limits on option purchase may only affect some stakeholders but not others

- Changes to the system made during option exercise can create liability concerns
- Fragmentation of stakeholders affiliated with an option can create liability issues for stakeholders even if they are not the option holder and hence do not make a decision on option exercise

Figure 9-21 Summary of pragmatic concerns dealing with the legal and liability issues associated with options

The following section synthesizes the results presented above. More generalized lessons concerning the limitations on options due to practical considerations are presented.

9.9   LESSONS LEARNED ABOUT "COMPLEX" REAL OPTIONS IN COMPLEX SYSTEMS: THE ITS CASE STUDY

The sections above present the results for each of the interview questions that were discussed with interviewees. This section synthesizes the above results and presents the set of generalized lessons learned about "complex" real options in complex systems.

Five major lessons learned are presented below. These include; new uses of flexibility, unanticipated consequences from using flexibility, stakeholder dependant costs, new choices for opponents of flexible systems, and considerations for option design. Each are discussed in a separate section below.

9.9.1   ALTERNATIVE USES FOR FLEXIBILITY

Real options have been presented as a way to increase value over the life-cycle of the system by explicitly coping with uncertainties. As the uncertainties are resolved, the real option is exercised in a manner that maximizes the value of the system. In this thinking, the real option and the decision to exercise are made with system value maximization in mind. In the literature the value that is being maximized is typically an economic value.

In practice, many other reasons beside economic value seem to motivate the purchase and exercise of options. This does not mean that the real options do not have value. On the contrary, the examples presented below demonstrate that the real options "in" systems concept can create value along new dimensions, such as political benefits.

Below is a discussion of the alternative examples for using real options that were found from the discussions with the interviewees.

- **Mechanism for fighting political battles, reaching compromise and creating political cover** – Instead of being designed and evaluated in a manner consistent with maximizing system economic value, multiple examples of options were given that seemed designed to resolve a conflict through compromise or postpone a political battle. In the Katy Freeway HOT lane to LRT line conversion option, multiple powerful stakeholders were against any Metro LRT line in the Katy Freeway. The result of this pressure caused Metro to abandon plans to build LRT lines on the HOV right-of-way. After another elected official entered into the battle, a compromise was reached that created the flexibility for Metro to pursue an LRT line at a latter date.

  In addition to providing the possibility of a future rail line in the Katy corridor, the compromise also created political cover for both parties. The option made it appear publicly that both sides were being reasonable by not dismissing a future rail line outright.

  Another example given by multiple interviewees was the Silver Line construction in Massachusetts. The Silver Line, a BRT line, is partially underground and partially above ground, as shown in Figure 9-22 and Figure 9-23. Massachusetts has the option in the future to dig tunnels and create a completely underground BRT line. The option to bury the remainder of the line was created as a political compromise between the state of Massachusetts and the federal government, where the state wanted to bury the entire line using federal dollars and the federal government did not want to pay for burying any of the line. Due to political maneuvers, money for half of the funding was eventually agreed to, with the alignment created to keep open the option of burying the remainder of the line in the future. The option created a compromise and allowed the postponement of a political battle likely to revolve around securing funding for burying the remainder of the Silver Line.

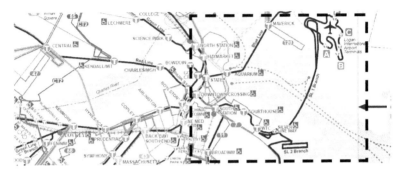

Figure 9-22 Map of downtown Massachusetts rail and BRT lines. Box denotes close-up shown in Figure 9-23. Figure from Massachusetts Bay Transit Authority.

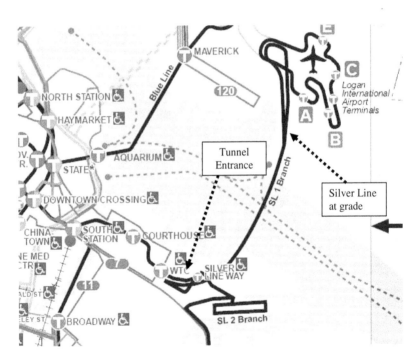

Figure 9-23 Close up of Silver Line in Massachusetts. Call out boxes denote tunnel entrance and at grade portions of Silver Line. Figure from Massachusetts Bay Transit Authority.

398

- **Mechanism for creating pressure** – A classic real option described in the literature is the option to create a pilot program. If the pilot program goes well, it would be expanded into a full program and if not, the pilot it abandoned. The option to expand is only exercised if the pilot goes well. As one interviewee described, pilot programs were often created and funded in that organization as a way to create political pressure to secure more funding. The end state of a full program had already been decided upon as the optimum choice by organization, though no funds had been allocated to it. To secure the funding, the pilot program would be funded at low levels for some length of time until its capabilities could be unveiled. After the anticipated successful unveiling, it was presented as an option of either providing funding to expand the program, or don't provide funding and lose the demonstrated beneficial capabilities. The argument to provide funding would be further strengthened by unveiling the pilot to other competing organizations first and then using the needed funding as a point of competitive pride, i.e. "without funding, look what they can do that we will not be able to do anymore". Here, the potential to exercise the option to abandon the project was presented as a "bad choice" for the purpose of increasing the probability that the option would be exercised in the pre-determined preferred direction.

- **Moving forward with second best alternative** – As with the case above, this example describes an instance where the organization has already decided on a course of action, but may have difficultly executing that course because of outside constraints. In the BRT to LRT line conversion example described above in Section 9.6.2, multiple localities had already decided that LRT was their preferred transportation mode, despite the fact that they could not secure funding for LRT lines. Instead, these localities secured funding for BRT and options to upgrade the BRT lines to LRT lines in the future. In this way, the components of the system common to BRT and LRT can be purchased today, moving the LRT line one step closer to reality. The example mentioned by interviewees of laying rail tracks and then covering over them with asphalt to be dug up later, is an extreme example of using option funding as a cover for a predetermined choice.

Two lessons learned can be drawn from this discussion. First, the way options are being used in practice are not always the same as the way that they are discussed in the literature on real options. In fact, some of the ways described above that options are being used in practice violate the reasons given in the literature for using options in the first place.

The second lesson learned is that options can be designed to address political issues. This is a use of options that has not been seen in the real options literature. The benefits of using real options "in" a system are already challenging to quantify. It may not be possible to quantify the benefits associated with real options "in' systems when the benefits are political.

9.9.2 Unanticipated Consequences of Using Flexibility in Systems

A major consequence of using "complex" real options in complex systems is the appearance of consequences from the flexibility that are not present when considering "standard" real options. The consequence of additional uncertainty being created when deploying flexible systems is discussed below. Uncertainty created for stakeholders other than the option holder is first discussed, followed by a discussion of additional uncertainty created for the option holder.

9.9.2.1 Uncertainty as a Result of Flexibility: Uncertainty for other Stakeholders

As seen from the Westpark Tollway example, the inclusion of flexibility in the system can affect other stakeholders by adding uncertainty to the system from their perspective.

The uncertainty that is added is influenced by the option expiration date and the option exercise timing. In the Westpark Tollway, land developers experienced increased uncertainty due to the Metro option. The uncertainty was of importance to the land developer because there was a high probability it would not be resolved when the decision on appropriate grade crossing would need to be made to complete the development. The uncertainty caused by Metro's option would not pose the same problem to the developers if the option expiration were of a shorter time frame, meaning the option would expire and either be exercised or not, resolving the uncertainty for the developer.

The option exercise is important in this case because of the relative clockspeeds involved between stakeholders.

Metro, as a government agency, likely has a slower clockspeed and longer time horizon until option expiration than a land developer trying to finish a particular development that it has started. In this case, the Metro option creates uncertainty that remains unresolved while the developer makes decisions.

The opposite case does not seem to be an issue. For example, interviewees discussed land development practices in Texas. These practices allow developers to buy land that is currently slated as part of the alignment for a future facility, before the facility construction begins or the government purchases the right-of-way. The developer has the option to build on the land immediately or delay a build decision for some time in the future. However, the developer often exercises the option at some point before a transportation agency moves forward with their plans. Here, the faster clockspeed of the developers' land options creates uncertainty on where future developments. This in turn can cause uncertainty on the actual future alignment of the proposed facility. However, the developer, with a faster clockspeed, exercises the option and resolves the uncertainty before the government agency need make a decision on final alignment of the facility. Therefore, once stakeholder's option creating uncertainty for another stakeholder is not an issue in this case, because of the relative clockspeeds involved.

9.9.2.2 Uncertainty as a Result of Flexibility: New Uncertainty for the Option Holder

An option is purchased as a means of coping with some identified uncertainties in the system, allowing different decisions to be made depending on how the uncertainties are resolved. The inclusion of flexibility, as discussed above, can create additional uncertainty for other stakeholders in the system.

Flexibility can also create additional uncertainties for the option holder as well.

In the Westpark Tollway example, ITS capabilities allowing for a switch in toll operations between flat pricing and congestion pricing were included in the system , for the purpose of switching to congestion pricing if the demand reached a high enough level. While the service level is currently a level F, the congestion pricing capabilities have not been exercised. As interviewees stated, there is some fear from HCTRA from the uncertainty surrounding the possible public response. HCTRA is also not certain they can count on maintaining political support in the existence of widespread or intense public resistance, as political pressure has forced other transportation agencies to abandon pricing changes that encountered public resistance. While the option was created to cope with uncertainty regarding future traffic demand, it has also created uncertainty regarding public response, which in turn affect the ability to successfully exercise the option. Additionally, public resistance could have a spillover effect and crate a precedent on pricing strategies for other HCTRA operated toll roads as well. In this example, the feedback created from the option has the potential to affect not only the Westpark Tollway, but also HCTRA operations and plans system-wide.

The lesson learned from this discussion is that the inclusion of "complex" real options in a complex system can create unanticipated consequences; in this case the creation of additional uncertainty into the system. What stakeholder is affected by this uncertainty and what effect the uncertainty has depends on specifics of the option and the relationship between the stakeholders.

9.9.3 STAKEHOLDER DEPENDANT COSTS

Examples from the qualitative analysis were found that costs associated with flexibility were not constant across stakeholders. This means that for the exact same system and the exact same flexibility in the system, the cost of managing and exercising the flexibility in the system differ across stakeholders. The specific costs that were found in this research to differ between stakeholders were political costs. In this case, the political costs for managing and exercising a flexible system, such as political costs associated with public resistance to raising tolls, differed between stakeholders. Public transportation agencies seemed to be the most sensitive to political costs, as public agency actions could be very directly influenced by elected officials. Private enterprises seem the least sensitive to political costs. Examples were shown where privatization of a toll road was either completed (such as in Chicago) or considered (in Houston), in part to allow less politicization of changes in tolls or changes in tolling schemes (such as from flat to congestion pricing).

Two major lessons learned come from this discussion. The first is that design and evaluation of "complex" real options in complex systems can not be properly completed without some knowledge of the stakeholder characteristics of the option owner. Second, some options may be better suited for specific stakeholders and not for others.

9.9.4 NEW WAYS TO OPPOSE FLEXIBLE SYSTEMS

In an institutional environment that has many stakeholders with different viewpoints and priorities, such as a regional transportation system, it is common that stakeholders will resist changes to the system that conflict with their own interests. For non-flexible systems political battles are fought of system changes, such as major construction that adds new capacity to the transportation system. Typically, opponents to such a change will fight to prevent the system deployment from occurring. Opponents can fight the changes during the design and the approval process and can continue the fight right up to the time of system deployment. However, once a non-flexible system is deployed, active opposition to the system typically ends. For example, once a road is built, stakeholders opposed to the road typically do not start to advocate the road being ripped up. The battle ends once the system is deployed.

For flexible systems, opponents to the system have new means to resist the system. As a flexible system can continue to change and evolve over time, past the date of deployment, opponents to the system can continue the fight beyond deployment. Instead of being limited to resisting system changes only during the design and deployment phase, opponents of flexible systems can continue resistance indefinitely. This means that opponents can resist the active management of the system and any attempt to exercise the flexibility built into the system.

Opponents to the flexible system can resist option exercise along multiple dimensions. These could include trying to change exercise conditions, increasing exercise costs, or resisting the active monitoring of the system.

The major lesson learned from this discussion is that the active management and long life-cycle of a flexible system creates additional opportunities for opponents of the system to resist option exercise. Additionally, opponents to the system can resist option exercise along multiple dimensions.

9.9.5 OPTION DESIGN CONSIDERATIONS

A quantitative analysis of "complex" real options in complex systems is not sufficient to determine what options are worthwhile to pursue. Examples were found in the interviews of options that appear worthwhile on paper, such as right-of-purchase, but in practice can not actually be purchased for legal reasons.

Additionally, two views on appropriate option design were found from the interviews. In one case, the political costs associated with an option had to be paid initial as part of the option purchase price. This was because if the option is open long enough, the government administration that supported the original purchase of the option may have been replaced with a new administration. Unless the option represented a high priority for the new administration, this new administration would likely be unwilling to spend the political capital necessary to exercise the option. If the political groundwork had already been laid by the previous administration, the probability that the new administration would consider exercising the option would increase.

In this case, the political costs associated with exercising an option were seen as more important than the economic costs. As such, it was advocated that political costs be paid as soon as possible, as a new option owner may be unwilling to pay these political costs as part of the option exercise cost.

The second view of an appropriate option design was much different. In this view, the technology and economic costs should be paid first. Once the flexible system was deployed political leaders could be lobbied to exercise the option. The lobbying to exercise the option was seen as potent because all costs had already been paid and the system was deployed. All that remained was the political will to exercise the option.

In this case, paying the technical and economic costs initial were seen as a way to create the political will so that the political costs could be both postponed until option exercise and reduced. This assumed that political costs would be reduced if the economic costs had already been paid for the system was deployed, requiring only that the elected official "flip the switch" to exercise the option.

Two lessons learned were had from this discussion. The first is that additional analysis is needed to ensure that options that appear worthwhile on paper are feasible when practical concerns are taken into account. The second is that the timing when to pay the costs associated with option design is important. There did not seem to be a general rule on when it was best to pay the specific costs associated with the flexible system. Likely, this will be not only dependant on the specific system and institutional environment, but also on the preferred management style of the option holder.

A summary of the lessons learned are presented in Table 9-6.

Table 9-6 Summary of major lessons learned from ITS case study qualitative analysis.

Alternative uses of options
Options are currently be used in ways not described in the real options literature. Specifically, they seem to be commonly used as a tool to resolve political considerations.
Unanticipated consequences of options
A flexible system can create uncertainty for stakeholders
Stakeholder dependant costs
Costs associated with the same option will vary across stakeholders. Private enterprises will likely face lower political costs than public enterprises
New ways to oppose flexible systems
Opponents of flexible systems can continue resistance to a system past the date of system deployment
Dimensions of resistance can include: • Changing option exercise decision rule   • Change option exercise cost   • Prevent active management and monitoring of the system
Option design considerations
Quantitative analysis of "complex" real options in complex systems is not sufficient to determine if the option is worthwhile or even possible
Qualitative analysis is necessary to determine how the option should be designed and how the costs should be structured. Two ways of structuring the costs were found: • Pay for the political costs initial in the option purchase price to facilitate option exercise by an option holder different from the stakeholder who purchased the option   • Pay for the economic costs initial and delay the political costs in the hope that political costs will be reduced if all other costs have already been paid

9.10 **REFERENCES**

ABC7. (2004) Chicago officials present massive security network, ABC7Chicago.com, Nov. 2004.

Altshuler, A. and D. Luberoff. (2003) Mega Projects: The Changing Politics of Urban Public Investment, Brookings Institution Press, Washington DC.

Banks, J. (2002) Introduction to Transportation Engineering, 2nd Ed. McGraw Hill, New York.

Brewer, S. and R. Sallee. (2002) Metro Action Spurs Legal Threat; Radack Resents Interference with Katy Freeway Widening Project, Houston Chronicle, March 26, 2002.

Canon, K. (2003) Residents Push for Light Rail Extension to Suburbs, Houston Chronicle, May 22, 2003.

Canon, K. (2002) Culberson, Constituents Trade I-10 Barbs; Congressman Calls Lawsuit to Halt Freeway Expansion 'Frivolous', Houston Chronicle, October 24, 2002.

Chicago Tribune. (2003) "Chicago Surveillance Cameras to be fitted with listening devices", Chicago Tribune, April 7, 2004.

City of Houston. (2007) City of Houston: Department of Public Works and Engineering, http://www.publicworks.cityofhouston.gov/

Crossley, D. (2004) Gulf Coast Institute Comments on HGAC 2025 Plan, found at http://www.gulfcoastinstitute.org/reports/gci_comments.pdf

CTA Press release (2004) www.transitchicago.com.

Dodder, R. (2006) Air Quality and Intelligent Transportation Systems: Understanding Integrated Innovation, Deployment and Adaptation of Public Technologies, Dissertation at MIT, Massachusetts.

Goodin, G. (2005) Managed Lanes: The Future of Freeway Travel, Institute of Transportation Engineers. ITE Journal, Feb. 2005.

Governor's Business Council. (2006) Shaping the Competitive Advantage of Texas Metropolitan Regions: The Role of Transportation, Housing and Aesthetics, Texas Governor's Business Council.

Greater Houston Partership. (2006) Transportation Funding memo.

Gulf Coast Institute. (2006) How a Transportation Project is Developed, Gulf Coast Institute Brochure.

Harris Country. (2007) Harris County website, http://www.co.harris.tx.us/

H.B. 3588. (2003) Comparison of House Bill 3588 and House Bill 2702, found on TxDOT website: http://www.dot.state.tx.us/publications/government_business_enterprises/3588_2702_co mparison.pdf

HCTRA. (2007) Harris County Toll Road Authority website, hctra.com

HCTRA Financial Statement. (2006) Harris County Toll Road Authority Basic Financial Statements, Harris County, Texas, hctra.com.

HCTRA Financial Statement. (2005) Harris County Toll Road Authority Basic Financial Statements, Harris County, Texas, hctra.com.

HCTRA Financial Statement. (2004) Harris County Toll Road Authority Basic Financial Statements, Harris County, Texas, hctra.com.

HCTRA / Metro. (2002) A Memorandum of Understanding by and Among the State of Texas (State), The County of Harris (County), and the Metropolitan Transit Authority of Harris County (Metro) for the operation of Transit Along the Katy Freeway, August 20, 2002.

HCTRA / TxDOT. (2003) Agreement by and Among the State of Texas, the County of Harris, and the Federal highway Administration for Funding, Design, and Reconstruction Relating to the Interstate Highway 10.

H-GAC. (2007) Houston – Galveston Area Council metropolitan planning organization website, www.h-gac.com/

H-GAC. (2006) Envision + Houston Region: Shaping Our Future Together.

H-GAC (2005) 2025 Regional Transportation Plan, Houston-Galveston Area.

Houston Chronicle. (2002) Two Way Street: Katy Freeway Design should allow Light Rail Option, March 29, 2002.

Hunter, F. (1953) Community Power Structure: A Study of Decision Makers, University of North Carolina Press, North Carolina.

Johnson, W. (1997) Urban Planning and Politics, Planners Press, Washington DC.

Judd, D. and T. Swanstrom. (2004) City Politics: Private Power and Public Policy, 4th ed., Pearson Longman, New York.

Katy Freeway Organization (2007) Katy Freeway Organization website, http://www.katyfreeway.org/

Katy Program. (2004) Katy Program Newsletter, v. 1 n. 1, Summer 2004.

Kirsner, S. (2004) Chicago moving to smart surveillance cameras, CNET.com, Sept. 2004.

Mehndiratta, S., D. Brand, and T. Parody. (2000) How Transportation Planners and Decision Makers Address Risk and Uncertainty, Transportation Research Record.

Metro. (2007) Metro HOV website, http://www.ridemetro.org/TransportationServices/HOV_locations/HOV_system.asp

Metro Phase II. (2003) Metro Phase II Study. Houston, Texas.

Metro Solutions. (2007) Metro Solutions website, http://metrosolutions.org/go/site/1068/

Morgan, D., R. England, J. Pelissero. (2007) Managing Urban America, 6th ed., Congressional Quarterly Press, Washington DC.

Parker, R. and J. Feagin. (1991). Houston: Administration by Economic Elites, in Big City Politics in Transition, edited by H. Savitch and J. Thomas, Sage, London, England.

Sallee, R. and S. Brewer. (2002) Gridlock Watch: Metro Wins Space for Rail on Katy; Plan Depends on cash, voters and Tom DeLay, Houston Chronicle, September 4, 2002.

Sallee, R., S. Brewer and J. Hindman. (2002) Metro Request for I-10 Panned; Some Fear a proposal by Transit Authority to Reserve Space on the Katy Freeway for a Light Rail Line will Delay Expansion Project, Houston Chronicle, March 23, 2002.

Studenski, P. (1930) Government of Metropolitan Areas, National Municipal League, New York.

TexasFreeway.com (2001) Westpark Tollway, found on: http://www.texasfreeway.com/houston/construction/westpark/westpark_tollway.shtml

Transtar. (2003) Houston Transtar Fact Sheet, found at: http://www.houstontranstar.org/about_transtar/docs/2003_fact_sheet_1.pdf

TxDOT. (2007) Texas Department of Transportation website, www.dot.state.tx.us/

USA Today. (2006) Foreign companies buying U.S. roads, bridges, USA Today, July 15, 2006.

USDOT. (2007) United State Department of Transportation website, www.dot.gov/

Zhao, T., S Sundararajan and C. Tseng3. (2004) Highway Development Decision-Making under Uncertainty: A Real Options Approach, Journal of Infrastructure Systems, March 2004.

10 FINDINGS AND CONCLUSIONS

Chapter 10 provides a set of twelve major findings and conclusions for the dissertation, which builds on the previous work presented in this dissertation. Chapter 2 introduced the concept of uncertainty, the "standard" real options used to cope with uncertainty in systems, the "standard" real options analysis techniques used to evaluate these real options, and a rationale why these techniques are not adequate to design, evaluate, and manage "complex" real options in complex systems. Chapter 3 then introduces two of the main contributions of this research. The first is the notion that a Life-Cycle Flexibility (LCF) Framework is necessary to evaluate "complex" real options in complex systems, as it takes into account technical and social system considerations along the entire life-cycle of a real option. The second is the idea of dual value design (DVD), which suggests that some technologies and technical architectures are capable of providing both inherent benefits as well as flexibility benefits.

The six chapters, Chapters 4 – 9, present two individual case studies, each case study providing an example of "complex" real options in a complex system. The two case studies spanned a range of physical and social systems; a blended wing body (BWB) type aircraft in a commercial aircraft manufacturing enterprise and Intelligent Transportation Systems (ITS) capabilities on managed roads in a regional transportation system composed of public and private enterprise stakeholders. These case studies are represented in Figure 10-1. Together, they provided a vehicle for testing out the LCF Framework and the DVD concept. Each case study contained both quantitative and qualitative aspects. The purpose of the quantitative evaluation was to better understand the flexibility in each system and estimate the value of flexibility. The purpose of the qualitative evaluation was to better understand the practical challenges through the life-cycle associated with "complex" real options in a complex system.

Figure 10-1 The two case studies in this research, each an example of "complex" real options in complex systems.

The relationship of Chapter 10 to the remainder of the dissertation is presented in Figure 10-2. This chapter contains four main sections; a summary of the overall research, major findings associated with each of the two research questions, a discussion on the validation of the Life-Cycle Flexibility (LCF) Framework, and conclusions from the research. The chapter then ends with a discussion of potential future work and some concluding thoughts.

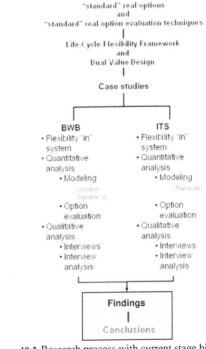

Figure 10-2 Research process with current stage highlighted.

The following section presents a summary of the research that appears in this dissertation.

10.1 <u>SUMMARY OF RESEARCH</u>

Designing flexibility in a system is one method for managing uncertainty. A great deal of previous work has been done to forward the concept and the evaluation of real options as a way to deal with uncertainty. Most of the work available in the real options literature concerns the use of real options "on" systems, as opposed to real options "in" systems. This distinction, made by de Neufville (de Neufville 2004), differentiates options where options "in" systems require a detailed technical understanding of the physical system. In options "on" systems, there is no need for considering the technical system as anything other than a black box.

The consideration of real options in the real options literature has primarily been concerned with "standard" real options. "Standard" real options are presented as relatively straightforward modifications or additions to a system to create flexibility. Additionally, "standard" real options can be evaluated with "standard" real option evaluation techniques, such as the Black-Scholes equation or binomial lattices.

This research considers two questions:

Research Question 1: How do "complex" real options and "standard" real options differ across the life-cycle of an option, including design, evaluation and management activities?

Research Question 2: How should real option processes be modified to systematically and comprehensively design, evaluate and manage "complex" real options?

For the research considered here, "complex" real options in complex systems are of interest. A "complex" real option is envisioned as being composed of more than a single or simple change or addition to a system to create flexibility. Rather, the "complex" real option is likely composed of interconnecting technological, organizational and process components. A "complex" real option may then be embedded in a complex system, which has technical and social system components and the behaviors that go along with this.

To meet the need for considering flexibility in complex systems, a new framework was created that takes a systematic and comprehensive view of the entire system, including both the technical and social systems. This Life-Cycle Flexibility Framework considers both the physical and social systems and spans the entire life-cycle of an option, starting with activities to ready the enterprise for creating flexible systems through the option exercise decision process and option deployment.

A second concept was presented in this research: dual value design (DVD) technology or technical architecture. The DVD concept is presented as a way for fully realizing the value associated with some technologies and technical architectures. The DVD concept forwards the idea that some technologies and technical architectures will have a dual value stream; one stream of benefits from the inherent value of the technology or technical architecture and one stream of benefits from flexibility. This concept allows for a more complete evaluation of the benefits associated with a technology or technical architecture, which may otherwise be overlooked.

The two case studies looked at in this research, BWB aircraft and Intelligent Transportation Systems (ITS), were chosen to allow contrast between case studies. While the two case studies both involve "complex" real options in complex systems, the technologies, technical architectures and enterprise architectures for each case study are quite different. For the BWB case study, flexibility is created with a technical architecture, the use of blending the wing and the body of the aircraft together. For the ITS case study, flexibility is created with a technology, ITS. For the BWB case study the primary enterprise of interest is a single, private enterprise aircraft manufacturer. For the ITS case study an extended enterprise architecture is of interest, consisting of multiple public and private enterprises.

The case studies were chosen to act as a test bed to exercise the LCF Framework and DVD concept and to better understand flexibility in these respective case study domains.

10.2 MAJOR FINDINGS
The following section presents the twelve major findings for this research. These twelve findings can be divided into two categories related to each of the two research questions.

A summary of these findings are presented in Table 10-1 and Table 10-2.

Table 10-1 Summary of major research findings related to the first research question: differences between "standard" and "complex" real options.

Major Findings: Research Question 1
Q1-1. Significant differences in purpose and behavior of flexibility exist between "standard" and "complex" real options.
Q1-2. The case studies provided a deeper understanding of the interaction between technical, organizational and process components of "complex" real options in complex systems.
Q1-3. The plurality of flexibilities that were found across stakeholders, with flexibilities addressing technical, funding and political uncertainties, often seem beyond the uses of flexibility as a way of dealing with uncertainty discussed in the research literature.
Q1-4. Sophisticated quantitative modeling was needed to better evaluate flexibility associated with "complex" real options in complex systems.
Q1-5. A strong relationship exists between enterprise architecture and flexibility.
Q1-6. The quantitative value of flexibility is not absolute, but relative to metrics, enterprise architecture, and enterprise goals / strategies.
Q1-7. Politics in flexible systems seem to present greater challenges than in non-flexible systems.
Q1-8. Flexibility can create externalities across stakeholders and over time.
Q1-9. Fragmentation of stakeholders creates perverse incentives for option design and evaluation, and creates additional barriers to designing, purchasing and exercising options.

Table 10-2 Summary of major research findings related to the second research question: what type of framework is needed to design, evaluate and manage "complex" real options.

Major Findings: Research Question 2
Q2-1. A new multi-dimensional framework is required for "complex" real options in complex systems, such as the LCF Framework.
Q2-2. The DVD concept was useful in determining instances where significant value from flexibility has not been considered in existing technologies and technical architectures, pointing to the need for the DVD concept to help fully value systems.
Q2-3. The case studies provided a first-order validation of the LCF Framework.

Each of these findings is discussed below. Findings associated with the first research question are presented, followed by findings associated with the second research question.

10.2.1 FINDINGS FOR RESEARCH QUESTION 1

The findings for the first research question are presented in this section. As a reminder, the research question introduced in Chapter 1 is repeated here.

Research Question 1: How do "complex" real options and "standard" real options differ across the life-cycle of an option, including design, evaluation and management activities?

Q1-1. Significant differences in purpose and behavior of flexibility exist between "standard" and "complex" real options.

As shown in Table 10-3, several combinations of real options and systems exist. In the literature, "standard" real options in "standard" systems are the primary focus. The real options that are of interest are typically relatively simple modifications or additions that create flexibility in the system. To evaluate these "standard" real options, "standard" real option evaluation techniques such as the Black-Scholes equation or binomial lattices are used, for which a rich literature exists.

Table 10-3 "Standard" and "Complex" real options and systems.

System Type	Option Type	
	"Standard" Real Option	"Complex" Real Option
"Standard" System	Discussed in literature. Examples include dual-fuel industrial steam-boiler and variable level parking garage.	NA
"Complex" System	Discussed in literature. Examples include option to expand water supply systems or the variable level parking garage in a more realistic setting.	Discussed in this research. Examples include the use of ITS in managed lanes and the use of BWB type aircraft to gain commonality across airplane families.

"Complex" real options in complex systems were the type of flexibility of interest in this research. The options for this type of flexibility were not single or simple modifications to a system. Rather, these options had technological, organizational and process components and implications. To evaluate these types of options, more sophisticated and comprehensive evaluation techniques were found to be needed. The LCF Framework is a first attempt at providing such a framework; it is discussed in the next finding.

Significant differences in purpose and behavior of flexibility exist between "standard" and "complex" real options. The definition used in "standard" real options is that:

The option holder has a right, but not the obligation, to take some action now or in the future at a predetermined cost

In "complex" real options, every part of this "standard" real options definition is called into question.

"The option holder..." – In "complex" real options fragmentation in the social system results in multiple stakeholders being associated with the option. Instead of a single option holder, there are a multitude of stakeholders involved including option purchasers, option owners and option holders, each having their own role in the life-cycle of the option.

- **Option purchaser** – This stakeholder puts up the funding to purchase the option. For example, the federal government will often fund state and local transportation initiatives.
- **Option owner** – This stakeholder owns the option, even if they did not purchase it. For example, TxDOT owns the right-of-ways on the interstates in Houston, though mainly federal money went into their construction.
- **Option holder** – This stakeholder controls the option and the exercise decision. For example, Houston Metro operates the managed lane network in Houston, although it is built on TxDOT right-of-way.

"...has a right but not an obligation..." – Politics that exist in the enterprise or between stakeholders associated with the option exist. The result is that some stakeholders may be actively working against deployment or exercise of the option. Whether or not the option holder will actually be able to exercise an option under these circumstances is questionable.

"...to take some action..." – The "action" that needs to be taken is actually multiple actions that span several dimensions. Actions taken over technical, organizational and process dimensions will be necessary during the design of the option and during the management of the option. Taking only one "action" will not be sufficient when deploying or exercising the option.

"... now or in the future..." – The action that can be taken may change over time. The change in action, meaning a change in option design or in option management for exercise, could be necessary because conditions have changed. For example, the state of the art in technology may change, which may require an updating of technological options before they are exercised. Or the change could be due to active involvement of stakeholders, enterprise architecture issues or legal/liability concerns. For example, stakeholders seeking to resist option exercise may seek to change the exercise outcome to one that is undesirable so that the option will not be exercised. The actions of HCTRA in trying to change the proposed LRT line to an expensive, entirely elevated LRT line could be interpreted as an example of this.

"...at a predetermined cost." – The cost of a "complex" real option may change over time. This could be due to the complexity in appropriately analyzing the option; as the analysis progresses, the cost estimate can also change as more is learned. Or the environment in which the option was to be exercised may have changed. This is especially true if transaction costs are included, such as political transaction costs. For example, in the Westpark Tollway, the ITS technology is present to exercise the option to change the tolling scheme from flat tolls to congestion pricing. However, the politics of the situation have changed and the option has not been exercised to date, although it would be beneficial.

Instead of an option being a contractual obligation with discrete initial deployment and exercise events, the "complex" real option in complex systems is constantly changing in design and value as the social system changes around it.

In addition to the behavior changes associated with the option, the very purpose of using "complex" real options in systems may be different. Instead of using these real options to address uncertainty associated with the system, real options can be designed in systems to accomplish other objectives, such as reaching a compromise between stakeholders. Or the uncertainty that is addressed may be different than that appearing in the literature on real options, such as using real options in systems to cope with uncertainties in political priorities.

The result of these changes in purpose and behavior of the option is that the presence of flexibility may not always be beneficial. In the real options literature, flexibility is implicitly seen as a "good" system characteristic that can add value. From this research, it is concluded that this is not always the case; in some cases the presence of flexibility can negatively affect the system. Three categories of the negative effects on the system from flexibility were found:

1. **Increased uncertainty** – Because of multiple stakeholders involved in the system, options held by one stakeholder create uncertainty for other stakeholders, due to the uncertain outcome state resulting from an option exercise decision. For example, the Metro option of delaying a decision on HOV lanes or a LRT line on the Westpark Tollway created uncertainty for land developers nearby.

2. **Value Destruction** – Because of multiple stakeholders involved with the option, the exercise of the option can result in value destruction for a stakeholder. For example, the decision to exercise the conversion of HOT lanes to a LRT line on the Katy Freeway removes a lucrative value stream for HCTRA. Combined with the uncertainty created by options, the potential for value destruction due to

future option exercise can prevent investments by other stakeholders from being undertaken in the first place.

3. **Friction between Stakeholders** – The flexibility from an option can change the behavior of the option holder. For example, the presence of the Texas H.B. 3588 / 2702 created flexibility for TxDOT in choosing to build roads as "gas-tax" roads or toll roads. Given this flexibility, they now approach each new facility build decision as a contingent decision. This has changed their relationship with other stakeholders, such as HCTRA, that were used to a standard operating procedure. Under the new contingent decision making, friction has been created between HCTRA and TxDOT. Whether this new friction degrades relationships between stakeholders remains to be seen.

These differences between "standard" and "complex" real options in complex systems points to the need for a framework, such as the LCF Framework, that systematically takes these differences into account, as discussed in the next finding.

Figure 10-3 diagrammatically depicts the logic of this section.

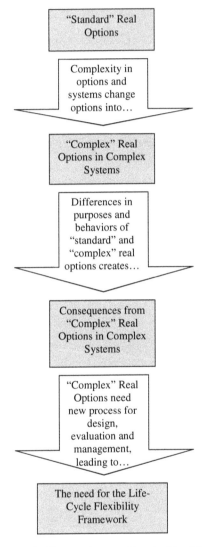

Figure 10-3 Summary of differences between "standard" and "complex" real options leading to need for Life-Cycle Flexibility Framework.

Q1-2. The case studies provided a deeper understanding of the interaction between technical, organizational and process components of "complex" real options in complex systems.

The interaction between technology, organizations and processes was apparent throughout the research. In the quantitative analysis, quantitative values could not be determined using "standard" real option evaluation techniques. Instead, explicit consideration of organizations and processes had to be incorporated into the quantitative evaluation process. For example, in the BWB case study, the quantitative analysis included consideration of corporate strategy, product line decisions, response to competitor actions, enterprise architecture and different accounting methods (i.e. program level costs and benefits versus enterprise level costs and benefits). In the ITS case study, the quantitative analysis included valuation with different metrics and related enterprise architectures. The quantitative results generated were in part determined by these social system considerations.

During the interview phase of the research, multiple examples were raised by stakeholders that attested to the existence of practical considerations that affected the hoped-for flexibility. Without considering the interaction of the technologies, organizations and processes involved in "complex" real options in complex systems, it seems unlikely that a realistic value can be determined for the benefits provided from flexibility. More importantly, without these considerations it is unlikely that flexibility could be designed such that it would be worthwhile, when taking practical considerations into account. For example, in the BWB case study, the enterprise's program-centric architecture (PCA) makes cross-family derivatives difficult to implement in practice, regardless of the value calculated from the quantitative analysis.

Q1-3. The plurality of flexibilities that were found across stakeholders, with flexibilities addressing technical, funding and political uncertainties, often seem beyond the uses of flexibility as a way of dealing with uncertainty discussed in the research literature.

Multiple types of flexibilities were found in use across the range of stakeholders that were interviewed. These flexibilities included flexibilities such as:
- Options that also appeared in the literature in detail, such as aircraft derivatives,
- Options that have only started to become identified in the literature, such as the use of ITS managed lanes for operational flexibility,
- Options that have received no attention in the literature, such as the use of real options in systems to create political compromise.

These options also spanned multiple classes of options, including:
- "Standard" real options, such as the Katy HOT to LRT conversion,

419

- More complex options (though not at the level of complexity examined in this research), such as the conversion of the Westpark Tollway from flat tolls to congestion pricing,
- Options that have not been defined in the literature, such as the use of real options in systems to provide political benefits as the primary purpose.

These multiple types of flexibilities appearing in practice point to the need for additional study and analysis. For example, there are currently non-trivial issues associated with evaluating real options quantitatively. Trying to quantitatively evaluate an option that has political benefits as the primary value stream adds to the difficultly in the evaluation.

In the ITS case study, alternative uses for flexibility were discovered. *In these examples, real options "in" systems were found to be applied to a number of challenging situations and were not limited to just coping with the types of uncertainty examined in the literature.*

Alternative uses for options that were found include: a mechanism for fighting political battles or compromising, a way to move forward with a second best solution and a tool for forcing option exercise. No alternative uses of flexibility were observed in the BWB case study.

Political Fights and Compromises

Political battles being fought over large system decisions are not uncommon for complex systems, especially in systems with multiple stakeholders with fragmented goals. *During interviews for the ITS case study, multiple examples were presented by interviewees on the use of flexibility as a means of continuing a political battle or as a compromise that could postpone further political fighting.* In the Katy Freeway HOT lane to LRT line conversion option example, Metro had already lost a political battle with HCTRA and county officials for maintaining control over the right-of-way. However, the intervention of state-wide elected officials on the side of Metro reintroduced the possibility of a future LRT line. The political battle dimensions were changed from trying to immediately build the LRT line, to one in which the option for a future LRT line was preserved. HCTRA and county officials fought against this inclusion and continue to issue public statements against the exercise of this option by Metro, a position confirmed by multiple interviewees. But the inclusion of the option keeps open the possibility that a future conversion could occur, though it is not inevitable. As the outright conversion of the existing HOV lanes into a LRT line was not feasible, nor was the postponement of conversion to HOT lanes, flexibility was introduced into the design as a means of postponing the immediate issues, but continuing the larger political battle between HCTRA and Metro supporters.

Flexibility can also be used to form a compromise or to postpone future political fighting. Multiple interviewees at the Volpe Center in Massachusetts and MIT described the current configuration of the Silver Line Bus Rapid Transit (BRT) in Boston, Massachusetts as a compromise between state and federal transportation officials.

Currently, the Silver Line right-of-way is half underground and half at-grade. The original desire by the state was to place the entire line underground, while the federal government did not want to fund any below grade line. The resulting solution of half below and half at-grade line, with the right-of-way where the line emerges from below ground to the surface placed to allow a future decision to sink the remainder of the line was a political compromise to avoid continuing political battles. In this example, the flexibility to sink the remainder of the line could postpone further fighting over funding to sometime in the future, when a future administration could take up the issue.

Second Best Alternative

Flexibility was also observed as a way to move forward with deployment of a project that could not receive funding. Instead, similarities between the project that could not be funded and other projects that could be funded, or second-best projects, were found. Funding was then applied for and the second best system was deployed with flexibility that would allow an upgrade to the preferred system at some time in the future.

Multiple interviewees applied this thinking to the current status of localities and states applying for federal transit funding. Interviewees described the current Bush Administration as being mostly against providing funding for LRT systems, preferring instead to fund BRT systems, given lower costs. However, localities prefer the more expensive, but perceived to be superior, LRT systems. Given that BRT and LRT system share some commonalities, such as similar right-of-ways, transit stations and perhaps power systems, multiple interviewees have described efforts of states and localities to apply for BRT systems with flexibility built in that would allow for upgrade to the preferred LRT systems.

While the rationale given is that upgrade could occur if future demand warranted, the interviewees felt that the flexibility being included in the design went beyond that needed for a future upgrade. Instead, it was an attempt to disguise the actions of states and localities trying to fund a LRT system under a BRT funding proposal. While few localities have gone through with exercising the flexibility to upgrade to the BRT system, interviewees felt that as soon as the administration changed to one more amenable to LRT systems, many of the options would be exercised.

In this example, flexibility was used to cope with uncertainty, but in this case it was uncertainty in future political priorities, rather than the demand uncertainty that was used as a reason for the need to fund the flexibility to upgrade from a BRT to LRT system. Interviewees gave an extreme example of one locality considering laying rail and then paving over the rail with asphalt to obtain the BRT funding, leaving only the costs of the trains to be funded by the state or locality. In this example, since the cost of the trains would be low with respect to the cost of the right-of-way and laying rail, funded under the BRT proposal, the options could be exercised almost immediately. *This example illustrates that the "flexibility" built into the system may not be intended to cope with uncertainty, or at least not the stated uncertainty, but rather as a way to disguise actions to move forward with the stakeholder's true objective.*

Forcing Option Exercise

In the real options literature, it is assumed that options will be exercised when they are "in the money"; exercising an option "out of the money" is assumed to be worthless. However, in practice, the value of the option depends on the stakeholder. For instance, exercising an option to build a system may not be the most beneficial outcome to society at large but could be beneficial to a particular stakeholder. Additionally, the benefits derived from a system are not just measured in economic terms, but also in other terms, such as prestige.

In the ITS case study, it was found that flexibility was used as a means to try and force exercise of the option to achieve a desired end state, where the desired end state was known a priori and was invariant with external conditions. Interviewees gave examples of developing pilot programs slowly over time to build up a set of capabilities, even if the funding was not available to directly fund the capabilities desired. Once a set of capabilities was created and operational in a limited form, other stakeholders would be invited to view the capabilities. If officials with the power to influence funding decisions were shown the capabilities, and were impressed, they would be notified of the "flexible" status of the program. That is, the program was only at a pilot stage, and had the option of being expanded into a full-scale program or aborted. If no funds were provided and the program was therefore aborted, the capabilities that had just previously been used to impress the stakeholder would also be terminated.

In this example, the flexibility to expand or terminate a program was used as an incentive to create the momentum to generate more funding to expand the program. The existence of flexibility, the possibility that the program could possibly be terminated, was used as a motivator to generate funding that had not been available previously. This would then allow for option exercise and funding for an expanded program, which had been the goal from the outset.

Q1-4. Sophisticated quantitative modeling was needed to better evaluate flexibility associated with "complex" real options in complex systems.

This research found that "standard" real options analysis techniques described in the real options literature were not sufficient to evaluate the "complex" real options in complex systems that were of interest to this research. The options of interest involved complex interactions of technologies, organizations and processes that influenced the option value during the analysis process. For example, in the BWB case study, corporate strategy, enterprise architecture, product design, competitive response and evaluation metrics all had to be considered during the evaluation process. In the ITS case study, enterprise architecture and evaluation metrics were considered during the evaluation process.

As a result, instead of "standard" real option analysis techniques, there was a need for more sophisticated modeling techniques that could incorporate aspects from both the technical system as well as the social system, as represented in Figure 10-4 and Figure 10-5. Trying to evaluate the flexibilities in both case studies was judged not to be possible, without significant simplifying assumptions that could change the character of the system. To overcome this, more sophisticated modeling techniques and the inclusion of social system considerations directly in the analysis was needed.

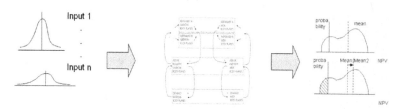

Figure 10-4 Quantitative analysis process for the BWB case study, using a system dynamics model of the aviation industry.

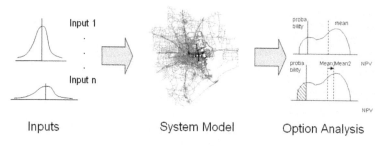

Figure 10-5 Quantitative analysis process for the ITS case study, using a transportation demand model.

Q1-5. A strong relationship exists between enterprise architecture and flexibility.

During the course of the research, a strong link was found between enterprise architecture and flexibility, which extended through the entire life-cycle of the option. Both the private enterprise in the BWB case study and the set of public and private enterprises in the ITS case study had barriers to the inclusion and use of real options in systems resulting from the enterprise architecture.

In the design of the option, for example, in the BWB case study, cross-family derivatives would not even be considered, as the enterprise architecture was program-centric and cross-family derivatives did not create benefits at the program level initially.

During evaluation of the option, enterprise architecture considerations also existed. For example, the fragmentation of stakeholders in the Houston transportation system resulted in options being created, like the Metro option to delay construction in the Westpark corridor, which created flexibility value for Metro but increased uncertainty for nearby land developers.

Enterprise architecture considerations also existed at option exercise. For example, the Metro HOT lane to LRT line conversion would require HCTRA to give up its HOT lanes, causing HCTRA and local political allies to take steps to prevent Metro from ever exercising the option.

In the BWB case study, multiple interviewees noted the fact that, historically, aerospace companies have been driven by programs. One interviewee referred to this fact as within aerospace companies, the "program is king". This program-centric architecture (PCA) creates many benefits, in terms of devolving responsibility and resources close to the decision making level within a program, where the product is being designed and built. However, the downside to a PCA is the lack of integration across-programs.

The lack of integration in a PCA creates challenges for flexibility that crosses programs or lasts for time periods beyond the current program. In these cases, flexibility may benefit other programs or even the same program, but only in the future, and perhaps the distant future. *The inclusion of flexibility in the system creates value at the enterprise level. However, at the program level, the program that includes the flexibility in the system for the first time experiences only the cost of the flexibility.* The future benefit stream will not affect it.

In a PCA, if individual program metrics are critical and overall corporate metrics are only the sum of the individual programs, there is no incentive for the initial program to embed flexibility in the system and every incentive for flexibilities that don't immediately benefit the program to be excluded. Why should the first program suffer the penalties for supporting flexibility that other programs will benefit from if there is no reward to the program, but still negative impacts on current performance? *If there are few or no metrics that create incentives at the program level to provide flexibility despite the penalty, while there may be disincentives due to the performance penalty being present, program managers have no reason to include flexibility in the system.*

This is further reinforced by the culture and interconnections that exist, or do not exist, within a PCA. Under a PCA, budgetary, personnel and political resources must be expended to create links with other programs, creating a cross-program infrastructure from scratch. As one interviewee described, this is not in the job description of the program managers and they just don't have the time or resources to make this happen, even if they wanted to.

In the ITS case study, the transportation system is influenced by a very fragmented set of stakeholders, spanning government bureaucracies, elected officials, private enterprises and citizen groups. A result of this fragmentation is different benefits and costs associated with the system for each stakeholder. The effect is each stakeholder pursues an agenda that will be the most beneficial to themselves. Note that this effect of fragmentation occurs in both non-flexible and flexible systems.

For flexible systems, the benefits and costs of an option are distributed differently for each stakeholder. In some cases, the option held by one stakeholder creates value at the expense of another stakeholder. For example, the Metro option to convert the HOT lanes on the Katy Freeway to a LRT line creates benefits for Metro upon exercise but harms HCTRA by removing one of their revenue streams.

To make the best use of flexibility that spans programs, either a new enterprise architecture that emphasizes enterprise level value is needed to replace the PCA or some "patch" is needed to fix the existing PCA to make it more compatible with cross-program flexibility.

These examples show that without aligning the real option design and the enterprise architecture, the value from flexibility may not be recognized or properly evaluated. Perhaps it is not used at all.

Q1-6. The quantitative value of flexibility is not absolute, but relative to metrics, enterprise architecture, and enterprise goals / strategies.

During the course of the quantitative analysis for each of the case studies a dependency between the values calculated for flexibility and a variety of social system considerations was observed. Social system consideration such as selection of metric, enterprise architecture and enterprise goals and strategies were all determined to affect the value of flexibility. Further these social system considerations were not independent, but coupled to one another.

In both cases, without the explicit consideration of the social system, the quantitative analysis would have been simplified to the point of not being useful or representative of how the option would be used in actuality.

For example, in the BWB case study, multiple instances of taking social system considerations into account when performing the quantitative analysis were necessary. These included:
- corporate strategy and decision processes (what markets to contest and what level of competition is acceptable),
- product line decisions (commonality across product lines or product line optimization),
- enterprise architecture (program vs corporate accounting),

425

- responses to competitor actions or competitor responses to one's own actions (competitor product offering design and timing and design and timing of responding products).

Consideration of these social factors helped shape the analysis and drive system value. For example, if a competitor will not contest a market, the need for commonality and derivative aircraft decreases, as a company can achieve monopoly product status and avoid the need to exercise an option to update the product. However, if a competitor is actively competing in a market niche, this will increase the need for options to create new derivatives capable of improving aircraft performance and maintaining, regaining or increasing market share.

The consideration of the social system in the quantitative analysis took two forms. First, the value of flexibility in a system varied as a function of the social system the flexible system was embedded within. Second, one option can simultaneously create benefits and costs for different stakeholders.

Relative Value of Flexibility

The valuation of the flexibility in the two case studies varied as a function of the metric of interest. As the flexibility of interest was a "complex" real option in a complex system, multiple possible metrics could be chosen from which to value the flexibility. The value of the flexibility will therefore be relative to the selected metric.

As an example of how these social system considerations affect the value of the flexibility, the flexibility in the BWB case study was found in the quantitative analysis to have different benefits when evaluated under different corporate strategies adopted by the aircraft manufacturer. The difference between a corporate strategy with the goal of just contesting a market niche to prevent a competitor from gaining monopoly status and a corporate strategy with the goal of trying to dominate the competitor in a market niche will lead to different valuations of flexibility. This is because the rules associated with when to exercise the flexibility in the system will be different, leading to different outcomes in response to the same competitor actions.

In the ITS case study, the option value for the ability to switch between HOT and TOT lanes varied significantly based on the metric chosen. When maximizing societal benefits was of interest, it was found that the long-term operation of the managed lane as a HOT lane was most beneficial. However, when maximization of toll revenues was the important metric for deciding option exercise, the long-term operation of the managed lane as a TOT lane was found to be superior. These differences in valuation due to the metric used to evaluate the option were found to have repercussions on the enterprise architecture and how stakeholders perceived the value of the option.

In these cases the valuation of the flexibility will be relative not only to the system design and the uncertainty the design is coping with, but also the metric used by the social system that the technical system is embedded within. In effect, the same flexibility "in" a system can be valued differently under different social system conditions.

Option Value Varied Across Stakeholders

Since different stakeholders employ different metrics when making decisions based on option purchase and exercise, and the option value varies for each metric, the value of the same option varies between stakeholders. Further, the option belonging to one stakeholder can affect another stakeholder's value in the system.

In the BWB case study, cross-family derivatives were seen as creating flexibility that had a positive value for the aircraft manufacturer, measured at the corporate level. However, the costs associated with designing commonality into the initial plane and the subsequent performance penalty was viewed by the initial aircraft program only as costs. However, the same option was seen as a benefit to later programs that could exercise the option, if worthwhile. In this case, the individual programs had to account for costs and benefits, as opposed to an enterprise-level metric that would track costs and benefits across the entire enterprise.

This differential valuation of the same flexibility is also evident in the ITS case study. For example, in the decision to use a HOT lane to delay infrastructure expansion, the value generated by deploying a HOT lane is dependant on the benefits perceived by a particular stakeholder. Public transportation agencies may perceive value from societal benefits, such as value of time savings, while a private enterprise operator may only perceive value from tolls collected. For the same option, this would lead the managed lane to be operated differently over time as a function of the enterprise in charge of the lane.

As another instance of differential value from the same option, the Metro option to delay the decision to build a tollway or a rail link in the existing Westpark right-of-way, created value for Metro but destroyed value for a local land developer. For Metro, the option to delay allows them to wait to determine what their needs will be in the future. However, this option destroys value for the land developer who is faced with additional uncertainty that can not be resolved until Metro has decided whether to exercise their delay option.

Yet another example is the Metro option for converting HOT lanes on the Katy Freeway into a light rail transit line. Exercising this option would allow Metro to increase their rail system into west Houston, but would reduce or eliminate the HOT lane revenue stream that would have been enjoyed by the HOT lane operator, HCTRA.

With a fragmented set of stakeholders associated either directly or indirectly with a flexible system, real options in the system will have different values for each stakeholder; the exercise or even the presence of the option can both create and destroy value for different stakeholders simultaneously.

427

These examples show that for the same option designed in the same physical system, the value calculated for the option will vary on multiple social system considerations, such as metrics, enterprise architecture and enterprise goals and strategies. Without taking into account the social system context of the option, an appropriate value can not be calculated.

Q1-7. Politics in flexible systems seem to present greater challenges than in non-flexible systems.

Because of the fragmentation of stakeholders in a system and the differential benefits and costs associated with flexibility for each, it is likely that stakeholders will fight to ensure that they receive a favorable distribution of benefits and costs. *While political fighting over benefits and costs is common in non-flexible systems, it creates a greater challenge in flexible systems.*

For non-flexible systems, political fighting over system design decisions mostly ends after system implementation. Once a large and complex system has been deployed, it is unlikely to be dismantled. For example, there may be political fighting over the decision to build a road. If the road is actually built, the fighting does not typically continue with opponents pushing for the road to be removed or even for the road to go unused.

For flexible systems, the same type of political fighting experienced in a non-flexible system does not have to end with system deployment. Rather, as the flexible system is actively managed, opponents can continue to resist further changes to the system brought about by option exercise past the date of initial deployment. *In this manner, political fighting can continue for the entire life-cycle of the system.*

In the ITS case study, the presence of politics affected option decision making throughout the option's life-cycle, from purchase decisions through exercise decisions. For example, the Metro option for converting HOT lanes to LRT lanes by increasing the strength of bridge supports was originally not going to be included into the design plans by Metro. HCTRA and county officials opposed the presence of rail in the Katy corridor and acted politically to remove its presence, and succeeded. Under previous agreements Metro had planned to abandon the right-of-way on the Katy Freeway that it had operated as a HOV lane to HCTRA, which has plans to operate the same right-of-way as HOT lanes. Through intervention of elected officials, Metro became re-integrated into the design plans for the Katy Freeway expansion, through the funding of an option to strengthen the bridge supports. The new presence of the option to convert the managed lanes into a LRT line has also shifted the tactics of the opposition. Initially, rail opponents resisted rail in the corridor outright. Then they resisted the inclusion of the option to convert the managed lanes into a LRT line in the system design. Currently, there are plans to resist the exercise of the option in the future, through various means such as trying to change the exercise conditions (requiring a public referendum), the exercise price (uncertain payoff from Metro to HCTRA), or proposing new, low feasibility outcomes that make option exercise unlikely (building a wholly elevated train running parallel to the freeway).

In this manner, opponents to a flexible system have two new strategies for resistance at their disposal. First, resistance can continue for a longer amount of time, over the life of the option, with opponents trying to prevent option exercise or change the outcomes of option exercise. Second, new tools are available for opposition; increase exercise costs, change exercise decision rules, delay exercise decisions, etc.

In the BWB case study, no examples of politics affecting flexibility decisions were found. One interpretation of this absence of political considerations could be that since the commercial aviation industry operates on such tight profit margins in a private enterprise, decisions are made on rational, economic considerations, with only choices that will improve the bottom line being made.

However, in discussions with multiple interviewees this proved not to be the case. As described by multiple interviewees, the decision process in the late 1990's and early 2000's on whether to bring to market either a BWB plane or the Sonic Cruiser, a tube and wing plane capable of increased flight speeds, was based much more on political considerations within the Boeing Company than technical considerations. In the end the Sonic Cruiser was offered over the BWB. One of the driving political reasons given by interviewees for this choice was a difference in cultures that create political conflict; the BWB originated from personnel associated with the old Douglas Aircraft Company, a former competitor and eventual acquisition of Boeing, while the Sonic Cruiser was from "Boeing proper". Due to cultural differences that still persist, interviewees described a desire to "kill" the BWB based mainly on these culturally-based political considerations. In the end, the Sonic Cruiser concept was met with little enthusiasm from airlines and in its place the 787 Dreamliner, an ultra-efficient aircraft, was offered.

This example, while not pointing to political considerations in flexibility decision making, still points to the strong possibility that company "politics" could still play a deciding role in creating barriers to effectively using flexibility in systems.

Q1-8. Flexibility can create externalities across stakeholders and over time.

During the case study research, the existence of externalities associated with the use of flexibility was observed. These externalities created costs external to the stakeholders buying and holding the option. Additionally, "externalities" also appeared for the option holder as well, with new unanticipated costs appearing later in time.

In the ITS case study, the Metro option to delay a decision on whether to develop their Westpark right-of-way as a HOV lane or a LRT line has created value through flexibility for Metro. However, the delay of this decision has created uncertainty for other stakeholders, such as nearby land developers who can not determine what type of crossing to build for the right-of-way until Metro determines which transportation mode they will develop.

Another example in the ITS case study was the Metro option to convert the HOT lanes on the Katy Freeway to a LRT line. The conversion option has benefit for Metro, but would result in the loss of the toll revenue for HCTRA, the operator for the HOT lanes.

Also in the ITS case study, the creation of "externalities" for the option holder later in time and along an unexpected dimension were also observed. In the Westpark Tollway, HCTRA deployed ITS capabilities with the option to switch to congestion pricing if needed. However, this option has created additional political uncertainty for HCTRA now that they want to exercise the option, as elected officials are wary of potential negative public backlash to such a conversion.

Q1-9. Fragmentation of stakeholders creates perverse incentives for option design and evaluation, and creates additional barriers to designing, purchasing and exercising options.

Fragmentation of stakeholders was found to create fragmentation in the concept of an "option holder" as described in the real option literature. Stakeholder fragmentation instead creates option purchasers, option owners and option holders, where each plays a role in the option life-cycle. Additionally, the externalities that can be created with flexibility generates incentives for additional stakeholders to try and influence the purchase or exercise of an option.

In the BWB case study, the desire to use cross-family derivatives in a program-centric enterprise architecture is difficult because of fragmentation between the option purchaser and the option holder. The initial aircraft developed will pay the development and performance costs associated with including commonality in the design. However, a future aircraft program reaps the benefits of this and can choose whether or not to exercise the option to leverage the commonality or create a new, optimized plane. Because the costs and benefits are fragmented across programs and because the enterprise architecture is program-centric, the result is that cross-family derivatives are not considered, even though there is value in the flexibility they provide at the enterprise level.

In the ITS case study, the fragmentation of stakeholders associated with the transportation system creates conflict in the design, evaluation and management of flexibility. For example, in the Katy Freeway HOT lane to LRT line conversion option, since the costs and benefits are distributed unequally among stakeholders, namely HCTRA and Metro, there is resistance from HCTRA to the inclusion of the flexibility in the system design or the potential exercise of the option by Metro.

As another example, the fragmentation in the ITS case study on who pays the option purchase price and who designs and holds the option creates the potential for wasteful designs. The design of BRT systems with the flexibility to upgrade to LRT systems in the future were given by interviewees as examples of wasteful flexibility. In the worst example given, rail lines were to be laid and paved over immediately, to be uncovered at some future date. This type of wasteful flexibility was possible because the federal government would pay for BRT systems with flexibility, but not LRT systems, which is what local transportation agencies really wanted. The fragmentation of option purchaser (the federal government) and option holder (local transportation agencies) created perverse incentives to create flexibility whose cost-benefit relationship created an investment of questionable value.

These examples show that the fragmentation of the stakeholders associated with options creates the potential for perverse incentives and barriers associated with design, evaluation and management activities. This fragmentation of stakeholders if different from the enterprise architecture as stakeholders can continue to be fragmented with different views and priorities under different enterprise architectures.

The major findings associated with the second research question are presented below.

10.2.2 FINDINGS FOR RESEARCH QUESTION 2
The findings for the second research question are presented in this section. As a reminder, the research question introduced in Chapter 1 is repeated here.

Research Question 2: How should real option processes be modified to systematically and comprehensively design, evaluate and manage "complex" real options?

Q2-1. A new multi-dimensional framework is required for "complex" real options in complex systems, such as the LCF Framework.

Due to the interaction of technological, organizational and process considerations in "complex" real options in complex systems, "standard" real option analysis techniques are not adequate for evaluation purposes. What is needed is a multi-dimensional framework that addresses the different considerations of the "complex" real options in complex systems.

Considerations of interest that drive the need for a multi-dimensional framework include:
- **Consideration of the physical system** – Technical knowledge of the physical system is necessary to adequately design flexibilities "in" systems, where the technology and technical architecture of the physical system may be changed.
- **Consideration of the social system** – Consideration of the social system is needed, as consideration of stakeholder objectives, enterprise architecture and political interactions can all create barriers for the use of options throughout their life-cycle. Figure 10-6 shows the relationship between a physical system embedded in a social system.

431

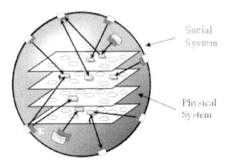

Figure 10-6 CLIOS Representation of Nested Complexity: Physical system "nested", or embedded, within a social system. Figure modified from (Sussman et al. 2007)

- **Consideration of the two types of uncertainty:**
  - **Statistically characterized** – The type of uncertainty commonly addressed in the real options literature, the ability to design a flexible system that can respond to well known possible outcomes is needed.
  - **Unknown unknowns** – A type of uncertainty not addressed in the real options literature, which may require a fundamentally different type of flexibility, where the flexibility may be required in the enterprise or institutional architectures, as opposed to flexibility "in" a system.

- **Consideration of the life-cycle** – The life-cycle of the option may be long lasting, with the option remaining open and the final decision on configuration of the system delayed for years or even decades. Since the final system configuration is not set after the initial implementation, this creates additional opportunities for opponents of the system to resist potential changes to the system that would be made through option exercise. Figure 10-7 shows the different phases of the life-cycle of an option.

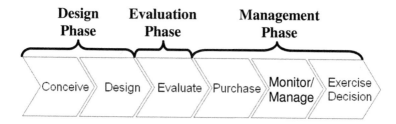

Figure 10-7 Life-cycle of an option.

The LCF Framework provides a first attempt at a multi-dimensional framework that is appropriate for evaluating "complex" real options in complex systems. The LCF Framework incorporates machinery that explicitly addresses the four considerations just mentioned: physical systems, social systems, different types of uncertainty and life-cycle considerations.

The LCF Framework calls for both quantitative and qualitative evaluation techniques in an attempt to better understand and evaluate the technical and social components of the option. The LCF Framework also proceeds temporally. It starts before the design of the option with activities to make the enterprise ready to support a flexible system and continues past the initial option deployment, through management activities to consider exercise decision considerations. Finally, the LCF Framework explicitly calls for the consideration of unknown unknowns in the process, highlighting the potential need for flexibility different than the "complex" real option in complex system variety; flexibility designed into the enterprise or institutional architecture may be necessary.

The validation of the LCF Framework is presented in Section 10.3 .

Figure 10-8 presents the LCF Framework.

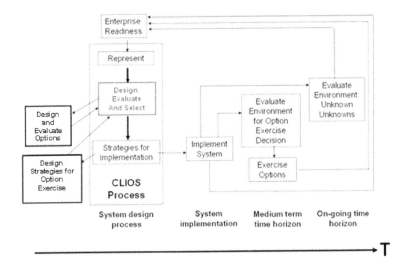

Figure 10-8 LCF Framework.

Q2-2. The DVD concept was useful in determining instances where significant value from flexibility has not been considered in existing technologies and technical architectures, pointing to the need for the DVD concept to help fully value systems.

The dual value design concept is presented as a way for fully realizing the value associated with select technologies and technical architectures. The DVD concept forwards the idea that some technologies and technical architectures will have a dual value stream; one stream of benefits from the inherent value of the technology or technical architecture and one stream of benefits from flexibility, as shown in Eq. 10-1. This concept allows for a more complete evaluation of the benefits associated with a technology or technical architecture, which may otherwise be overlooked. Additionally, the DVD concept allows a greater understanding of the balance in value between inherent and flexibility value associated with a system.

$$\text{Eq. 10-1} \quad \begin{array}{c} \text{DVD} \\ \text{value} \end{array} = \begin{array}{c} \text{inherent value} \\ \text{from technology} \end{array} + \begin{array}{c} \text{value from} \\ \text{flexibility} \end{array}$$

The weight of the inherent and flexible value streams was found to change from technology to technology, and even varied for different applications of the same technology. For example, during the quantitative evaluation of the ITS case study, the

434

ITS capabilities used to create the option to delay infrastructure created significant flexibility benefits. However, the same technology created only marginal flexibility benefits when the option to switch between HOT and TOT lanes was considered.

The DVD concept was found to be a useful construct for differentiating between inherent and flexible value streams. For "complex" real options in complex systems, it is not always immediately apparent what part of the value from a particular technology or technical architecture is attributed to the inherent value and which to the value of flexibility. If flexibility is of interest, with the required calculations to support the investment in a flexible system, the DVD concept is useful in helping to understand how much of the value from the technology or technical architecture comes from flexibility, as opposed to the inherent value.

Q2-3. The case studies provided a first-order validation of the LCF Framework.

The two case studies undertaken at in this research, BWB aircraft and Intelligent Transportation Systems (ITS), were chosen to allow contrast and represent a range of physical and social systems; with the range enabling the testing of the LCF Framework and the DVD concept under a variety of systems. While the two case studies both involve "complex" real options in complex systems, the technologies, technical architectures and enterprise architectures for each case study are different. For the BWB case study flexibility is created with a technical architecture, the use of blending the wing and the body of the aircraft together. For the ITS case study flexibility is created with a technology, ITS. For the BWB case study the primary enterprise of interest is a single private enterprise, primarily an aircraft manufacturer. For the ITS case study an extended enterprise architecture is of interest, consisting of multiple public and private enterprises.

These differences are summarized in Figure 10-9. The differences between case study technologies, technical architectures and enterprise architectures allowed the LCF Flexibility concept to be tested on very different systems. Additional discussion on the validation of the LCF Framework is provided in Section 10.3.

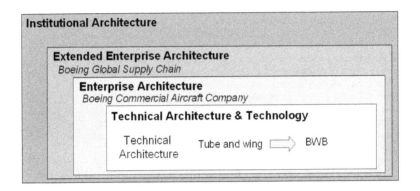

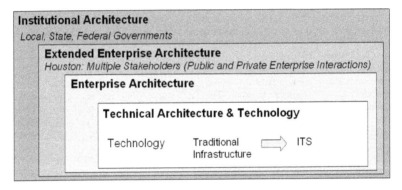

Figure 10-9 Characteristics of case studies on the dimensions of: technical architecture and technology, enterprise architecture, extended enterprise architecture and institutional architecture.

The following section discussed the validity of the LCF Framework.

10.3 <u>LIFE-CYCLE FLEXIBILITY REVISITED</u>

The Life-Cycle Flexibility Framework, as presented in Chapter 3 and used and discussed throughout this research, is a first attempt at creating a framework that allows designers and decision makers a systematic process for designing, evaluating, and managing "complex" real options in complex systems. As such, the LCF Framework is based on an existing process, the CLIOS Process, for analyzing complex systems, including the technical and social components of the system. The LCF Framework extends the CLIOS Process by recognizing the need to extend the implementation of a flexible system beyond a single implementation event, caused by the repeated nature of decisions on whether to exercise the option or not, where option exercise will change the system.

Now, at the end of the research, the Life-Cycle Flexibility Framework is revisited in this section to determine if the LCF Framework is useful and valid and to also analyze limitations and potential improvements. As addressed in the preceding section, the LCF Framework, or a similar type of framework, is needed for the analysis of flexibility "in" complex systems. The validation of the LCF Framework is presented below, followed by a discussion of its limitations.

10.3.1 VALIDATION OF THE LCF FRAMEWORK

As a framework designed to improve system design and analysis processes, the LCF Framework is difficult to conclusively validate. As discussed in Goldenson (Goldenson et. al 1996), there have been a "dearth" of studies assessing the effectiveness of processes, such as systems engineering or CMMI (Capability Maturity Model Integration). The studies that have occurred have largely been empirical in nature, assessing the benefits derived from the use of these types of processes in already completed programs. As the LCF Framework has not been used in practice, there is no empirical data from which to judge the effectiveness of the LCF Framework. Rather, instead of validating the LCF Framework concept through its effectiveness, the evidence of LCF validity is proposed through the following two methods.

The two major arguments are presented as evidence of the LCF Framework's validity.

1. **Intellectual basis in previous literature** – The LCF Framework has been partially validated through the thinking and logic that have gone into its creation and use, consulting the literature on individual parts of the LCF Framework and basing the LCF Framework in part on pre-existing processes.

   The soundness of the different pieces on which LCF is built can be found in the literature. Each of the individual pieces that are used in the LCF Framework has links to various literatures. While this does not guarantee that the LCF Framework in totality is sound, each of the individual steps and processes that form the foundation of the LCF Framework are sound, which is a necessary first step towards overall framework validity.

   The literature on other frameworks and processes has been consulted and compared to the LCF Framework. Indeed, the LCF Framework exists largely as an extension and integration of existing complex system processes, such as the CLIOS Process, and existing real option analysis processes presented in the literature.

The individual pieces of the LCF Framework are grounded in the literature and the LCF Framework in its entirety appears to be a rational integration of these pieces.

The resulting framework has been presented to different academic audiences familiar with complex systems multiple times, with feedback provided from the audience incorporated back into the framework.

2. **Validation of the LCF Framework through the research case studies** – As demonstrated in this research through the two case studies selected, there is a strong need for the thinking advocated in the LCF Framework. Both case studies demonstrated behaviors that may not have been evident using existing real option processes or existing complex system processes, such as the CLIOS Process. Rather, using the LCF Framework brought out important characteristics of each case study that otherwise may have been overlooked.

During the course of the quantitative analysis for the two case studies it was found that "standard" real options analysis techniques described in the real options literature were not sufficient to evaluate the "complex" real options in complex systems that were of interest to this research. The options of interest involved complex interactions of technologies, organizations and processes that influenced the option value during the analysis process. For example, in the BWB case study, corporate strategy, enterprise architecture, product design and evaluation metrics all needed to be considered to evaluate flexibility. In the ITS case, enterprise architecture and evaluation metrics had to be explicitly considered during the quantitative evaluation process. "Standard" real option processes were not able to take these considerations into account. There has been some work in the literature to try and adapt these "standard" analysis techniques to consider more complex systems. Examples include use of real options analysis and game theory (Smit and Trigeogris 2004) or the application of real options to policy analysis (Dixit and Pindyck 1996).

However, in these cases, the analysis techniques could be considered more as "standard" real options in complex systems, instead of the full "complex" real options in complex system addressed in this research. Since quantitative analysis techniques did not exist in the literature that were deemed appropriate for evaluating "complex" real options in complex systems, a new quantitative analysis methodology was instead used. This methodology was based on sophisticated modeling techniques, such as system dynamics and traffic demand modeling. As such, they followed previous work done by (Tufano and Moel 1997, Clemons and Gu 2003, Greden et al. 2005, and Miller 2006). However, it was found that for "complex" real options in complex systems, social system considerations had to be taken explicitly into account. Therefore, the modeling techniques were extended to explicitly incorporate some social system considerations. For example, in the system dynamics model developed for the BWB case study, different cost structures and decision rules could be incorporated directly into the model to represent different enterprise architectures, corporate strategies and metrics used in option decision making. In the ITS traffic demand model, considerations such as the use of public or private enterprise architectures and the appropriate metric for each enterprise architecture could be used as input into the demand model to determine the effects on the transportation system.

Additionally, through the course of the interviews, many additional social system considerations were found to be important and commonplace in "complex" real options in complex systems. Without the use in this research of LCF Framework, these types of social system considerations would not have been addressed.

Together, this experience during the case study process points to the need for the LCF Framework. The LCF Framework is not put forward as the final word in evaluating "complex" real options in complex systems. Rather, it is put forward as a first attempt which can be built on or may inspire or invoke thoughts in similar flexibility research in complex systems. Additionally, it is hoped that the LCF Framework help illuminate some additional differences between "standard" real options in "standard" systems and "complex" real options in complex systems.

The following section discusses further thoughts for the LCF Framework.

10.3.2 LIMITATIONS OF THE LCF FRAMEWORK
The LCF Framework was designed specifically to address "complex" real options in complex systems. As such it has a number of limitations for a more generic application.

First, the LCF Framework has been designed around the paradigm of a complex system being composed of a technical and social system. For "standard" real options in "standard" systems, there is likely no need for the LCF Framework, as it would be "overkill". Rather, a "standard" real options analysis technique could be more appropriate. For complex systems without a strong technical component, the need for the LCF Framework, or at least the need for much of the machinery of the framework, is questionable. However, the analysis of complex systems without a sizable technical system is outside the scope of this research.

Second, the LCF Framework was designed around the paradigm of flexibility created by real options. Traditionally, real options have been applied to systems where the uncertainties are known a priori, can be statistically characterized and the desired responses for particular outcomes are also known a priori. This limits the application of LCF Framework to only statistically characterized phenomenon. The applicability to other types of uncertainties is questionable. A need to extend the LCF Framework to address these other types of uncertainties has been incorporated into the framework and addressed in Section 3.2.7. It is envisioned that the ability to address uncertainties such

439

as unknown unknowns may require significantly different approaches than those discussed in this research, and all other research that the author has seen to date. It is anticipated that a greater reliance on flexible enterprises will be needed to address uncertainties such as unknown unknowns. Also, if other types of uncertainties are to be addressed by flexibility "in" the system, significant changes to design processes, both for the system and for the flexibility, are anticipated. While unknown unknowns were addressed in the LCF Framework, much more work is needed to adequately address this type of uncertainty.

Third, the LCF Framework is currently a generic framework and is not in a state that is easily applicable to any organization interested in using such a framework. Additional work is needed to make the LCF Framework operational outside the research community. Additionally, it is likely that the framework would need modifications for use at any specific organization, to tailor the framework for a particular organization's needs. Some of this work would be needed in streamlining the framework. As the LCF Framework in its current state was an attempt to be comprehensive in addressing all aspects of flexibility, the resulting framework needs tuning to be directly used in practice.

Finally, the LCF Framework assumes that some process exists for making tradeoffs between flexibility and other methods of addressing uncertainty, such as robustness, and that some process exists for helping to identify possible flexible solutions in the system. Both of these are critical needs and neither is currently addressed in the framework.

Additional suggestions for future areas of work are addressed in Section 10.5.

The following section re-visits the original two research questions and provides a set of conclusions for each question.

10.4 RESEARCH QUESTIONS AND CONCLUSIONS
Revisiting the two research questions originally introduced in Chapter 1, each is addressed in the following two sections in turn with major conclusions that were drawn from this research.

10.4.1 CONCLUSIONS FOR THE FIRST RESEARCH QUESTION
This section presents the conclusions for the first research questions. As a reminder, the research question is re-stated below.

How do "complex" real options and "standard" real options differ across the life-cycle of an option, including design, evaluation and management activities?

This question was answered by comparing the literature on "standard" real options with the findings drawn from the two case studies.

As defined in Section 2.6, the difference between "standard" and "complex" real options was defined as the extent of the change in the system required to create flexibility. For "standard" real options, the option requires only a relatively simple modification or addition to the system to create flexibility. For "complex" real options, the option may be substantially more involved. In the "complex" real option case, interactions between technology, organizational considerations and processes must all be considered to proceed with option deployment and exercise. As a reminder, the following definition for a "complex" real option was proposed.

> "A complex option is composed of multiple components across a variety of dimensions, such as technical, financial, political, organizational and legal. All components are necessary for the option to be deployed and exercised; no single component is sufficient.

Because of the presence and interaction of these different components in a "complex" real option, the considerations and activities that must be dealt with throughout the option's life-cycle differ between "standard" and "complex" real options. The comparison between "standard" and "complex" real options was considered over the three main phases the author identified as composing an option's life-cycle: design, evaluation and management. A discussion of the phases in a real option's life-cycle was provided in Section 3.1.2.

The differences between "standard" and "complex" real options that were found in the two case studies conducted for this research are summarized below in Table 10-4 and Table 10-5. A brief discussion then follows. Pointers to previous sections in the dissertation are also included, if the reader is interested in additional detail concerning these points.

Table 10-4 Summary of differences between "standard" and "complex" real options found in the two case studies.

Option Life-Cycle Phases	"Standard" Real Options in Systems	"Complex" Real Options in Complex Systems: Case Studies	
		BWB/Boeing Base Study	ITS/Houston Case Study

Design	• Design of options in physical system	• Physical system
		  ○ 250 and 450 passenger BWB
		• Enterprise-centric design decisions
			• Physical system
			  ○ ITS in managed lanes: HOT, BRT and TOT lanes
			• Enterprise architecture/Management processes

Evaluation	• Financial
	  ○ Monetary
	• Evaluation techniques
	  ○ "Standard" techniques such as Black-Scholes or binomial lattices
		• Financial
		  ○ NPV of aircraft sales
		• Evaluation techniques
		  ○ System dynamics model
		• Competitive environment
		• Corporate strategy/Metrics
			• Financial
			  ○ NPV of societal benefits and tolls
			• Evaluation Techniques
			  ○ Regional transportation traffic demand model
			• Network effects
			• Public vs. Private operator metrics

Management	• Managerial flexibility assumed	• Program-Centric Architecture vs. Enterprise-Centric Architecture needed for "cross-family" derivatives • Corporate strategy / culture	• Politics from fragmentation of multiple stakeholders and objectives • Politics from the fragmentation of the "option holder" role • Externalities from flexibility

Differences between "standard" and "complex" real options in the design phase lead to the need to consider enterprise architecture issues in parallel with the option design.

For "standard" real options in systems, the primary consideration in the design phase of the option's life-cycle centers on the technical aspects of how the system is designed to provide flexibility. For a "complex" real option in a complex system, it was found from the case studies that more than just the technical aspects of the option must be considered. The technical nature of the options for the BWB and ITS case studies are provided in Sections 4.4 and 7.7. Additional non-technical considerations are presented below.

In the BWB case study, an enterprise-centric design decision process was needed to adequately design the cross-family derivatives that were of interest. Current design processes are made from the "bottom up", where programs have the freedom to make design decisions that are best for the program, with little regard to how these design could affect other existing or future programs. For flexibility enabled by commonalty across families, design decisions will need to be made that will have a direct impact on other programs. This can lead to trade-offs between program level and enterprise level metrics. Commonality across programs can create flexibility and lead to lower costs of future programs, but at an expense to current programs. Without an enterprise-centric decision making process for design choices, the flexibility provided in "cross-family" derivatives will never be built into existing aircraft. In this case, enterprise level changes must be made to enable consideration and design of the options examined in the BWB case study. The reader is referred to Section 6.7 for additional discussion.

In the ITS case study, enterprise architecture considerations that lead to a change in road network management processes is needed. Historically, most road network improvement projects have involved construction of additional traditional infrastructure, such as new lanes or bridges. Once built, these have required little or no management, save for periodic maintenance activities. ITS-based solutions allow the road network to be managed. This management requires that transportation organizations that have historically built and maintained roads develop new competencies in facility and network management as well. This is especially important when using ITS to create flexibility, as the facility and network will need to be actively managed. Here, active management means that the operations of the road may change over time, such as between a HOT lane and a TOT lane. This is compared to static management where the facility may be managed as a single function type, such as a HOT lane. The active management requires even more attention to operations, collection of information about the usage of the network, and the authority to make changes in the network (i.e. switch between a HOT lane and a TOT lane for example). Without a simultaneous design of the enterprise architecture to provide for capabilities in active management, the deployed ITS technologies will not be able to provide the intended flexibility value. The reader is referred to Section 7.1 for additional discussion.

Differences between "standard" and "complex" real options in the evaluation phase lead to the need for more sophisticated analysis techniques to allow system characteristics to be adequately considered.
For "standard" real options, a monetary evaluation metric is used to determine the value and costs of the option. To provide this evaluation, "standard" real option evaluation techniques are employed, such as the Black-Scholes equation or binomial lattices.

For "complex" real options, a monetary metric may not be always appropriate. For example, in the BWB case study a monetary metric was appropriate (revenues and costs from aircraft), but in the ITS case study various metrics could be used, such as societal benefits or toll revenues. Additional discussion of metrics for the two case studies are presented in Sections 5.2.4 and 8.2.3.

443

It may also not be possible to analyze "complex" real options using only "standard" real option evaluation techniques. In the BWB case study a system dynamics model was needed to allow multiple attributes of the system to be analyzed, such as multiple sources of uncertainty, competitor responses, and changes in airline operating strategies. In the ITS case study a regional traffic demand model was needed to allow facility and network effects to be observed. Additional discussion of the quantitative evaluation techniques used for the two case studies are presented in Sections 5.1 and 8.1.

In the BWB case study, additional considerations not found in "standard" real option evaluation techniques were necessary when evaluating the options. First, the competitive nature of the aircraft market had to be taken into account. This included planning for and reacting to competitive responses, as well as making decisions based on prior and expected competitor actions. Second, corporate strategy and the relevant metrics were also critical when evaluating the options. Corporate strategies such as wanting to dominate a market, contesting a market or ceding a market drove the analysis of the results from the evaluation process. This means that developing a new aircraft may seem like a good investment under some corporate strategies, such as contesting a market, but the same aircraft design would not seem like a good investment with other corporate strategies, such as dominating a market. Metrics were also important in making a decision on the value of a new plane. For this case program-level and corporate-level metrics were considered, with the same plane designs having different level of benefits when considered from a program or corporate viewpoint. Without these additional considerations of the competitive environment, corporate strategy and appropriate metrics, the evaluation of the "complex" real option could not be conducted. Additional discussion on these evaluation considerations for the BWB case study can be found in Sections 5.3.2.

In the ITS case study, additional considerations not found in "standard" real option evaluation techniques were necessary when evaluating the options. First, the network effects of the addition of the ITS capabilities should be considered, in addition to the facility level effects. This is because the facility is integrated into a larger system, the regional road network, and gains in the facility through improved traffic flow could be offset by degraded flow elsewhere in the network. Second, the consideration of the type of operator managing the managed lane drove the metrics that would be appropriate for evaluating the facility. For example, if the operator is a public enterprise, societal benefits may be the appropriate metric, while toll revenues may be the preferred metric for a private enterprise operator. Without consideration of the additional considerations of the network effects and the type of enterprise that will be operating the facility, the evaluation of the "complex" real option could not be properly conducted. Additional discussion on these evaluation considerations for the ITS case study can be found in Sections 8.3.1.1 and 8.3.2.

Differences between "standard" and "complex" real options in the management phase lead to the need to consider the option from the perspective of the multitude of stakeholder involved in the system, each with a unique interest in the outcome of the option.

For "standard" real options it is assumed that managerial flexibility exists, meaning that the option holder can exercise the option at will. In the "complex" real options observed for the two case studies, the assumption of managerial flexibility for purchasing, managing or exercising the option completely broke down for multiple reasons.

In the BWB case study, two main considerations lead to the lack of managerial flexibility in even purchasing the options. First, the enterprise architecture of the Boeing Company was observed to be very program-centric, with program being described as "king". This resulted in program-level responsibility and authority, but also in program-centric metrics. Enterprise-level metrics appeared to be the sum of program-level metrics. This meant that any attempt at creating flexibility across aircraft families, each with their own program, was difficult to impossible, because of the nature of the program-centric architecture.

Second, the program-centric architecture was reinforced by both the corporate strategy and the corporate culture. The corporate strategy and culture at Boeing is centered around being able to offer the latest technologies for each new program. Under this strategy and culture, flexibility through the use of commonality to create "cross-family" derivatives was not seen as a positive value, as it constrained the use of new technologies in new programs and created performance penalties in the aircraft. This type of corporate strategy and culture is exactly opposite of that of Airbus, which regularly uses commonalty for "cross-family" derivatives. Because of the enterprise architecture, corporate strategy and corporate culture, the flexibility from "cross-family" derivatives could not even be "purchased" in the Boeing Company. Additional discussion of these management challenges can be found in Sections 6.7 and 6.8 for the BWB case study.

In the ITS case study, three main considerations lead to the lack of managerial flexibility in purchasing, managing and exercising the ITS in managed lane options. First, the fragmentation of stakeholders (such as transportation agencies, business interests, citizen interests, environmental interests, political officials, etc.) and the differing goals of each created political pressure that could prevent or delay the purchasing or exercising the option. The exercise of the option would represent a change to the system from the status quo, which may be resisted by stakeholders. For example, the exercise of the option to move to a congestion pricing system on the Westpark Tollway was resisted by the public, which was then resisted by local elected officials, making it difficult for the county tollroad authority to switch the facility operations from a flat toll to a congestion priced system. The purchase of the option was also resisted as it was recognized by stakeholders to introduce the *possibility* of change.

Second, the fragmentation of the "option holder" role made it difficult to purchase, manage and exercise the option. For similar reasons as just discussed with the fragmentation of stakeholders in general, the fragmentation of multiple transportation agencies also created conflicting goals and priorities that severely constrained managerial flexibility. This was especially the case where different agencies had conflicting claims on the same facility. For example, on the Katy Freeway managed lane, HCTRA, the county toll authority, wanted to use the facility as a HOT lane and opposed the option to convert the facility to a LRT line, held by Metro the regional transit authority. The result was political battles along the entire life-cycle of the option, from purchase, management and exercise.

Third, the existence of flexibility creates externalities for other stakeholders which will then resist the presence of flexibility in the first place. One stakeholder's flexibility creates uncertainty for other stakeholders that can only be resolved at the time of the exercise of the option. Because of the fragmentation of stakeholders, fragmentation in the option holder role and the creation of externalities from flexibility, managerial flexibility was severely constrained in the ITS case study. Additional discussion of these constraints for the ITS case study can be found in Sections 9.8 and 9.9.

In addition to these changes associated with "complex" real option, the very purpose of using real options in systems may be different.

"Complex" real options can be designed to cope with uncertainties not appearing in the real options research literature or even to accomplish objectives not associated with coping with system uncertainty at all.

Table 10-5 summaries the uses for "complex" real options found in the case studies.

Table 10-5 Difference in uses between "standard" and "complex" real options as found from the two case studies.

Uses for Options	"Standard" Real Options	"Complex" Real Options: Case Studies	
		BWB/Boeing Base Study	ITS/Houston Case Study
"Standard" Uses	• Means to cope with uncertainty	• Means to cope with uncertainty ○ Passenger demand growth rate ○ Fuel prices	• Means to cope with uncertainty ○ Travel demand growth ○ Relative travel demand growth between modes (single passenger, 2 passenger, 3 passenger and freight)
"Alternative" Uses	• None	• None found	• Means to fight political battles / compromise • Means to achieve second best solution • Mechanism to aid in option exercise

"Standard" real options are described in the literature as a means for addressing uncertainty. From the case studies, it was found that "complex" real options may be used for multiple purposes; the "standard" purpose of addressing uncertainty or "alternative" purposes as well. The "standard" purpose of addressing uncertainty for each case study is described in Sections 4.4 and 7.7 for the BWB and ITS case studies.

In the ITS case study, three alternative uses for real options were found. First was the use of flexibility to solve political battles and reach a compromise. Political battles fought over competing alternative designs would be won or lost with the adoption of a single alternative. Flexibility was seen as a way for the "loser" to keep open the possibility that their alternative could be adopted in the future. By forcing the winning alternative to include options that if exercised would change the system to the "losing" alternative, the supporters of this alternative could continue to fight the same political battle in the future. Conversely, flexibility was seen as a way to postpone a political battle by including the option to switch between alternatives in the future, in effect a compromise between multiple stakeholders with preferences for different alternatives.

Second, flexibility was seen as a mechanism to gain a second best solutions. In situations where the desired system could not be obtained because of funding issues, such as a LRT line, a similar system that was cheaper, such as a BRT line, was sought. Included in the second best solution would be options to upgrade it in the future to the preferred solution. This allowed stakeholders to move forward towards the preferred solution through the inclusion of options to upgrade or expand from the second best solutions.

Third, options were seen as a means to exercise the same option. For options such as the expansion of a pilot program to a full program or abandonment of the pilot program, the possibility that the capabilities developed in the pilot program could be lost if the program is not expanded was used as a rationale to expand the program. In this case, the expansion of the program was the desired outcome and the possible option outcome of abandonment was used as a reason to exercise the option in a certain direction, that of program expansion.

These three examples from the ITS case study demonstrate how "complex" real options can be used for uses beyond those discussed in the literature on "standard" real options. Additional discussion of these "alternative" uses for flexibility can be found in Section 9.9

The difference between "standard" and "complex" real options can be further illustrated by re-examining the definition of a "standard" real option. This shows how each part of the "standard" real option definition changes when considering the design, evaluation and management activities of a "complex" real option.

The definition used in "standard" real options is that:

> *The option holder has a right, but not the obligation, to take some action*
> *now or in the future at a predetermined cost*

For "complex" real options, every part of this "standard" real options definition is called into question, as summarized in Figure 10-10.

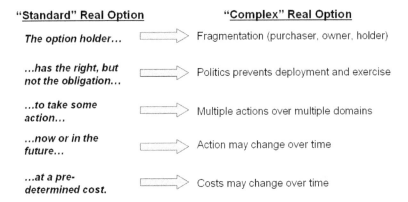

"Standard" Real Option	"Complex" Real Option
The option holder...	Fragmentation (purchaser, owner, holder)
...has the right, but not the obligation...	Politics prevents deployment and exercise
...to take some action...	Multiple actions over multiple domains
...now or in the future...	Action may change over time
...at a pre-determined cost.	Costs may change over time

Figure 10-10 Summary of Differences between "Standard" and "Complex" Real Options.

The recognition of these challenges not only affects the value of the option but can, and should, influence the design of an option. As in any design process, the final design is often arrived at in a manner resembling more art than science, dominated by creativity and followed by analysis and fine tuning. Flexible systems are no different in the leeway that exists for choosing the option design. Not taking into account the additional challenges posed by the requirements imposed or implied by the social system can result in an option design that has no real chance of being adopted or properly used.

This has implications for how real options are designed, evaluated and managed. Physical system and social system considerations are necessary for successfully designing, evaluating and managing "complex" real options. Without understanding the differences in "standard" and "complex" real options, the value of the option will likely not be realized, if it can be deployed at all.

The conclusions for the second research question are presented in the next section.

10.4.2 CONCLUSIONS FOR THE SECOND RESEARCH QUESTION

This section presents the conclusions for the second research questions. As a reminder, the research question is re-stated below.

How should the real option process be modified to systematically and comprehensively design, evaluate and manage "complex" real options?

From the research it was found that challenges associated with "complex" real options occurred throughout the life-cycle of an option from both technical system and social system considerations. The LCF Framework incorporates machinery during the design, evaluation and management of the option that explicitly addresses the three considerations just mentioned: physical & social systems, life-cycle considerations and different types of uncertainty.

The LCF Framework aids in activities related to the design, evaluation and management of the "complex" real option, considering both technical and social system components.

The LCF Framework provides a first attempt at a multi-dimensional framework that is appropriate for evaluating "complex" real options in complex systems. The LCF Framework calls for both quantitative and qualitative evaluation techniques in an attempt to better understand and evaluate the technical and social components of the option. The LCF Framework also explicitly calls for the consideration of unknown unknowns into the process, highlighting the potential need for flexibility different than the "complex" real option in complex system variety; flexibility designed into the enterprise or institutional architecture may be necessary.

The LCF Framework provides a methodology for systematically integrating the technical and social system considerations over the entire life-cycle of the "complex" real option.

Previous work in the real options literature emphasizes the financial analysis of the option. In most cases, this "standard" real options analysis mostly or wholly neglects life-cycle considerations and the interaction of technical and social system considerations.

The LCF Framework proceeds temporally. It starts before the design of the option with activities to make the enterprise ready to support a flexibility system and continues past the initial option deployment, through management activities to consider exercise decision considerations.

Figure 10-11 presents the LCF Framework. A more detailed description of the LCF Framework is presented in Chapter 3.

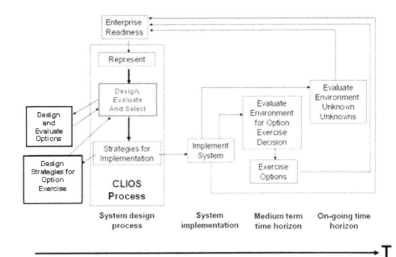

Figure 10-11 LCF Framework.

Given the results found from the first research question on the differences between "standard" and "complex" real options, "standard" real option analysis techniques are not adequate in designing, evaluating and managing "complex" real options. The LCF Framework is seen as an improvement over existing techniques as the LCF Framework calls for a comprehensive set of activities to address the entire life-cycle of an option, while "standard" real option analysis techniques concentrate primarily on the financial analysis of the option. The set of activities called for in the LCF Framework are presented below, arranged by the phases of the option's life-cycle: design, evaluation and management. The individual activity labels are mapped back to the LCF Framework shown in Figure 10-12.

Design Phase
a. Addressing social system considerations before the design of the option. See Section 3.2.8 for more details.
b. Addressing physical and social system considerations during the design of the option. See Sections 3.2.3 through 3.2.5 for more details.
c. Anticipating social system challenges (i.e. political responses, legal issues, etc.) associated with managing the option and modifying the physical or social system response before the option is deployed. See Section 3.2.5 for more details.

Evaluation Phase

d. Evaluating the option with quantitative and qualitative analysis techniques. See Section 3.2.3 for more details.

Management Phase

e. Addressing physical and social system consideration during deployment of the option. See Section 3.2.5 for more details.
f. Providing for evaluation of the system and the environment post-deployment. See Section 3.2.6 for more details.
g. Consideration of decision process for option exercise along with actions related to option exercise. See Section 3.2.6 for more details.
h. Feedback from changes occurring in the system due to option exercise into modifications needed in the physical and social system to support the post-option exercise system. See Section 3.2.8 for more details.
i. Consideration of unknown unknown uncertainties. See Section 3.2.7 for more details.

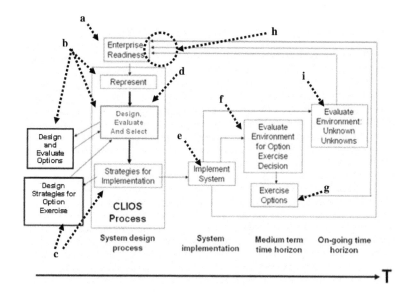

Figure 10-12 LCF Framework with specific activities called out.

Given that, one, "standard" real options and "complex" real options differ significantly, two, this difference makes "standard" real options analysis techniques inadequate when designing, evaluating and managing "complex" real options, and three, the LCF Framework provides a means to address physical and social system considerations across the entire option life-cycle; it therefore seems that the LCF Framework is a step in the right direction for creating a process for the design, evaluation and management of "complex" real options.

The following section presents suggestions for future research.

10.5 FUTURE RESEARCH
This research has studied the role of flexibility "in" complex systems. A framework was developed, two specific cases studied, and a new concept in designs creating value along multiple dimensions proposed. However, much work still remains to be done in the area of flexibility "in" complex systems. Below are some suggestions where more work would be valuable.

1. **Additional case studies.** For this research, only two case studies were chosen. Additional case studies should be looked at and the scope of the case studies broadened. For example, the case studies selected did not touch such areas as technical systems that looked at continuous flow processes, such as refineries, or were more based in information transfers, such as IT networks, nor did it fully explore social system constructs, such as public-private partnerships or non-profit organizations. It is assumed that the concepts discussed here would find application in these other areas as well, but it is expected that additional case studies and additional breadth in the case studies selected would extend and refine the results presented here.

2. **Improved integration of technical and social considerations.** For this research, the LCF Framework explicitly considers both technical and social considerations. However, this research only took the first steps at including the social considerations into the quantitative model. While the utility of trying to incorporate each of the social considerations raised in this research directly into the model is questionable, it would be valuable to include these considerations as part of a scenario analysis and sensitivity analysis of the system. This would help uncover how important these different barriers are towards maintaining system value. In this research, a quantitative analysis was conducted, followed in sequence by a qualitative evaluation. More iteration and integration of these two types of analyses would likely affect the system design and evaluation.

3. **Additional consideration of dual value design and extension to multiple value design.** This research introduced the concept of dual value designs as a means of more fully accounting for the benefits in a system. More in-depth study of the DVD concept is warranted. Additionally, the "dual" portion of the dual value design concept is arbitrary. There seems to be no reason why the two value streams described in this research, from inherent and flexibility benefits, should be the only value streams present. Rather, it may be possible to create a "multi-value design (MVD). What the "multi" value streams are would be dependant on the specific application of interest. For example, if political benefits are needed, the system may be able to be designed to continue to meet whatever the inherent

452

need for the system is, while simultaneously providing the political benefits. How this would be done would be application specific. But in essence it may be possible to create a situation that additional value streams can be created in the system for low marginal costs, essentially creating "something for nothing".

4. **Operationalizing of LCF type framework.** A framework for considering both technical and social processes was created for this research. The ideas behind the framework appear to be sound and useful, but the literature is replete with frameworks where the idea appears to be "good". Additional study on how to better operationalize the LCF Framework, moving it from a research tool to a process that would be useful in practice, is needed.

5. **Additional work on unknown unknowns** – While the LCF Framework addressed unknown unknown uncertainties, this was not a major focus of the research. As such, it is thought that considerable more work is needed in fleshing out a process for coping with unknown unknowns. It is envisioned that this type of future study could take two different directions. First, is additional study in enterprise architecture and behavior. How to design and operate an enterprise that is capable of regular or constant assessment of itself and the environment so that unknown unknowns can be identified and dealt with is an open question. It is thought that some hints on how to do this can be found in the innovation literature.

Second, how to technically design a physical system so that it can cope with unknown unknowns is also an area where much work can be accomplished. It is thought that the design of real options is much better suited for coping with statistically defined unknowns where outcomes are known a priori. It is not clear if real options "in" a system can be modified to cope with unknown unknowns or if a new design paradigm is needed altogether. Or even if a design capable of coping with unknown unknowns is fully realizable.

6. **Additional work on design of flexible systems** – The options studied in this research were the result of "creative" thinking by the author. While the options considered in this research appear valid (from the quantitative analysis and from discussions with interviewees), it is not believed that these options represent a complete, or even the most innovative or useful, set of options that could be found with the BWB and ITS systems. A more systematic way of identifying where flexibility would be useful in a system would be helpful. As seen in the quantitative analysis conducted for this research, flexibility values differed for the same technologies. This means that the technology is more or less useful at providing flexibilities in some situations and less so in other situations. Some process that allows a design to "scan" the system and determine where the flexibility would be most useful is needed.

7. **Additional work on trade-offs between different strategies for coping with uncertainty** – This research concentrated on flexibility as a means for coping with uncertainty. However, this is only one strategy. Robustness, agility, resiliency, versatility, upgradability and others also exist. How to make the trade-off between strategies and choose which would be the best for a particular systems is an area that has not been focused on in the research literature.

Additionally, the relationship between these different strategies is not completely understood either. A "flexible" system may only be flexible at a certain level. For example, to achieve its flexibility, the "flexible" system may depend on "robust" subsystems. Conversely, the "flexible" system may be a component in a larger system-of-systems, which is itself versatile. The relationship between these system levels is unclear and blurs the distinction between these different types of strategies.

10.6 CONCLUDING THOUGHTS

For this research "complex" real options in complex systems were of interest. A "complex" real option was envisioned as being composed of more than a single or simple change or addition to a system to create flexibility, as characterizes a "standard" real option. Rather, a "complex" real option is likely composed of interconnecting technological, organizational and process components. A "complex" real option may be embedded in a complex system, which has technical and social system components and the behaviors that go along with this.

This additional complexity in real options and systems was found to create a need for a new way of considering and evaluating flexible systems. The Life-Cycle Flexibility (LCF) Framework was created to flexibility from "cradle to grave" in a socio-technical system over multiple types of uncertainty.

In the end, it is hoped that this research provides some insight, and is helpful in generating some ideas for future insight by others, in the design, evaluation and management of "complex" real options in complex systems.

10.7 REFERENCES

Clemons, E. and B. Gu. (2003) Justifying Information Technology Investments: Balancing the Need for Speed of Action with Certainty Before Action, Proceedings of the 36t h Hawaii International Conference on System Sciences. Honolulu, Hawaii.

Datar, v. and S. Mathews. (2004) European Real Options: An Intuitive Algorithm for the Black-Scholes Formula, Journal of Applied Finance, Spring/Summer 2004.

Dixit, A. and R. Pindyck. (1994) Investment Under Uncertainty, Princeton University Press, New Jersey.

Goldenson, D., K. El Emam, J. Hersleb, and C. Deephouse. (1996) Empirical Studies of Software Process Assessment Methods, in Software Process Assessments and Improvements, edited by T. Rout, Computational Mechanics.

Greden, L., L. Glicksman, and G. Lopez-Betanzos. (2005). A Real Options Methodology for Evaluating Risk and Opportunity of Natural Ventilation. Proceedings of 2005 International Solar Energy Conference. August 6-12, 2005, Orlando, Florida.

Hastings, D. and H. McManus. (2004) A Framework for Understanding Uncertainty and its Mitigation and Exploitation in Complex Systems, Engineering Systems Symposium, MIT, Massachusetts.

Miller, B. (2005) A Generalized Real Options Methodology for Evaluating Investments Under Uncertainty with Application to Air Transportation, MIT Doctoral Dissertation, Massachusetts.

Nightingale, D. (2005) Class notes for Integrating the Enterprise Architecture course, taught at MIT, Massachusetts.

Ramirez, N. (2002) Valuing Flexibility in Infrastructure Developments: The Bogotá Water Supply Expansion Plan, MIT Masters Thesis, Massachusetts.

Sussman, J., R. Dodder, J. McConnell, A. Mostashari, S. Sgouridis. (2007) The CLIOS Process: A User's Guide, Working Paper.

Smit, H. and L. Trigeorgis. (2004) Strategic Investment: Real Options and Games, Princeton University Press, New Jersey.

Stirling, A. (1998) Risk at a Turning Point? Journal of Risk Research, v. 1 n. 2.

Tufano, P. and A. Moel (1997). Bidding for Antamina, Harvard Business School Case No. 9-297-054. Rev. Sept. 15, Massachusetts.